Teacher's Lesson Guide

 **Wright Group**

www.WrightGroup.com

 **Wright Group**

Printed in the United States of America.
Send all inquiries to:
Wright Group/McGraw-Hill
P.O. Box 812960
Chicago, IL 60681

ISBN 978-0-07-657447-6
MHID 0-07-657447-4
3 4 5 6 7 8 9 RMN 16 15 14 13 12 11

WRIGHT GROUP

LEAD21™

LITERACY EQUITY ACCELERATION DIFFERENTIATION

Transforming Literacy Instruction

WRIGHT GROUP

LEAD 21 ™

Transforming Literacy Instruction

The Name Says It All

LITERACY EXPANDED

So that all fourth-grade students not only learn reading basics, but also are proficient in the strategies and skills 21st century readers and thinkers need.

EQUITY ENSURED

So that all fourth-grade students have access to grade-level content.

ACCELERATION ACHIEVED

Through a built-in step-by-step instructional plan — designed to bring all fourth-grade students beyond progress toward proficiency.

DIFFERENTIATION REFINED

Through innovative texts, technologies, and effective scaffolded instruction designed to engage all fourth-grade students.

21st CENTURY

21st Century Literacies for 21st Century Learners.

21ˢᵗ Century Students and Teachers

Optimal Instruction for 21st Century Students

The Basics...

Wright Group LEAD21 includes all foundational literacies fourth-graders need:

- **Oral Language Development**
- **Phonics**
- **Fluency**
- **Vocabulary**
- **Comprehension**
- **Writing and Language Arts**

And Beyond...

Wright Group LEAD21 expands literacy instruction to equip fourth-graders for the 21st century by building stamina through inquiry-based instruction:

- **Accessing Information**
- **Evaluating Information**
- **Collaborating to Understand Information**
- **Creating New Information**
- **Presenting Information**

Unit 7 Contents

Week 3

21st CENTURY SKILLS

Week 4

21st CENTURY SKILLS

Writing and Language Arts

literature for this unit

Theme Reader

Differentiated Readers

Intensive

Strategic

Benchmark

Advanced

Unit 7 Planner overview

THEME Question

What makes the West exceptional?

In Unit 7, students will be learning the **social studies** concepts of geography and its relation to economy, regional characteristics, and life in the Mountain States and Pacific States. Each week students will address one essential Focus Question related to the Unit Theme: *The Wide-Open West.*

Weekly Focus Questions

Week 1

How are geography and economy connected in the Mountain States?

Week 2

How are geography and economy connected in the Pacific States?

Week 3

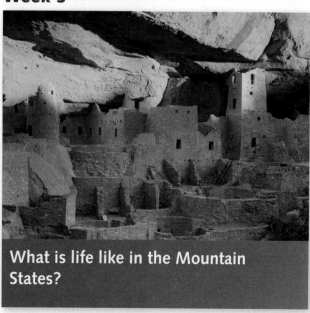

What is life like in the Mountain States?

Week 4

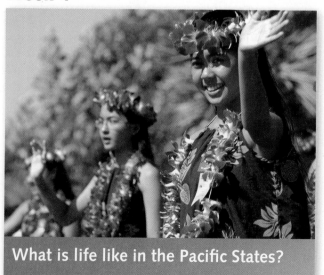

What is life like in the Pacific States?

THEME-RELATED
Resources

Online Resources

Log on to www.wgLEAD21.com for online resources to support instruction and professional development.

Bibliography

A Leveled Theme Bibliography appears on pages 304–305.

CURRICULUM
Connections

Literacy and Social Studies

Selections in this theme build content-area literacy in social studies. Reading about these big ideas provides an opportunity to reinforce or enhance your social studies instruction.

- The connection between geography and economy
- Life in the Mountain States and Pacific States
- Regional characteristics of the West

Unit 7 Planner
resources

Differentiated Reading

	Level	Leveling Highlights
INTENSIVE *Westward EXPEDITIONS* 	14	**Language and Sentences** • Unfamiliar key vocabulary usually defined in context • Use of Idioms, similes, metaphors **Content** • Inference implied and required to predict events • Many episodes built around a single plot
STRATEGIC *VOYAGE TO THE WEST*	18	**Language and Sentences** • Important key vocabulary usually defined in context • Use of hyperbole **Content** • Inference implied and required to predict events • Complex characters and events
BENCHMARK *Passage to the West*	19	**Language and Sentences** • Important key vocabulary usually defined in context • Literary language integral to story **Content** • Reasoning beyond text required • Assumes prior knowledge
ADVANCED *Westward Bound*	23	**Language and Sentences** • Important key vocabulary defined in context • Complex sentence structures **Content** • Reasoning beyond text required • Unfamiliar concepts or setting

See the inside back covers of the Differentiated Readers for corresponding guided reading levels.

Concepts and Literature

THEME READER

Practice

PRACTICE COMPANION

Practice Companion
VOLUME **2**

STUDY STATION FLIP CHARTS

Book Corner · Writer's Desk · Word World · Vocabulary Central

VOCABULARY AND WORD STUDY

epractice
• word study games
• vocabulary activities

Teaching Support

TEACHER'S LESSON GUIDE WITH ELL SUPPORT

RESOURCE MASTERS

ASSESSMENT HANDBOOK

Home Connection

HOME CONNECTION

Assessment

GROUP PLACEMENT AND READING PROGRESS ASSESSMENTS

DIFFERENTIATED UNIT ASSESSMENT

QUARTERLY BENCHMARK ASSESSMENT

Use with Benchmark Week, Unit 8.

ASSESSMENT DATA AND REPORTS

Digital 21

Unit at a Glance

Unit 7 Planner
curriculum mapping

	Oral Language	Theme Vocabulary	Comprehension	Word Study
Week 1	**Listening and Speaking** Focus Question: How are geography and economy connected in the Mountain States? **Viewing** Virtual Field Trip Theme Reader	**Theme Vocabulary** ✔ extremes irrigated arid **Vocabulary Strategy** ✔ Synonyms	**Strategy** ✔ Review Visualize **Skills** ✔ Review Generalize Text Features: Line Graphs	**Skill** ✔ Negative Prefixes
Week 2	**Listening and Speaking** Focus Question: How are geography and economy connected in the Pacific States? **Viewing** Theme Reader	**Theme Vocabulary** ✔ missionary film rugged **Vocabulary Strategy** ✔ Context Clues	**Strategy** ✔ Review Monitor Comprehension **Skills** ✔ Review Identify Cause and Effect Text Features: Captions	**Skill** ✔ Contractions
Week 3	**Listening and Speaking** Focus Question: What is life like in the Mountain States? **Viewing** Theme Reader	**Theme Vocabulary** ✔ fulfill treasure exchange **Vocabulary Strategy** ✔ Descriptive Language	**Strategy** ✔ Review Make Predictions **Skill** ✔ Review Sequence Events **Literary Elements** ✔ Plot—Conflict and Resolution	**Skill** ✔ Review Negative Prefixes
Week 4	**Listening and Speaking** Focus Question: What is life like in the Pacific States? **Viewing** Theme Reader	**Theme Vocabulary** ✔ Review **Vocabulary Strategy** ✔ Review	**Strategy** ✔ Review Determine Important Information **Skill** ✔ Review Recall and Retell	**Skill** ✔ Review Contractions

Skills Trace

Comprehension Strategies

Visualize
Grade 4: Taught Unit 3, Weeks 1, 2; Reviewed Units 5, 7

Monitor Comprehension
Grade 4: Taught Unit 2, Weeks 1, 2; Reviewed Units 5, 7

Make Predictions
Grade 4: Taught Unit 2, Weeks 3, 4; Reviewed Units 5, 7

Determine Important Information
Grade 4: Taught Unit 1, Weeks 1, 2; Reviewed Units 5, 7

Comprehension Skills

Generalize
Grade 4: Taught Unit 3, Weeks 1, 2; Reviewed Unit 7

Identify Cause and Effect
Grade 4: Taught Unit 5, Weeks 3, 4; Reviewed Unit 7

Sequence Events
Grade 4: Taught Unit 1, Weeks 3, 4; Reviewed Unit 7

Recall and Retell
Grade 4: Taught Unit 2, Weeks 3, 4; Reviewed Unit 7

Spelling	Fluency	Writing Process	Grammar	Inquiry	Digital Literacy/ Study Skills	Assessment
Pattern ✓ Words with VV Pattern	**Genre** Advertisement "The Great Potato State"	**Genre** Science Fiction Story **Writing Traits** ✓ Organization Ideas Conventions Voice	**Skills** ✓ Review Adverbs That Compare (-er/-est) Review Adverbs That Compare (more/ most)	**Process** 1. Generate Ideas and Questions 2. Make a Conjecture 3. Make Plans to Collect Information	**Skill** ✓ Listening Skills	**Wrap Up** Fluency ✓ Presentation Spelling ✓ Posttest
Pattern ✓ Final e + l Sound	**Genre** Procedural Text "Hiking in Redwood"	**Genre** Science Fiction Story **Writing Traits** ✓ Voice Organization Sentence Fluency Conventions Presentation	**Skills** ✓ Prepositions Prepositional Phrases	**Process** 4. Organize and Synthesize Information 5. Confirm or Revise Your Conjecture	**Skill** ✓ Collaboration	**Wrap Up** Fluency ✓ Presentation Spelling ✓ Posttest
Skill ✓ Three-Syllable Words	**Genre** Interview "Roaring Downriver"	**Genre** Autobiography **Writing Traits** ✓ Organization Ideas Conventions Voice	**Skills** ✓ Review Prepositions Review Prepositional Phrases	**Process** 6. Develop Presentation	**Skill** ✓ Evaluate Sources	**Wrap Up** Fluency ✓ Presentation Spelling ✓ Posttest
Skill ✓ Silent Consonants	**Genre** Journal Entry "At the Trail's End"	**Genre** Autobiography **Writing Traits** ✓ Word Choice Sentence Fluency Conventions Presentation	**Skills** ✓ Avoid Double Negatives Recognize Troublesome Word Groups	**Process** 7. Deliver Presentation	**Skill** ✓ Consider Your Audience	**Wrap Up** Fluency ✓ Presentation Spelling ✓ Posttest Inquiry ✓ Presentation

Skills Trace

Word Study

Negative Prefixes
Grade 3: Taught Unit 1
Grade 4: Taught Unit 7, Week 1
Reviewed Unit 7, Week 3
Grade 5: Taught Unit 1

Contractions
Grade 3: Taught Units 4, 7
Grade 4: Taught Unit 7, Week 2
Reviewed Unit 7, Week 4
Grade 5: Taught Unit 7

Language Arts

Prepositions
Grade 4: Taught Unit 7, Week 2
Reviewed Unit 7, Week 3
Grade 5: Taught Unit 6

Prepositional Phrases
Grade 4: Taught Unit 7, Week 2
Reviewed Unit 7, Week 3
Grade 5: Taught Unit 6

Avoid Double Negatives
Grade 3: Taught Unit 7
Grade 4: Taught Unit 7, Week 4
Reviewed Unit 8, Week 1
Grade 5: Taught Unit 7

Recognize Troublesome Word Groups
Grade 3: Taught Unit 5; Reviewed Unit 6
Grade 4: Taught Unit 7, Week 4
Reviewed Unit 8, Week 1

Week 1 Planner

Interactive Reading
WHOLE GROUP | 25–35 mins.

tested ✓

	Oral Language	Vocabulary	Read Together	Comprehension	Word Study and Phonics	Spelling	Fluency
Day 1	Introduce the Theme	Introduce Theme Vocabulary ✓	• Model • Share • Read Theme Reader, pp. 380–391	Read about geography and economy in the Mountain States.	Introduce ✓ Words with VV Pattern	Spelling ✓ Pretest Introduce Words with VV Pattern	Introduce and Model "The Great Potato State"
Day 2	Reinforce the Theme	Reinforce ✓ Theme Vocabulary	Read Theme Reader, pp. 392–395	Review ✓ Comprehension Strategy Visualize	Reinforce ✓ Words with VV Pattern	Practice ✓ Words with VV Pattern	Shared Choral Reading "The Great Potato State"
Day 3	Reinforce the Theme	Introduce ✓ Vocabulary Strategy Synonyms	Reread Theme Reader, pp. 380–395	Review ✓ Comprehension Skill Generalize	Introduce ✓ Negative Prefixes practice	Practice ✓ Words with VV Pattern	Paired Reading "The Great Potato State"
Day 4	Extend the Theme	Extend ✓ Theme Vocabulary	Reread Theme Reader, pp. 380–395	Reinforce ✓ Comprehension Strategy Visualize	Reinforce ✓ Negative Prefixes practice	Practice ✓ Words with VV Pattern	Personal Rehearsal "The Great Potato State"

Day 5	Inquiry and 21st Century Skills ⓔtools 21 inquiry project

21st CENTURY SKILLS

Introduce the Project
Connect to the Theme

Model the Inquiry Process
1. Generate Ideas and Questions
2. Make a Conjecture
3. Make Plans to Collect Information

Minilesson: Listening Skills Review

Begin Inquiry Group Work
Assign Inquiry Groups
Choose Discussion Roles
Monitor Student Progress

Theme Reader   Pages 380–395

Weekly Vocabulary

extremes
irrigated
arid

ⓔbook
online coach

Selection 1: Differentiated Readers   Pages 6–29

Intensive

Weekly Vocabulary

range
barbed
endure
integral
supplement
widespread
preserve
initiative

ⓔbook
online coach

Strategic

Weekly Vocabulary

sustain
mesa
pillar
surge
ominous
adobe
astounding
devise
hue

ⓔbook
online coach

Differentiated Reading
SMALL GROUPS | 60–80 mins.

Read and Comprehend

Reinforce Theme Vocabulary ✓

Reread Theme Reader,
pp. 380–391

Introduce Differentiated Vocabulary ✓
Read about canyons and deserts, the Rockies, mountain plains, or the Colorado River in the first half of Selection 1.

Reinforce Comprehension Strategy ✓
Visualize

Introduce Differentiated Vocabulary ✓
e practice
Read about canyons and deserts, the Rockies, mountain plains, or the Colorado River in the second half of Selection 1.

Reinforce Comprehension Skill ✓
Generalize

Extend Vocabulary
e practice

Reread Differentiated Readers,
pp. 6–29

Reinforce Comprehension Strategy ✓
Visualize

Mixed Groups

Cross-Text Sharing

Think Back

Connect to Inquiry

Wrap Up
WHOLE GROUP | 5–10 mins.

Share, Connect, Assess

Share Text Connections

Daily Writing

Student Self Assessment

Daily Progress Monitoring

Home Connection

Share Text Connections

Daily Writing

Student Self Assessment

Daily Progress Monitoring

Home Connection

Share Text Connections

Daily Writing

Student Self Assessment

Daily Progress Monitoring

Home Connection

Share Text Connections

Daily Writing

Student Self Assessment

Daily Progress Monitoring

Home Connection

Weekly Assessment

Fluency Presentation ✓

Spelling Posttest ✓

Student Self Assessment

Weekly Progress Monitoring

Writing and Language Arts
WHOLE GROUP | 30 mins.

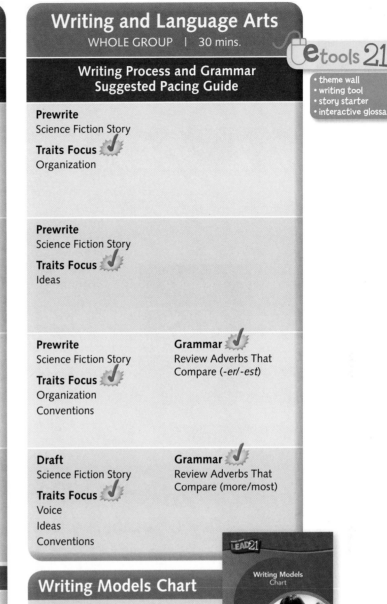

• theme wall
• writing tool
• story starter
• interactive glossary

Writing Process and Grammar
Suggested Pacing Guide

Prewrite
Science Fiction Story
Traits Focus ✓
Organization

Prewrite
Science Fiction Story
Traits Focus ✓
Ideas

Prewrite
Science Fiction Story
Traits Focus ✓
Organization
Conventions

Grammar ✓
Review Adverbs That Compare (-er/-est)

Draft
Science Fiction Story
Traits Focus ✓
Voice
Ideas
Conventions

Grammar ✓
Review Adverbs That Compare (more/most)

Writing Models Chart

Writing Model
Science Fiction Story,
pp. 48–51

Target Literacy Skills

Comprehension Strategy ✓
Visualize

Comprehension Skill ✓
Generalize

Vocabulary Strategy ✓
Synonyms

Selection 1: Differentiated Readers
Pages 6–29

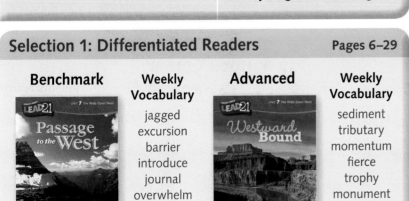

Benchmark

Passage to the West

Weekly Vocabulary
jagged
excursion
barrier
introduce
journal
overwhelm
dedicate
maintain

e book
online coach

Advanced

Westward Bound

Weekly Vocabulary
sediment
tributary
momentum
fierce
trophy
monument
vicinity
achievement
retain

e book
online coach

Week 1 Planner

Daily Small-Group Rotation

	Small-Group, Teacher-Led Instruction	Independent Practice	Self-Selected Reading	Study Station Flip Charts
	When the teacher is with these groups…	these groups rotate through independent activities.		
Session 1	Intensive	Advanced	Benchmark	Strategic
Session 2	Strategic	Intensive	Advanced	Benchmark
Session 3	Benchmark	Strategic	Intensive	Advanced
Session 4	Advanced	Benchmark	Strategic	Intensive

Study Station Flip Charts, page 25

Day 1: Vocabulary Central

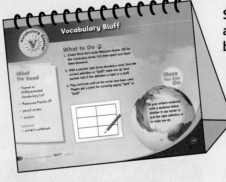

Students play a vocabulary bluffing game.

Day 2: Writer's Desk

Students write a friendly e-mail.

Day 3: Word World

Students make books containing words with prefixes.

Day 4: Book Corner

Students read silently and make a poster about a place they read about.

Week 1 Day 1

Lesson Highlights

- Introduce the Theme
- Introduce Theme Vocabulary: extremes, irrigated, arid
- Spelling Pretest: Words with VV Pattern
- Prewrite a Science Fiction Story, pp. 130–131

Materials

	Teacher's Lesson Guide	Student Components	Digital 21
Interactive Reading	pp. 10–15	• Theme Reader, pp. 380–391 • Practice Companion, pp. 185–186, 190–191	etools 21 theme wall · virtual field trip · ebook online coach
Differentiated Reading	pp. 16–21	• Theme Reader, pp. 380–391 • Resource Masters 6, 13, 14, 20	ebook online coach
Wrap Up	p. 22	• Resource Masters 1–3	etools 21 · theme wall · writing tool · story starter
Writing and Language Arts	pp. 130–131	• Writing Models Chart, pp. 48–49 • Practice Companion, pp. 220–221 • Resource Master 23	

Tips for Success

- Introduce the Theme and Focus Questions, the Inquiry Project, and the Question Board.
- You may wish to have students begin the Weekly Planner on Practice Companion page 185.
- Introduce the Study Stations (Flip Charts, p. 25) and arrange materials for the week.
- Set up the science fiction writing process lesson (pp. 128–145), so students know what they will be working on this week and what the end product will be.

Oral Language and Vocabulary

Interactive Reading whole group

Objectives
Students will:
• Discuss the theme
• Use theme vocabulary

Introduce the Theme

To introduce the theme, discuss the unit title from the Theme Reader Unit Opener (p. 377).

**Theme Reader
Pages 377–438**

The title of the unit is *The Wide-Open West.* This is the part of the United States that is in the western part of the country.

Encourage students to tell what they know about the western part of the United States, such as names of states or cities. Have students tell what they know about the geography and economy of the Western Region. Ask:

• What does the picture on page 379 make you think this unit will be about?

• What do the pictures on pages 378 and 379 show us about different aspects of geography and how people interact with the land?

Introduce the Theme and Focus Questions below (pp. 378–379). Explain that these questions will guide learning throughout the unit. **a**

Unit 7: The Wide-Open West

Theme Question: What makes the West exceptional?

	FOCUS QUESTIONS
Week 1	How are geography and economy connected in the Mountain States?
Week 2	How are geography and economy connected in the Pacific States?
Week 3	What is life like in the Mountain States?
Week 4	What is life like in the Pacific States?

Launch the Virtual Field Trip to build background.

Introduce the Inquiry Project

21ST CENTURY SKILLS

Tell students that they will begin a new Inquiry Project on Day 5 this week. Each Inquiry Group will choose a new Inquiry Question to investigate.

Encourage students to post Theme-related questions, answers, concepts, and images to the Question Board. A possible list of relevant information that students might post includes:

• Maps of the Western Region.

• News articles about the Western Region.

• Artwork depicting the Old West.

Remind students that they can post to the Question Board at any time during the unit. They should feel free to respond to someone else's question.

etools 21 *theme wall* — Students can also use the Theme Wall to post ideas and images.

Activate Prior Knowledge

Ask students to name words that relate to geography and economy. Write their ideas on the board. The lists might include words such as these:

Geography: land, mountain, hill, river, ocean, country, state, place, weather, plants

Economy: money, trade, jobs, manufacturing, products, factory, worker, stock market

Then ask:

• What do you know about the geography in different parts of the country?

• Where have you visited that had interesting or unusual geography? What was it like?

• What types of jobs do you know about that are connected to geography?

Introduce Theme Vocabulary

Theme Vocabulary
extremes
arid
irrigated

Use the following vocabulary routine to introduce the theme vocabulary words that students will read this week in their Theme Readers. These words will help students answer the Theme and Focus Questions. **b**

Vocabulary Routine	
Help students scan the selection to find the highlighted theme vocabulary words, and have them read and pronounce the words after you. Then use the vocabulary routine below to discuss the meaning of each word.	
Define	**Extremes** (p. 382) are the farthest points, complete opposites.
Example	The hottest summer temperatures and the coldest winter temperatures are extremes.
Ask	What kinds of weather extremes have we experienced so far this year?

Irrigated (p. 387) means "being watered through streams, pipes, or other means." *The irrigated crops were taller than the crops that didn't have water.* Why would *irrigated* crops be taller than crops that didn't receive water?

Arid (p. 389) is land that gets very little rain. *The arid desert is hot and dry.* What are other characteristics of an *arid* desert?

ASSIGN PRACTICE COMPANION **186**

scaffolding options

a ELL Support

CONCEPT DEVELOPMENT
Some English language learners may have difficulty with the word *exceptional* in the Theme Question: *What makes the West exceptional?* Explain that *exceptional* means "very good, and different from anything else." Give examples of familiar things that are exceptional, such as a very successful sports team or a book that is better than any other. Then have students rephrase the Theme Question. (What makes the West a very nice place and different from other places?)

b ELL Support

COGNATES
Point out the following Spanish cognates of the theme vocabulary words:

English	Spanish
extreme	extremo(a)
arid	árido(a)

ebook onlinecoach
Literacy Builder

Students can use the eBook version of the Theme Reader for building literacy.

Read and Comprehend

Objectives
Students will:
• Read about the Western Region

Prepare to Read

Build Background

Today students read pages 380–391 of *A Tour of the Western Region*, a nonfiction selection about the western part of the United States.

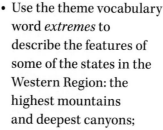

Theme Reader Pages 380–381

• Explain that the Western Region is made up of many different states.

• Use the theme vocabulary word *extremes* to describe the features of some of the states in the Western Region: the highest mountains and deepest canyons; hottest and coldest temperatures.

• Point out that in the Western Region, bodies of water are used for irrigation. Explain that people also use rivers, lakes, and oceans to send goods to other parts of the country and the world. **a**

Preview and Predict

Use the Theme Reader (pp. 380–381) to start previewing the selection. Model your thinking:

think aloud The Chapter 1 title tells me that we will read about the Mountain States of the Western Region. The words *geography* and *economy* make me think that this chapter will be about the land and how people make a living in the Mountain States.

• Continue previewing the introduction and Chapter 1 with students, pointing out the titles, subheads, maps, photographs, captions, and highlighted words.

• Have students tell what they think they might learn from this section of the selection. Discuss ideas that are familiar or interesting to them.

Set Purposes

Remind students that setting a purpose before reading helps readers focus their attention.

• Students will find answers to the Theme Question.

• Students will set their own purposes, based on their own interests. Model setting a purpose:

think aloud What are my reasons for reading *A Tour of the Western Region*? First, I want to find answers to the Theme Question: *What makes the West exceptional?* I also want to learn more about the interesting places in the Western Region.

MODELED AND SHARED READING

Read Together

Begin reading the introduction and Chapter 1 of *A Tour of the Western Region*. Model reading pages 382 and 383 as students follow along. As you read, model your thinking.

think aloud The second paragraph says that the Western Region contains eight Mountain States, states along the Pacific Ocean, and the states of Hawaii and Alaska. I can see the areas highlighted on the map on page 383.

Continue reading and sharing your thinking. Pause periodically to check understanding of the theme concepts and vocabulary.

PAGES 383–385 Look at these photographs. What are they photographs of, and why are these landforms important? *(Possible responses: Red Rock Canyon is visited by a million people each year; these lands are used for mining.)* **b**

PAGES 386–387 On these pages, we read about the ranches and farm land of the Mountain States. What are some different ways that people in the area use the land? *(Possible responses: They raise cattle. They grow potatoes.)*

PAGES 388–391 Have students look at the photographs on these pages and read the captions.

How do you think the photographs are related? How does this relate to the Focus Question? *(Possible responses: They all show unique features of the area. The geography of the land, such as the Colorado River, helps the area's economy through tourism or making power.)*

Respond

Review the predictions students made and the purposes they set before reading. Monitor understanding by discussing students' ideas and encourage them to use the theme vocabulary words in their answers.

- What did you think you would learn from this part of the selection? Were your predictions correct? What examples from the text support your predictions? If your predictions were not accurate, how did your ideas change as you read the text?

- What was your purpose for reading? Did you achieve this purpose? If not, do you think that rereading this section would help? Do you think reading the next part of the selection will help you achieve your purpose?

Talk About Text

Promote discussion about the author's purpose in the selection. Ask:

- What do you think the author's purpose is for this selection? Why do you think so? *(Possible response: The author's purpose is to inform the reader about the Mountain States of the United States. I know this because she uses facts, photographs, maps, and charts.)* **c**

a Literacy Builder

CONCEPT DEVELOPMENT
Build additional understanding of how people interact with and depend on geography. Ask students to think about how people in the Western States utilize the natural resources around them. Before students begin reading, ask them to answer the following questions:

- How do mountains affect life in the Western States? *(tourism, mining)*

- How do rivers and canyons affect life in the Western States? *(tourism, rafting, creating power)*

Have students jot down their predictions and look back on them after they read the selection.

b Intervention for Acceleration

USE GRAPHIC SOURCES
Ensure that students can interpret the map on page 384. Ask questions, such as:

- What do the orange and pink colors on the map tell you? *(whether a state is in the Mountain States or on the Pacific Ocean)*

- In which area is New Mexico? What about Montana? *(both are in the Mountain States area)*

c Challenge

CONCEPT DEVELOPMENT
Challenge students to describe the features that distinguish a region. Encourage them to think about regions of the United States or regions in other countries around the world. Have students discuss how a region is different from a country. Also discuss the similarities between regions.

Word Work and Fluency

Interactive Reading *whole group*

Objectives
Students will:
- Spell words with the VV pattern
- Analyze words with the VV pattern
- Practice fluent reading

Spelling and Word Study

Pretest Words with the VV Pattern

Say each word from the list, read the sentence, and say the word again. Then have students write the word.

1. **idea** My *idea* for my science project is to build a model of the solar system.
2. **lion** We heard a *lion* roar in the distance while we were on safari.
3. **unusual** Monique found an *unusual* book she had never seen before.
4. **radio** My sister enjoys listening to music on the *radio* in the morning.
5. **liar** No one wants to be called a *liar*.
6. **poem** The class listened to the teacher read the funny *poem*.
7. **India** *India* is a country in Asia.
8. **piano** Olivia's hands ran up and down the keys of the *piano*.
9. **fuel** Most cars need *fuel* to operate.
10. **diary** I enjoy writing my thoughts in my *diary*.
11. **violin** I have always wanted to learn how to play the *violin*.
12. **period** Don't forget to add a *period* at the end of the sentence.
13. **cereal** There is a prize in the box of *cereal*.
14. **video** We can't play the *video* game because our TV is broken.
15. **meteor** The scientist studied the *meteor* that landed on Earth.
16. **February** Valentine's Day is in *February*.

Review Words

17. **explain** You need to *explain* how that cat got into the box!
18. **sandwich** David likes to put cheese on his *sandwich*.

Frequently Misspelled Words

19. **they're** *They're* going to the river today.
20. **right** Take a *right* at the corner to find the library.

Explain that these words may seem easy to spell, but they are often misspelled by fourth-graders.

Help students self-correct their tests.

- Say each word, spell it aloud, and say the word again.
- Students checkmark each correctly spelled word.
- Students circle each misspelled word and write the correct spelling next to it. Encourage students to note these words as the ones they should pay extra attention to this week.

Teach Words with the VV Pattern

Explain that when two vowels appear next to each other and are not digraphs or diphthongs, they make two separate sounds. In these words, syllables are divided between the vowels. Demonstrate this pattern, using the spelling word *idea*.

- Write *idea* on the board.
- Label each letter as a vowel or consonant.
- Ask students to identify the VV pattern.
- Model dividing the word into syllables: I|de|a.

Practice/Apply

Word Sort Invite students to use word cards to sort words with the VV pattern into piles of words with two syllables or three syllables. **a**

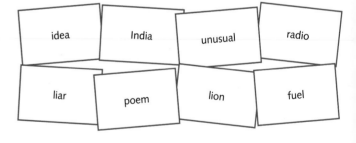

Fluency

Introduce and Model

Introduce the fluency selection, "The Great Potato State" on Practice Companion page 190. Tell students

Practice Companion Pages 190–191

that throughout the week, they will read the advertisement to practice fluency.

- To activate prior knowledge and build background, show Idaho on a map and discuss its climate in relation to your own state.

- Explain that potatoes are an important crop in Idaho.

- Introduce, pronounce, and discuss words that may be unfamiliar, such as *robust, locales,* and *delighted.*

Read the selection aloud two or three times. Model using good phrasing, pacing, and expression. Ask:

- Did you enjoy the advertisement? What did you like about it?

- Does this advertisement make you want to visit Idaho? Why or why not?

- How is this similar to other advertisements you've seen? How is it different?

Practice

Lead an echo reading of the selection, followed by a line-a-student choral reading, assigning one or two lines of text to each student.

---

scaffolding options

a Challenge

SPELLING
Divide the class into teams. Challenge teams to think of as many words as they can that contain the VV pattern. After a set time limit, have each team write the words they thought of in a list on the board. Compare the lists teams made, and declare the team that thought of the most correct words as the winner.

b Intervention for Acceleration

WORD STUDY
Help students better understand unfamiliar words by naming synonyms and antonyms such as these:

- precipitous (steep, sheer, gradual)
- robust (healthy, hearty, strong, weak)
- locale (setting, area, backdrop)
- delighted (pleased, happy, thrilled, unhappy)
- pondered (thought about, considered)

Differentiated Reading small groups

Objectives
Students will:
- Reinforce the theme
- Reinforce theme vocabulary
- Reread about the Western Region

Prepare to Read

Build Background

Remind students of the Theme Question: *What makes the West exceptional?* Ask questions to help students

eBook

online coach

Theme Reader
Pages 380–391

recall key concepts from the first quarter of the selection. For example, ask:

What is the land like in the Western Region? What things are produced or made in the Western Region?

List student ideas on the board. Have partners reread the list and find a fact or graphic from their Theme Reader that supports each idea.

Reinforce Theme Vocabulary ✓*tested*

To reinforce and assess students' understanding of the theme vocabulary, have them raise their right hand if they agree and their left hand if they disagree. Discuss student responses after each statement.

- Tall mountains and deep valleys are **extremes** of the landscape.
- An iceberg is a feature of an **arid** environment.
- **Irrigated** plants don't typically get a lot of rain.

Ask students to create a Venn Diagram (Resource Master 13) about the Western Region. Label the circles *Geography* and *Economy*. Have students reread each vocabulary word and guide them to decide where to write it. Prompt students to add additional words to the diagram that support the idea of how geography and economy are connected.

ASSIGN | RESOURCE MASTER | **13**
| PRACTICE COMPANION | **186**

Set Purposes

Students will reread *A Tour of the Western Region* to:

- Notice information or details they missed during the first reading.
- Help them understand parts of the text that didn't make sense the first time they read.
- Find answers to the Theme Question.

Emphasize that rereading helps us think more deeply about a topic and understand how ideas fit together. Encourage students to suggest information they want to understand better after rereading the selection.

Read

Explain that students will hear pages 380–391 again, but this time they will be closely guided to respond.

To help students get started, model your thinking as you read pages 382–383.

think aloud From the map on page 383, I can guess that the text will be about the places and states pictured. When I read page 382, I see many words to describe places and locations.

Guide Comprehension

Have students use sticky notes to write down questions they have as they follow along and listen to you reread. After reading, have partners ask and answer the questions they wrote. Monitor students' understanding by pausing periodically to reinforce the theme concepts and vocabulary.

PAGES 385–387 The caption on page 386 says that ranching is an important part of Wyoming's culture.

Write the following prompt on the board and have students respond on a sticky note:

One landform that is important to the region is . . . . *(Responses will vary.)*

PAGES 388–391 There are many places named on these pages. Look back and find each one on a map.

How does the land help the economy of the Western Region? *(Students should respond by giving information about how the land of the Western Region is used to help the economy of the area.)*

Check Comprehension

1. One important idea in this section is that the Western Region is a good place to farm. What is one detail that supports this idea? *(Possible response: The irrigated soil around the Snake River makes the land good for farming.)* IDENTIFY MAIN IDEAS AND DETAILS

2. What did you learn about the importance of the Colorado River? *(Possible response: The power that it holds helps create and supply energy to many people in the Western Region.)* SUMMARIZE

3. Why do people want to visit the Western Region? *(Possible response: The landscape is beautiful and there are many places to ski and participate in fun activities.)* MAKE INFERENCES **c**

Respond and Write

1. Ask students which part of the rereading they found the most interesting, and how the selection helps answer the Theme Question.

2. Have students reread the list of key concepts they made before reading. Have them discuss with a partner whether the list is complete, adding additional key concepts as they feel necessary. Discuss as a class what students wrote, revising the list on the board.

scaffolding options

a Intervention for Acceleration

COMPREHENSION: MAKE CONNECTIONS
Have partners discuss people they know or know about who live in the communities mentioned. You may need to help students think about people who typically live in the West, such as ranchers. Ask questions to prompt discussion, such as:

- What are some typical activities these people participate in? How are these people the same and different from people in other places?
- How do the people interact with the geography of where they live?

b ELL Support

PICTURE CLUES
Have partners look at the photographs and maps in this section of the text, identifying landforms and waterways they see. Then ask them to scan the introduction and identify geographical terms. Have them match up the photographs with appropriate terms from the text. Remind students that looking at photographs and maps can give us clues about the reading.

c Intervention for Acceleration

FEEDBACK
As partners share their sticky notes, circulate and listen for their ideas and answers. Ask leading questions to help them answer each prompt as needed. Take note of any responses that will help generate group discussion of each prompt or question.

ebook **online coach**

Intervention for Acceleration

Students can use the support features in the eBook version of the Theme Reader.

Read and Comprehend Strategic

Objectives
Students will:
• Reinforce the theme
• Reinforce theme vocabulary
• Reread about the Western Region

Prepare to Read

Build Background

Review the Theme Question with students: *What makes the West exceptional?* To ensure students understand

**Theme Reader
Pages 380–391**

the concept of the Western Region, have each student describe an aspect of the region or name one of its states or geographical features. Elicit that the Western Region is divided into several parts. Then have students write down questions that they still have about the geography and economy of the Western Region. Remind students to look for the answers as they read.

Reinforce Theme Vocabulary

To reinforce and assess students' understanding of the theme vocabulary, ask the following questions. Have students write their responses on a piece of paper.

• Freezing rain followed by a drought is an example of weather _____ . *(extremes)*

• _____ environments need lots of extra water. *(Arid)*

• _____ land will have a better chance of producing healthy crops. *(Irrigated)*

Have students answer the following questions by raising their right hand for the first choice given or their left hand for the second choice.

• Which description goes with **extremes**: *normal* or *different*?

• Which word goes with **arid**: *wet* or *dry*?

• Which action goes with **irrigated**: *provide* or *take away*?

ASSIGN   **PRACTICE COMPANION   186**

Set Purposes

Students will reread pages 380–391 of *A Tour of the Western Region* to:

• Notice information they might have missed the first time they read.

• Help them better understand parts of the text that were confusing.

• Find answers to the Theme Question.

Emphasize that rereading helps us understand how ideas fit together and think about a topic more deeply. Encourage students to suggest what they hope to understand better after rereading the text.

Read

Explain that students heard pages 380–391 read, but now they will read it together with some guidance. To help students get started, model reading pages 382–383 as students follow along. As you read, model your thinking. **c**

think aloud When I look at page 382, the first thing I see is the introduction title, "The Western Region." I know that an introduction should tell what the whole selection is about, so I will skim the page to find out more. I see a list of words at the bottom: *geography, economy, history,* and *culture.* Now I know what we'll learn about in this selection.

Guide Comprehension

Have partners continue reading. Circulate and listen as they read. Pause them periodically to monitor understanding of the theme concepts and vocabulary.

PAGES 384–387 Read the captions. Now look at the photographs and think about the concepts you're learning this week. Talk with your partner about the concepts the photographs represent. *(Responses will vary, but students should discuss how the geography of the Western Region is unique and how it contributes to the economy.)*

PAGES 388–389 There is an important word highlighted on page 389. How does the word *arid* relate to the geography of the Western Region? *(Possible response: Some of the land in the Western Region is desert land and it is* arid.*)*

PAGES 390–391 Reread the first sentence on page 391. This is the main idea of this section. What are three details in this section that support this idea? Remember to reread the captions and the paragraphs before you answer. *(Possible responses: There are great places to ski all around Colorado and Utah; Yellowstone National Park is in this region; many visitors come to the desert states to enjoy their warm weather and wonderful scenery.)*

Check Comprehension

1. What is Chapter 1 mostly about? *(Possible response: how the geography and economy of the Mountain States are related)* IDENTIFY MAIN IDEAS AND DETAILS

2. Look at the small photo on page 389. How does this photograph relate to the economy of the Western Region? *(Possible response: The Hoover Dam provides water that is used to make power. The electricity allows places such as Las Vegas to prosper and grow.)* MAKE INFERENCES

3. Choose one of the photographs from these pages and explain how it shows the connection between economy and geography. *(Possible response: The photo on page 390 shows rafters in the Grand Canyon. These rafters help support the tourism part of the Mountain States' economy by renting or buying a raft.)* MAKE CONNECTIONS

Respond and Write

1. Have students reread the questions they wrote at the beginning of the lesson. Have students discuss with a partner any answers they found to the questions. Call on volunteers to share their questions and answers with the class.

2. Invite students to write in their journals how the introduction and Chapter 1 have answered the Theme Question.

---

scaffolding options

a Intervention for Acceleration

CONCEPT DEVELOPMENT
To help students better understand how geography and economy are connected, help them complete a T-Chart (Resource Master 14). Write *geography* above one column and *economy* above the other. Have students list geographical features of the region and brainstorm ways each can effect the economy.

ASSIGN RESOURCE MASTER **14**

b Challenge

COMPREHENSION: MAKE CONNECTIONS
Challenge students to use Resource Master 20 to make connections to one of the theme vocabulary words. Encourage students to use examples from personal experience and from sources beyond the classroom, such as museums, television programs, and magazines.

ASSIGN RESOURCE MASTER **20**

c Literacy Builder

ACADEMIC LANGUAGE
Review the word *introduction* as it is used in the context of a reading selection. Discuss the type of information that is usually found in the introduction to a book. An introduction usually gives an overview of the topic, but sometimes it may tell why the author chose to write about the topic, or how he or she went about it.

Intervention for Acceleration

Students can use the support features in the eBook version of the Theme Reader.

Read and Comprehend

Differentiated Reading *small groups*

Objectives
Students will:
• Reinforce the theme
• Reinforce theme vocabulary
• Reread about the Western Region

Prepare to Read

Build Background

Ask students to think about the Theme Question: *What makes the West exceptional?* and the key concepts presented in the whole-group session. Have students draw a sketch that shows one way the Western Region's geography and economy are related. Have students explain their drawing to the group.

Theme Reader
Pages 380–391

Reinforce Theme Vocabulary

To reinforce and assess students' understanding of the theme vocabulary, ask them to complete a Word Map (Resource Master 6) about one of the theme vocabulary words: *extremes, arid, irrigated.* Have students add a drawing, a definition, examples, non-examples, and a sentence about the word. Have partners share what they wrote. **a**

ASSIGN	RESOURCE MASTER	6
	PRACTICE COMPANION	186

Set Purposes

Students will reread pages 380–391 of *A Tour of the Western Region* to:

• Find and note details that will help them answer the Theme Question as they read.

• Notice information they missed the first time, and think more deeply about how ideas fit together.

Read

To set reading expectations, model your thinking as you read page 382.

think aloud

The introduction says I'll learn more about the geography, economy, history, and culture of the Western Region. I'm most interested in finding out how people make a living, and learning about their way of life.

Guide Comprehension

Have students continue reading independently. Pause them periodically to monitor understanding of theme concepts and vocabulary.

PAGES 380–387 Have students summarize why agriculture prospers in the Western Region. *(Possible response: The climate and irrigation helps things grow.)* SUMMARIZE

PAGES 388–391 Have students explain how the geography of the Western Region plays a role in its economy. MAKE CONNECTIONS

Respond and Write

1. Have students use details from the text to add to their drawing about the Western Region. Ask them to write phrases and sentences describing what they drew, and then share their work with the group.

2. Have students respond to the Theme Question. **b**

scaffolding options

a Challenge

VOCABULARY
Have students use each vocabulary word to write a sentence about a topic other than the Western Region. Have partners exchange sentences and evaluate whether the meaning of each vocabulary word remains the same within the context of the new sentence.

b Critical Thinking

EVALUATE IDEAS
Have students list the agricultural assets of the Western Region and of another region they have read about. Have them analyze which factors the two regions have in common, and then decide whether one region is better able to produce more crops or livestock.

Differentiated Reading · small groups

Objectives
Students will:
- Reinforce the theme
- Reinforce theme vocabulary
- Reread about the Western Region

Prepare to Read

Build Background

Ask students to discuss key concepts and the Theme Question: *What makes the West exceptional?* Have

Theme Reader Pages 380–391

students draw a flow chart that shows an example of how geography and economy are connected in the Western Region. Have students explain their charts to the group.

Reinforce Theme Vocabulary

To reinforce and assess students' understanding of the theme vocabulary *(extremes, arid, irrigated)*, have students make word associations. Ask them to think of an action, item, event, or example associated with each word, and then share their ideas with a partner.

ASSIGN | **PRACTICE COMPANION** | **186**

Set Purposes

Students will reread pages 380–391 of *A Tour of the Western Region* to:

- Find details that help answer the Theme Question.
- Think more deeply about the topic, and to try to understand how ideas fit together.
- Achieve purposes they set for themselves.

Read

To set reading expectations, model your thinking.

Before reading the text, I take a look at the photos and read the captions. They tell me about the geography and economy of the Western Region. From this, I can predict that the text will discuss ways that the economy and geography of the Western Region are related.

Guide Comprehension

Have students continue reading silently. After they read, discuss the theme concepts and vocabulary.

PAGES 382–387 Have students discuss the main ideas on each page and point out details that help explain each idea or give further examples. IDENTIFY MAIN IDEAS AND DETAILS

PAGES 388–391 Discuss as a group how information from the text can be used to help describe communities and landscapes students know personally or have learned about elsewhere. SYNTHESIZE **a**

Respond and Write

1. Have students write a summary explaining the flow chart they drew, using details from the text to support their ideas. Have them share their work. **b**

2. Have students respond to the Theme Question by using details from the selection.

scaffolding options

a Critical Thinking

ANALYZE EXAMPLES
To help students answer the question, have them analyze a community they know well and use it as a model (or anti-model) for the Western Region community they describe.

b ELL Support

WORD STUDY
Encourage English language learners to identify five unknown words from the selection and define each one. Then have students write sentences that demonstrate each word's meaning, and share what they wrote with a partner.

Share, Connect, Assess

Objectives
Students will:
- Use key concepts and vocabulary
- Make text-to-self connections
- Write about a photo from the Theme Reader
- Monitor their progress

Share Text Connections

Make Text-to-Self Connections Bring students back together from their small groups to share what additional things they learned while reading about the West.

- Encourage students to use theme and other academic vocabulary as they share their own insights about key concepts.
- Ensure that students from all groups have a chance to contribute to the discussion.
- Ask students to share their thoughts on how what they've read connects to their personal experiences.

etools 21
theme wall

Daily Writing

Have students choose a photo from the Theme Reader pages they read today. Have them write a description of what they see in the photo. Does it make them want to visit that place?

For additional writing practice, remind students to access the Story Starter from their student Home Page.

etools 21
- writing tool
- story starter

Student Self Assessment

- Remind students that they are responsible for their learning and that it is helpful to be aware of how well they understand what they are reading, writing, talking, and thinking about in the classroom.
- You may want students to reflect on their reading and learning by using their Personal Reading Logs and My Daily Progress sheets (Resource Masters 1, 3).

ASSIGN RESOURCE MASTER **1, 3**

Daily Progress Monitoring

To ensure that students have mastered the day's skills and strategies, monitor their success in completing the following independent work:

- **Vocabulary:** Practice Companion, p. 186
- **Spelling:** Practice Companion, p. 188
- **Fluency:** Practice Companion, p. 190
- **Study Station Work Record:** Resource Master 2
- **Self Assessment:** Resource Masters 1, 3

Home Connection

Distribute the Unit 7 Letters Home from the Home Connection book. Tell students to share with their caregivers what they will be learning in this unit.

Day at a Glance

Lesson Highlights

- Review Comprehension Strategy: Visualize

- Spelling and Word Study: Words with VV Pattern

- Introduce the Differentiated Readers

- Prewrite a Science Fiction Story, pp. 132–133

Materials

	Teacher's Lesson Guide	Student Components	Digital 21
Interactive Reading	pp. 24–27	• Theme Reader, pp. 392–395 • Practice Companion, pp. 186, 188, 190, 192–193 • Resource Masters 11, 14, 25	ebook online coach
Differentiated Reading	pp. 28–33, 288–291 (ELL)	• Differentiated Readers • Resource Masters 4, 11, 12	ebook online coach
Wrap Up	p. 34	• Resource Masters 1–3	etools 21 • theme wall • writing tool • story starter
Writing and Language Arts	pp. 132–133	• Writing Models Chart, pp. 48–49 • Practice Companion, pp. 220–221 • Resource Master 23	

Tips for Success

- Guide students to make connections between reading and writing (p. 25).

- Distribute the Differentiated Readers and allow students time to explore and get excited about their new books for the unit.

- Remind students to use their Study Station Work Records (Resource Master 2) throughout the week.

Oral Language and Vocabulary

Objectives
Students will:
• Reinforce the theme
• Reinforce theme vocabulary

Reinforce the Theme

Use pages 378-379 of the Theme Reader to reinforce the theme. Remind students of the unit title, *The Wide-Open West*, and discuss how the photographs on these pages illustrate aspects of the Western Region. Ask:

ebook
online coach

**Theme Reader
Pages 377–438**

• What do you notice about these photographs?

• What do they tell you about the Western Region?

Prompt students to use the words *extremes*, *arid*, and *irrigated* during their discussion.

Activate Prior Knowledge

Explain that the Western Region was inhabited by Native Americans when Europeans began exploring the area. People began to settle in the area to have their own land and farm, and towns were founded. The West continued to grow, and today it has a unique culture.

• Invite students to share what they know about the history and culture of the West.

• Show students historical images of the Mountain States. Then ask:

What do you think it would have been like to settle in the West at this time?. **a**

• Have students tell what they know about the Native Americans and early explorers of the West.

Reinforce Theme Vocabulary

Theme Vocabulary	
extremes	the farthest points, complete opposites
arid	land that gets very little rain
irrigated	being watered through streams, pipes, or other means

As a class, brainstorm ideas to write a story or a scenario using the theme vocabulary words they are learning this week.

• For example, students might write a realistic story about a family moving West and trying to start a farm. Or they may wish to write a science fiction story about a colony on another planet. Encourage students to be creative.

• You may wish students to use Resource Master 25 as a sequence chart to plan the scenario. **b**

ASSIGN

RESOURCE MASTER	**25**
PRACTICE COMPANION	**186**

model
read share

Read and Comprehend

REVIEW **COMPREHENSION STRATEGY**

Visualize

Define

Remind students that readers visualize what they read by using the words on the page to create pictures in their minds.

To check understanding, have students turn to a partner and name and define the strategy.

Model

Use a T-Chart (Resource Master 14) to model visualizing what you read. Write the text that you use in the first column and what you visualized in the other column.

 The author describes how the Grand Canyon was formed on page 390. I can use the words on the page to picture it in my mind. I visualize a fast moving river cutting through the land and making the canyon deeper and deeper as time passes.

Visualize	
What I Read	What I Visualize
p. 390: how the Colorado River formed the Grand Canyon	I picture a river cutting through the land, making a canyon.

Collaborative Practice

• Have students reread page 390 and sketch what they visualize. Guide students by asking:

  • What does the author tell about on page 390?

  • Have you ever seen anything like that?

  • As you read, what do you picture in your head?

• Have students share their sketches and explain them to the class. **c**

Reading/Writing Connection

Writers use vivid language to help readers visualize. Ask:

  What descriptive words does the author of *A Tour of the Western Region* use?

ASSIGN

RESOURCE MASTER	14
PRACTICE COMPANION	192–193

scaffolding options

a ELL Support

BUILD ORAL LANGUAGE
Some English language learners might struggle to share their prior knowledge orally. Invite them to jot their ideas down first, and then share with a partner before trying out their ideas with the whole class.

b Challenge

VOCABULARY
Challenge partners to deepen their understanding of the theme vocabulary words by creating a sentence for each word that conveys its meaning. Ask students to build each sentence around the word *because*. For example, *Travelers need to be aware of the temperature extremes before they travel to the desert, because not packing the right clothes can ruin a trip.* Before students share their sentences with another pair, have them remove the vocabulary words so the pair can fill in the blanks.

c Intervention for Acceleration

COMPREHENSION STRATEGY: VISUALIZE
If students have difficulty visualizing what they read, provide partners with books from the classroom library that are photograph or illustration-heavy. One partner describes the image to the other partner, who draws what he or she visualises. Encourage the first students to use vivid, rich words in their descriptions. At the end of the activity, have partners compare the original image with the student's visualization. Have them discuss the similarities and differences between the images, and how rich language helped them visualize.

Read and Comprehend (continued)

Objectives
Students will:
- Read about the history and culture of the Western Region
- Reinforce visualizing

Prepare to Read

Build Background

Remind students that in the first part of *A Tour of the Western Region*, they learned about the geography and

Theme Reader
Pages 392–395

economy of the Western Region. Explain that today they will learn about the history and culture of the region.

- Draw a Concept Web (Resource Master 11) on the board with the word *history* in the center. Guide students to add related words to the web. Then, draw a second web for the word *culture* and do the same.

- Show students images from the early West. Explain that as settlers began to move to the West, they made farms, cleared land, and founded towns and cities.

ASSIGN | RESOURCE MASTER **11**

Preview and Predict

Preview Chapter 2 of *A Tour of the Western Region*. Point out the chapter title, subhead, photographs, chart, and captions. Ask students questions to help them make predictions:

- What does the photograph on page 392 make you think this section will be about? *(Possible response: The homes people built in the West.)*

- Look at the header "History and Culture" and the photos. Will this section be about the past or the present? How do you know?

Set Purposes

Students will read to find answers to the Theme Question: *What makes the West exceptional?*

Students should also skim Chapter 2 to set a purpose for their own reading, such as to learn more about something that looks interesting to them.

Read Together

Share your thinking as you begin reading Chapter 2 of *A Tour of the Western Region*. Have partners continue reading. Pause them periodically to discuss theme concepts and vocabulary.

PAGES 392–393 Let's look at the photo and read the caption. This photo shows the Ancestral Pueblo cliff dwellings in Colorado. I know from the caption that this area is about 800 years old. How would you describe the buildings in this picture? Try to use your new vocabulary words in your description. *(Possible response: The buildings look very simple and the land appears arid. Living in houses that are built of rock connected to a cliff would be very different from living in the types of houses we live in today.)*

PAGES 394–395 Have partners summarize what they learned about settlers in the West. Discuss the most important ideas as a group.

Respond

Have students look at their concept webs from the beginning of the lesson and tell which aspects of the web the chapter discussed. Talk about the purposes students set for themselves, and whether they achieved those purposes. Have students share how visualizing helped them understand what they read.

Partner Talk ★★

Provide the discussion points below:

- Talk about the part of the chapter that was most interesting.

- Tell your partner about one scene that you visualized while reading, adding many details to help your partner "see" the scene.

- Discuss how the chapter answered the Theme Question.

Word Work and Fluency

Objectives
Students will:
- Practice the VV pattern
- Practice fluent reading

Spelling and Word Study

Practice Words with the VV Pattern
Review the VV pattern with students. Then have students use their spelling lists to write a sentence for each word, and then read their sentences to a partner. The partner spells the word and gives its meaning. **b**

ASSIGN | PRACTICE COMPANION **188**

Fluency

Shared Choral Reading
Ask students to revisit the first paragraph of "The Great Potato State" (Practice Companion, p. 190) and look for the rich language used to describe aspects of Idaho's geography.

- What words does the author use to describe Idaho's geography? *(green, snow-covered, sparkling)*
- How do these words improve your reading experience?
- What words could you use to describe the geography in our area?

Explain that today students will pay special attention to phrasing, or the way readers chunk sentences into parts to help them understand the text. Tell students that you will read the advertisement, pausing periodically to explain your phrasing. Ask students to pay special attention to how you chunk words into meaningful segments.

Read the selection once, pausing for explanation; then reread it without pausing. Close the lesson by leading a choral reading of the speech. Remind students to pay attention to their own phrasing during the choral reading. **c**

ASSIGN | PRACTICE COMPANION **190**

---

scaffolding options

a Critical Thinking

ANALYZE FACTS AND DETAILS
Once students have completed their discussions about settlers in the West, split the class into groups of four and ask them to compare and contrast the settlers in the West and settlers in New England, which they read about in *A Tour of the Atlantic States* in Unit 3. Then have students detail the hardships each group faced. Bring the class back together and have each group share an item from their discussion.

b Literacy Builder

WORD STUDY
Ask student pairs to search Chapter 2 of *A Tour of the Western Region* to identify other words with the VV pattern. Have pairs organize the words into two lists (one syllable vs. multiple syllables) and record the page number where each word is found. Invite pairs to share their words in a whole-group discussion. When a pair says a word, invite volunteers to tell which sound or sounds it includes.

c ELL Support

FLUENCY
If English language learners have difficulty understanding the selection, ask your native English speakers to act out the selection as others chorally read it.

Differentiated Reading
small groups

Objectives
Students will:
- Use differentiated vocabulary
- Reinforce visualizing
- Read about working and living in the Mountain States

Prepare to Read

Build Background

Read with students the Focus Question: *How are geography and economy connected in the Mountain States?* (Differentiated Reader, p. 5).

This week students will read about living and working in the Mountain Plains. Ask:

How does using the land of an area help its economy?

Differentiated Reader Pages 6–17

Then read together the title, *Living and Working in the Mountain Plains* (p. 6).

- Explain that the Mountain Plains is an area at the base of the Rocky Mountains. Encourage students to tell what they know about plains areas. Have them use the photograph on page 6 to help them.

- Start a Concept and Word Web (Resource Master 11) about the word *plains* on chart paper. Have students suggest ideas to add to the web.

ASSIGN   RESOURCE MASTER **11**

Introduce
Differentiated Vocabulary *tested!*

Have students complete the Vocabulary Rating Sheet (Resource Master 4).

- Find and pronounce with students the highlighted differentiated vocabulary words (pp. 6–17).

- Use the following routine to discuss each word's meaning.

- For each word, have students jot down and explain answers to prompts.

Vocabulary Routine

Define	**Range** (p. 15) means "an area of open land where livestock can move and graze."
Example	Many herds of cattle can be found on the range.
Ask	What else might be raised on the range?

Barbed (p. 16) means "having sharp points." *Rusty snagged his shirt on the barbed wire fence.* Where would you find *barbed* wire? **a**

ASSIGN   RESOURCE MASTER **4**

Preview and Predict

Have students preview the selection, focusing on chapter titles, photos, captions, and other text features. Ask them what they think they might learn from reading this selection, and why they think so.

Set Purposes

Remind students that setting a purpose will help them focus their attention and read more deeply.

- Students will add new information and details to the concept web.

- Students should also look for answers to the Focus Question.

REINFORCE COMPREHENSION STRATEGY

Visualize

Remind students that when readers visualize, they picture things in their minds. Have students tell why readers use this strategy. *(to better understand what they read)*

To reinforce visualizing, you may wish to use page 7 to model your thinking.

> **think aloud** This paragraph asks us what we picture when we think of the Mountain States. I picture tall, majestic mountains. I see people skiing on these mountains and enjoying the steep slopes. What do you picture? **b**

ASSIGN   PRACTICE COMPANION **192–193**

Read

Today students will read pages 6–17 of *Living and Working on the Mountain Plains*. To help them get started, model your thinking as you read page 7.

> **think aloud** The picture on this page looks like something I would see in a magazine! That almost makes me want to live there. As I read, I see that there are many natural features that could make someone want to live in the Mountain Plains.

Guide Comprehension

Invite partners to continue reading. Pause them periodically to monitor understanding of key concepts and vocabulary. Have students discuss each prompt with their partner before sharing with the group.

PAGES 6–8 Have students look at the map on page 8. Invite them to describe what information the key provides.

PAGES 9–12 Have partners read the **Strategy Tool Kit** on page 12 and give oral descriptions to answer the question. Have volunteers share what they visualized with the group.

PAGES 13–17 Have partners analyze the text for ways that geography and economy are connected. *(Students should mention that farmers and ranchers use the land to grow their crops and raise their livestock.)*

Check Comprehension

1. What do we learn about on page 12? How do the temperatures affect the people living there? *(the changes in temperatures throughout the year in Cheyenne, Wyoming; droughts and extreme temperatures can hurt the farm land)* IDENTIFY MAIN IDEA

2. Why do you think people enjoy living and working in the Mountain Plains? MAKE INFERENCES

3. What things happen throughout the year on the range? SEQUENCE EVENTS

Respond and Write

1. Have partners discuss **Stop and Think** on page 17.

2. Have students add new information to the Concept Web you began as a group earlier. Have them include specific details to support ideas they've already added to the web.

3. Discuss how the first half of the selection has helped students answer the Focus Question.

scaffolding options

ELL Support

See page 288 of this Teacher's Lesson Guide for vocabulary and instructional support of English language learners at the Intensive level.

a Literacy Builder

VOCABULARY: WORD RELATIONSHIPS
Invite students to work in pairs to familiarize themselves with the underlined words in *Living and Working in the Mountain Plains*. Before reading, have partners list the underlined words on pages 6–17, record the definition for each, and use each in a sentence. Then, have pairs write an antonym, synonym, or example of each word and use it to quiz another pair of students. For example, *What might have slopes? (mountains)*

b Intervention for Acceleration

USE GRAPHIC SOURCES
If students have trouble visualizing, encourage them to use the photographs in the Differentiated Reader as a starting point. Ask them questions about each photo to help them describe what they see. Then, ask them to imagine what they might hear, smell, taste, and touch if they were a participant in each photograph.

ebook online coach

Intervention for Acceleration

Students can use the support features in the eBook version of the Differentiated Reader.

Read and Comprehend

Objectives
Students will:
- Use differentiated vocabulary
- Reinforce visualizing
- Read about the canyons and deserts of the Mountain States

Differentiated Reading

small groups

Prepare to Read

Build Background

Read with students the Focus Question: *How are geography and economy connected in the Mountain States?* (Differentiated Reader, p. 5). This week students will read about the history of the canyons and deserts of the Mountain States.

Differentiated Reader Pages 6–15

Read together the title, *Canyons and Deserts of the Mountain States* (p. 6).

- Explain that the geography of the Mountain States is full of extremes, from dry deserts to rushing rivers and hot desert temperature to cold mountain temperatures. Encourage students to tell what they know about the geography of the Mountain States.

- Have students examine a map that shows the Western Region of the United States. Point out states that belong to the Mountain States. Have them start a quickwrite describing the Mountain States.

Introduce
Differentiated Vocabulary

Have students complete the Vocabulary Rating Sheet (Resource Master 4).

- Find and pronounce with students the highlighted differentiated vocabulary words (pp. 6–15).

- Use the following routine to discuss each word's meaning.

- For each word, have students jot down and explain answers to prompts.

Vocabulary Routine	
Define	**Sustain** (p. 9) means "to support or keep living."
Example	It doesn't take much rain to sustain vegetation in the desert.
Ask	What is an antonym for sustain?

A **mesa** (p. 11) is a hill or mountain with a flat top. *The mesa extended out of the desert floor.* What is another characteristic of a *mesa*?

Continue the routine with *pillar* (p. 11), *surge* (p. 12), and *ominous* (p. 15), using the Glossary definitions and sentences and asking questions.

ASSIGN RESOURCE MASTER **4**

Preview and Predict

Have students preview the selection, focusing on chapter titles, photos, captions, and other text features. Ask them what they think they might learn from reading this selection, and why they think so.

Set Purposes

Remind students that setting a purpose will help them focus their attention and read more deeply.

- Students will read to revise their quickwrites with new information.

- Students should also look for answers to the Focus Question.

REINFORCE COMPREHENSION STRATEGY

Visualize

Remind students that when readers visualize, they picture things in their minds. Have students tell why readers use this strategy *(to make sense of what they read).*

think aloud This first paragraph on page 7 describes what the Painted Desert looks like. The author says the land is rainbow-colored. These words help me picture the area in my mind. There must be a lot of different colors in the hills, like in a rainbow. I visualize hills that are striped in the colors of the land.

ASSIGN PRACTICE COMPANION **192–193**

Read

Tell students that today they will read pages 6–15 of *Canyons and Deserts of the Mountain States.* To help them get started, model your thinking as you read page 6.

 This paragraph includes two highlighted words: *extreme* and *arid.* I know the meanings of these two words from our earlier discussion. I think that this story will tell us more about the extreme conditions in the mountain states and how arid some of the land can be.

Guide Comprehension

Have partners continue reading. Pause them periodically to monitor understanding of key concepts and vocabulary. **a**

PAGES 6–9 Have partners read the **Strategy Tool Kit** on page 9. Ask students if they used a fix-up strategy to monitor their comprehension and if so, which one they used. Have volunteers share their responses to the question with the group.

PAGES 10–11 Have students revisit the text in order to visualize the deserts of the Mountain States. Have students share their visualizations with a partner.

PAGES 12–15 Ask students to retell what they learned about canyons.

Check Comprehension

1. What are the most important ideas on each page from pages 7–15? *(Possible response: Page 7: The Mountain States have many natural features. Pages 8–11: Desert land can be found in the Mountains States. It is hot and dry. Pages 11–15: The Mountain States have long, deep canyons too.)* DETERMINE IMPORTANT INFORMATION

2. Summarize what you've read about today. SUMMARIZE

3. What is an area of the world that has land features similar to those of the Mountain States? MAKE CONNECTIONS

Respond and Write

1. Have partners discuss **Stop and Think** on page 15, citing examples from the text. **b**

2. Have partners revisit their quickwrites and add anything new they learned in the selection.

3. Ask students how the selection up to this point has helped answer the Focus Question.

scaffolding options

ELL Support

See page 289 of this Teacher's Lesson Guide for vocabulary and instructional support of English language learners at the Strategic level.

a Intervention for Acceleration

USE ON-PAGE SUPPORTS
Point out the underlined word on page 9. Tell students that underlined word are usually important to the understanding of the story. Underlined words also allow the reader to read more fluently without having to pause to use a dictionary. Have students reread the sentence that contains an underlined word, and then reread it substituting the word given below.

b Intervention for Acceleration

REREAD
Before students answer **Stop and Think** on page 15, ask them to reread pages 6–15. Remind students that rereading helps them understand and remember the key concepts and events in a story. Remind students that as they reread, they should look for the most important information that will help them answer the question.

ebook online coach
Intervention for Acceleration

Students can use the support features in the eBook version of the Differentiated Reader.

Read and Comprehend

Differentiated Reading *small groups*

Objectives
Students will:
- Use differentiated vocabulary
- Reinforce visualizing
- Read about the majestic Rockies

Prepare to Read

Build Background

Introduce the Focus Question: *How are geography and economy connected in the Mountain States?*

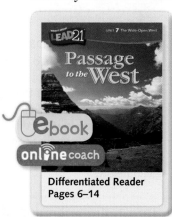

Differentiated Reader Pages 6–14

- Elicit what students already know about this topic. Read together the title, *The Majestic Rockies* (p. 6). Have students use the photos on pages 6–14 to describe the Rocky Mountains and tell what *majestic* means.

- Ask students to do a 30-second quickwrite on the topic of mountain areas.

Introduce Differentiated Vocabulary *tested*

Have students complete the Vocabulary Rating Sheet (Resource Master 4).

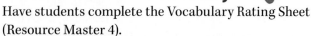

Vocabulary Routine	
Define	**Jagged** (p. 7) means "having a sharp, uneven edge or surface."
Example	We had to watch out for the jagged rocks as we walked along the river bank.
Ask	What kinds of things can be jagged?

An **excursion** (p. 9) is a pleasure trip. *We enjoyed our excursion to the Grand Canyon.* Where would you like to go on an *excursion*?

Partners continue the routine with *barrier* (p. 12), using the Glossary definition and sentence and asking questions.

ASSIGN RESOURCE MASTER **4**

Preview/Predict/Set Purposes

Students preview the selection and predict what they will learn. They read to answer the Focus Question and add information to their quickwrites.

Read

Guide Comprehension

Partners will read pages 6–14 of *The Majestic Rockies*. You may wish to monitor understanding of theme concepts and vocabulary with the prompts below. Remind students to visualize while they read.

PAGES 6–10 Have students use the map on page 8 to discuss the regions of the Rocky Mountains.
USE TEXT FEATURES **a**

PAGES 11–14 Have students pause during reading to ask their partner questions. ASK AND ANSWER QUESTIONS

Respond and Write

Have students check their predictions of what they would learn, and then respond to the Focus Question and add information to their quickwrites.

scaffolding options

ELL Support

See page 290 of this Teacher's Lesson Guide for vocabulary and instructional support of English language learners at the Benchmark level.

a Literacy Builder *tested*

COMPREHENSION: VISUALIZE Challenge partners to give imaginative oral descriptions of what they are reading about. For example, on page 9, students might describe what it would be like to be in the Canadian Rockies in the summertime.

Differentiated Reading
small groups

Objectives
Students will:
- Use differentiated vocabulary
- Reinforce visualizing
- Read about the Colorado River

Prepare to Read

Build Background

Introduce the Focus Question: *How are geography and economy connected in the Mountain States?* and have students read the title on page 6.

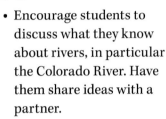

**Differentiated Reader
Pages 6–13**

- Encourage students to discuss what they know about rivers, in particular the Colorado River. Have them share ideas with a partner.

- Have students make a KWL Chart (Resource Master 12) and complete the "What I Know" column.

ASSIGN | RESOURCE MASTER **12**

Introduce
Differentiated Vocabulary *tested*

Have students complete the Vocabulary Rating Sheet (Resource Master 4).

Vocabulary Routine	
Define	**Sediment** (p. 7) is the rocks, dirt, and other matter that is carried and then left by water, wind, or glaciers.
Example	Sediment can be found at the bottom of rivers.
Ask	What do you think sediment looks and feels like?

Partners continue the routine with *tributary* (p. 8), and *momentum* (p. 13), using the Glossary definitions and sentences and asking questions.

ASSIGN | RESOURCE MASTER **4**

Preview/Predict/Set Purposes

Have students preview and make predictions. Then students will complete the "What I Want to Know" column of their KWL charts. They will complete their charts and answer the Focus Question.

Read

Guide Comprehension

Students will read pages 6–13 of *The Colorado River in the Mountain West* on their own and visualize as they read. After they read, discuss selection concepts.

PAGES 6–9 Prompt students to make connections between the map of the Colorado River and the text on these pages. MAKE CONNECTIONS

PAGES 10–13 Have students summarize what they learned from this part of the story about how the lakes along the Colorado River help support the area's economy. SUMMARIZE

Respond and Write

1. Invite students to discuss their predictions and how the selection helps answer the Focus Question.

2. Ask students to complete the "What I Learned" column of their KWL charts.

scaffolding options

ELL Support

See page 291 of this Teacher's Lesson Guide for vocabulary and instructional support of English language learners at the Advanced level.

Literacy Builder *tested*

COMPREHENSION: VISUALIZE
Have students visualize participating in a recreational activity on the Colorado River. Have them describe to a partner what they are doing, using details such as how things feel, sound, smell, and appear.

Share, Connect, Assess

Objectives
Students will:
- Use key concepts and vocabulary
- Make text-to-text connections
- Write about land features of the West
- Monitor their progress

Wrap Up
whole group

Share Text Connections

Building Classroom Community

Make Text-to-Text Connections Bring students back together from their small groups to talk about their Differentiated Reader selections.

- Invite students to share the topic of their selections and something interesting they've read so far. Encourage them to share some of the differentiated vocabulary words they read.

- Ask students what they know about the topics that other groups are reading about. As they discuss the texts, point out connections. For example, compare the picture of mountains in *Living and Working in the Mountain Plains* (p. 10) with the picture of the Rockies in *The Majestic Rockies* (p. 10).

- Have students share how what they've read and discussed answers the week's Focus Question.

etools 21
theme wall

Daily Writing

Have students write a paragraph about the land features of the part of the West they read about today. Encourage them to provide descriptive details.

For additional writing practice, remind students to access the Story Starter from their student Home Page.

etools 21
- writing tool
- story starter

Student Self Assessment

- Remind students that they are responsible for their learning and that it is helpful to be aware of how well they understand what they are reading, writing, talking, and thinking about in the classroom.

- You may want students to reflect on their reading and learning by using their Personal Reading Logs and My Daily Progress sheets (Resource Masters 1, 3).

ASSIGN RESOURCE MASTER **1, 3**

Daily Progress Monitoring

To ensure that students have mastered the day's skills and strategies, monitor their success in completing the following independent work:

- **Vocabulary:** Practice Companion, p. 186
- **Comprehension:** Practice Companion, pp. 192–193
- **Spelling:** Practice Companion, p. 188
- **Fluency:** Practice Companion, p. 190
- **Study Station Work Record:** Resource Master 2
- **Self Assessment:** Resource Masters 1, 3

Home Connection

Distribute the Unit 7 Take-Home Activities from the Home Connection book. Tell students to complete the activities with their caregivers.

Day at a Glance

Lesson Highlights

- Introduce Vocabulary Strategy: Synonyms
- Review Comprehension Skill: Generalize
- Use Text Features: Line Graphs
- Introduce Word Study: Negative Prefixes
- Prewrite a Science Fiction Story, pp. 134–135

Materials

	Teacher's Lesson Guide	Student Components	Digital 21
Interactive Reading	pp. 36–39	• Theme Reader, pp. 380–395 • Practice Companion, pp. 189–190, 194–197 • Resource Masters 14, 24	ebook online coach · epractice word study games
Differentiated Reading	pp. 40–45, 288–291 (ELL)	• Differentiated Readers • Resource Master 4	ebook online coach · epractice vocabulary activities
Wrap Up	p. 46	• Resource Masters 1–3	etools 21 • theme wall • writing tool • story starter
Writing and Language Arts	pp. 134–135	• Writing Models Chart, pp. 48–49 • Practice Companion, pp. 220–221, 223 • Resource Masters 15, 23	

Tips for Success

- Guide students to make connections between reading and writing (p. 37).
- Use the Writing Models Chart to show a model of a science fiction story.
- Use the Theme Reader or other classroom books to point out examples of line graphs.

Interactive Reading whole group

Objectives
Students will:
- Reinforce the theme
- Use synonyms

Reinforce the Theme

Use the images on Theme Reader pages 378–391 to recall the Theme Question: *What makes the West exceptional?* Ask:

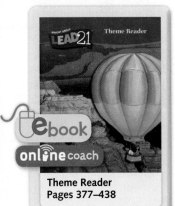

**Theme Reader
Pages 377–438**

- What is special about the geography of the Western Region? *(Possible response: There are plains, mountains, valleys, and canyons.)*

- What is special about the economy of the Western Region? *(Possible response: Ranchers raise livestock, and the beautiful landscape brings tourists. Both help the economy.)*

Point out the images on Theme Reader pages 392–395 and ask:

- What is special about the history of the Western Region? *(Possible responses: Native Americans were the first inhabitants; Settlers created farms and towns.)*

- What is special about the culture of the Western Region? *(Responses will vary but students may mention arts, sports, music, mining towns, monuments, and so on.)*

Encourage students to use the new vocabulary words they've learned throughout the discussion.

INTRODUCE VOCABULARY STRATEGY

Use Synonyms

Define and Model

Tell students that a strategy they can use to expand their understanding of words is using synonyms. Explain:

> Synonyms are words that have almost the same meaning. Finding synonyms can help readers better understand the meaning of words as used in the text and help them learn new words.

Reread page 388 of the Theme Reader. Have students identify a pair of words that are synonyms having to do with the Colorado River (*twists, turns*).

You may wish to choose other words from this section of text, such as *mighty*, *arid*, and *prosper*, and ask students to come up with synonyms.

Practice

Have partners look at page 391 of the Theme Reader and use a T-Chart (Resource Master 14) to list words from the text and synonyms for those words.

Examples include:

Synonyms	
Word from Text:	Synonym:
interesting	exciting
well-known	popular
scenery	setting
attraction	activity

Have partners share their word pairs with the class, and list the pairs on the board.

Invite students to define each word and share how the definitions are similar and different.

ASSIGN

RESOURCE MASTER	14
PRACTICE COMPANION	194–195

model · read · share

Read and Comprehend

Objectives
Students will:
• Review generalizing

REVIEW **COMPREHENSION SKILL**

Generalize tested

Define and Model

Remind students that generalizing is a skill readers use to understand what they read. Say:

A generalization is a broad statement that combines different examples that are mostly alike. The words all, none, most, or many often appear in a generalization.

Use Resource Master 24 as you model generalizing with Theme Reader page 384.

think aloud I read that the Mountain States have many different geographical features, such as mountains, which are used for mines, and plains, which are used for farming. The Colorado River is good for tourism. I can make a generalization that many geographical features contribute to the economy of the Mountain States.

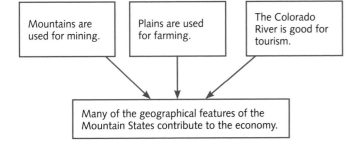

Practice

Ask students to make another generalization from many details or examples that are similar in Chapter 1. Use Resource Master 24 to record their ideas. **b**

Reading/Writing Connection

Explain that writers know that readers generalize to make sense of the text. Ask:

How might writers help readers generalize about certain ideas? *(Writers put common ideas together or compare and contrast ideas to help the reader.)*

ASSIGN
| RESOURCE MASTER | **24** |
| PRACTICE COMPANION | **196** |

---

scaffolding options

a Intervention for Acceleration

VOCABULARY: SYNONYMS
Some students may not be able to easily identify words that have commonly-used synonyms. For students who need additional prompts to complete the activity, help them by pointing out specific words in the text for which they should find synonyms. Have partners discuss each word and what it means, then offer words that could be suitable synonyms. Have students check their work using a dictionary or thesaurus, if desired.

b Challenge

COMPREHENSION: GENERALIZE
Challenge students to provide their own examples of generalizing. Ask them to think about the things they do every day and to try to come up with generalizations about the information. Have them first give examples of what they do and then describe their generalizations to the class. Ask the class to give feedback on the generalizations and determine if they are accurate, based on the examples students provided.

Interactive Reading whole group

Objectives
Students will:
• Use line graphs
• Reinforce generalizing

Prepare to Read

Use Text Features

Discuss how text features help readers understand concepts.

**Theme Reader
Pages 382–395**

• Have students name text features they know. Tell students that text features often provide additional information about a topic.

• Have students look through Chapters 1 and 2 to point out text features, such as captions, maps, sidebars, and charts.

Text Features Minilesson: Line Graphs

Study the line graph about Utah's population (p. 395). Explain that line graphs give information and help readers understand a topic more deeply.

• What is the line graph about? *(the history of Utah's population)*

• What happened to Utah's population over the years? *(It grew.)*

• How does the chart relate to what the text says? *(A large number of Mormons moved into Utah, which helped the population grow.)*

Ask students to revisit pages 382–395 and look for other parts of the selection in which a line graph would be helpful. *(Possible responses: tons of coal, silver, and gold mined each year; number of tourists per year; number of Native Americans still living in the West)*

Set Purposes

Students reread pages 382–395 to:

• Find out how text features add information to the text and help answer the Theme Question: *What makes the West exceptional?*

Read Together

Have students reread pages 382–395 of *A Tour of the Western Region*. After students read, discuss how text features add to the text's meaning. Share any generalizations they identified or made as they read. **b**

PAGES 382–387 How does the map on page 384 help you understand what the Western Region is? *(It clearly shows the states that make up the region.)*

PAGES 388–391 What examples of cause and effect can you find in the captions? *(Possible response: The movement of an underground salt bed caused the creation of a sandstone formation in Arches National Park in Utah.)*

PAGES 392–393 How does the text help you visualize what it was like to live during the early history of the West? *(Possible response: The text describes what the Native American houses were made of, this helps me visualize what they looked like.)*

PAGES 394–395 Who first explored some of the Mountain States? How has the area changed since that time? *(Lewis and Clark first explored the Mountain States in the 1880s. Since then, the fur trade moved to the area, Mormons settled in Utah, and mining towns expanded rapidly. Now the West hosts many tourists.)*

Respond

After students read, ask them to share how text features help them answer the Theme Question: *What makes the West exceptional?* **c**

Talk About Text ★★★

Encourage students to discuss the role of text features in nonfiction:

• How do text features help you understand the text?

• What kinds of text features do you find most useful when reading nonfiction?

• What are some ways that authors use line graphs in nonfiction texts?

Word Work and Fluency

Objectives
Students will:
- Practice the VV pattern
- Analyze prefixes *un-, de-, dis-, counter-, mis-*
- Practice fluent reading

Spelling

Practice Words with the VV Pattern
Have students turn to page 189 in their Practice Companions. Explain that students will proofread the paragraph to find and correct the misspelled words.

ASSIGN PRACTICE COMPANION **189**

Word Study

Introduce Negative Prefixes
Explain that the prefixes *un-, de-, dis-, counter-,* and *mis-* have negative meanings, such as "not" or "away." Using prefixes helps readers figure out the meaning of words.

Teach/Model
Write the following words on the board and have students identify their meanings based on their prefixes.

> *undecided* (not decided)
> *decline* (to turn something down)
> *detach* (remove from)
> *dismayed* (not happy)
> *counter-clockwise* (not clockwise)
> *mismatched* (not matched)
> *mistreat* (treat poorly)

Practice/Apply
Ask students to think of additional words with prefixes with negative meanings and add them to the list.

ASSIGN PRACTICE COMPANION **197**
epractice
word study games

Fluency

Paired Reading
Read "The Great Potato State" (Practice Companion, p. 190) to model appropriate expression. Have partners practice reading the selection with expression.

ASSIGN PRACTICE COMPANION **190**

---

scaffolding options

a Challenge

USE TEXT FEATURES
Invite students to gather information and use it to create their own line graph. For example, students might track the amount of fruit students ate each day, or they may track the temperature each day for a week.

Discuss how creating a line graph helped them analyze and interpret the data.

b Literacy Builder

COMPREHENSION: GENERALIZE
Have students discuss the generalizations they made as they read. Keep a list of generalizations on the board. Discuss which generalizations help answer the Theme Question.

c Critical Thinking

EVALUATE TEXT FEATURES
Have small groups of students discuss what they've learned so far from the selection. Ask:
- If you were writing a short summary of Chapters 1 and 2, what single text feature would you include to support your summary?

Encourage groups to consider a variety of text features that would best convey the most important information, such as maps and charts.

Read and Comprehend　　Intensive

Differentiated Reading small groups

Objectives
Students will:
- Use differentiated vocabulary
- Reinforce using synonyms
- Reinforce generalizing
- Reinforce using text features
- Read about working and living in the Mountain States

Prepare to Read

Review

Review pages 6–17 of *Living and Working on the Mountain Plains* by asking questions, such as:

Differentiated Reader Pages 18–27

- What kinds of things do people do as they live and work in the mountain plains?
- Why do you think ranchers still use the range like they did more than 100 years ago? What are some words you would use to describe the range?

Have students share what they found out about the Focus Question: *How are geography and economy connected in the Mountain States?*

Introduce Differentiated Vocabulary

Have students complete the Vocabulary Rating Sheet (Resource Master 4).

- Find and pronounce with students the highlighted differentiated vocabulary words (pp. 18–27).
- Use the following routine to discuss each word's meaning. For each word, have students jot down and explain answers to prompts.

Vocabulary Routine	
Define	**Endure** (p. 18) means "to continue to exist."
Example	The building has endured many strong hurricanes.
Ask	What is another word for *endure*?

Integral (p. 19) means "necessary and important." *Teachers are an integral part of a student's education.* Why are teachers an *integral* part of education?

Continue the routine with *supplement* (p. 21), *widespread* (p. 23), *preserve* (p. 23), and *initiative* (p. 25), using the Glossary definitions and sentences and asking questions.

ASSIGN　**RESOURCE MASTER 4**　 vocabulary activities

Set Purposes

Display the Concept Web the group began on Day 2. Point to words in the Concept Web. Have the group read the items chorally.

- Students will look for additional words to add to the Concept Web as they read.
- Students will look for answers to the Focus Question.

REINFORCE COMPREHENSION SKILL

Generalize　tested ✓

Remind students that a generalization is a very general statement based on examples that are mostly alike. Students must first identify important information before they can study those examples and make a general statement about them.

To review generalizing, use pages 15–17 to model your thinking:

> **think aloud** Theses pages include text that explains that ranchers have raised cattle on the Mountain Plains for more than one hundred years. What generalization can you make about the importance of the range to the area?

ASSIGN　**PRACTICE COMPANION 196**

Read

Tell students that today they will finish reading *Living and Working on the Mountain Plains*. Remind them to use the skills and strategies they learned in whole group as they read. To help them get started, model your thinking as you read pages 18–19.

> **think aloud** I read in the caption on page 18 that cowboys herd hundreds of cattle in a roundup. I also see two highlighted words that are important to the concept of roundups. I will pay attention to these words as I read the chapter to help me understand the concept of a roundup.

Guide Comprehension

Invite students to continue reading silently. Circulate to reinforce theme concepts, skills, and strategies. Allow students to use sticky notes to make notes and write questions they may have about the text. **a**

PAGES 18–20 Have partners read the **Strategy Tool Kit** on page 19 and jot down their ideas. Then ask students to use details from the text to visualize which geographic features would make a good roundup location. **b**

PAGES 21–22 Have students jot down notes about how tourism is an important part of some ranchers' lives. *(Possible response: Some ranchers depend on tourism during the off-season, or when they aren't raising or moving cattle.)*

PAGES 23–27 Have students identify the importance of the Ranchers Stewardship Alliance and what they contribute to their community.

Check Comprehension

1. What is one generalization you can make about what you have read so far? GENERALIZE

2. Describe how helicopter cowboys are different from other types of cowboys. *(Helicopter cowboys round up the cattle using the noise of the helicopters. Other types of cowboys use horses to round up cattle.)* COMPARE AND CONTRAST

3. Make connections between the ranches described in the text and a ranch you have visited or seen in the movies or on television? What words might you use to describe the ranch? Write synonyms for these words. MAKE CONNECTIONS

Respond and Write

1. Have students return to their Concept Webs to add new information. Have partners compare webs and discuss how today's reading helps answer the Focus Question.

2. Have students write a persuasive paragraph or personal letter to convince a friend or family member to travel to the Western Region to visit a ranch. Have them include information from the text and add details that they've visualized. You may wish to have students complete their writing during Independent Practice.

scaffolding options

ELL Support

See page 288 of this Teacher's Lesson Guide for vocabulary and instructional support of English language learners at the Intensive level.

a Intervention for Acceleration

MONITOR COMPREHENSION
Encourage students to make note of which comprehension and fix-up strategies they use while reading and looking for answers to the Guide Comprehension questions. When they have finished the activites, have partners discuss which strategies they used the most and which they used the least. Have students explain why they used certain strategies more often than others.

b Intervention for Acceleration

USE ON-PAGE SUPPORTS
Remind students to take advantage of the On-Page Support feature on pages 18-19. To further comprehension of the underlined words, have students create sentences using *herd* and *branded*, and then share those sentences with partners.

ebook online coach
Intervention for Acceleration

Students can use the support features in the eBook version of the Differentiated Reader.

Read and Comprehend  Strategic

Objectives
Students will:
- Use differentiated vocabulary
- Reinforce using synonyms
- Reinforce generalizing
- Reinforce using text features
- Read about the canyons and deserts of the Mountain States

Prepare to Read

Review

Review pages 6–15 of *Canyons and Deserts of the Mountain States* by asking questions, such as:

ebook online coach

Differentiated Reader Pages 16–27

- Where are the Mountain States and what are they like?
- What types of land features can you find in the Mountain States?

Have students share what they found out about the Focus Question: *How are geography and economy connected in the Mountain States?*

Introduce
Differentiated Vocabulary

Have students complete the Vocabulary Rating Sheet (Resource Master 4).

- Find and pronounce with students the highlighted differentiated vocabulary words (pp. 16–27).
- Use the following routine to discuss each word's meaning. For each word, have students jot down and explain answers to prompts.

Vocabulary Routine	
Define	**Adobe** (p. 17) means "a sun-dried brick made from clay and straw."
Example	The houses in the historic Pueblo city are made of adobe.
Ask	Do you think houses made of adobe were easy to build?

Astounding (p. 20) means "causing surprise or amazement." *The Grand Canyon offers many astounding sights for visitors to see.* What are some *astounding* sights you have seen so far in this unit?

Devise (p. 21) means "to invent." *The team must devise a way to raise money for the field trip.* How can groups work together to *devise* plans?

Hue (p. 22) is a color. *At sunset, the sky has a yellow-orange hue.* What colors would you use to describe the *hue* of the sky during sunrise?

ASSIGN **RESOURCE MASTER 4** **epractice** vocabulary activities

Set Purposes

Remind students that setting a purpose helps readers focus their attention to get more out of their reading.

- Students will read to and add to the quickwrites they started the day before.
- Students will also read to find answers to the Focus Question.

REINFORCE COMPREHENSION SKILL

Generalize

Remind students that a generalization is a general statement based on examples that are mostly alike. Ask students why they must first identify important information before they can generalize.

Help students locate a generalization on page 14.

think aloud The text on page 14 says that many canyons still have rivers running through them today. The word *many* indicates a generalization.

ASSIGN **PRACTICE COMPANION 196**

Read

Tell students that today they will finish reading *Canyons and Deserts of the Mountain States*. Remind them to use the skills and strategies they learned in whole group as they read. To help them get started, model your thinking as you read page 16.

think aloud I see from the chapter title that I will read about people who live in the canyons and deserts in the Mountain States. I can tell by looking at the photo and reading the caption on page 16 that some people live in traditional Pueblo architecture. I wonder why they choose to live this way? I will keep this in mind as I read the second part of the selection.

Guide Comprehension

Have students continue reading silently. Circulate to reinforce theme concepts, skills, and strategies. Allow students to jot down their thoughts before answering your prompts.

PAGES 18–19 Have partners make generalizations about what they read on each page. Then have them jot down synonyms for the words *beautiful, rush,* and *settle. (Possible synonyms: gorgeous, stunning, pretty; hurry, race; live, remain, dwell)*

PAGES 20–21 Have partners read the **Strategy Tool Kit** on page 21 and jot down their ideas. Have partners discuss any connections they made with these pages.

PAGES 22–27 Have students read the captions on these pages and retell how they provide more information about the text. *(The captions provide specific examples of concepts discussed in the text.)*

Check Comprehension

1. What information does the graph on page 21 provide? *(The number of annual visitors to the Grand Canyon.)* USE TEXT FEATURES   **a**

2. How does tourism help the people of the Mountain States? *(It provides jobs for many of the locals, and visitors spend money in the area.)* SUMMARIZE

3. How is industry in the Mountain States different today than it was in the past? *(Industry used to focus on mining, but today the mines are mostly tourist attractions. Solar energy is a growing industry.)* COMPARE AND CONTRAST

Respond and Write

1. Ask students to tell about what part of the selection was the most interesting to them, and have them make a generalization about that section.   **b**

2. Have students complete their quickwrites and share them with the group. Then lead a group discussion about how today's reading helps answer the Focus Question.

scaffolding options

ELL Support

See page 289 of this Teacher's Lesson Guide for vocabulary and instructional support of English language learners at the Strategic level.

a Intervention for Acceleration

USE TEXT FEATURES: LINE GRAPH
To ensure comprehension, ask additional questions about the line graph on page 21:

What is the first date on the graph? The last? *(1960 and 2009)*

What year had the most visitors? *(2000)*

Approximately how many visitors did the Grand Canyon have in 1990? *(4 million)*

What is the source of this data? *(United States Department of National Parks)*

b Critical Thinking

AUTHOR'S PURPOSE
Ask students to review the photographs in the second half of the selection and explain why the author might have included them. Discuss with students how these photographs can be used to help them add to their descriptions of the Western Region.

ebook **online coach**
Intervention for Acceleration

Students can use the support features in the eBook version of the Differentiated Reader.

Read and Comprehend

Differentiated Reading
small groups

Objectives
Students will:
- Use differentiated vocabulary
- Reinforce using synonyms
- Reinforce generalizing
- Reinforce using text features
- Read about the Rocky Mountains

Prepare to Read

Review

Review with students pages 6–14 of *The Majestic Rockies.* Have students reference their quickwrites

from the previous day to help them explain key concepts they learned. Have them share what they found out about the Focus Question: *How are geography and economy connected in the Mountain States?*

Differentiated Reader Pages 15–27

Introduce
Differentiated Vocabulary *tested*

Have students use the Vocabulary Rating Sheet (Resource Master 4).

Vocabulary Routine	
Define	**Introduce** (p. 16) means "to bring in for the first time."
Example	The new student was introduced to her class.
Ask	Why is it important to introduce yourself to new people?

Partners continue the routine with *journal* (p. 18) *overwhelm* (p. 20), *dedicate* (p. 24), and *maintain* (p. 27), using the Glossary definitions and sentences and asking questions.

ASSIGN RESOURCE MASTER **4**   **epractice** vocabulary activities

Set Purposes

Have students tell what they want to learn from pages 15–27 of the selection.

- Students will read to add information to the quickwrites they started at the beginning of the selection.

- Students will read to answer the Focus Question.

Read

Guide Comprehension

As students finish reading *The Majestic Rockies,* remind them to use skills and strategies they learned in whole group. Circulate to reinforce concepts, skills, and strategies. **a**

PAGES 16–25 Have students explain how the sidebars, charts, and captions help them understand what life is like in the Rocky Mountains. **USE TEXT FEATURES**

PAGES 26–27 Ask students to generalize the information on each page. Then have them make a generalization about the entire selection. **GENERALIZE**

Respond and Write

Have students finish their quickwrites by adding information they learned in today's reading. Have them include ideas that answer the Focus Question.

scaffolding options

ELL Support

See page 290 of this Teacher's Lesson Guide for vocabulary and instructional support of English language learners at the Benchmark level.

a Challenge

VOCABULARY: SYNONYMS
Choose a variety of challenging words from the reading and list them on the board. Have students use context clues to formulate definitions for each word, and then have them list synonyms for each. Have partners compare their notes.

Differentiated Reading
small groups

Objectives
Students will:
- Use differentiated vocabulary
- Reinforce using synonyms
- Reinforce generalizing
- Reinforce using text features
- Read about the Colorado River

Prepare to Read

Review

Review with students pages 6–13 of *The Colorado River in the Mountain West.* Have students use the KWL charts they began the previous day to discuss the key concepts they've learned so far. Have them share what they found out about the Focus Question: *How are geography and economy connected in the Mountain States?*

Differentiated Reader
Pages 14–27

Introduce Differentiated Vocabulary

tested

Have students use the Vocabulary Rating Sheet (Resource Master 4).

Vocabulary Routine	
Define	**Fierce** (p. 14) means "wild."
Example	The fierce lion wanted to attack its prey.
Ask	What is another animal that might be considered fierce?

A **trophy** (p. 16) is a prize usually awarded for a victory. *The baseball team won the state trophy.* Why might a team win a *trophy*?

Partners continue the routine with *monument* (p. 18), *vicinity* (p. 20), *achievement* (p. 23), and *retain* (p. 26), using the Glossary definitions and sentences and asking questions. Ⓐ

ASSIGN   RESOURCE MASTER   4
epractice
vocabulary activities

Set Purposes

Discuss what students want to learn from the selection and elicit why setting a purpose for reading is helpful.

- Students will read to complete the KWL charts they started during the previous lesson.
- Students will read to answer the Focus Question.

Read

Guide Comprehension

Students will finish reading *The Colorado River in the Mountain West.* As students read independently, encourage them to use the skills and strategies they learned in whole group. After students read, use the following prompts:

PAGES 14–19 Have students make generalizations about the national parks described on these pages. **GENERALIZE**

PAGES 20–27 Have students explain how the captions, sidebars, and chart help the reader better understand the text on these pages. **USE TEXT FEATURES**

Respond and Write

Have students complete their KWL charts by adding information they learned to the last column. Have them discuss answers to the Focus Question.

scaffolding options

ELL Support

See page 291 of this Teacher's Lesson Guide for vocabulary and instructional support of English language learners at the Advanced level.

Ⓐ Challenge

VOCABULARY: SYNONYMS
Challenge students to use a dictionary to find synonyms for the differentiated vocabulary words. Then have students write a short story using both the vocabulary words and at least one synonym for each word.

Share, Connect, Assess

Wrap Up
whole group

Objectives
Students will:
- Summarize selections
- Make text-to-world connections
- Write about using a map or GPS
- Monitor their progress

Share Text Connections

Building Classroom Community

Make Text-to-World Connections Bring students back together from their small groups to summarize their selections.

- Encourage students to use theme and other academic vocabulary in their summaries.

- As students discuss the texts, help them to make connections between texts and the world. For example, the map in *The Colorado River in the Mountain West* (p. 9) helps readers understand features of the Colorado River Basin. Similarly, drivers use maps to learn more about an area.

- Ask students to share the activities they completed during Respond and Write.

- Have students share how what they've read answers the week's Focus Question.

etools 21
theme wall

Daily Writing

Have students write about a time they used a map or GPS to navigate. Encourage them to tell how the map or GPS helped them, and what they learned from it.

For additional writing practice, remind students to access the Story Starter from their student Home Page.

etools 21
- writing tool
- story starter

Student Self Assessment

- You may want students to reflect on their reading and learning by using their Personal Reading Logs and My Daily Progress sheets (Resource Masters 1, 3).

ASSIGN RESOURCE MASTER **1, 3**

Daily Progress Monitoring

To ensure that students have mastered the day's skills and strategies, monitor their success in completing the following independent work:

- **Vocabulary:** Practice Companion, pp. 194–195
- **Comprehension:** Practice Companion, p. 196
- **Word Study:** Practice Companion, p. 197
- **Spelling:** Practice Companion, p. 189
- **Fluency:** Practice Companion, p. 190
- **Study Station Work Record:** Resource Master 2
- **Self Assessment:** Resource Masters 1, 3

epractice
reporting

Home Connection

Distribute the Unit 7 Take-Home Activities from the Home Connection book. Tell students to complete the activities with their caregivers.

Week 1 Day 4

Lesson Highlights

- Extend Theme Vocabulary
- Reinforce Comprehension Strategy: Visualize
- Use Text Evidence
- Reinforce Word Study: Negative Prefixes
- Draft a Science Fiction Story, pp. 136–137

Materials

	Teacher's Lesson Guide	Student Components	Digital 21
Interactive Reading	pp. 48–51	• Theme Reader, pp. 380–395 • Practice Companion, pp. 187–188, 190–193, 197 • Resource Masters 14, 21	ebook online coach · epractice word study games
Differentiated Reading	pp. 52–57, 288–291 (ELL)	• Differentiated Readers • Resource Masters 14, 16	ebook online coach · epractice vocabulary activities
Wrap Up	p. 58	• Resource Masters 1–3	etools 21 • theme wall • writing tool • story starter
Writing and Language Arts	pp. 136–137	• Writing Models Chart, pp. 48–49 • Practice Companion, pp. 220, 224 • Resource Master 17	etools 21 writing tool

Tips for Success

- Introduce the methods for using text evidence that students will use throughout the unit.
- Guide students to use multiple strategies as they read (Model Multiple Strategies, p. 49).
- As students work on their science fiction stories, encourage them to make connections between reading and writing as they Talk About Text

Oral Language and Vocabulary

Objectives
Students will:
- Extend the theme
- Extend theme vocabulary

Interactive Reading
whole group

Extend the Theme

Recall the Theme Question: *What makes the West exceptional?* Have students name concepts that they discussed this week, such as geography, economy, history, and culture. List their ideas on the board.

LEAD21
Theme Reader

 ebook
online coach

Theme Reader
Pages 377–438

Challenge students in small groups to use each of these words in a discussion that answers these questions:

- How do these concepts relate to our community?

- How are economy and geography connected in our community?

Encourage students to draw conclusions that demonstrate a generalization about the Mountain States. Demonstrate what's expected by modeling how to start a conversation such as:

think aloud Our city is close to a ski resort. Many people enjoy skiing there in the winter. The ski resort employs a lot of people in the area. People spend money at the ski resort and at neighboring businesses. I can make a generalization that the ski resort is important to our area's economy.

- Ask volunteers to summarize the outcomes of their small-group discussions.

- Have the class decide which concepts are most important to your area.

Extend Theme Vocabulary

To extend understanding of the theme vocabulary, complete a word association activity. To help the class get started, model the first response.

think aloud When I hear the word *extremes,* the first word I think of is *desert.* Desert can be really hot during the daytime and extremely cold at night. Deserts experience the extremes in temperatures. My word association for *extremes* is *desert.*

Continue by using the following procedure:

- Say the word *extremes* and ask a volunteer to say the first word that comes to mind. Invite them to share the way this word connects to *extremes.*

- Record the student's response on the board, and ask another volunteer to share a word that he or she associates with the previous student's response.

- Continue in this way until students cannot provide any more word associations. Then use the same routine for *arid* and *irrigated.*

As a class, review the list of words generated during the activity, and discuss how the words are related (synonyms, antonyms, examples, word parts).

ASSIGN | PRACTICE COMPANION **187**

model
read
share

Read and Comprehend

Objectives • Reinforce visualizing
Students will:

REINFORCE COMPREHENSION STRATEGY

Visualize

Define

Have students tell what it means to visualize and ask them why readers use visualizations to help them understand the text.

Remind students that readers use more than one strategy when they read. Invite students to recall strategies they know.

Model Multiple-Strategy Use

Model multiple-strategy use with Theme Reader page 384.

 This page talks about how visitors come year round to enjoy the Rocky Mountains and all that they have to offer. I can infer that many people depend on the Rocky Mountains to support the area's economy. I can also make a connection between the text and the fact that this region is called the Mountain States. The mountains are obviously very important to this area.

Guided Practice

Have students continue rereading Chapter 1, working with a partner to complete Use Multiple Strategies (Resource Master 21). Circulate to guide students. Discuss as a class what partners wrote. Remind students to use multiple strategies as they read today. **c**

Independent Practice

Students continue to reread the selection independently, recording on Resource Master 21 the strategies they use.

Reading/Writing Connection

Explain that writers use descriptive words and specific examples to help readers visualize something and understand how it is unique. Ask:

Why would a writer describe an area as frigid, mountainous, and rugged, instead of cold, tall, and rocky? *(Possible response: The first set of words makes the reader think of more specific images and feelings.)*

ASSIGN

RESOURCE MASTER	21
PRACTICE COMPANION	192–193

scaffolding options

a Critical Thinking

ANALYZE VOCABULARY

Have students compare the word-association lists they created for each vocabulary word. Have them identify words that were included on multiple lists. For example, the word *extremes* may be related to *opposites, weather, and unpredictable*. Have students use the interconnected words to create oral explanations of how each vocabulary word is linked to *extremes*. Model an example:

 There can be extremes in the weather. Weather can also be unpredictable. Extreme weather can be opposite of the weather the day before, such as when there is an ice storm in Texas one day, and then the next day it is 90 degrees.

b Literacy Builder

WORD RELATIONSHIPS

After the word association game, have pairs or small groups discuss whether connecting words that are related is a helpful tool for building vocabulary. Ensure that students explain their opinions.

c Intervention for Acceleration

MULTIPLE-STRATEGY USE

Review with students some of the strategies they've learned so far. Have students list the strategies on a note card and jot down a word or two that helps them remember how to use the strategy. For example, students may draw an icon of an eye for visualizing, or they may write the formula "Text + What I Know" for making inferences. Have students pause periodically while reading to review their note cards and see if they can apply any of the strategies to the text.

Interactive Reading whole group

Objectives
Students will:
• Reread to find text evidence
• Reinforce visualizing

Prepare to Read

Use Text Evidence

Remind students that they have been reading *A Tour of the Western Region* to help them answer the Theme Question: *What makes the West exceptional?*

**Theme Reader
Pages 380-395**

• Explain that readers can use evidence from the text to support their ideas or answers to questions about the text.

• Suggest that skimming and scanning are two helpful methods for finding text evidence. Invite volunteers to explain each of the techniques. Then say:

I like to scan the chapter titles and section headings to help me quickly locate information related to a specific topic.

• Tell students that they will use a T-Chart (Resource Master 14) with the headings *Page Number* and *Text Evidence* to record text evidence and the page number where it is found. **a**

ASSIGN RESOURCE MASTER **14**

Set Purposes

Students will reread Chapters 1 and 2 today to gather information to help them answer the Theme Question.

Read Together

Begin rereading, modeling how to skim and scan for text evidence. Record the example on chart paper:

 think aloud When I skim page 384, I can see information is provided about the geography and economy of the Western Region. The caption explains that Red Rock Canyon attracts one million people each year. That is definitely something that makes the West exceptional.

Ask partners to continue to read, using their T-charts to record text evidence that will help them answer the Theme Question.

Stop periodically and ask volunteers to add text evidence they've recorded on the chart paper, and discuss it as a class.

A Tour of the Western Region, Pages 380-395	
What makes the West exceptional?	
Page #	**Text Evidence**
384	One million people visit Red Rock Canyon each year.
386	Sheep and cattle use 70 percent of Wyoming's land for grazing.
388	The intersection of Utah, Colorado, Arizona, and New Mexico is the only place in the nation where four states come together at one place.

Respond

Partners will discuss how the text evidence they gathered helps them answer the Theme Question.

Discuss how visualizing details in the selection helped students understand why the West is exceptional.

Writer's Response

Have students choose one activity:

• Choose an example of text evidence and provide more detail about how it relates to the Theme Question.

• Which part of the West would you be interested in visiting, and why?

Have students discuss their thoughts with a partner before jotting down their responses.

Word Work and Fluency

Objectives
Students will:
- Practice the VV pattern
- Reinforce prefixes *de-, un-, dis-, counter-, mis-*
- Practice fluent reading

Spelling

Practice Test

Have partners dictate the spelling words to one another. Then have them self-correct their papers. Remind them to focus their attention on any words they misspelled.

ASSIGN PRACTICE COMPANION **188**

Word Study

Reinforce Negative Prefixes

Remind students that the prefixes *de-, un-, dis-, counter-,* and *mis-* have negative meanings. Write the following words on the board. Have volunteers provide the meaning of each word based on its prefix.

depart	counterfeit
unharmed	disappear
misuse	demote

Practice/Apply

Have pairs choose one word with each prefix and write a sentence for each.

ASSIGN PRACTICE COMPANION **197** word study games

Fluency

Personal Rehearsal

Model reading "The Great Potato State" (Practice Companion, p. 190) with appropriate pacing. Read it again at a fast pace. Ask how pacing affects comprehension.

Have students rehearse the selection and complete the Reading Response Form (Practice Companion, p. 191). **c**

ASSIGN PRACTICE COMPANION **190–191**

---

scaffolding options

a Intervention for Acceleration

KEY WORDS
Suggest to students that they can make skimming and scanning the text even easier by identifying key words to look for. If students are trying to answer the Focus Question, for example, they might scan the text for the word *geography* because that word is a key word in the question. Encourage students to share any tricks they use to help them identify important information in a selection.

b Literacy Builder

WORD STUDY
Have students use a dictionary or thesaurus to find additional words that begin with the prefixes *de-, un-, dis-, counter-,* and *mis-.* Caution students to pay attention to the meanings of the words, as not all words that begin with these prefixes contain a negative connotation.

c Intervention for Acceleration

FLUENCY PRACTICE
After students have practiced reading the passage with fluent pacing, have them choose another selection to practice fluent reading. Have partners read the selection once together, deciding which parts should have a faster or slower pace and discussing why. Then have them reread the selection, using the pace they chose. You may wish to monitor pacing and provide feedback.

Read and Comprehend

Objectives
Students will:
- Extend vocabulary
- Reread to find text evidence
- Reinforce visualizing
- Reinforce generalizing

Differentiated Reading *small groups*

Prepare to Read

Extend Vocabulary

Explain that one way to expand vocabulary knowledge is to find relationships among words. Say:

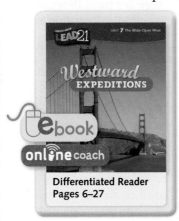

Differentiated Reader
Pages 6–27

- Words might be related because they are synonyms or antonyms, such as *tall/short* or *short/tall*.
- They might be related because one word is an example of another, such as *maple* and *tree*.

Write the following word pairs on the board:

range/field (S)	preserve/waste (A)
endured/quit (A)	initiative/program (EX)
integral/important (S)	barbed/soft (A)
supplement/extra (EX)	widespread/large (S)

Follow this procedure:

- Have each student write the words *synonym*, *antonym*, and *example* on separate index cards.
- After you read each pair, have students hold up the appropriate card. **a**
- Discuss the words' meanings and relationships.

 **epractice** vocabulary activities

Set Purposes

Students will revisit *Living and Working on the Mountain Plains* to find and record text evidence to support answers to the Focus Question: *How are geography and economy connected in the Mountain States?*

Use Text Evidence

Invite a volunteer to recall why using text evidence is important. Have students prepare a new T-Chart (Resource Master 14) with the headings *Page Number* and *Text Evidence*. When students find a fact or detail that might help them answer the Focus Question, they should record it in the chart.

Help students get started by reading aloud page 7. Model your thinking as you read.

think aloud On page 7, I read about the types of landforms that are included in the Mountain Plains. They are mountains, canyons, and flat lands that are covered with grasses called *prairies*. The last sentence states these are an important part of the geography and economy of the Mountain States. This answers the Focus Question. I will write this statement and page number in my chart.

ASSIGN RESOURCE MASTER **14**

Read

Guide Comprehension

Have partners continue rereading *Living and Working on the Mountain Plains*, working together to record text evidence in their charts. Students should share their notes with the group after each chapter. Use the prompts below to provide support as needed. **b**

CHAPTERS 1–2 Have students share what text evidence they found that helps them answer the Focus Question. *(Possible response: Some of the captions provide information about how the geography and economy are connected.)* USE TEXT EVIDENCE

CHAPTERS 3–4 Have students connect the vocabulary words from Chapters 3 and 4 to the chapters' most important ideas. *(Possible response: The word* endured *describes how ranchers have survived conditions in the Mountain Plains for many years. It relates to the overall feeling of how ranching is such an important or integral part of the economy and geography of the area.)* DETERMINE IMPORTANT INFORMATION

CHAPTER 5 Ask students to make a generalization about how people of the Western States are looking toward the future. Have them explain how this generalization connects to the ideas of geography and economy. GENERALIZE

Respond and Write

Have students look over the text evidence they've gathered and share one or two items with the group. Guide students to understand how the information from the text helps them answer the Focus Question.

Prepare to Share

Tell students they will discuss the **Think Back** activities on page 28 of their Differentiated Readers tomorrow with their mixed groups.

1. **Check Understanding** Have students review the T-charts they have been using to record text evidence. For discussion tomorrow, ask them to identify ways that the plains are important to the economy of the Mountain States.

2. **Understand Text Features** Explain that when students meet tomorrow in their mixed groups, they will share their ideas about how graphs are helpful in presenting information to readers.

3. **Share and Compare** Review the list of ways in which geography and economy are connected in the selections that have been read so far in this unit.

4. **Think Critically** Complete this activity as a group. Emphasize details from the selection that point to why the West is exceptional. Guide students in making generalizations from these details.

scaffolding options

ELL Support

See page 288 of this Teacher's Lesson Guide for vocabulary and instructional support of English language learners at the Intensive level.

a Intervention for Acceleration

PARTNER FOR ACCELERATION
As an alternate procedure for the Extend Vocabulary activity, you might have students work with partners to discuss each word pair before they hold up their note cards. Or, the whole group might discuss each word's meaning before students identify the relationship and hold up their cards.

b Intervention for Acceleration

COMPREHENSION SKILL: VISUALIZE
Remind students to visualize while they reread the selection to enhance comprehension. If they have difficulty visualizing the text, encourage them to use the photographs as a starting point for their visualizations. Encourage them to note the colors of the sky, mountains, rivers, and grasses. Ask them to imagine the sounds of native animals and the way the earth and wind smell.

ebook online coach
Intervention for Acceleration

Students can use the support features in the eBook version of the Differentiated Reader.

Read and Comprehend   Strategic

Objectives
Students will:
- Extend vocabulary
- Reread to find text evidence
- Reinforce visualizing
- Reinforce generalizing

Prepare to Read

Extend Vocabulary

Suggest that one way to expand vocabulary knowledge is to understand how words are related. Explain that words

Differentiated Reader Pages 6–27

can be linked because they are synonyms or antonyms, because one word is an example of another word, or because they share similar word parts.

- Distribute to each student Resource Master 16. Have students use the headings *Synonyms, Antonyms, Examples,* and *Word Parts.*

Write the following word pairs on the board:

sustain/keep (S)	astounding/boring (A)
mesas/formations (EX)	hue/color (S)
pillars/columns (S)	ominous/dark (S)
surged/shrunk (A)	adobe/house (EX)
devised/developed (S)	

Read the word pairs aloud, discussing the meanings of any unfamiliar words. Have students record the word pairs in the appropriate column of their charts. Afterward, encourage a group discussion about how the words pairs are related.

ASSIGN RESOURCE MASTER **16**
e practice vocabulary activities

Set Purposes

Students will reread *Canyons and Deserts of the Mountain States* to find and record text evidence to support responses to the Focus Question: *How are geography and economy connected in the Mountain States?*

Use Text Evidence

Ask students to recall why using text evidence is a helpful strategy. Then, have them create a new T-Chart (Resource Master 14) with the headings *Page Number* and *Text Evidence.* Ask students to record in the chart any facts or details that might help them answer the Focus Question.

Help students get started by reading aloud pages 6–7. Model your thinking as you read.

> **think aloud** These pages share what types of landforms are found in the Mountain States. They also include a map of this area. The first paragraph on page 7 states that many people visit the canyons and deserts of this area to see the beautiful land. This is an answer to the Focus Question. I will write this detail, along with the page number, in my chart.

ASSIGN RESOURCE MASTER **14**

Read

Guide Comprehension

Have partners continue to reread *Canyons and Deserts of the Mountain States* and work together to record text evidence in their charts. Use the prompts below to provide support as needed.

PAGES 6–17 Discuss with students how the map on page 11 connects with the photographs on pages 8 and 9. Have students put their fingers on the map to point out the areas shown in the photographs. *(Possible response: The map shows the location of desert areas in the Mountain States.)* USE TEXT FEATURES **a**

PAGES 18–27 Visualize a sunset over the desert mesas and plateaus. Why do you think artists are inspired by what they see? How are the arts related to the Focus Question? *(Possible response: Artists are inspired by the beauty of the unique landscape of the West. Artists make things to trade and to sell to tourists to help the area economy.)* VISUALIZE

Respond and Write

Have students look over the text evidence they've gathered and share one or two items with the group. Guide students to understand how the information from the text helps them answer the Focus Question.

Prepare to Share

Tell students they will discuss the **Think Back** activities on page 28 of their Differentiated Readers tomorrow with their mixed groups.

1. **Check Understanding** Have students review the T-charts they have been using to record text evidence. For discussion tomorrow, ask students to identify ways that the canyons and deserts help the economy of the Mountain States.

2. **Understand Text Features** Explain that when students meet tomorrow in their mixed groups, they will share their ideas about how graphs are helpful in presenting information to readers.

3. **Share and Compare** Review the list of ways in which geography and economy are connected in the selections that have been read so far in this unit.

4. **Think Critically** Complete this activity as a group. Emphasize details from the selection that point to why the West is exceptional. Guide students in making generalizations from these details. **b**

scaffolding options

ELL Support

See page 289 of this Teacher's Lesson Guide for vocabulary and instructional support of English language learners at the Strategic level.

a Intervention for Acceleration

COMPREHENSION SKILL: GENERALIZING
Challenge students to make a generalization based on the information from pages 6–7. If students struggle, point out that even though the geography of the Mountain States varies and can be extreme, all of the landforms have one thing in common. (*The geography of the Mountain States benefits the economy of the area and its people.*)

b Critical Thinking

SYNTHESIZE CONCEPTS
Point out that this question is closely related to the Theme Question. Remind students to combine what they have learned from their reading of the selection with their understanding of what makes the West exceptional. Explain that all of the information they have learned to answer the Theme Question can be combined to discuss the **Think Critically** activity tomorrow in mixed groups.

ebook online coach

Intervention for Acceleration

Students can use the support features in the eBook version of the Differentiated Reader.

Read and Comprehend   Benchmark

Objectives
Students will:
- Extend vocabulary
- Reread to find text evidence
- Reinforce visualizing
- Reinforce generalizing

Prepare to Read

Extend Vocabulary

Point out that one way to expand vocabulary knowledge is to understand how words are related.

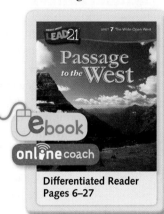

Explain that words are related if they are synonyms or antonyms, if one word is an example of another word, or if two words share the same or similar word parts.

Differentiated Reader Pages 6–27

Read the following clues. Have students name and write down the vocabulary word that is related. **a**

- *Mountains* are an example of this word. *(jagged)*
- *A cruise* is an example of this word. *(excursion)*
- *Wall* is a synonym for this word. *(barrier)*
- *Present* is an synonym for this word. *(introduce)*
- *Diary* is a synonym for this word. *(journal)*
- *Calm* is an antonym for this word. *(overwhelmed)*
- *Give* is an synonym for this word. *(dedicate)*
- *Cease* is an antonym for this word. *(maintain)*

vocabulary activities

Set Purposes

Students will revisit *The Majestic Rockies* to find and record text evidence to support responses to the Focus Question: *How are geography and economy connected in the Mountain States?*

Use Text Evidence

Have students create a T-Chart (Resource Master 14) with the headings *Page Number* and *Text Evidence*. Students will record facts that help them answer the Focus Question. Invite volunteers to find and share an example of text evidence.

ASSIGN   **RESOURCE MASTER 14**

Read

Guide Comprehension

Students work independently to gather text evidence and complete their charts. Monitor students' progress with the following prompts.

CHAPTERS 1–2 Have students identify and record rich language that helps them visualize the text. VISUALIZE

CHAPTER 3 Have students make a generalization about how tourism and mining affect the economy of the Rocky Mountains. GENERALIZE

Respond and Write

1. Have students use the text evidence they found today to write a response to the Focus Question.

2. Have students prepare answers to the **Think Back** activities for discussion in mixed groups tomorrow.

ELL Support

See page 290 of this Teacher's Lesson Guide for vocabulary and instructional support of English language learners at the Benchmark level.

a Challenge

VOCABULARY
Challenge students to choose four vocabulary words and find one more example of a related word. Have them use each vocabulary word and its related word in a sentence that explains how they are related.

Differentiated Reading
small groups

Objectives
Students will:
- Extend vocabulary
- Reread to find text evidence
- Reinforce visualizing
- Reinforce generalizing

Prepare to Read

Extend Vocabulary

Point out that one way to expand vocabulary knowledge is to understand how words are related.

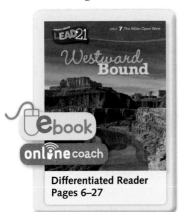

**Differentiated Reader
Pages 6–27**

- One way words are related is if they are synonyms or antonyms. What is a synonym for *sediment?* What is an antonym for *rugged?*

- You may also identify examples of a word. What is an example of a *tributary?*

- Some words share the same or similar word parts. What word shares a word part with *momentum?*

Write the following on the board:

fierce *(Example)*	retain *(Word Part)*
trophy *(Synonym)*	momentum *(Antonym)*
monument *(Example)*	sediment *(Synonym)*
vicinity *(Synonym)*	tributary *(Synonym)*
achievement *(Antonym)*	

Have students work independently to give examples of related words as stated. Then have them share and compare their examples in pairs or small groups.

Set Purposes

Students will revisit *The Colorado River in the Mountain West* to record text evidence to answer the Focus Question: *How are geography and economy connected in the Mountain States?*

Use Text Evidence

Have students create a T-Chart (Resource Master 14) with the headings *Page Number* and *Text Evidence*. Tell students that, as they read, they should note facts that will help them answer the Focus Question.

ASSIGN   RESOURCE MASTER 14

Read

Guide Comprehension

Have students revisit the selection independently to record text evidence. After they read, use the following points of discussion. **a**

CHAPTERS 1–2 Select a geographic feature mentioned in these chapters and summarize how it affects the economy of the Western Region. **SUMMARIZE**

CHAPTER 3 Ask students to share generalizations about how the Colorado River's power helps the area's economy. **GENERALIZE**

Respond and Write

1. Have students use the text evidence they found today to write a response to the Focus Question.

2. Have students prepare answers to the **Think Back** activities for discussion in mixed groups tomorrow.

scaffolding options

ELL Support

See page 291 of this Teacher's Lesson Guide for vocabulary and instructional support of English language learners at the Advanced level.

a Challenge

VISUALIZE
Challenge students to select a paragraph from the text that is difficult to visualize. Have students rewrite the paragraph, using rich language to boost the reader's comprehension. Share as a group.

Share, Connect, Assess

Objectives
Students will:
- Use key concepts and vocabulary
- Use text evidence to answer essential questions
- Make text-to-text connections
- Write about finding text evidence
- Monitor their progress

Wrap Up
whole group

Share Text Connections

Building Classroom Community

Make Text-to-Text Connections Bring students back together from their small groups to share how the text evidence they gathered from their Differentiated Reader selections helped them to answer the Focus Question: *How are geography and economy connected in the Mountain States?*

- Encourage students to use theme and other academic vocabulary as they share their responses.

- Ensure that students from all groups have a chance to contribute to the discussion.

- As students share text evidence, help them make connections between texts. For example, both *The Colorado River in the Mountain West* and *The Majestic Rockies* discuss national parks and what people can see when they visit the parks.

etools 21
• theme wall

Daily Writing

Have students write briefly about the strategy and method they used to find text evidence. Encourage them to describe how the text evidence helped them to answer the Theme and Focus Questions.

For additional writing practice, remind students to access the Story Starter from their student Home Page.

etools 21
• writing tool
• story starter

Student Self Assessment

- Remind students that they are responsible for their learning and that it is helpful to be aware of how well they understand what they are reading, writing, talking, and thinking about in the classroom.

- You may want students to reflect on their reading and learning by using their Personal Reading Logs and My Daily Progress sheets (Resource Masters 1, 3).

ASSIGN **RESOURCE MASTER 1, 3**

Daily Progress Monitoring

To ensure that students have mastered the day's skills and strategies, monitor their success in completing the following independent work:

- **Vocabulary:** Practice Companion, p. 187
- **Comprehension:** Practice Companion, pp. 192–193
- **Word Study:** Practice Companion, p. 197
- **Spelling:** Practice Companion, pp. 188–189
- **Fluency:** Practice Companion, pp. 190–191
- **Study Station Work Record:** Resource Master 2
- **Self Assessment:** Resource Masters 1, 3

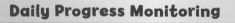

epractice
reporting

Home Connection

Distribute the Unit 7 Take-Home Activities from the Home Connection book. Tell students to complete the activities with their caregivers.

21st **CENTURY SKILLS**

Week 1 Day 5

Lesson Highlights

- Introduce the Project
- Assign Inquiry Groups
- 21st Century Skills Minilesson: Listening Skills
- Cross-Text Sharing
- Fluency Presentation
- Spelling Posttest

Materials

	Teacher's Lesson Guide	Student Components	Digital 21
Inquiry	pp. 60–63	• Practice Companion, pp. 174, 198–200, 370–372 • Resource Masters 8, 33–35	etools 21 inquiry project
Cross-Text Sharing	pp. 64–65	• Differentiated Readers • Practice Companion, p. 201 • Resource Masters 14, 35	ebook online coach
Wrap Up	pp. 66–67	• Assessment Handbook, pp. 13–14, 140 • Differentiated Reader, p. 29 • Practice Companion, p. 202 • Resource Master 1	etools 21 • theme wall • writing tool • story starter

Inquiry Process Guide

Week 1, Day 5	Week 2, Day 5	Week 3, Day 5	Week 4, Day 5
1. Generate Ideas and Questions 2. Make a Conjecture 3. Make Plans to Collect Information	Days 1–4: Collect Information 4. Organize and Synthesize Information 5. Confirm or Revise Your Conjecture	Days 1–4: Collect Information 6. Develop Presentation	Days 1–4: Collect Information 7. Deliver Presentation

Tips for Success

21st **CENTURY SKILLS** Form Inquiry Groups that include one member from each differentiated reading level.

- Provide Investigation Sheets (Resource Master 35) for students to use throughout the week on Days 1–5. Students will also begin Idea Tracker (Resource Master 34).

- Set out theme-related reference materials for students to use throughout the week on Days 1–5.

Generate Ideas

Objectives
Students will:
• Make connections between the theme question and the Inquiry project
• Review the Inquiry process
• Practice collaboration

Inquiry whole group

Introduce the Project

Connect to the Theme

Ask a volunteer to recall the Theme Question: *What makes the West exceptional?* and the Focus Question:

**Theme Reader
Pages 380–408**

How are geography and economy connected in the Mountain States? Say:

Think back to what you read about the Mountain States. How would you describe the Mountain States? What questions do you still have about living and working in these states?

• Have students revisit the Inquiry Self-Assessment Rubric they completed for Unit 6 (Practice Companion, p. 174) to review what they did well and what they would like to improve.

• Explain that, in Unit 7, students will learn about a time line as a possible format to share their Inquiry findings. Invite students to review the characteristics of a time line on Practice Companion page 200.

• Have students create a Unit 7 Inquiry folder.

etools 21 inquiry project

Be sure students know to access Inquiry Project online from their student Home Page.

ASSIGN PRACTICE COMPANION **174, 200**

Model the Inquiry Process

1. Generate Ideas and Questions

Brainstorm Questions Review the questions that students have posted on the Question Board this week. Model brainstorming questions using the Question Board:

Many of you wrote questions about the Grand Canyon. Some of you wondered how the Painted Desert got all of its different colors. That would be a good question to research. You might write it like this: Why are the layers of sediment in the Grand Canyon different colors?.

etools 21 theme wall

Students can refer to the Theme Wall to view other posted questions.

Decide on a Question Remind students to choose a question that is not too broad and can be researched easily. For example, *Where is Hollywood?* can be answered by looking at a map. However, *How did Hollywood become the center of the movie-making industry in the United States?* can be researched in more depth. Ask:

How could you change the question *What is the weather like in the Mountain States?* to make it a stronger Inquiry Question? *(How does climate affect the Mountain States?)*

Other possible Inquiry Questions for Unit 7 include

• How was the Moffat Tunnel through the Rocky Mountains built?

• How was the Grand Canyon formed?

2. Make a Conjecture

Write on the board or display on chart paper the following sample Inquiry Question:

How did Hollywood become the center of the movie-making industry in the United States?

Remind students that a conjecture is made before research has been conducted, so it may change. It can be revised as research and understandings progress.

Model making a conjecture for the sample question.

 I think what I know about California can help me make a guess about how Hollywood became the center of the movie industry. The weather is warm and sunny in California, which is probably good for filming movies outdoors, because you can film all year long. I think one reason Hollywood became the center of the movie-making industry is that the weather there is good for filming.

Encourage students to comment on your conjecture and offer their own conjectures. Ask students to explain how they arrived at their conjectures. **a**

3. Make Plans to Collect Information

Remind students that each group member should plan to do research independently next week. Have students list several topics to research. Tell them to divide up the topics and compromise so that everyone is researching something of interest. Have them refer to the Information Finder (Practice Companion, p. 371) and discuss other possible sources of information. Say:

When you work in a group, you can find more information if each group member researches a part of the topic. Each group member should still use a variety of sources, however. For information on the movie-making industry in Hollywood, I could search Web sites. I could also reference an encyclopedia for quick facts about the location and demographics of the area. **b** **c**

ASSIGN   PRACTICE COMPANION   371

21st CENTURY SKILLS

Minilesson: Listening Skills Review

Discuss good listening skills with students. Say:

When someone is speaking, you should listen quietly and wait until that person is finished so that you don't miss out on important information.

Invite a volunteer to speak and model attentive listening and asking clarifying questions. Ask:

What characteristics of good listening did I observe? *(good eye contact, not interrupting)*

Have students work in groups to write a list of rules for good listening. Then have them share their lists with the class as the other groups demonstrate good listening. Invite volunteers to tell what rules for good listening they followed.

scaffolding options

a Intervention for Acceleration

SUPPORT CONJECTURES
Discuss with students how to make a conjecture about a topic they don't know much about. Say:

Sometimes you may have to make a conjecture about a question you don't know much about. When this happens, start by writing all of the things that you do know about the topic. Use one of these as a basis for a conjecture, and remember that you can always add to your conjecture or revise it as you become more knowledgeable.

b Literacy Builder

BUILD INTEREST
If a student does not exhibit interest in his or her group's Inquiry Question, tell that student that even if the Inquiry Question isn't his or her first choice, he or she can still choose a part of personal interest to research. Help these students choose specific topics or questions related to their groups' Inquiry Questions that both support the collective research efforts and are personally rewarding.

c ELL Support

CONCEPTS AND VOCABULARY
Invite English language learners to work with partners to list specific words and phrases they might use to research their individual parts. Have pairs write the words together and, if needed, check the spelling in dictionaries so that students are using accurate words to search for information.

Collaborate and Communicate

Objectives
Students will:
• Choose discussion roles
• Choose an Inquiry question and make a conjecture
• Make plans to collect information
• Collaborate in Inquiry groups

Inquiry *mixed groups*

Begin Inquiry Group Work

The following Resource Masters and Practice Companion pages will be used in this lesson.

Step	Resource Master	Practice Companion
All	Collaboration Rubric 39 Evaluation Rubric A 40	Week 1 Inquiry Checklist, p. 198 Time Line, p. 200 Group Roles, p. 370
2.	Idea Tracker 34	
3.	Investigation Sheet 35	Inquiry Planner, p. 199 Information Finder, p. 371 Evaluating Sources, p. 372

Assign Inquiry Groups

Assign new Inquiry Groups for Unit 7 and ask students to move into their groups. Try to include at least one student from each differentiated reading level in each group. Students may want to name their groups.

Choose Discussion Roles

Review the group discussion roles *(Questioner, Checker, Recorder, Discussion Monitor)* and have students choose their roles for their projects. See Group Discussion Roles (Practice Companion, p. 370). Encourage each student to choose a new or different role for this project.

ASSIGN **PRACTICE COMPANION 370**

Monitor Student Progress

Use the Collaboration Rubric (Resource Master 39) and the Inquiry Evaluation Rubric A (Resource Master 40) to monitor student progress throughout the project. Review the project expectations with students before beginning Inquiry Group work.

USE **RESOURCE MASTER 39, 40**

Inquiry Groups

1. Generate Ideas and Questions   *critical thinking* `make connections, evaluate`

Brainstorm Questions Students use the pages they read in their Theme Readers this week or the questions posted on the Question Board to recall the theme-related ideas that they would like to learn more about.

• Groups should collaborate to formulate at least three questions, based on shared interests. **a**

• Suggest that students write all their ideas and then underline or mark the ones they like best.

• Students fill in their Inquiry Checklist (Practice Companion, p. 198) as they complete each step. Prompt each group Checker to make sure each checklist item is being addressed.

ASSIGN **PRACTICE COMPANION 198**

Decide on a Question Circulate to help students strengthen their questions.

• Tell students to choose a question that is open-ended and relates to the theme.

• Remind groups to use what they have learned about compromise and cooperation to reach a consensus about their Inquiry Questions.

• Prompt the group Discussion Monitor to help the group stay on topic and make sure everyone is collaborating.

2. Make a Conjecture   *critical thinking* `evaluate`

• Remind students that there are no wrong conjectures, so they should share their ideas freely.

• Point out that students can use the words *I think* and *maybe* to start their conjectures.

• Have each group choose a conjecture that synthesizes everyone's ideas. **b**

• Point out that the group Questioner can prompt others to express their ideas by asking them questions.

- The Recorder for each group should fill in the Idea Tracker (Resource Master 34) to record the group's main discussion points this week.

- Remind each group to post its question and conjecture on the Question Board. Groups can update their questions and conjectures as their understandings evolve.

 Students can refer to the Theme Wall to view other posted questions.

- Help students wrap up their discussions to prepare them to transition to the next step.

ASSIGN RESOURCE MASTER 34

3. Make Plans to Collect Information
critical thinking *analyze, evaluate*

- Tell students to make a list of information they will gather by making a list of topics or specific questions related to their Inquiry Projects. Have them divide up the topics or questions among their group members.

- Remind them that the theme library may have information and resources they can use.

- Have copies of the Investigation Sheet (Resource Master 35) available in the classroom where students can access them.

- Remind students to use the Evaluating Sources Checklist (Practice Companion, p. 372) as they collect information.

- Each student should complete his or her Action Plan for the next week on the Inquiry Planner (Practice Companion, p. 199). c d

- Each group's Checker should make sure all Week 1 Inquiry Checklist items have been completed. Students place Inquiry materials into their Unit 7 Inquiry folders.

ASSIGN RESOURCE MASTER 35
PRACTICE COMPANION 199, 372

scaffolding options

a Literacy Builder
21st CENTURY SKILLS

BRAINSTORMING
Have students use a Concept and Word Web (Resource Master 11) to brainstorm ideas related to the theme. Have students write down all of their ideas and then choose their three favorite concepts.

ASSIGN RESOURCE MASTER 11

b ELL Support

CONCEPTS AND VOCABULARY
English langauge learners may find it helpful to partner with native English speakers for group discussions. Encourage them to ask their partners questions about any unfamiliar words or concepts, but remind them that they should also practice good listening skills and wait until each speaker is finished before talking with their partners.

c Literacy Builder
21st CENTURY SKILLS

ONLINE RESEARCH
To help students collect information, encourage them to use their student Home Page at www.wgLEAD21.com to access Inquiry Project online, where they will find links and tips for locating theme-related Web sites. If possible, arrange for Internet access time and allow students to sign up for time slots. Review with students the Internet Safety Agreement (Resource Master 33).

ASSIGN RESOURCE MASTER 33

 inquiry project

ebook online coach

d Intervention for Acceleration

COLLECT INFORMATION
As a source option, students can use the support features in the eBook version of the Differentiated Readers to access texts at higher reading levels.

Connect Ideas

Objectives
Students will:
- Share information across texts
- Use speaking and listening skills
- Make connections between the Differentiated Readers and the Inquiry project

Cross-Text Sharing
mixed groups

CONNECT DIFFERENTIATED READERS

Cross-Text Sharing

While students stay in their Inquiry Groups, announce Cross-Text Sharing time. Remind students that they have read about how geography and economy are connected in the Mountain States.

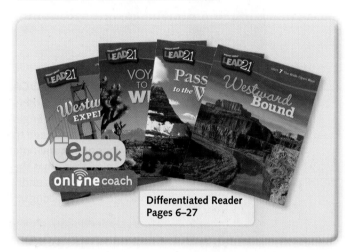

Differentiated Reader
Pages 6–27

- Remind students that all Differentiated Readers can be considered a source of information to answer their Inquiry Questions.

- Have students from each differentiated group share the title of the selection they read, summarize the main ideas, and display photographs from the selection to discuss what they learned. Have students share any information that can be used to help answer their groups' Inquiry Questions. **a**

- If a group lacks a representative from one or more of the differentiated levels, combine groups so that each level is represented within a group.

- Make sure each group has access to all four Differentiated Readers. Summarize selections for students, as needed.

Monitor Student Progress

As you observe and work with each group, fill in your observations using the Collaboration Rubric (Resource Master 39).

USE RESOURCE MASTER **39**

Think Back

- Have students turn to **Think Back** page 28 in their Differentiated Readers.

- Tell students they will complete Practice Companion page 201 as they do Cross-Text Sharing.

ASSIGN PRACTICE COMPANION **201**

Check Understanding

Have students write on Practice Companion page 201 some of the ways that geography and economy are connected in the Mountain States. Intensive and Strategic-level students can expand on the lists they prepared on Day 4 during Prepare to Share.

Understand Text Features

Form mixed-level pairs within each Inquiry Group. Have the mixed-level pairs take turns explaining their line graphs to partners. To facilitate the discussion, ask:

- What is the title of your line graph?
- What information does the graph give?
- How does the information in the line graph connect to the text?

Share and Compare

Have students use a T-Chart (Resource Master 14) to compare their lists of how geography and economy are connected in the selections they read. Then have them look for similarities in their connections. Tell them to use these similarities to summarize how geography and economy are connected. **b** **c**

ASSIGN RESOURCE MASTER **14**

Think Critically

Have each student give examples from his or her reading to answer the Theme Question: *What makes the West exceptional?* For ideas, students can use the ideas they gathered during the week's reading. Students can fill in their ideas on Practice Companion page 201.

Connect to Inquiry

Before wrapping up Cross-Text Sharing, ask groups to connect what they learned in their sharing to their Inquiry Questions. Ask:

What connections can you make between the ideas that were shared in your discussion and your Inquiry Question?

- Have students discuss their ideas, take notes, and put their notes into their Inquiry folders.
- Remind students to continue to work on their Inquiry Projects during Independent Practice and Self-Selected Reading time.
- Point out the location of the copies of the Investigation Sheet (Resource Master 35). Explain that each group member will need to collect information and have it ready to share with the group next week on Day 5. **d**

ASSIGN RESOURCE MASTER 35

a Intervention for Acceleration

SUMMARIZE
Tell students that headings and subheadings give the main idea of a section of text. Have students write each heading in sequence and use them to help them summarize the selections.

b Critical Thinking

SYNTHESIZE
Tell students that when they look for connections with their partners' ideas, they are synthesizing. Students may find it helpful to draw lines or arrows between related ideas and then write or say a sentence that tells the relationship between the ideas.

c Challenge

SYNTHESIZE
Challenge students to create a drawing that illustrates how the geography and economy of the Mountain States are connected. Students may use one of the comparisons from their T-chart or they can brainstorm a different connection. Ask for volunteers to share their drawings with the class.

d Literacy Builder

COLLABORATION
Emphasize to students that it is important that they come to each group meeting prepared and with the information they agreed to collect. Explain that the success of their projects depends on each group member making a contribution.

Share, Connect, Assess

Objectives
Students will:
- Perform fluent reading
- Spell words with the VV pattern

Wrap Up the Week *whole group*

Fluency Presentation

Have students turn to "The Great Potato State" on Practice Companion page 190. Each student will perform a reading of the advertisement for the class to demonstrate using good phrasing, expression, and pacing. Explain:

- Today we will be sharing the advertisement we have been working on all week by presenting it to the class. As you read aloud the advertisement, read with expression. Remember to use your voice to persuade the audience.

- When you present the advertisement to the class, make sure to use an appropriate pace and volume so that everyone in the class can hear and understand.

- Students may choose another selection to perform for the class.

- You may wish to give students the option of performing this week's or another fluency selection to a caregiver at home.

- As students perform, use Assessing Oral Reading, Assessment Handbook pages 13–14, to evaluate and record each student's oral reading performance.

USE **ASSESSMENT HANDBOOK 13–14**

Spelling Posttest

Remind students that their spelling words have the VV pattern. Say a word, use it in a sentence, and say the word again. Students will write each word.

1. **idea** My *idea* for my science project is to build a model of the solar system.
2. **lion** We heard a *lion* roar in the distance while we were on safari.
3. **unusual** Monique found an *unusual* book she had never seen before.
4. **radio** My sister enjoys listening to music on the *radio* in the morning.
5. **liar** No one wants to be called a *liar*.
6. **poem** The class listened to the teacher read the funny *poem*.
7. **India** *India* is a country in Asia.
8. **piano** Olivia's hands ran up and down the keys of the *piano*.
9. **fuel** Most cars need *fuel* to operate.
10. **diary** I enjoy writing my thoughts in my *diary*.
11. **violin** I have always wanted to learn how to play the *violin*.
12. **period** Don't forget to add a *period* at the end of the sentence.
13. **cereal** There is a prize in the box of *cereal*.
14. **video** We can't play the *video* game because our TV is broken.
15. **meteor** The scientist studied the *meteor* that landed on Earth.
16. **February** Valentine's Day is in *February*.

Review Words
12. **explain** You need to *explain* how that cat got into the box!
13. **sandwich** David likes to put cheese on his *sandwich*.

Frequently Misspelled Words
14. **they're** *They're* going to the river today.
15. **right** Take a *right* at the corner to find the library.

Objectives
Students will:
- Use key concepts
- Make text-to-self connections
- Write a description of a Mountain State
- Monitor their progress

Share Text Connections

Make Text-to-Self Connections Ask students to share the theme connections they made during Cross-Text Sharing time. On chart paper, begin a Theme Concept Web for Unit 7.

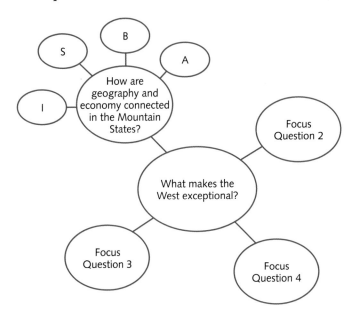

Write the Theme Question in the center circle and this week's Focus Question in one of the four connecting circles.

- For each Differentiated Reader, have students share a concept or main idea that connects to the Focus and Theme Questions.

- As students discuss their connections from their Differentiated Readers, fill in the outermost circles.

- Have students think about how this helps them address the Theme Question. Ask:

  What is the connection between geography and economy in the Mountain States? How do the Mountain States help make the West exceptional?

- Save the Theme Concept Web and build on it over the next three weeks.

Think Ahead

Have students open their Differentiated Readers to page 29 and begin thinking about the selection they will read next week.

Read aloud next week's Focus Question: *How are geography and economy connected in the Pacific States?* Then read the **Selection Connection** and **Show What You Know** activities. Have students write their answers to these activities on Practice Companion page 202.

ASSIGN | PRACTICE COMPANION **202**

Daily Writing

Encourage students to imagine that they are giving a guided tour of an area of the West. Have them write what they would tell the people in the group.

Student Self Assessment

- You may want students to reflect on their learning by using My Daily Progress sheet, Resource Master 1.

- Remind students to note the concepts and skills for which they could use more support.

ASSIGN | RESOURCE MASTER **1**

Weekly Progress Monitoring

Use the following assessment tools to check students' weekly progress following independent and mixed-group work:
- **Practice Companion:** pp. 186–197
- **Fluency Presentation**
- **Spelling Posttest**
- **Think Back** and **Think Ahead, Differentiated Reader:** pp. 28–29
- **Assessing Oral Reading, Assessment Handbook:** pp. 13–14
- **Weekly Observation Record, Assessment Handbook:** p. 140

Week 2 Planner

Interactive Reading
WHOLE GROUP | 25–35 mins.

	Oral Language	Vocabulary	Read Together	Comprehension	Word Study and Phonics	Spelling	Fluency
Day 1	Discuss the Theme	Introduce Theme Vocabulary ✓	• Model • Share • Read Theme Reader, pp. 396–403	Read about geography and economy in the Pacific States.	Introduce ✓ Final *Schwa* + *l* Sound	Spelling ✓ Pretest Introduce Final *Schwa* + *l* Sound	Introduce and Model "Hiking in Redwood"
Day 2	Reinforce the Theme	Reinforce ✓ Theme Vocabulary	Read Theme Reader, pp. 404–408	Review ✓ Comprehension Strategy Monitor Comprehension	Reinforce ✓ Final *Schwa* + *l* Sound	Practice ✓ Final *Schwa* + *l* Sound	Shared Choral Reading "Hiking in Redwood"
Day 3	Reinforce the Theme	Introduce ✓ Vocabulary Strategy Context Clues	Reread Theme Reader, pp. 396–408	Review ✓ Comprehension Skill Identify Cause and Effect	Introduce ✓ Contractions *e*practice	Practice ✓ Final *Schwa* + *l* Sound	Paired Reading "Hiking in Redwood"
Day 4	Extend the Theme	Extend ✓ Theme Vocabulary	Reread Theme Reader, pp. 396–408	Reinforce ✓ Comprehension Strategy Monitor Comprehension	Reinforce ✓ Contractions *e*practice	Practice ✓ Final *Schwa* + *l* Sound	Personal Rehearsal "Hiking in Redwood"

Day 5 — Inquiry and 21st Century Skills *e*tools 21 · inquiry project

21st CENTURY SKILLS

Review Project Plan
Connect to the Theme
Discuss Previous Week

Model the Inquiry Process
Continue to Collect Information
4. Organize and Synthesize Information
5. Confirm or Revise Your Conjecture

Continue Inquiry Group Work
Review Discussion Roles
Monitor Student Progress

Minilesson: Collaboration

Theme Reader   Pages 396–408

Weekly Vocabulary

missionary
film
rugged

*e*book
online coach

Selection 2: Differentiated Readers   Pages 30–55

Intensive

Weekly Vocabulary

differ
carve
variety
contribute
tremendous
leisurely
balmy
accustomed

*e*book
online coach

Strategic

Weekly Vocabulary

frequent
inland
origin
critical
pasture
occur
bushel
reservoir

*e*book
online coach

Differentiated Reading
SMALL GROUPS | 60–80 mins.

Read and Comprehend

Reinforce Theme Vocabulary ✓

Reread Theme Reader,
pp. 396–403

Introduce Differentiated Vocabulary ✓
Read about farming, California, Hawaii, or technology in the first half of Selection 2.

Reinforce Comprehension Strategy ✓
Monitor Comprehension

Introduce Differentiated Vocabulary ✓
🖱 epractice
Read about farming, California, Hawaii, or technology in the second half of Selection 2.

Reinforce Comprehension Skill ✓
Identify Cause and Effect

Extend Vocabulary
🖱 epractice

Reread Differentiated Readers,
pp. 30–55

Reinforce Comprehension Strategy ✓
Monitor Comprehension

Mixed Groups

Cross-Text Sharing

Think Back

Connect to Inquiry

Wrap Up
WHOLE GROUP | 5–10 mins.

Share, Connect, Assess

Share Text Connections
Daily Writing
Student Self Assessment
Daily Progress Monitoring
Home Connection

Share Text Connections
Daily Writing
Student Self Assessment
Daily Progress Monitoring
Home Connection

Share Text Connections
Daily Writing
Student Self Assessment
Daily Progress Monitoring
Home Connection

Share Text Connections
Daily Writing
Student Self Assessment
Daily Progress Monitoring
Home Connection

Weekly Assessment

Fluency Presentation ✓
Spelling Posttest ✓
Student Self Assessment
Weekly Progress Monitoring

Writing and Language Arts
WHOLE GROUP | 30 mins.

Writing Process and Grammar
Suggested Pacing Guide

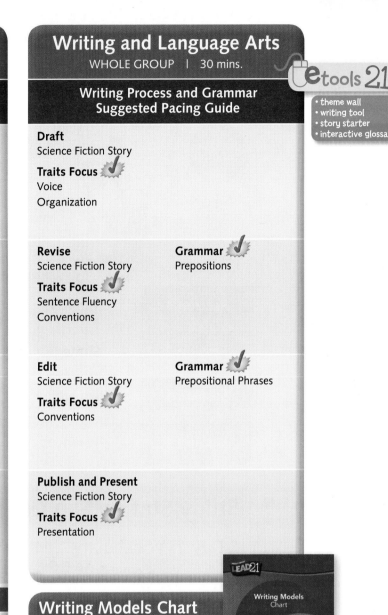

🖱 etools 21
• theme wall
• writing tool
• story starter
• interactive glossary

Draft
Science Fiction Story
Traits Focus ✓
Voice
Organization

Revise   **Grammar** ✓
Science Fiction Story   Prepositions
Traits Focus ✓
Sentence Fluency
Conventions

Edit   **Grammar** ✓
Science Fiction Story   Prepositional Phrases
Traits Focus ✓
Conventions

Publish and Present
Science Fiction Story
Traits Focus ✓
Presentation

Writing Models Chart

Writing Model
Science Fiction Story,
pp. 48–51

Selection 2: Differentiated Readers   Pages 30–55

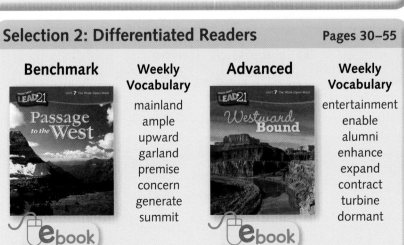

Benchmark	Weekly Vocabulary	Advanced	Weekly Vocabulary
Passage to the West	mainland ample upward garland premise concern generate summit	*Westward Bound*	entertainment enable alumni enhance expand contract turbine dormant

🖱 ebook
onl●ne coach

🖱 ebook
onl●ne coach

Target Literacy Skills

Comprehension Strategy ✓
Monitor Comprehension

Comprehension Skill ✓
Identify Cause and Effect

Vocabulary Strategy ✓
Context Clues

Week 2 Planner

Daily Small-Group Rotation

	Small-Group, Teacher-Led Instruction	Independent Practice	Self-Selected Reading	Study Station Flip Charts
	When the teacher is with these groups…	these groups rotate through independent activities.		
Session 1	Intensive	Advanced	Benchmark	Strategic
Session 2	Strategic	Intensive	Advanced	Benchmark
Session 3	Benchmark	Strategic	Intensive	Advanced
Session 4	Advanced	Benchmark	Strategic	Intensive

Study Station Flip Charts, page 26

Day 1: Vocabulary Central

Students play a game with vocabulary words.

Day 2: Writer's Desk

Students write a story about meeting a visitor from the West Coast.

Day 3: Word World

Students fill in a contractions chart.

Day 4: Book Corner

Students read with a partner and summarize the selection.

Day at a Glance

Lesson Highlights

- Discuss the Theme
- Introduce Theme Vocabulary: missionary, film, rugged
- Spelling Pretest: Final *e* + *l* Sound
- Draft a Science Fiction Story, pp. 138–139

Materials

	Teacher's Lesson Guide	Student Components	Digital 21
Interactive Reading	pp. 72–75	• Theme Reader, pp. 396–403 • Practice Companion, pp. 203–204, 208–209	ebook online coach
Differentiated Reading	pp. 76–81	• Theme Reader, pp. 396–403	ebook online coach
Wrap Up	p. 94	• Resource Masters 1–3	etools 21 • theme wall • writing tool • story starter
Writing and Language Arts	pp. 138–139	• Writing Models Chart, pp. 48–49 • Practice Companion, pp. 220–221	etools 21 writing tool

Tips for Success

- You may wish to have students begin the Weekly Planner on Practice Companion page 203.
- Introduce the Study Stations (Flip Charts, p. 26) and arrange materials for the week.
- **21st CENTURY SKILLS** Remind students to work on their Inquiry Projects during Independent Practice or Self-Selected Reading time.
- Set out theme-related reference materials for students to use during the week. Refer also to the Theme Bibliography, pages 304–305.

Oral Language and Vocabulary

Interactive Reading whole group

Objectives
Students will:
- Discuss the theme
- Use theme vocabulary

Discuss the Theme

Have students recall the Theme Question: *What makes the West exceptional?*

**Theme Reader
Pages 377–438**

- Have students scan pages 380–395 of *A Tour of the Western Region* to share ideas that stood out to them, and why.

- Invite each student to select one image or a sentence that shows one way the West is exceptional and share it with the class.

Discuss the Inquiry Project

 **21st CENTURY SKILLS**

Have students recall the Inquiry Questions they chose last week. Tell them that they will continue their investigation this week.

- Remind students to collect information during Independent Practice or Self-Selected Reading time.

- Encourage students to continue to post their ideas and questions on the Question Board.

etools 21 theme wall | Students can also use the Theme Wall to post ideas and images.

Activate Prior Knowledge

Explain that the Pacific States, like the Mountain States, have many landforms. Agriculture is an important part of the economy.

Name the Pacific States and ask students to share what they know about these states, including the climate, landforms, or anything else they find interesting.

Introduce Theme Vocabulary

Theme Vocabulary
missionary
film
rugged

Introduce the theme vocabulary words that students will read this week in their Theme Readers. These words will help students answer the Theme and Focus Questions. **a**

Vocabulary Routine	
\multicolumn{2}{l}{Help students scan the selection to find the highlighted theme vocabulary words, and have them read and pronounce the words after you. Then use the vocabulary routine below to discuss the meaning of each word.}
Define	A **missionary** (p. 405) is someone sent by a group to spread their beliefs, usually religious.
Example	The missionary helped the people in the village learn about a new religion.
Ask	What else might a missionary teach a village?

Film (p. 402) means "to use a motion-picture camera to take pictures." *The movie director is ready to film the scene.* What kind of things would you like to *film*?

Rugged (p. 400) means "being rough or irregular." *Mount Everest is a rugged landform.* Name something else that might be considered *rugged*.

ASSIGN | PRACTICE COMPANION **204**

Read and Comprehend

Objectives
Students will:
- Read about the Pacific States

Prepare to Read

Build Background

Explain that today students will learn about the geography and economy of the Pacific States.

Theme Reader Pages 396–403

Explain that farming, fishing, and natural resources are all important industries in the Pacific States.

Preview/Predict/ Set Purposes

Preview Chapter 3 of *A Tour of the Western Region.* Encourage students to predict what they might learn. Students will read to answer the Theme Question.

MODELED AND SHARED READING

Read Together

Share your thinking as you model reading page 396. Pause periodically to check understanding of theme concepts and vocabulary.

PAGES 396–397 Let's look at the photographs. What do you think the climate is like in these places? Does it look like things grow well here?

PAGES 398–403 How does water affect the economy in this area?

Respond

Review the predictions students made and the purposes they set. Revisit the Theme Question.

Partner Talk ★★

Have partners discuss one of the following questions:

How does the geography of the Pacific States differ from that of the Mountain States?

How does today's reading help you answer the Theme Question?

---

scaffolding options

a ELL Support

COGNATES
Point out the Spanish cognates of the theme vocabulary.

English	Spanish
film	filmar
missionary	el/la misionero(a)

b Challenge

COMPREHENSION: DETERMINE IMPORTANT INFORMATION
Challenge students to think about what is the most important thing the author wants them to learn in Chapter 3.

c Intervention for Acceleration

PARTNER FOR ACCELERATION
Pair students at the Intensive or Strategic level with students at the Benchmark or Advanced level. Invite the Benchmark and Advanced-level students to reread Chapter 3 while their partners follow along. Pause after each page and invite partners to discuss the important information.

Literacy Builder

Students can use the eBook version of the Theme Reader for building literacy.

Word Work and Fluency

Objectives
Students will:
- Spell words with the final schwa + *l* sound
- Analyze words with the final schwa + *l* sound
- Practice fluent reading

Spelling and Phonics

Pretest the Final Schwa + *l* Sound

Say each word from the list, read the sentence, and say the word again. Then have students write the word.

1. **towel** Don't forget your *towel* when you go to the beach.
2. **pedal** Malik put his foot on the bicycle *pedal*.
3. **riddle** My brother told me a funny *riddle*.
4. **metal** The *metal* pipe stuck out of the ground.
5. **simple** I had no problem doing the *simple* activity.
6. **ankle** She broke her *ankle* during the race.
7. **eagle** The *eagle* built a nest high in the tree.
8. **special** We had a *special* dinner for my brother's birthday.
9. **trouble** My little sister was in *trouble* for coloring on the wall.
10. **marvel** The Grand Canyon is a *marvel* of nature.
11. **gravel** The new road was made out of *gravel* and sand.
12. **gentle** We enjoyed the *gentle* breeze as it blew through the trees.
13. **barrel** The wooden *barrel* was once used to hold water for horses.
14. **squirrel** The young *squirrel* searched for food for the winter.
15. **model** He was recognized as a *model* citizen in the community.
16. **tangle** The necklace chain has a small *tangle* in it.

Review Words

17. **violin** I have always wanted to learn how to play the *violin*.
18. **cereal** *Cereal* is my favorite breakfast food.

Frequently Misspelled Words

19. **around** The small dog ran *around* in circles.
20. **having** I enjoyed *having* my grandfather come to visit me on Saturday.

Explain that these words may seem easy to spell, but they are often misspelled by fourth-graders.

Help students self-correct their tests:
- Say each word, spell it aloud, and repeat the word.
- Students checkmark each correctly spelled word.
- Students circle each misspelled word and write the correct spelling next to it. Encourage students to note these words as the ones they should pay extra attention to this week.

Teach the Final Schwa + *l* Sound

Explain that words with the final schwa + *l* sound are spelled different ways.

- Write the words *ankle, towel,* and *special* on the board.
- Help students underline the letters that spell the final schwa + *l* sound.
- Point out that *ankle* has a silent *e* at the end of the word. [a]

Practice/Apply

Word Sort Distribute word cards with the spelling words on them. Have students sort the cards into three groups based on the spelling of their final sound. Check answers as a class. [b]

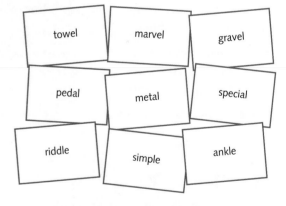

Fluency

Introduce and Model

Introduce the fluency selection, "Hiking in Redwood," on Practice Companion page 208. Remind students that fluent readers are better able to understand what they read. Tell them that throughout the week, they will practice reading the procedural text to be a fluent reader.

To activate students' prior knowledge and build background, ask them to share if they have ever been on a hike or a nature walk. Invite students to describe their experiences.

Practice Companion Pages 208–209

- Explain that students will read a procedural selection that will tell them how to hike through the Redwood forests.

- Introduce, pronounce, and discuss some possibly unfamiliar words, such as *stately, rustic, scenic,* and *bluff.*

Read aloud the selection two or three times as students follow along. Demonstrate good phrasing, expression, and pacing. Ask:

- What interests you about the selection?
- What did you visualize as you listened to me read?
- Would you like to hike this trail?

Practice

Lead an echo reading of the passage, followed by a choral reading. **c**

scaffolding options

a Intervention for Acceleration

WORD STUDY
For further reinforcement of these sounds, have students look through their Theme Readers for words with the endings *-el, -al,* and *-le.* Have partners take turns pronouncing these words.

b Challenge

EXPAND VOCABULARY
Have students define each word from the word cards. Then have them randomly draw two of the word cards and create a sentence that uses both words. Have students share their sentences with a partner or the class.

c Intervention for Acceleration

FLUENCY
You may wish to have students complete additional practice of their weekly fluency skills by choosing another selection from the classroom library to read with a partner.

Read and Comprehend Intensive

Objectives
Students will:
• Reinforce the theme
• Reinforce theme vocabulary
• Reread about the Pacific States

Differentiated Reading
small groups

Prepare to Read

Build Background

Remind students of the Theme Question: *What makes the West exceptional?* Have students recall key concepts from pages 380–395. Then have them name landforms, activities, or other items that were already familiar to them.

Theme Reader
Pages 396–403

• List student ideas on the board.

• Have students chorally read the list back, and then discuss the ideas with a partner.

Reinforce Theme Vocabulary

To reinforce and assess students' understanding of the theme vocabulary, have them work as a group to complete a Word Map (Resource Master 6) about the word *missionary.*

• Draw a Word Map on chart paper. Have volunteers label it with the vocabulary word and draw or paste a picture of an area where a missionary might travel to today or a place missionaries have traveled to in the past, in the center.

• Ask students to suggest a definition, examples, and non-examples. Record their ideas in the Word Map.

• Have partners write sentences using the word and share them with the group. Have students choose one sentence to write on the Word Map.

• Have partners continue the exercise with *film* and *rugged.*

ASSIGN

RESOURCE MASTER	6
PRACTICE COMPANION	204

Set Purposes

Students will reread Chapter 3 of *A Tour of the Western Region* to:

• Notice details they missed when reading the first time through.

• Help them understand information that didn't make sense or was confusing.

• Find answers to the Theme Question.

Encourage students to suggest information they want to better understand after rereading the section.

Read

Explain that students will hear Chapter 3 again, but this time each student will be closely guided to respond. To help students get started, model reading pages 396–397 as they follow along. As you read, model your thinking.

think aloud The first thing I notice is the chapter title, "The Pacific States: Geography and Economy." The photograph shows a very large, snowy mountain and forest land. I bet that this area gets lots of rain and snow each year. As I begin reading page 396, I learn that I am correct. I will keep reading to find out more about this area and its geography.

Guide Comprehension

Ask students to use a piece of paper to jot down their answers to questions you pose. Have them follow along as you reread the chapter. Monitor students' understanding by pausing throughout the selection to reinforce theme concepts and vocabulary.

PAGES 396–397 There is a map on page 396. How is this map important to the reader? What information does it provide? *(Possible response: The map is important because it tells the reader where the Pacific States are located in relation to other states.)*

PAGES 398–399 The captions and side bars on these pages tell about natural resources found in the Pacific States. What kinds of resources can be found in these areas? *(water, lumber)*

PAGES 400–401 There is an important word highlighted on page 400. What did you find out today about *rugged* cliffs? *(Students should respond by giving information about how the coastline of California looks.)*

PAGES 402–403 Did anything surprise you or particularly interest you on these pages? Explain why you were surprised or interested? Tell how you could find more information on the topic. *(Responses will vary.)* **c**

Check Comprehension

1. What does Chapter 3 mostly talk about? *(Possible responses: the geography and economy of the Pacific States; the landforms and products of the Pacific States.)*
IDENTIFY MAIN IDEA AND DETAILS

2. What are some examples of how the geography of the Pacific States affects its economy? *(Possible response: Agriculture provides jobs; the waterways make trade easier for the area; tourism is an important part of the area's economy.)* **ANALYZE**

Respond and Write

1. Ask students to tell whether they think they would enjoy living in the Pacific States. Have them give reasons explaining why or why not.

2. Have students reread the list of information that was already familiar to them that they made before reading. Have them discuss whether they read any additional information that they already knew about and make notes of their ideas. Discuss as a class what partners wrote, adding to the list on the board.

scaffolding options

a ELL Support

PICTURE CUES
Encourage students who are not very familiar with the geography of the United States to browse through books that feature photographs of the Pacific States. Help students name important landforms, plants, animals, and other objects shown in the photos.

b Intervention for Acceleration

FLUENCY
Tell students that repeated reading helps build their fluency, and that being fluent readers helps them better understand what they read. Model reading aloud page 396 a couple of times. Then have students read it through several times to practice building fluency.

c Critical Thinking

EVALUATE TEXT
Have students evaluate the effectiveness of this informational text. Ask them to consider whether:
- The selection includes mostly facts.
- The facts are supported by details.
- The text features enhance understanding.
- A different approach might have helped readers take away more information from the text.

Intervention for Acceleration

Students can use the support features in the eBook version of the Theme Reader.

Read and Comprehend   Strategic

Differentiated Reading small groups

Objectives
Students will:
• Reinforce the theme
• Reinforce theme vocabulary
• Reread about the Pacific States

Prepare to Read

Build Background

Recall the Theme Question: *What makes the West exceptional?* Have students recall key concepts from

**Theme Reader
Pages 396–403**

pages 380–395. Then have them tell what questions they still have.

• List their questions on the board.

• Have students chorally read the list back, and then discuss with a partner whether they can answer any of the questions.

Reinforce Theme Vocabulary

To reinforce and assess students' understanding of the theme vocabulary, have them complete a Word Map (Resource Master 6) about the word *rugged*.

• Have students fill in the Word Map with a drawing, a definition, examples, and non-examples. Then have them write a sentence using the word.

• Have students also complete Word Maps for *film* and *missionary*, and then share their charts with the group.

ASSIGN

RESOURCE MASTER	6
PRACTICE COMPANION	204

Set Purposes

Students will reread Chapter 3 of *A Tour of the Western Region* to:

• Notice details they missed when reading the first time through.

• Help them understand information that didn't make sense or was confusing.

• Find answers to the Theme Question.

Encourage students to suggest information they want to better understand after rereading the chapter.

Read

Explain that students heard Chapter 3 read, but now they will read it together with some guidance. To help students get started, model reading pages 396–397 as they follow along. As you read, model your thinking.

think aloud From the title, I see that we'll be reading about the geography and economy of the Pacific States. I remember from Chapter 1 that this region is west of the Mountain States. The ocean probably affects people's way of life and is an important resource to them.

Guide Comprehension

Have partners continue reading Chapter 3. Circulate and listen as they read. Pause them periodically to help monitor their understanding of theme concepts and vocabulary. **a** **b**

PAGES 396–398 How does water affect the economy of the Pacific Northwest? *(Water is used for fishing, recreation, power, and irrigation. The Grand Coulee Dam makes more than one quarter of the hydroelectric power in the United States.)*

PAGES 399–401 Look at the sidebar at the bottom of page 399. How does it relate to the information on the rest of the page? *(It gives details about the history of parts of Washington that aren't mentioned in the text. It tells about the economy of the state.)*

PAGES 402–403 What do the economies of Alaska and Hawaii have in common? *(They both rely heavily on tourism.)*

Check Comprehension

1. What role does tourism play in the Pacific States? *(Students should mention that many people come to the area to see all the natural features and take part in the interesting industries that it has to offer.)*
SUMMARIZE **c**

2. What are the main products that come from the Pacific States? *(apricots, rice, pistachios, timber, fishing, electronics, airplanes, dairy, and cherries)* DETAILS/FACTS

Respond and Write

1. Have students reread the questions they wrote at the beginning of the lesson. Tell students to discuss with partners any answers they found. Call on volunteers to share their questions and answers with the class.

2. Invite students to write in their journals how Chapter 3 of *A Tour of the Western Region* has helped answer the Theme Question.

---

scaffolding options

a Intervention for Acceleration

MISCUES
As students partner-read, circulate and listen for their miscues. Use one of their miscues for immediate feedback to the whole group about what type of error to avoid.

b ELL Support

PICTURE CLUES
Suggest to students that the author took great care to choose photographs that would support the text. Encourage students to skim Chapter 3 and carefully study the photographs. After rereading, pair English language learners with native speakers and have students discuss how each photo further explains the text on the page.

c Intervention for Acceleration

COMPREHENSION: SUMMARIZE
Some of your students might have difficulty summarizing the chapter. Provide students with Resource Master 27. Have them list the main topic of the chapter in the first box, and the most important details about that topic in the other boxes. Then guide them to use that information to create their summary.

ASSIGN RESOURCE MASTER **27**

ebook **online** coach

Intervention for Acceleration

Students can use the support features in the eBook version of the Theme Reader.

Differentiated Reading
small groups

Read and Comprehend | Benchmark

Objectives
Students will:
- Reinforce the theme
- Reinforce theme vocabulary
- Reread about the Pacific States

Prepare to Read

Build Background
Ask students to recall the Theme Question: *What makes the West exceptional?* and the key concepts

Theme Reader Pages 396–403

discussed in the whole-group session. Encourage students to make a list of facts they found interesting in the selection so far. Have students share their list with the group.

Reinforce Theme Vocabulary

To reinforce and assess students' understanding of the theme vocabulary, ask them to complete a Word Map (Resource Master 6) about the word *rugged*. Have students add a drawing, a definition, examples, non-examples, and a sentence about the word. Ask students to continue the procedure with *film* and *missionary*. Have partners share what they wrote.

ASSIGN	RESOURCE MASTER	6
	PRACTICE COMPANION	204

Set Purposes
Explain that one reason to reread is to notice details that were missed the first time. Students will reread Chapter 3 of *A Tour of the Western Region* to:

- Help them better understand parts of the text that didn't make sense the first time.

- Find more information and details to help them answer the Theme Question.

Read

To set reading expectations, model your thinking as you read pages 396–397.

think aloud The caption on page 397 states that cherry season in Washington and Oregon starts in June and ends in August. That's a pretty short time frame. I wonder if this has an impact on their economy. I will keep this in mind as I reread the chapter.

Guide Comprehension
Have students continue reading the chapter independently. Pause them periodically to monitor understanding of the theme concepts and vocabulary.

PAGES 396–399 Have students make text-to-text connections with other stories or selections they've read about the Pacific States. **MAKE CONNECTIONS**

PAGES 400–401 Ask students to imagine that they have traveled to Hollywood. Encourage them to describe what they hear, see, smell, and feel. **VISUALIZE**

Respond and Write

1. Invite students to add interesting facts to the list they started at the beginning of class. **a**

2. Have students respond in writing to the Theme Question: *What makes the West exceptional?* **b**

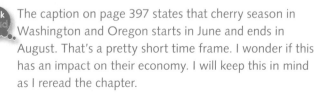

scaffolding options

a Challenge

EXTEND THE TOPIC
As students read, have them write down any questions they have that are not answered in the text. Challenge students to use additional resources to find the answers to their questions, and then report what they learned to the class.

b Critical Thinking

EVALUATE PHOTOGRAPHS
Have students evaluate and discuss the selection photographs.

- How does each photo relate to the text on the same page?

- Do the photos add to your understanding? Explain.

Differentiated Reading
small groups

Objectives
Students will:
- Reinforce the theme
- Reinforce theme vocabulary
- Reread about the Pacific States

Prepare to Read

Build Background

Ask students to discuss the key concepts and the Theme Question: *What makes the West exceptional?*

**Theme Reader
Pages 396–403**

- Have students work independently to fill in a Concept and Word Web (Resource Master 11) on the topic of geography and economy. Encourage them to use examples from the text they have read so far.

- When they are finished, invite students to share the webs with the group or partners.

ASSIGN   RESOURCE MASTER   **11**

Reinforce Theme Vocabulary   *tested* ✓

To reinforce and assess students' understanding of the theme vocabulary, ask each student to think of a sentence for each vocabulary word *(film, rugged, missionary)* that conveys its meaning. Have students write their sentences before sharing them with partners. **a**

ASSIGN   PRACTICE COMPANION   **204**

Set Purposes

Students will reread Chapter 3 of *A Tour of the Western Region* to note additional details that answer the Theme Question.

Students should also set their own purposes for reading.

Read

Guide Comprehension

Have students continue rereading the chapter silently. After they read, use the following prompts to guide discussion of theme concepts and vocabulary.

PAGES 396–398 Have students debate whether the first part of Chapter 3 contains facts or opinions. *(Responses will vary, but students should be able to distinguish between facts and opinions and offer evidence to support their answers.)* DISTINGUISH FACT AND OPINION

PAGES 400–403 Ask students what would happen to the economy of the Pacific States if there were no more precipitation. *(Possible response: This would greatly affect the lumber. apple, cherry and farm industry. The trees, fruit, and crops would not grow well and couldn't be sold to support the economy.)* SUMMARIZE **b**

Respond and Write

1. Have students add new words and ideas to their concept webs. Invite students to share the completed webs with the group.

2. Ask students to write a few sentences about how Chapter 3 answers the Theme Question.

scaffolding options

a Challenge

VOCABULARY
Challenge students to include in their sentences words such as *if, but,* and *because* to demonstrate a deeper understanding of each vocabulary word. Suggest that their sentences explain *how* or *why* as related to the vocabulary word.

b ELL Support

COMPREHENSION STRATEGIES
Remind students to apply comprehension strategies to help them understand the text. Suggest strategies, such as ask and answer questions or monitor comprehension, for students who are struggling to understand the selection.

Share, Connect, Assess

Objectives
Students will:
- Use key concepts and vocabulary
- Make text-to-self connections
- Write about the Pacific States
- Monitor their progress

Share Text Connections

Building Classroom Community

Make Text-to-Self Connections Bring students back together from their small groups to share what additional things they learned while reading about the Pacific States.

- Encourage students to use theme and other academic vocabulary as they share their own insights about key concepts.

- Ensure that students from all groups have a chance to contribute to the discussion.

- Ask students to share their thoughts on how what they've read connects to their personal experiences.

etools 21
theme wall

Daily Writing

Have students write a paragraph about a place they would like to visit in the Pacific States. Why? What is interesting about that place?

For additional writing practice, remind students to access the Story Starter from their student Home Page.

etools 21
- writing tool
- story starter

Student Self Assessment

- Remind students that they are responsible for their learning and that it is helpful to be aware of how well they understand what they are reading, writing, talking, and thinking about in the classroom.

- You may want students to reflect on their reading and learning by using their Personal Reading Logs and My Daily Progress sheets (Resource Masters 1, 3).

ASSIGN   RESOURCE MASTER   **1, 3**

Daily Progress Monitoring

To ensure that students have mastered the day's skills and strategies, monitor their success in completing the following independent work:

- **Vocabulary:** Practice Companion, p. 204
- **Spelling:** Practice Companion, p. 206
- **Fluency:** Practice Companion, p. 208
- **Study Station Work Record:** Resource Master 2
- **Self Assessment:** Resource Masters 1, 3

Home Connection

Distribute the Unit 7 Take-Home Activities from the Home Connection book. Tell students to complete the activities with their caregivers.

Week 2 Day 2

Lesson Highlights

- Review Comprehension Strategy: Monitor Comprehension
- Spelling and Phonics: Final Schwa + *l* Sound
- Revise a Science Fiction Story, pp. 140–141

Materials

	Teacher's Lesson Guide	Student Components	Digital 21
Interactive Reading	pp. 84–87	• Theme Reader, pp. 404–408 • Practice Companion, pp. 204, 206, 208, 210–211 • Resource Master 18	ebook / online coach
Differentiated Reading	pp. 88–93, 292–295 (ELL)	• Differentiated Readers • Resource Masters 4, 7, 8, 11, 12, 14	ebook / online coach
Wrap Up	p. 94	• Resource Masters 1–3	etools 21 • theme wall • writing tool • story starter
Writing and Language Arts	pp. 140–141	• Writing Models Chart, pp. 50–51 • Practice Companion, pp. 222, 225	etools 21 interactive glossary

Tips for Success

- Guide students to make connections between reading and writing (p. 85).
- Remind students to use their Study Station Work Records (Resource Master 2) throughout the week.
- If students work on their writing during Independent Practice, have them use the Evaluation Rubric on Practice Companion page 221.

 Remind students to work on their Inquiry Projects during Independent Practice or Self-Selected Reading time.

Oral Language and Vocabulary

Interactive Reading *whole group*

Objectives
Students will:
- Reinforce the theme
- Reinforce theme vocabulary

Reinforce the Theme

To reinforce the theme, have students describe what they see in the photo on Theme Reader page 380. Ask:

eBook
online coach

**Theme Reader
Pages 377–438**

What do you think a desert is like? Do you think it is difficult to live there? What geographical features can you see in the photo?

- Prompt students to discuss how farmland and the range relate to the geography and economy of the Western Region.

- Then have them name other unique aspects of the Western Region that they've learned about as they've read the selection.

Activate Prior Knowledge

Remind students that in Chapter 2, they learned about the history and culture of the Mountain States. Explain that today they will learn about the history and culture of the Pacific States.

- Ask students to share what they know about the history of the Pacific States.

- Guide students to share what they know about the California Gold Rush. Point out that this time in history was very important in shaping the area as we know it today.

- Have students tell what they know about the cultural aspects of the Pacific States. Ask students to name foods, music, and special places and events they know about.

Reinforce Theme Vocabulary

Theme Vocabulary	
missionary	someone sent by a group to spread their beliefs, usually religious
film	to use a motion-picture camera to take pictures
rugged	being rough, irregular

To help students reinforce the theme vocabulary, have them write clues to help their classmates guess each word.

- Review the definitions of the theme vocabulary with students.

- Write each word on a note card.

- Divide the class into two teams.

- Have a student from one team draw a card, then think of clues to describe the word's meaning without using the word itself. That student's team gets 30 seconds to guess the word. If they don't guess it in time, the other team has a chance to guess the word. **b**

ASSIGN PRACTICE COMPANION **204**

Read and Comprehend

REVIEW **COMPREHENSION STRATEGY**

Monitor ✓tested Comprehension

Define

Have students recall that readers monitor their comprehension as they read. If they don't understand something, they can use fix-up strategies. Write the following fix-up strategies on chart paper and guide students to recall how to use each one. **c**

Monitor Comprehension: Fix-up Strategies	
Reread	Use images as clues
Read on	Seek help
Adjust reading rate	

Model

Use the Theme Reader (p. 403) to model monitoring comprehension and using fix-up strategies.

 think aloud After I read this page, I'll pause and recall what I read to make sure I understood everything. I'm still not quite sure what the major industries are in Alaska. I'll go back and reread the paragraph slowly to make sure I understand.

Collaborative Practice

As students use page 403 to practice monitoring comprehension, prompt them to pause and sum up what they've read to check understanding. Invite students to suggest fix-up strategies readers could use if they did not understand.

Reading/Writing Connection

Explain that writers monitor comprehension as they write. They reread what they have written to make sure it is clear, and they revise to clarify any confusing parts. Ask students to identify complex concepts in the Theme Reader that the writer may have revisited to make sure they were clear to the reader.

ASSIGN   PRACTICE COMPANION   210–211

scaffolding options

Objectives
Students will:
• Read about the Pacific States
• Reinforce monitoring comprehension

Prepare to Read

Build Background
Remind students that in Chapter 3 of *A Tour of the Western Region*, they learned about the geography and economy of the Pacific

States. Explain that today they will learn about its history and culture.

ebook online coach

**Theme Reader
Pages 404–408**

• Draw a concept web on the board with the words *history* and *culture* in the center.
• Write information the students already know about the Pacific States.

• Add important concepts they did not mention, such as Lewis and Clark, the Northern Pacific Railroad, and Pearl Harbor.

Preview and Predict
Preview Chapter 4 of *A Tour of the Western Region*. Point out the chapter title, subheads, photographs, illustration, captions, and highlighted word. Ask students for their observations:

• What do you think is happening in the illustration on page 405? Do you think this was an exciting time in the history of the region? *(Possible response: People are shoveling and using pick axes. They seem to be looking for something, maybe gold.)*
• What are the main topics you will read about? How do you know? *(The history and culture of the region; the title and headings tell what each section is about.)* **a**

Set Purposes
Students will read to find answers to the Theme Question: *What makes the West exceptional?*

Students should also set their own purposes for reading, and skim the chapter to find something they might want to learn more about.

Read Together

Have partners read Chapter 4 of *A Tour of the Western Region*. Remind students to monitor their own comprehension as they read. Pause them periodically to discuss theme concepts and vocabulary.

PAGES 404–405 Let's look at the captions and images first. What do you think the text will be about after reading the captions and looking at the images? *(Possible response: the Inuit of Alaska; how the Gold Rush helped shape California.)*

After reading, have students tell whether their predictions were correct and what additional information they learned.

PAGES 406–407 Encourage students to summarize what they learned about the states of Alaska and Hawaii.

Invite students to think about the Theme Question, and tell what they learned about the unique culture in the Pacific States.

Respond

Have students talk about the purposes they set for themselves and whether they achieved those purposes. Ask students to share facts or ideas from the selection that surprised or interested them.

Have students tell how monitoring comprehension helped them understand what they read.

> **Partner Talk** ★ ★
>
> **Provide the discussion points below:**
>
> • Talk about the part of the chapter that was most interesting to you.
> • Tell your partner about one way that you monitored your own comprehension as you read.
> • Discuss how the chapter answered the Theme Question.

model
read   share

Word Work and Fluency

Spelling and Phonics

Practice the Final Schwa + *l* Sound

Remind students that words with the final schwa + *l* sound can be spelled in more than one way. Review the spelling patterns.

Have students use their spelling lists to write a sentence for each word and then read their sentences to a partner. The partner spells the word and gives its meaning.

ASSIGN PRACTICE COMPANION **206**

Fluency

Shared Choral Reading

Have students turn to "Hiking in Redwood" on page 208 of their Practice Companions. Ask students to recall the topic of the procedural text. Ask:

- What types of things would you see on a hike through Redwood National Park?

Explain that *phrasing* means breaking text into smaller, meaningful chunks to make the passage easier to understand.

- Read the procedural text, pausing to explain your phrasing.

- Read the selection again without pausing. Have students discuss the difference between the two readings.

- Have students read the procedural text chorally. Remind them to pay special attention to their phrasing. **c**

ASSIGN PRACTICE COMPANION **208**

---

scaffolding options

a ELL Support

USE PICTURE CLUES
Have students pay special attention to the photos and illustration to help them make predictions about what they will read. Guide students to describe what they see in each image and connect the images with heads, highlighted words, captions, and other text features in the chapter.

b Intervention for Acceleration

COMPREHENSION: SEQUENCE EVENTS
As students read, have them take notes of important events and the dates they happened. After reading, have partners construct a time line that gives an overview of the events in Chapter 4. Students may wish to use Resource Master 18 to complete this activity.

ASSIGN RESOURCE MASTER **18**

c Intervention for Acceleration

FLUENCY
Distribute to students a photocopy of the fluency selection "Hiking in Redwood." Suggest that students use highlighter pens to mark up the procedural text to help them read more fluently. For example, students can color each period red to indicate a full stop. Have students practice reading the marked-up procedural text to each other.

Read and Comprehend [Intensive]

Objectives
Students will:
• Use differentiated vocabulary
• Reinforce monitoring comprehension
• Read about the California coastline

Prepare to Read

Build Background

Read with students the Focus Question: *How are geography and economy connected in the Pacific States?*

online coach

Differentiated Reader Pages 30–39

(Differentiated Reader, p. 5) Read together the title, *The California Coast* (p. 30).

• Tell students that this week they will read about California's coast. Explain that California's coast brings many visitors to the state and is an important part of its economy.

• Encourage students to tell what they know about coastlines and about California. Show photographs and maps to aid student participation.

• Start a KWL Chart (Resource Master 12) on chart paper. Have students complete the "What I Know" column together.

ASSIGN [RESOURCE MASTER **12**]

Introduce
Differentiated Vocabulary *tested*

Have students complete the Vocabulary Rating Sheet (Resource Master 4).

• Find and pronounce with students the highlighted differentiated vocabulary words (pp. 30–39).

• Use the following routine to discuss each word's meaning.

• For each word, have students jot down and explain answers to prompts.

Vocabulary Routine	
Define	To **differ** (p. 31) is to be different.
Example	My brother and I differ in our taste in books, because he likes science fiction and I don't.
Ask	What is another word for differ?

To **carve** (p. 32) is to cut or shape as if by cutting. *My grandfather likes to carve the turkey each Thanksgiving.* Which would you be more likely to *carve*: a chicken or a balloon? Why?

Continue the routine with *variety* (p. 34), *contribute* (p. 34), *tremendous* (p. 36), and *leisurely* (p. 38), using the Glossary definitions and sentences and asking questions.

ASSIGN [RESOURCE MASTER **4**]

Preview and Predict

Encourage students to preview the selection, looking at the chapter titles, photos, and other text features. Ask students what they think they might learn.

Set Purposes

Setting a purpose helps readers focus their attention to understand more of what they read.

• Students should look for answers to the Focus Question.

• Students will complete the "What I Want to Know" column of their KWL chart, and share their ideas.

REINFORCE COMPREHENSION STRATEGY

Monitor *tested*
Comprehension

Remind students that when readers monitor comprehension, they make sure they understand what they're reading. Have students tell why readers use this strategy. *(to get more out of their reading and use fix up strategies when they don't understand the text)*

To reinforce monitoring comprehension, you may wish to use page 31 to model your thinking.

think aloud The first paragraph on page 31 includes an underlined word: *jagged*. I do not quite know what that word means. I will go back and use the word substitute provided at the bottom of the page to understand that *jagged* is similar to the word "uneven." This helps me understand that the coastline of California is uneven with many bays and coves.

ASSIGN [PRACTICE COMPANION **210–211**]

Read

Tell students that today they will read pages 30–39 of *The California Coast.* To help them get started, model your thinking as you read page 30.

 The first paragraph tells me that California is the third-largest state with more than 163,700 square miles of land. That is really big! As I read the first half of the story, I will think about what a state that size must do with all that land and what it has to offer visitors.

Guide Comprehension

Have partners continue reading. Pause them periodically to monitor understanding of key concepts and vocabulary. Have students jot down ideas about the prompts before discussing them with their partners.

PAGES 30–35 Read the **Strategy Tool Kit** on page 33 with students. Have partners jot down their ideas before discussing the questions with the group.

How do you think the coastal habitats contribute to the economy of California?

PAGES 36–39 Have partners define *tremendous* and describe how its meaning relates to the topic of these pages.

Check Comprehension

1. What created the coastline of California?
IDENTIFY CAUSE AND EFFECT

2. What additional information do the side bars on pages 32 and 38 provide? USE TEXT FEATURES

3. How have people worked to preserve the redwood trees? SUMMARIZE

Respond and Write

1. Have partners discuss **Stop and Think** on page 39. Then ask students to think about how these features compare with the geographic features of the Mountain States. **b**

2. Have students complete the "What I Learned" column of the KWL chart you began as a group. Have them discuss what they still want to find out, and add their ideas to the "What I Want to Know" column.

3. Discuss how today's reading has helped students answer the Focus Question.

scaffolding options

ELL Support

See page 292 of this Teacher's Lesson Guide for vocabulary and instructional support of English language learners at the Intensive level.

a Literacy Builder

WORD STUDY
To help students better understand the vocabulary, have them choose a word and complete a Word Skeleton (Resource Master 7). Have students work in pairs or independently, then share their work with the group.

ASSIGN RESOURCE MASTER **7**

b Critical Thinking

SYNTHESIZE
Have students apply the **Stop and Think** on page 39 to your area. Encourage them to think about geographic features that are popular tourist attractions in your area, or geographic features that would make good attractions. Have partners discuss their ideas.

ebook online coach

Intervention for Acceleration

Students can use the support features in the eBook version of the Differentiated Reader.

Differentiated Reading
small groups

Objectives
Students will:
- Use differentiated vocabulary
- Reinforce monitoring comprehension
- Read about farming in the Pacific Northwest

Prepare to Read

Build Background

Read with students the Focus Question: *How are geography and economy connected in the Pacific States?*

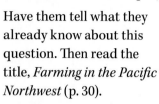

(Differentiated Reader, p. 5)

Have them tell what they already know about this question. Then read the title, *Farming in the Pacific Northwest* (p. 30).

Differentiated Reader Pages 30–41

- Explain that this week students will read about what types of farming contribute to the economy of the Pacific Northwest. Tell students that much of the food that we eat every day comes from the Pacific Northwest.

- Encourage students to tell what they know about the climate of the states of the Pacific Northwest.

- Invite students to complete a Concept and Word Web (Resource Master 11) about farming in the Pacific Northwest. Have students share ideas.

ASSIGN   RESOURCE MASTER **11**

Introduce Differentiated Vocabulary

Have students complete the Vocabulary Rating Sheet (Resource Master 4).

- Find and pronounce with students the highlighted differentiated vocabulary words (pp. 30–41).

- Use the following routine to discuss each word's meaning.

- For each word, have students jot down and explain answers to prompts.

Vocabulary Routine	
Define	**Frequent** (p. 31) means "happening often."
Example	The river frequently floods, so the nearby houses are built atop hills.
Ask	What is the opposite of frequently?

Inland (p. 32) is the inner part of a country, away from the coast. *Many rivers and streams run inland from the ocean.* What is the opposite of *inland*?

Continue the routine with *origin* (p. 35), *critical* (p. 37) and *pasture* (p. 41), using the Glossary definitions and sentences and asking questions.

ASSIGN   RESOURCE MASTER **4**

Preview and Predict

Have students preview the selection, focusing on photographs, headings, captions, and other text features. Ask them what they think they might learn from reading this selection, and why they think so.

Set Purposes

Remind students that setting a purpose will help them focus their attention and read more deeply.

- Students will add new information and details to their Concept and Word Webs.

- Students should also look for answers to the Focus Question.

REINFORCE COMPREHENSION STRATEGY

Monitor Comprehension

Remind students that experienced readers monitor comprehension by stopping to make sure they understand what they've read. Have students tell why readers use this strategy. *(to get deeper meaning out of their reading and use fix up strategies when they don't understand the text)*

To reinforce monitoring comprehension, you may wish to use page 31 to model your thinking.

think aloud
The first paragraph on page 31 tells about the types of food that are grown in the Pacific Northwest. I like to eat these foods. I wonder what other foods are grown in this region? I will keep this question in mind as I read the first half of the selection.

ASSIGN   PRACTICE COMPANION **210–211**

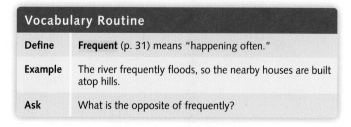

Read

Students will read pages 30–41 of *Farming in the Pacific Northwest*. To help them get started, model your thinking as you read page 31.

 The first paragraph on page 31 asks me to think about where the foods in my lunch come from. I've never really thought about that before. The text says a lot of food comes from the Pacific Northwest. I wonder what other products I use originate there.

Guide Comprehension

Have partners continue reading. Pause them periodically to monitor understanding of key concepts and vocabulary.

PAGES 30–35 Have partners read the **Strategy Tool Kit** on page 35 and give oral descriptions to answer the question. Have volunteers share which strategies they used to monitor their comprehension of the text.

PAGES 36–39 Have partners discuss the importance of the Columbia River to the people of the Pacific Northwest. Then have a volunteer from each pair summarize for the group. **b**

PAGES 40–41 Ask students to scan the text and identify why Oregon is a good place to grow crops and raise livestock. *(Possible response: a lot of open land and the climate make it easier to grow crops and raise livestock.)*

Check Comprehension

1. Look at the photographs on pages 38–39. How do they help you understand the importance of water routes to the people of the Pacific Northwest? **USE GRAPHIC SOURCES**

2. How do the mountains in the Pacific Northwest affect the climate of the area? **IDENTIFY CAUSE AND EFFECT**

3. What are the most important ideas on each page from pages 30–41? **DETERMINE IMPORTANT INFORMATION**

Respond and Write

1. Have partners discuss **Stop and Think** on page 41. Ask students to compare the geography of the Pacific Northwest to that of your area or of another area, and determine which area is best for farming.

2. Ask students if what they learned matched their predictions. Discuss how the selection to this point has answered the Focus Question.

3. Have students revisit the Concept Webs they started at the beginning of the lesson and add new information they learned from the selection.

scaffolding options

ELL Support

See page 293 of this Teacher's Lesson Guide for vocabulary and instructional support of English language learners at the Strategic level.

a Intervention for Acceleration

READ CHALLENGING TEXT
Have students work with a partner to apply the comprehension strategy to a higher level Differentiated Reader. Encourage students to use Resource Master 14 to help them monitor their comprehension of the selection. Invite partners to share which strategies worked best for them as they read the more challenging text.

ASSIGN **RESOURCE MASTER 14**

b Intervention for Acceleration

CONCEPT DEVELOPMENT
Help students understand the concept of waterways by doing a concept brainstorm with them (Resource Master 8). Have students list words they associate with waterways. Then, ask partners to choose the six words they think are most important in defining the concept. Discuss student ideas as a group.

ASSIGN **RESOURCE MASTER 8**

ebook onlinecoach

Intervention for Acceleration

Students can use the support features in the eBook version of the Differentiated Reader.

Read and Comprehend

Differentiated Reading *small groups*

Objectives
Students will:
- Use differentiated vocabulary
- Reinforce monitoring comprehension
- Read about Hawaii

Prepare to Read

Build Background

Introduce the Focus Question: *How are geography and economy connected in the Pacific States?* and the selection title, *Hawaii: The*

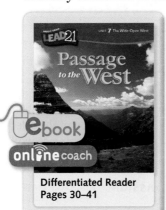

Differentiated Reader Pages 30–41

Beautiful Island State (pp. 5, 30). Elicit what students already know about Hawaii or other islands. Explain:

Hawaii is a string of islands. The geography and climate can differ between the islands.

Have students make a list of what they know, and then share their ideas with a partner. Discuss their responses as a group.

Introduce Differentiated Vocabulary

Have students complete the Vocabulary Rating Sheet (Resource Master 4).

Vocabulary Routine	
Define	**Mainland** (p. 30) is the main part of a continent.
Example	Tourists can travel from the mainland to the island of Hawaii.
Ask	What is the difference between a mainland and an island?

Ample (p. 32) means "plentiful." *We had an ample amount of food on the Thanksgiving dinner table.* What foods would you enjoy an *ample* supply of?

Partners continue with *upward* (p. 40), using the Glossary definition and sentence and asking a question.

ASSIGN   RESOURCE MASTER **4**

Preview/Predict/Set Purposes

Students preview the selection to see what they will learn. They read to answer the Focus Question and add to their list of what they know about Hawaii.

Read

Guide Comprehension

Partners will read pages 30–41 of *Hawaii: The Beautiful Island State*. You may wish to monitor understanding of theme concepts and vocabulary with the prompts below. Remind students to monitor comprehension as they read.

PAGES 30–35 How does the geography of Hawaii contribute to its tourism industry? MONITOR COMPREHENSION

PAGES 36–41 Have students identify the characteristics of Hawaii's main islands. IDENTIFY DETAILS AND FACTS **a**

Respond and Write

1. Ask students to share new information they learned that can help them answer the Focus Question.

2. Have students add new details to their list of information about Hawaii.

scaffolding options

ELL Support

See page 294 of this Teacher's Lesson Guide for vocabulary and instructional support of English language learners at the Benchmark level.

a Challenge

COMPREHENSION: ASK AND ANSWER QUESTIONS
Challenge partners to think more deeply about the text by asking each other questions about information they don't understand. Remind students to use strategies like rereading and reading on to find answers while monitoring their comprehension.

Differentiated Reading — small groups

Objectives
Students will:
- Use differentiated vocabulary
- Reinforce monitoring comprehension
- Read about technology in the Pacific States

Prepare to Read

Build Background

Introduce the Focus Question: *How are geography and economy connected in the Pacific States?* and the selection title, *Technology in the Pacific States* (pp. 5, 30). Ask students how they use technology. Elicit what students know about the Pacific States and how technology might be used there. Have them begin a Concept and Word Web (Resource Master 11) that gives their responses. Discuss their responses as a group.

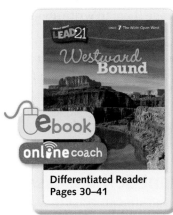

ebook
online coach

Differentiated Reader
Pages 30–41

ASSIGN   RESOURCE MASTER **11**

Introduce Differentiated Vocabulary *tested*

Have students complete the Vocabulary Rating Sheet (Resource Master 4).

Vocabulary Routine	
Define	**Entertainment** (p. 30) is amusement or performances.
Example	Watching movies is a form of entertainment.
Ask	What is your favorite form of entertainment?

Enable (p. 32) means "to make something possible or easy." *Studying and doing my homework enables me to do well on math tests.* What kinds of things can you do to *enable* a healthy body?

Partners continue the routine with *alumni* (p. 33), using the Glossary definition and sentence and asking a question.

ASSIGN   RESOURCE MASTER **4**

Preview/Predict/Set Purposes

Have students preview the selection. They will add information to their concept webs and answer the Focus Question.

Read

Guide Comprehension

Students will read pages 30–41 of *Technology in the Pacific States* on their own. Remind them to monitor comprehension as they read. After they read, discuss vocabulary and key concepts.

PAGES 30–37 Why is technology an important aspect of the economy of the Pacific States? SUMMARIZE

PAGES 38–41 Have students explain how the film industry has changed over the years. Have them write down which strategies they used to find the information. MONITOR COMPREHENSION

Respond and Write

Invite students to add information to their concept webs and discuss how this selection has helped them answer the Focus Question.

scaffolding options

ELL Support

See page 295 of this Teacher's Lesson Guide for vocabulary and instructional support of English language learners at the Advanced level.

a Challenge

COMPREHENSION: SUMMARIZE
Challenge students to think about the important information they identified in the first half of the selection and use it to write a summary of what they have read so far. Remind them to include only the most important information.

Share, Connect, Assess

Objectives
Students will:
- Use key concepts and vocabulary
- Make text-to-text connections
- Write about opening a tourist attraction
- Monitor their progress

Wrap Up
whole group

Share Text Connections

Building Classroom Community

Make Text-to-Text Connections Bring students back together from their small groups to talk about their Differentiated Reader selections.

- Invite students to share the topic of their selections and something interesting they've read so far. Encourage them to share some of the differentiated vocabulary words they read.

- Ask students what they know about the topics that other groups are reading about. As they discuss the texts, point out connections. For example, both *Hawaii: The Beautiful Island State* and *The California Coast* describe why visitors would want to visit and what they can do while there.

- Have students share how what they've read and discussed answers the week's Focus Question.

etools 21
- theme wall

Daily Writing

Have students write about a tourist attraction that they would like to open in a place they have read about. Encourage them to write about why they chose this attraction and who will help them get started with it.

For additional writing practice, remind students to access the Story Starter from their student Home Page.

etools 21
- writing tool
- story starter

Student Self Assessment

- Remind students that they are responsible for their learning and that it is helpful to be aware of how well they understand what they are reading, writing, talking, and thinking about in the classroom.

- You may want students to reflect on their reading and learning by using their Personal Reading Logs and My Daily Progress sheets (Resource Masters 1, 3).

ASSIGN **RESOURCE MASTER 1, 3**

Daily Progress Monitoring

To ensure that students have mastered the day's skills and strategies, monitor their success in completing the following independent work:

- **Vocabulary:** Practice Companion, p. 204
- **Comprehension:** Practice Companion, pp. 210–211
- **Spelling:** Practice Companion, p. 206
- **Fluency:** Practice Companion, p. 208
- **Study Station Work Record:** Resource Master 2
- **Self Assessment:** Resource Masters 1, 3

Home Connection

Distribute the Unit 7 Take-Home Activities from the Home Connection book. Tell students to complete the activities with their caregivers.

Day at a Glance

Lesson Highlights

- Introduce Vocabulary Strategy: Context Clues
- Review Comprehension Skill: Identify Cause and Effect
- Use Text Features: Captions
- Introduce Word Study: Contractions
- Edit a Science Fiction Story, pp. 142–143

Materials

	Teacher's Lesson Guide	Student Components	Digital 21
Interactive Reading	pp. 96–99	• Theme Reader, pp. 396–408 • Practice Companion, pp. 207–208, 212–215	ebook online coach / epractice word study games
Differentiated Reading	pp. 100–105	• Differentiated Readers • Resource Masters 4, 6, 14	ebook online coach / epractice vocabulary activities
Wrap Up	p. 106	• Resource Masters 1–3	etools 21 • theme wall • writing tool • story starter
Writing and Language Arts	pp. 142–143	• Writing Models Chart, pp. 50–51 • Practice Companion, pp. 221, 226	etools 21 • writing tool • interactive glossary

Tips for Success

- Guide students to make connections between reading and writing (p. 97).

- You may wish to set out the Writing Models Chart where students can see it and refer to it during their Independent Practice.

 Remind students to work on their Inquiry Projects during Independent Practice or Self-Selected Reading time.

Oral Language and Vocabulary

Interactive Reading whole group

Objectives
Students will:
- Reinforce the theme
- Use context clues

Reinforce the Theme

Use the images on Theme Reader pages 396 and 397 to recall the Theme Question: *What makes the West exceptional?* Ask:

**Theme Reader
Pages 377–438**

- What is special about the history of the Pacific States? *(Responses will vary, but students may mention Native Americans, the Gold Rush, and hunting.)*
- What is special about the culture of this area? *(Responses will vary, but students may mention cities, art, architecture, music, food, wide-open spaces, and influences from other cultures and countries.)*

Have students look at the photos and illustration in Chapters 3 and 4 of the selection and ask questions about each one to get students to share their thoughts. Ask questions such as:

- What does this image remind you of?
- How do you think the people in this image are feeling?
- What does this image tell you about the West?

During the discussion, encourage students to use new vocabulary words they've learned in this unit.

INTRODUCE VOCABULARY STRATEGY

Use Context Clues

Define and Model

Remind students that there are many strategies they can use to understand unfamiliar words when they read. Ask students to recall strategies they know and use when they read. Then explain: **a**

> Context clues are words or pictures that give information about the meaning of a word. When you come across an unknown word, scan the sentence and paragraph for details, synonyms, and other clues to the word's meaning.

Have students turn to page 402 in their Theme Readers. Read aloud the paragraph and write the words *movie industry* on the board. Model your thinking:

think aloud
> The phrase *movie industry* is unfamiliar to me. I know what a movie is because I like to watch them at home. I am not sure of the meaning of the word *industry* though. As I keep reading, I see that the text tells me that some movies are produced and filmed in Hollywood, California and that the geography of the region is used for the sets of movies. I think *movie industry* means all of the things involved in making movies.

Practice

Have students continue reading page 403 to practice looking for context clues.

- Have partners define the meanings of *elevation* and *prominent,* identifying phrases and text features that helped them figure out the words.

- As a class, discuss what students found.

- You may wish to have partners continue practicing looking for context clues in the rest of the selection. Have them identify unknown words, discuss with a partner, and then check their ideas with the class or in a dictionary.

ASSIGN | PRACTICE COMPANION 212–213

model
read
share

Read and Comprehend

Objectives
Students will:
• Review identifying cause and effect

REVIEW **COMPREHENSION SKILL**

Identify Cause and Effect

Define and Model

Remind students that an *effect* is something that happens, and a *cause* is the reason it happens. Draw a T-chart on chart paper and model your thinking as you read page 397 in the Theme Reader.

There is a large amount of metal found in mines in the Pacific Northwest. Because of the abundance of metal, airplane manufacturing is one of the most important industries in the area. The reason airplanes are manufactured in the area is that metal is found nearby.

Identify Cause and Effect

Cause	Effect
large amount of metal is found in the region	important airplane manufacturing industry
area is located on waterways	waterways ship goods all over the world and help the economy
freshwater runs through dams	power is generated

Practice

Have partners revisit the chapter for other examples of cause and effect. Circulate to provide support. After students are finished reading, have the class suggest causes and effects and add them to the T-charts. **b** **c**

Reading/Writing Connection

Writers use key words to signal to the reader that they are describing a cause-and-effect relationship, such as *because*, *due to*, *as a result*, and *if/then*.

Invite students to page through the Theme Reader to find examples of key words and the cause-and-effect relationships they signal.

ASSIGN   **PRACTICE COMPANION 214**

---

scaffolding options

a ELL Support

ACADEMIC LANGUAGE
Some students may need more help understanding the concept of *context*. Explain that *context* is the situation, setting, or ideas surrounding a word or circumstance. Point out, for example, that we often say "taken out of context" to refer to an idea that doesn't make sense unless we know the whole story.

b Intervention for Acceleration

RETEACH
If students are struggling with the practice activity, provide additional scaffolding by listing several familiar examples of cause and effect, such as a room being messy, not being able to find anything, losing homework, and so on. Review each relationship and help students understand how they are related. Then list several different causes and effects and have students match up each pair. Have students explain how they are related. Next, list two or three initiating causes and have students name an effect for each one.

c Challenge

COMPREHENSION: CAUSE AND EFFECT
Ask students to identify other examples of cause and effect relationships in the Theme Reader or their Differentiated Reader that help them understand how geography and economy in the Western Region are related.

Interactive Reading whole group

Objectives
Students will:
• Use captions
• Reinforce identifying cause and effect

Prepare to Read

Use Text Features

Discuss how text features help readers understand concepts.

Theme Reader Pages 396–408

• Have students name text features they know.

• Tell students that text features often give the readers clues to what they will read about.

• Have students look back through Chapters 3 and 4 to point out text features, such as captions, maps, and sidebars.

Text Features Minilesson: Captions

Have students read the captions on pages 406 and 407 of the Theme Reader. Point out that captions give information about the photographs.

• How do the captions relate to what we read about in this chapter? *(They tell the reader about the culture and history of Hawaii and Alaska.)*

• How do the captions help you understand the text more clearly? *(Possible response: They provide more information about the topics on the pages. They also help to clarify what is pictured on the pages.)*

Set Purposes

Students reread Chapters 3 and 4 to find out how captions help them better understand unit concepts and the Theme Question: *What makes the West exceptional?*

Read Together

Have students reread Chapters 3 and 4 of *A Tour of the Western Region.* After students read, discuss how text features add to the text's meaning, and share cause-and-effect relationships they identified.

PAGES 396–397 How do the captions relate to the text on each page? *(One gives more information about the mountain in Washington pictured on the page. The other gives more information about the important cherry industry in the state.)*

PAGES 398–399 How might you use an encyclopedia or dictionary to better understand the information in each sidebar? *(Possible response: Both would provide more details and a better understanding about the two topics for example, an encyclopedia might tell how or when the Grand Coulee dam was built.)*

PAGES 400–403 What do the chapter heads make you think you will read about? *(Students should mention things to see and do in the Pacific States - California, mountains and valleys, movies, islands.)*

What examples of cause and effect can you find in this section? *(Possible responses: the amount of rainfall that the area receives makes timber an important industry.)*

PAGES 404–408 How do the photographs and illustration enhance the text? *(Possible response: they show examples of the culture and the area mentioned in the text.)*

Respond

After students read, ask them to share how chapter heads and other text features add meaning to the text and help them answer the Theme Question: *What makes the West exceptional?*

Talk About Text ★★★

Have students talk about an author's use of opinions in informational text:

• Why might authors include their opinions in informational text? Do the opinions help readers better understand the important information?

• Do you think authors should include their opinions in informational text? Why or why not?

Word Work and Fluency

Objectives
Students will:
- Practice spelling words with the final schwa + *l* sound
- Analyze contractions
- Practice fluent reading

Spelling

Practice the Final Schwa + *l* Sound

Have students turn to page 207 in their Practice Companions. Explain that students will proofread the paragraph to find and correct the misspelled words. **b**

ASSIGN | PRACTICE COMPANION **207**

Word Study

Introduce Contractions

Tell students that they will learn about contractions with *have, had, would,* and *not.* Explain that recognizing these words helps readers understand a text's meaning.

Teach/Model

Point out the word *wouldn't* on page 402 of the Theme Reader. Say:

> The word *wouldn't* is short for *would* and *not.* The whole phrase, *wouldn't be complete,* tells me that something would not be complete.

Have students use the word *wouldn't* in a sentence about their area. **c**

Practice/Apply

Ask partners to identify the contractions in the following sentences and tell what each one means:

- I haven't had time to go to the store yet.
- I would've come to your party if I had finished my homework.

ASSIGN | PRACTICE COMPANION **215**

epractice
word study games

Fluency

Paired Reading

Read "Hiking in Redwood" (Practice Companion, p. 208), modeling appropriate expression. Have partners take turns reading the procedural text with expression, and then discuss how it helped them better understand the selection.

ASSIGN | PRACTICE COMPANION **208**

---

scaffolding options

a Intervention for Acceleration

COMPREHENSION: DISTINGUISH FACT AND OPINION
Remind students as they read to consider whether statements are facts or opinions. Guide students by providing questions they can ask, such as:

- Can this statement be proved?
- What do I already know about the topic that can help me decide if this is a fact?
- Does this statement tell something that the author thinks or believes?

b Intervention for Acceleration

SPELLING
Provide students additional practice with the spelling words by having them write sentences with at least half of the words. Tell students that as they write their sentences, they should include two choices for the spelling word: one that is spelled correctly, and one that is not. Then have students exchange papers with a partner and have the partner choose the correct spelling of the word.

c Literacy Builder

WORD STUDY
Help students understand conditional statements with modal verbs, such as the phrase *would have come.* Explain that the phrase expresses the idea of possibility in the past. Review how to form the structure with students (modal + *have* + past participle), and explain that recognizing the *have* in contractions is important when identifying this verb tense.

Differentiated Reading
small groups

Objectives
Students will:
- Use differentiated vocabulary
- Reinforce identifying cause and effect
- Reinforce using context clues
- Reinforce using text features
- Read about the California coast

Prepare to Read

Review

Review pages 30–39 of *The California Coast* by asking questions, such as:

Differentiated Reader Pages 40–53

- What are characteristics of the California coast?
- What is the weather like in that area?

Have students share what they found out about the Focus Question: *How are geography and economy connected in the Pacific States?*

Introduce
Differentiated Vocabulary

Have students complete the Vocabulary Rating Sheet (Resource Master 4).

- Find and pronounce with students the highlighted differentiated vocabulary words (pp. 40–53).
- Use the following routine to discuss each word's meaning.
- For each word, have students jot down and explain answers to prompts.

Vocabulary Routine	
Define	**Balmy** (p. 49) means "warm and pleasant."
Example	Many people enjoy the balmy weather of southern California.
Ask	Are balmy and frigid the same? Why or why not?

Accustomed (p. 51) means "used to or familiar with." *He was accustomed to eating cereal for breakfast each day.* What are you *accustomed* to?

ASSIGN   RESOURCE MASTER **4**   **epractice** vocabulary activities

Set Purposes

Display the KWL chart that students began on Day 2.

- Point to words in the KWL chart. The group reads the items chorally.
- Invite students to add additional questions to the "Want to Know" column.
- Students will look for answers to their questions and read to find out more about the Focus Question.

REINFORCE COMPREHENSION SKILL

Identify Cause and Effect

Remind students that an effect is something that happens and a cause is what makes it happen. These concepts help readers better understand what they read.

To review identifying cause and effect, use page 32 to model your thinking.

 think aloud The text says that millions of years ago, rock plates shifted deep under the earth and collided, which formed the mountain ranges in what is now California. The cause is the rock plates shifting, and the effect is the formation of the mountain ranges.

ASSIGN   PRACTICE COMPANION **214**

Read

Tell students that today they will finish reading *The California Coast*. Remind them to use the skills and strategies they learned in whole group as they read. To help them get started, model your thinking as you read page 40.

think aloud This page mentions that tourism is important to the central coast of California. It also mentions some places in the central coast, such as Big Sur. The caption on this page tells me that surfers and artists like Big Sur. It must be a beautiful area with good waves for surfers.

Guide Comprehension

Invite students to continue reading silently. Circulate to reinforce theme concepts, skills, and strategies. Allow students to use sticky notes to make notes and write questions they may have about the text. **b**

PAGES 40–45 Ask partners to read the **Strategy Tool Kit** on page 45 and discuss their ideas. Have partners share which fix-up strategies they used to monitor their comprehension.

PAGES 46–48 What context clues help you figure out the meaning of the word *commercial* on page 47? *(Possible response: catch goes to homes, restaurants, and stores – that means it is being sold; fishing is big business.)*

Have students discuss how the photograph and its caption give more information about the text.

PAGES 49–53 Have students jot down notes about the causes and effects from this part of the selection. Have volunteers share their ideas with the group.

Check Comprehension

1. What can people see and do while visiting Monterey Bay? *(Possible response: They can watch the sea lions. They can go to the aquarium.)* SUMMARIZE

2. What clues in the text and side bar support the fact that San Francisco is a historic town with different cultures? *(Possible response: The text mentions Chinatown and says there are neighborhoods filled with history. The side bar mentions the first cable car and that they are still used today.)* IDENTIFY MAIN IDEA AND DETAILS

3. Would you like to visit a movie set? Why or why not? *(Possible response: I would like to visit a movie set to see how movies are made.)* MAKE CONNECTIONS

Respond and Write

1. Ask students how what they learned helped them answer the Focus Question.

2. Have students return to the KWL chart to add new information in the "What I Learned" column. Read the column chorally. Invite volunteers to share the most interesting fact or idea they learned.

3. Have students create a travel ad that explains why people should visit the California coast. You may wish to have students complete their ads during Independent Practice.

scaffolding options

ELL Support

See page 292 of this Teacher's Lesson Guide for vocabulary and instructional support of English language learners at the Intensive level.

a Literacy Builder

VOCABULARY

To reinforce the meaning of the word *accustomed*, have students complete a Word Map (Resource Master 6). To get them started, brainstorm a list of things to which a person might be accustomed. Have students draw a picture, define the word, and complete the rest of the Word Map. Ask students to share their Word Maps with a partner, then present their ideas to the group.

ASSIGN   RESOURCE MASTER **6**

b Intervention for Acceleration

COMPREHENSION: IDENTIFY CAUSE AND EFFECT

Provide students with a T-chart to use as they read. Have them record causes they read about in the left column, and the effects they read about in the right column. Explain that they will use their notes during Check Comprehension.

ASSIGN   RESOURCE MASTER **14**

ebook onlinecoach
Intervention for Acceleration

Students can use the support features in the eBook version of the Differentiated Reader.

Read and Comprehend   Strategic

Differentiated Reading
small groups

Objectives
Students will:
• Use differentiated vocabulary
• Reinforce identifying cause and effect
• Reinforce using context clues
• Reinforce using text features
• Read about farming in the Pacific Northwest

Prepare to Read

Review

Review pages 30–41 of *Farming in the Pacific Northwest* by asking questions, such as:

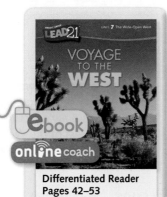

Differentiated Reader Pages 42–53

• What is one of the crops that is grown in the Pacific Northwest?
• Why does it rain so much in the area?
• How do people use water from the Columbia River?

Have students share what they found out about the Focus Question: *How are geography and economy connected in the Pacific States?*

Introduce
Differentiated Vocabulary

Have students complete the Vocabulary Rating Sheet (Resource Master 4).

• Find and pronounce with students the highlighted differentiated vocabulary words (pp. 42–53).
• Use the following routine to discuss each word's meaning.
• For each word, have students jot down and explain answers to prompts.

Vocabulary Routine	
Define	**Occur** (p. 48) means "to happen."
Example	A meteor shower might occur every 100 years.
Ask	What typical activity might occur every day?

A **bushel** (p. 49) is a measure equal to about 32 quarts. *Many types of food can be measured in bushels.* What is one food that can be measured in a *bushel*?

A **reservoir** (p. 51) is an artificial lake where water is collected and stored for use. *Our town gets our water from an underground reservoir.* Why might a *reservoir* be important to an area?

ASSIGN   RESOURCE MASTER **4**

vocabulary activities

Set Purposes

Remind students that setting a purpose helps readers focus their attention to get more out of their reading.

• Students will read to add information to the Concept and Word Webs they started the day before.
• Students will also read to find answers to the Focus Question.

REINFORCE COMPREHENSION SKILL

Identify Cause and Effect

Remind students that an effect is an action that happens, and a cause is why it happens. Identifying these relationships helps readers understand facts and events.

Model identifying cause and effect using page 38.

The last sentence in the first paragraph on page 38 tells me that inexpensive power from the Columbia River has drawn business to the Pacific Northwest. So, the cause of business coming to the area is because there is inexpensive power available.

ASSIGN   PRACTICE COMPANION **214**

Read

Explain to students that today they will finish reading *Farming in the Pacific Northwest*. Remind them to use the skills and strategies they learned in whole group as they read. To help them get started, model your thinking as you read page 42.

Page 42 continues to talk about farming in the Pacific Northwest. On this page, the caption tells me the photo is of a vineyard that is located in the Pacific Northwest. This is one example of farming in the local area. I will pay attention to other types of crops that are grown in the Pacific Northwest.

Guide Comprehension

Invite students to continue reading silently. Circulate to reinforce theme concepts, skills, and strategies. Have partners share their thoughts before answering your prompts in class discussion.

PAGES 42–44 Have students read the **Strategy Tool Kit** on page 44 and jot down their ideas. Have partners discuss their ideas. `a`

PAGES 45–49 Have students identify which information found in the captions is not available in the text. Ask partners to discuss the importance of this information, and why captions are important in an informational text. *(Possible response: Captions provide more specific details about the text as well as information about what is in photographs or illustrations.)*

PAGES 50–51 Have partners identify cause-and-effect relationships on these pages. `b`

PAGES 52–53 Direct students to the word *dairy* on page 52. Ask them which context clues they used to help them understand the meaning of that word. *(cows, milk)*

Check Comprehension

1. What is Willamette Valley known for? *(It is known for its rich soil. About half of Oregon's agricultural products are grown there.)* DETAILS/FACTS

2. Summarize what you learned in Chapter 3. SUMMARIZE

3. Why does the author state that caring for a fruit orchard is hard work? Is this sentence a fact or opinion? *(Possible response: The author wants the reader to know all of the work a farmer has to do to care for an orchard. This is the author's opinion that the work is hard.)* DISTINGUISH FACT FROM OPINION

Respond and Write

1. Ask students how what they learned helped them answer the Focus Question.

2. Have students add details to their Concept Webs. Discuss together how the ideas in the selection help them understand what the Pacific States are like.

3. Have students write a short paragraph about what they think it would be like to live or work on a farm in the Pacific Northwest. Have students share their ideas with the class.

scaffolding options

ELL Support

See page 293 of this Teacher's Lesson Guide for vocabulary and instructional support of English language learners at the Strategic level.

`a` Intervention for Acceleration

USE A THESAURUS
Have students look up the underlined word *plentiful* on page 43 in a thesaurus to learn synonyms and antonyms that will help them understand its meaning. Have partners create sentences with two or three synonyms from the thesaurus.

`b` Intervention for Acceleration

BUILD CONCEPTS
To help students understand the concept of irrigation, have partners imagine they want to irrigate a garden that is near a water source. Ask them to write down the steps they would take to get the water to the garden, and then have them discuss their ideas with the group. If possible, show students pictures of irrigation systems during the group discussion to help them understand how irrigation works.

ebook online coach
Intervention for Acceleration

Students can use the support features in the eBook version of the Differentiated Reader.

Read and Comprehend

Differentiated Reading small groups

Objectives
Students will:
- Use differentiated vocabulary
- Reinforce identifying cause and effect
- Reinforce using context clues
- Reinforce using text features
- Read about Hawaii

Prepare to Read

Review

Review with students pages 30–41 of *Hawaii: The Beautiful Island State*. Have students review the list they made the day before to remind them what they've already learned about Hawaii. Have them look back over the pages and restate the important concepts. Then have them share what they found out about the Focus Question: *How are geography and economy connected in the Pacific States?*

LEAD21 UNIT 7 The Wide-Open West
Passage to the West

ebook
online coach

Differentiated Reader
Pages 42–53

Introduce
Differentiated Vocabulary *tested*

Have students complete the Vocabulary Rating Sheet (Resource Master 4).

Vocabulary Routine	
Define	A **garland** (p. 45) is flowers or leaves tied together and worn around the neck or head as a decoration.
Example	I wore a garland at my parent's Hawaiian-themed party.
Ask	Would you be more likely to see garlands in Hawaii or on the mainland? Why?

Partners continue the routine with *premise* (p. 46), *concern* (p. 46), *generate* (p. 52), and *summit* (p. 52), using the Glossary definitions and sentences and asking questions.

ASSIGN RESOURCE MASTER **4**

practice
vocabulary activities

Set Purposes

Display the list that students created the day before. Have students tell what they want to learn from the second half of the selection.

- Students will read to add information to the lists they started yesterday.
- Students will read to answer the Focus Question.

Intensive — Self-Selected Reading
Strategic — Independent Practice
class manager
Advanced — Study Stations
Benchmark

Read

Guide Comprehension

As students finish reading *Hawaii: The Beautiful Island State*, remind them to use the skills and strategies they learned in whole group. Circulate to reinforce concepts, skills, and strategies. **a**

PAGES 42–45 Have students tell how the subhead and captions relate to the text and photos. USE TEXT FEATURES

PAGES 46–53 Have students state how agriculture and aquaculture are important to Hawaii's economy. The word *export* is on page 49. Ask students which context clues they used to help them understand the meaning of the word? SUMMARIZE

Respond and Write

Have students finish their list by adding information they learned during today's reading. Have them include ideas that answer the Focus Question.

scaffolding options

ELL Support

See page 294 of this Teacher's Lesson Guide for vocabulary and instructional support of English language learners at the Benchmark level.

a Literacy Builder *tested*

COMPREHENSION: IDENTIFY CAUSE AND EFFECT
Have students list causes and effects as they read, then discuss how the information helped them understand the topic more deeply. Invite students to tell whether any of the causes or effects were confusing, and if so, how they monitored their comprehension to understand what the author wanted to say.

Differentiated Reading
small groups

- Use differentiated vocabulary
- Reinforce identifying cause and effect
- Reinforce using context clues
- Reinforce using text features
- Read about technology in the Pacific States

Prepare to Read

Review

Review with students pages 30–41 of *Technology in the Pacific States.* Have students use the Concept Webs

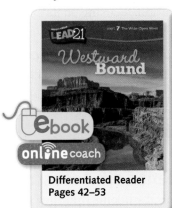

Differentiated Reader Pages 42–53

they began the day before to discuss the key concepts they've learned so far. Have them look back over the pages and restate the important concepts. Have them share what they found out about the Focus Question: *How are geography and economy connected in the Pacific States?*

Introduce
Differentiated Vocabulary

Have students use the Vocabulary Rating Sheet (Resource Master 4).

Vocabulary Routine	
Define	**Enhance** (p. 43) means "to increase or improve."
Example	The new stereo speakers enhance the sound of the music.
Ask	What is another word for enhance?

Partners continue the routine with *expand* (p. 47), *contract* (p. 47), *turbine* (p. 47), and *dormant* (p. 52), using the Glossary definitions and sentences and asking questions.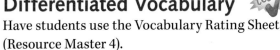

ASSIGN RESOURCE MASTER 4

epractice vocabulary activities

Set Purposes

Discuss what students want to learn from the selection and elicit why setting a purpose for reading is helpful.

- Students will read to complete the Concept Webs they started at the beginning of the selection.
- Students will read to answer the Focus Question.

Read

Guide Comprehension

Students will finish reading *Technology in the Pacific States.* Remind them to use the skills and strategies they learned in whole group. After students read, use the following prompts:

PAGES 42–48 Have students explain how text features help readers better understand the topic. USE TEXT FEATURES

PAGES 49–53 Have students discuss cause-and-effect relationships in Chapter 6. IDENTIFY CAUSE AND EFFECT

Respond and Write

Have students complete their Concept Webs by adding information they learned during today's reading. Have them discuss how the web helps them answer the Focus Question.

scaffolding options

ELL Support

See page 295 of this Teacher's Lesson Guide for vocabulary and instructional support of English language learners at the Advanced level.

Challenge

VOCABULARY: CONTEXT CLUES
Have students select a vocabulary word and use the word in a sentence that alludes to its meaning. Encourage students to avoid giving the definition outright, but to instead create context clues to provide meaning.

Share, Connect, Assess

Objectives
Students will:
- Summarize selections
- Make text-to-world connections
- Write about a place in the West
- Monitor their progress

Wrap Up
whole group

Share Text Connections

★★★ Building Classroom Community

Make Text-to-World Connections Bring students back together from their small groups to summarize their selections.

- Encourage students to use theme and other academic vocabulary in their summaries.

- As students discuss the texts, help them to make connections between texts and the world. For example, students read about the apples, wheat, and other crops produced in the Pacific Northwest. Point out that wheat bread and apples are staples of many Americans' diets.

- Ask students to share the activities they completed during Respond and Write.

- Have students share how what they've read answers the week's Focus Question.

etools 21
theme wall

Daily Writing

Have students draw a picture of a place in the West. Have them label the picture and write a sentence about the location, focusing on its agriculture, economy, or other details.

For additional writing practice, remind students to access the Story Starter from their student Home Page.

etools 21
- writing tool
- story starter

Student Self Assessment

- Remind students that they are responsible for their learning and that it is helpful to be aware of how well they understand what they are reading, writing, talking, and thinking about in the classroom.

- You may want students to reflect on their reading and learning by using their Personal Reading Logs and My Daily Progress sheets (Resource Masters 1, 3).

ASSIGN RESOURCE MASTER **1, 3**

Daily Progress Monitoring

To ensure that students have mastered the day's skills and strategies, monitor their success in completing the following independent work:

- **Vocabulary:** Practice Companion, pp. 212–213
- **Comprehension:** Practice Companion, p. 214
- **Word Study:** Practice Companion, p. 215
- **Spelling:** Practice Companion, p. 207
- **Fluency:** Practice Companion, p. 208
- **Study Station Work Record:** Resource Master 2
- **Self Assessment:** Resource Masters 1, 3

epractice
reporting

Home Connection
Distribute the Unit 7 Take-Home Activities from the Home Connection book. Tell students to complete the activities with their caregivers.

Day at a Glance

Lesson Highlights

- Extend Theme Vocabulary
- Reinforce Comprehension Strategy: Monitor Comprehension
- Use Text Evidence
- Reinforce Word Study: Contractions
- Publish and Present a Science Fiction Story, pp. 144–145

Materials

	Teacher's Lesson Guide	Student Components	Digital 21
Interactive Reading	pp. 108–111	• Theme Reader, pp. 396–408 • Practice Companion, pp. 205–206, 208–211, 215, 227–228 • Resource Masters 5, 14, 21	ebook online coach / epractice word study games
Differentiated Reading	pp. 112–117, 292–295 (ELL)	• Differentiated Readers • Resource Master 14	ebook online coach / epractice vocabulary activities
Wrap Up	p. 118	• Resource Masters 1–3	etools 21 • theme wall • writing tool • story starter
Writing and Language Arts	pp. 144–145	• Writing Models Chart, pp. 48–51 • Practice Companion, p. 221	

Tips for Success

- Guide students to use multiple strategies as they read (Model Multiple Strategies, p. 109).

- You may wish to use the Assessment on Practice Companion pages 227–228 to monitor student progress on skill and strategy use over the past two weeks.

 Remind students to work on their Inquiry Projects during Independent Practice or Self-Selected Reading time.

Oral Language and Vocabulary

Interactive Reading
whole group

Objectives
Students will:
- Extend the theme
- Extend theme vocabulary

Extend the Theme

Recall the Theme Question: *What makes the West exceptional?* and have students summarize what they have learned about the area. Say:

Theme Reader Pages 377–438

Suppose you wanted to describe the Western Region to a friend who had never been there but wanted to go there for a vacation. What would you tell them about the land, the people, and the culture? What interesting information about the history of the area would you share?

Have students share their thoughts in small groups. To help students get started, model your thinking:

> **think aloud** What if I had a friend who was thinking of visiting the Western Region? I asked myself what they and their family would want to know. They'd probably need to know about the types of attractions they could visit, like the Grand Canyon.

Have groups identify three pieces of information that they think are the most important in describing the Western Region. After groups have had sufficient time to share their thoughts, come back together for a whole class discussion. **a**

Extend Theme Vocabulary

To help students extend their knowledge of theme vocabulary, distribute Vocabulary Recording Sheets (Resource Master 5) to students.

- To help students get started, model how to fill out the sheet. Say:

> **think aloud** Let's begin with the first two columns, *Word* and *What It Means.* We already know the information that should be included in these columns. Write the word and its definition.

- As students fill their charts, write the word and the definition in the chart.

Vocabulary Recording Sheet			
Word	What It Means	My Sentence	Personal Connections
missionary	a person who is sent by a group to share their beliefs, usually religious	The missionary helped the people open a school in the village.	help, assist, helper

- Invite volunteers to create a sentence using the word *missionary.* Write it in column three, and ask students to do the same.

- Guide students in brainstorming a list of other words they associate with *missionary,* such as *help, assist, helper,* and so on. Record the list in column four.

- Have students continue with the words *film* and *rugged.* **b**

ASSIGN

RESOURCE MASTER	5
PRACTICE COMPANION	205

Read and Comprehend

Objectives
Students will:
- Reinforce monitoring comprehension

REINFORCE **COMPREHENSION STRATEGY**

Monitor Comprehension

Define
Ask students to recall that readers monitor comprehension by checking their understanding of what they read.

Then explain that readers often use multiple strategies as they read. Encourage students to share other strategies they know.

Model Multiple-Strategy Use
Use page 400 from the Theme Reader to model using multiple strategies to monitor comprehension.

 The text says that California's coastline offers sandy beaches. I visualize soft sand that is pushed through my toes as I walk on it. Then I saw the words *rugged cliffs*. I know *sandy* describes the beaches so *rugged* must describe the cliffs. I know that the coastline of California has cliffs that are uneven and jagged. I can make an inference that *rugged* means "uneven and jagged."

Guided Practice
Have partners use Resource Master 21 to record the strategies they use to monitor comprehension as they revisit Chapter 3 of *A Tour of the Western Region*.

Circulate to provide support as needed, suggesting strategies that may work and asking guiding questions. After partners have finished, lead a class discussion about the strategies they used as they read. **c**

Independent Practice
Have students independently continue to read the selection and apply multiple strategies. Have them add more information to Use Multiple Strategies (Resource Master 21).

ASSIGN

RESOURCE MASTER	21
PRACTICE COMPANION	210–211

scaffolding options

a Challenge

USE OUTSIDE RESOURCES
Encourage groups of four to write down a list of questions they have that were not answered by the text, as well as other information about the Western Region that they would like to know. Have them make a list of where they can find this information. Allow time during Independent Practice for groups to find answers to at least one of their questions and create a visual aid. Then have groups present their questions and answers to the class.

b Literacy Builder

VOCABULARY
Ask pairs of students to choose a vocabulary word and make a Concept and Word Web (Resource Master 11) using a combination of words and images. Encourage them to look through old magazines, Web sites, and other sources for visuals. Suggest that students even create their own images for inclusion in their word webs. Have pairs present their completed webs to the class.

ASSIGN   RESOURCE MASTER **11**

c ELL Support

MODEL MULTIPLE-STRATEGY USE
Some English language learners may have trouble accessing multiple strategies simply by name. To aid connections between words and concepts, list the strategies they have learned on the board and guide them to recall how each is used.

Read and Comprehend (continued)

Objectives
Students will:
• Reread to find text evidence
• Reinforce monitoring comprehension

Prepare to Read

Use Text Evidence

Remind students that they have been reading *A Tour of the Western Region* to answer the Theme Question:

What makes the West exceptional?

online coach

**Theme Reader
Pages 396–408**

• Explain that when readers read for specific information, they can use evidence from the text to support their answers. **a**

• Review with students why skimming and scanning are successful tools for locating text evidence (*readers can quickly locate specific information in the text*). **b**

• Tell students to continue using their T-Charts (Resource Master 14) with the headings *Page Number* and *Text Evidence* to record text evidence and the page number where it is found.

ASSIGN RESOURCE MASTER **14**

Set Purposes

Students will reread Chapters 3 and 4 to gather text evidence that answers the Theme Question: *What makes the West exceptional?*

Read Together

Begin rereading Chapters 3 and 4. Use the chart paper from the previous week as you model finding and recording text evidence from page 396.

think aloud As I skim the text on page 396, I see the sentence, "California has more than 1,000 miles of coastline." To me, this is pretty exceptional. I think this answers the Theme Question.

Have partners continue to read and complete their own charts. Prompt students to help them determine whether the information in the captions and sidebars is important.

PAGES 396–402 Does the information in the captions support the text, offer new information, or describe the photographs? Is this information helpful in answering the Theme Question?

PAGES 403–408 What do you learn from the captions about the history and culture of the Pacific States? Do these details help you answer the Theme Question?

Respond

Have students compare the text evidence they have gathered and then poll the class to find the most common examples.

Invite them to share places in the text where they applied fix-up strategies as they monitored their comprehension.

Writer's Response

Ask students to use the text evidence they have gathered to write a response to the Theme Question. Invite volunteers to share their paragraphs with the class.

Word Work and Fluency

Objectives
Students will:
- Practice spelling words with final *e* + *l* sound
- Reinforce analyzing contractions
- Practice fluent reading

Spelling

Practice Test

Have partners dictate the spelling words to one another. Then have them self-correct their papers. Remind them to focus their attention on any words they misspelled.

ASSIGN | PRACTICE COMPANION **206**

Word Study

Reinforce Contractions

Write examples of contractions on the board and have students identify the two words being contracted and determine the meaning of the contraction.

> haven't
> hadn't
> wouldn't
> would've

Practice/Apply

Have volunteers suggest examples of other contractions they may have heard of or used in the past. Write the suggestions on the board and have students tell which two words make the contraction.

ASSIGN | PRACTICE COMPANION **215**

epractice
word study games

Fluency

Personal Rehearsal

Model reading "Hiking in Redwood" (Practice Companion, p. 208) with appropriate pacing. Remind students that reading too fast or too slow makes it hard to understand what they read. **c**

Ask students to rehearse the procedural text and complete the Reading Response Form (Practice Companion, p. 209).

ASSIGN | PRACTICE COMPANION **208–209**

---

scaffolding options

a Intervention for Acceleration

CONCEPT DEVELOPMENT
For students who have difficulty identifying text evidence, remind them that evidence can come in many forms. Some evidence is obvious, such as images, charts, and factual statements in the text. Other evidence is not as obvious, such as inferences that readers make based on the author's tone.

b Literacy Builder

KEY WORDS
Remind students that they should not reread the entire slection as they look for text evidence. Point out that the key to scanning is to identify specific key words to look for in the text. These key words are related to the questions students want to answer. Have them brainstorm a list of key words to use when scanning the selection that will help them answer the Theme Question.

c Intervention for Acceleration

FLUENCY
Ask partners to choose a chapter or passage from their own Differentiated Reader selection and practice reading the piece aloud for each other with appropriate pacing. After several reads, encourage students to focus on a different aspect of fluency, such as expression or phrasing. Encourage partners to offer advice on how to improve fluency.

Read and Comprehend | Intensive

Differentiated Reading small groups

Objectives
Students will:
- Extend vocabulary
- Reread to find text evidence
- Reinforce monitoring comprehension
- Reinforce cause and effect

Prepare to Read

Extend Vocabulary *tested*

Explain to students that one way to expand vocabulary is by developing word associations through examples.

Differentiated Reader Pages 30–53

Tell students that you will ask them a question and they should record their responses.

Provide students with *yes/no* or *either/or* questions, such as the following:

- Would your opinion likely **differ** from your friend's? Why or why not?

- Can something be **carved** out of stone? Why or why not?

- Which word means the same as **variety**: *many* or *few*? Why?

- If you **contribute** something, do you give or take? Why?

- Which word goes better with **tremendous**: *tiny* or *huge*? Why?

- Would you **leisurely** make your bed if you wanted to go outside and play? Why or why not?

- Would you prefer **balmy** or chilly weather? Why?

- Which are you more **accustomed** to? School or a dentist's office? Why?

- Ask students to share their responses and discuss how they came to their conclusions.

- As the group discusses the activity, record any associated or related words that might help students retain their understanding of these differentiated vocabulary words. At the end of the discussion, have students copy your list.

epractice vocabulary activities

Set Purposes

Students will revisit *The California Coast* to find and record text evidence to support answers to the Focus Question: *How are geography and economy connected in the Pacific States?*

Use Text Evidence

Distribute Resource Master 14 and have students tell why using text evidence is important. Remind students that when they read a fact or detail that could help them answer the Focus Question, they should record it in their charts. Help students get started by reading aloud page 34. Model your thinking as you read. **a**

think aloud The Focus Question asks how geography and economy are connected. When I read page 34, I read that people from all over come to see the animals and wildlife that can be found along the California coastline. This is one way that geography and economy are connected.

ASSIGN   **RESOURCE MASTER 14**

Read

Guide Comprehension

Have partners continue to reread *The California Coast*. Pairs should work together to record text evidence in their charts. Students should share their notes with the group after each chapter. Use the prompts below to provide support as needed.

PAGES 30–41 How does the map, photographs, and captions help you understand the text better and provide evidence to help you answer the Focus Question? *(They help the reader visualize information; they show how geography and economy are connected.)* USE GRAPHIC SOURCES

PAGES 42–48 Have partners pause after each page to ask and answer questions to make sure they understand what they've read. If students still don't understand something, remind them to ask for help. MONITOR COMPREHENSION **b**

PAGES 49–53 Why do people want to live in Los Angeles and San Diego? *(Both places have great weather and beaches.)* IDENTIFY CAUSE AND EFFECT

Respond and Write

Have students look over the text evidence they've gathered and share one or two items with the group. Guide students to understand how the information from the text helps them answer the Focus Question.

Prepare to Share

Tell students they will discuss the **Think Back** activities on page 54 of their Differentiated Readers tomorrow with their mixed groups.

1. **Check Understanding** Make sure students understand that this question reflects the Focus Question. After students have completed the activity independently, bring students back together to share their ideas with the class.

2. **Understand Text Features** If necessary, remind students of the purpose of a caption. Encourage them to think about what the captions in the selection provided and how they offered more information about the text.

3. **Share and Compare** Explain that when students meet tomorrow with their groups, they will be comparing their ideas about which industries are dependent on land and/or water with a partner from another group.

4. **Think Critically** Complete the activity as a group. Point out that this question reflects the Theme Question and that students can use the notes they have taken to help them answer the question.

scaffolding options

ELL Support

See page 292 of this Teacher's Lesson Guide for vocabulary and instructional support of English language learners at the Intensive level.

a Intervention for Acceleration

USE TEXT FEATURES
Remind students that as they read, they should pay special attention to text features such as headings, captions, maps, and sidebars. Explain that text features often offer strong evidence to support ideas or information. Encourage students to include text features in their T-charts as appropriate.

b Critical Thinking

SYNTHESIZE CONCEPTS
Have students work in pairs or small groups to create a graphic organizer that summarizes the information in the selection. Ask students to present their finished products to the class, and challenge them to use visuals, such as photographs from the selection or their own drawings, in their presentations.

ebook online coach

Intervention for Acceleration

Students can use the support features in the eBook version of the Differentiated Reader.

Read and Comprehend   Strategic

Objectives
Students will:
- Extend vocabulary
- Reread to find text evidence
- Reinforce monitoring comprehension
- Reinforce cause and effect

Prepare to Read

Extend Vocabulary

Explain that one way to expand vocabulary knowledge is to make word associations through answering questions about words. Have students record their responses to the following prompts:

Differentiated Reader Pages 30–53

- Which word goes better with inland: *valley* or *beach*? Why?

- What word goes better with origin: *history* or *future*?

- Is an emergency an example of a critical situation? Why or why not?

- Which is more likely to graze in a field: a cow or a fish? Why?

- Where are you more likely to find a pasture: a farm or a city? Why?

- Which is more likely to occur after lunch: class time or a parade? Why?

- Is corn or beef more likely to be measured in a bushel? Why?

- Is concrete or water more likely to be found in a reservoir? Why?

Ask students to share their responses and discuss how they came to their conclusions. Record any associated or related words that the class discusses for each differentiated vocabulary word. **a**

epractice vocabulary activities

Set Purposes

Students will revisit *Farming in the Pacific Northwest* to find and record text evidence to support answers to the Focus Question: *How are geography and economy connected in the Pacific States?*

Use Text Evidence

While students prepare their T-charts, begin a group discussion about why text evidence is important. Remind students that when they read a fact or detail that could help them answer the Focus Question, they should record it in their charts. Help students get started by modeling your thinking as you read page 31.

 As I skim the text, I notice the word *geography* on page 31. I should reread this paragraph to see if it can help me answer the Focus Question. It talks about the geography of the Pacific States lending itself to agriculture. I already know that agriculture is tied to the economy. I think this information is important, so I'll record it in my chart.

ASSIGN   RESOURCE MASTER **14**

Read

Guide Comprehension

Have partners continue to reread *Farming in the Pacific Northwest*. Guide them to work together to record text evidence in their charts. Use the prompts below to provide support as needed.

PAGES 30–35 Why is agriculture so successful in the Pacific Northwest? *(The geography and climate are both excellent for farming. There is plenty of water.)* **USE TEXT EVIDENCE**

PAGES 36–44 Remind students that important information might be found in text features like captions and sidebars.

How does the caption on page 38 relate to the Focus Question? *(Possible response: The geographic location of the port helps to ship goods around the world, which helps the local economy.)* **USE TEXT FEATURES**

PAGES 45–53 Have students identify instances of cause and effect on these pages. *(Irrigation and good soil make Washington State an ideal place to grow crops; As snow melts in the mountains it causes the reservoirs to fill up.)* **IDENTIFY CAUSE AND EFFECT**

Respond and Write

Have students look over the text evidence they have gathered and share one or two items with the group. Guide students to understand how the information from the text helps them answer the Focus Question.

Prepare to Share

Tell students they will discuss the **Think Back** activities on page 54 of their Differentiated Readers tomorrow with their mixed groups.

1. **Check Understanding** Make sure students understand that this question reflects the Focus Question. After students have completed the activity independently, bring students back together to share their ideas with the class.

2. **Understand Text Features** If necessary, remind students of the purpose of a caption. Encourage them to think about what the captions in the selection provided and how they offered more information about the text.

3. **Share and Compare** Explain that when students meet tomorrow with their groups, they will be comparing their ideas about which industries are dependant on land and/or water with a partner from another group.

4. **Think Critically** Complete the activity as a group. Point out that this question reflects the Theme Question and that students can use the notes they have taken to help them answer the question. **b**

scaffolding options

ELL Support

See page 293 of this Teacher's Lesson Guide for vocabulary and instructional support of English language learners at the Strategic level.

a Literacy Builder

WORD STUDY

Encourage students to list words that are related to the differentiated vocabulary by using resources such as a dictionary or thesaurus. Help them analyze some of the words they've listed by asking questions such as these:

- What are different forms of this word?
- What root and prefix do you see in this word?
- How is this word related to the vocabulary word?

b Critical Thinking

SYNTHESIZE CONCEPTS

Encourage students to synthesize their notes from both Week 1 and Week 2 of the unit as they prepare their answers to **Think Critically**. Remind them that other students in their mixed groups might share information from the Theme Reader selection, but the information from the Differentiated selections will be new to their classmates from other groups.

ebook **online coach**

Intervention for Acceleration

Students can use the support features in the eBook version of the Differentiated Reader.

Share, Connect, Assess

Objectives
Students will:
- Use key concepts and vocabulary
- Use text evidence to answer essential questions
- Make text-to-text connections
- Write about finding text evidence
- Monitor their progress

Wrap Up
whole group

Share Text Connections

Building Classroom Community

Make Text-to-Text Connections Bring students back together from their small groups to share how the text evidence they gathered from their Differentiated Reader selections helped them to answer the Focus Question: *How are geography and economy connected in the Pacific States?*

- Encourage students to use theme and other academic vocabulary as they share their responses.

- Ensure that students from all groups have a chance to contribute to the discussion.

- As students share text evidence, help them make connections between texts. For example, *Hawaii: The Beautiful Island State* and *Farming in the Pacific Northwest* both discuss the importance of agriculture.

etools 21
theme wall

Daily Writing

Ask students to write briefly about the strategy and method they used to find text evidence. Encourage them to describe how the text evidence helped them to answer the Theme and Focus Questions.

For additional writing practice, remind students to access the Story Starter from their student Home Page.

etools 21
• writing tool
• story starter

Student Self Assessment

- Remind students that they are responsible for their learning and that it is helpful to be aware of how well they understand what they are reading, writing, talking, and thinking about in the classroom.

- You may want students to reflect on their reading and learning by using their Personal Reading Logs and My Daily Progress sheets (Resource Masters 1, 3).

ASSIGN RESOURCE MASTER **1, 3**

Daily Progress Monitoring

To ensure that students have mastered the day's skills and strategies, monitor their success in completing the following independent work:

- **Vocabulary:** Practice Companion, p. 205
- **Comprehension:** Practice Companion, pp. 210–211
- **Word Study:** Practice Companion, p. 215
- **Spelling:** Practice Companion, pp. 206–207
- **Fluency:** Practice Companion, pp. 208–209
- **Study Station Work Record:** Resource Master 2
- **Self Assessment:** Resource Masters 1, 3

epractice
reporting

Home Connection

Distribute the Unit 7 Take-Home Activities from the Home Connection book. Tell students to complete the activities with their caregivers.

Day at a Glance

21st CENTURY SKILLS

Lesson Highlights

- Review Project Plan
- 21st Century Skills Minilesson: Collaboration
- Cross-Text Sharing
- Fluency Presentation
- Spelling Posttest

Materials

	Teacher's Lesson Guide	Student Components	Digital 21
Inquiry	pp. 120–123	• Practice Companion, pp. 216–217, 370, 372 • Resource Masters 25, 33–36	**etools 21** • inquiry project • theme wall
Cross-Text Sharing	pp. 124–125	• Differentiated Readers • Practice Companion, p. 218 • Resource Masters 14, 35	**ebook** online coach
Wrap Up	pp. 126–127	• Assessment Handbook, pp. 13–14, 140 • Differentiated Reader, p. 55 • Practice Companion, p. 219 • Resource Master 1	**etools 21** • theme wall • writing tool • story starter

Inquiry Process Guide

Week 1, Day 5	Week 2, Day 5	Week 3, Day 5	Week 4, Day 5
1. Generate Ideas and Questions 2. Make a Conjecture 3. Make Plans to Collect Information	Days 1–4: Collect Information 4. Organize and Synthesize Information 5. Confirm or Revise Your Conjecture	Days 1–4: Collect Information 6. Develop Presentation	Days 1–4: Collect Information 7. Deliver Presentation

Tips for Success

- Provide Investigation Sheets (Resource Master 35) for students to use during the week.
- Provide Chain Organizers (Resource Master 36) for students to use while they organize and synthesize information, or have students choose another type of organizer.
- Monitor student weekly progress by using the Assessment on Practice Companion pages 227–228.

Develop Ideas

Objectives
Students will:
- Make connections between the theme question and the Inquiry project
- Review last week's Inquiry lesson
- Review the Inquiry process

Inquiry whole group

Review Project Plan

Connect to the Theme

Ask a volunteer to recall the Theme Question: *What makes the West exceptional?* and the Focus Question: *How are geography and economy connected in the Pacific States?* Say:

> Think about what you learned about the relationship between geography and economy in the Pacific States. What might you see if you visited this area? What kind of job might you have if you lived there?

 **etools 21**
inquiry project
Be sure students know to access Inquiry Project online from their student Home Page.

Discuss Previous Week

- Students take out their Inquiry folders.
- Review the Inquiry steps covered last week:

1. Generate Ideas and Questions

2. Make a Conjecture

3. Make Plans to Collect Information

- Verify that each group has completed the Week 1 Inquiry Checklist (Practice Companion, p. 198).

ASSIGN PRACTICE COMPANION 198

Model the Inquiry Process

Continue to Collect Information

Remind students that they were asked to collect information during independent time this week. Tell them they will have a few minutes today in class to continue collecting information.

- Remind students that nonfiction books, magazines, and Internet sources may all have information they can use to answer their questions.
- Review the Evaluating Sources Checklist (Practice Companion, p. 372). Model analyzing information to determine its value.

When you do an Internet keyword search, you will probably find more information than you need. Remember that one way you can quickly evaluate whether a Web site has the information you need is to scan the headings, photographs, and captions. If you don't see main ideas that relate to your question, move on to another site.

ASSIGN PRACTICE COMPANION 372

4. Organize and Synthesize Information

Organize Remind students that as they take turns sharing their research with their groups, they will need to organize it and think about how the ideas are related and build upon each other. Remind groups that they can use organizers, such as the Chain Organizer (Resource Master 36). Say:

> When you share information in your group, listen for how similar ideas are related. If you are discussing how Hollywood became the center of the movie-making industry, you could put information about the geography of the area in one chain and information about events leading up to the development of Hollywood in other chains. **b**

ASSIGN RESOURCE MASTER 36

Synthesize Write on the board the sample Inquiry Question and conjecture:

> *How did Hollywood become the center of the movie-making industry in the United States?*
>
> *I think one reason Hollywood became the center of the movie-making industry is because the weather there is good for filming.*

Review with students that synthesizing is putting ideas together to draw conclusions and form new ideas. Draw on the board the following chart:

Fact 1	Fact 2	My Synthesis
In the 1900s, film studios began moving to California because the weather was good for filming.	In 1910, director D. W. Griffith and his group of actors began making movies in Hollywood. They thought the people there were friendly and helpful.	Good weather and friendly people made directors want to make movies in Hollywood.

think aloud I have learned that movie makers first came to Hollywood because the weather there was good for filming. They found that the people there welcomed them and were friendly. I know that good weather and friendly people are helpful when you are making movies, so these are probably two reasons why Hollywood became the center of the movie-making industry in the United States.

5. Confirm or Revise Your Conjecture

Students should use their synthesized information as supporting or refuting evidence for their conjectures. Ask:

- Does my synthesis about Hollywood match my original conjecture? *(Yes, I found out that my original conjecture was one reason people came to Hollywood to make movies.)*

- Do I need to update my conjecture to match any new understandings? *(Yes, I can add other reasons people came to Hollywood to make movies, such as friendly people.)* **c**

Model for students how you could use what you've learned about Hollywood to make a time line. Draw on the board the following time line.

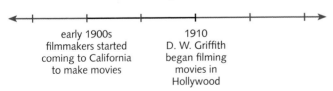

early 1900s
filmmakers started
coming to California
to make movies

1910
D. W. Griffith
began filming
movies in
Hollywood

A time line is a good way to show a sequence of events, or the order in which things happened. Time lines are usually arranged from left to right or top to bottom. It's important to label each event you include on a time line.

Invite students to come to the board and add dates to this time line or suggest ideas for additional time lines related to their Inquiry questions.

a Literacy Builder

INQUIRY CHECKLIST
If a group has not completed Inquiry steps 1–3 from its Week 1 Inquiry Checklist, coach group members to complete the remaining steps when the class breaks into Inquiry Groups. Give them periodic prompts during Inquiry Group work to help them keep pace.

b Intervention for Acceleration

ORGANIZE INFORMATION
Support students who are struggling to organize information into their Chain Organizers by having them write each piece of information on a slip of paper and arrange the slips into different information chains. Once they have the slips of paper arranged appropriately, they can transfer the information onto their Chain Organizers.

c Critical Thinking

EVALUATE CONJECTURE
Tell students that when they evaluate their conjectures, they should make sure they can point to information in their research that supports what they have written. If they can't, they need to change just the part that they can't support. Explain that they may need to change a word or idea or add a detail to make their conjectures match their research.

Collaborate and Communicate

Inquiry mixed groups

Objectives
Students will:
- Review discussion roles
- Practice collaboration
- Collect information
- Organize and synthesize information
- Confirm or revise conjectures
- Collaborate in Inquiry groups

Continue Inquiry Group Work

The following Resource Masters and Practice Companion pages will be used in this lesson.

Step	Resource Master	Practice Companion
All	Investigation Sheet 35 Collaboration Rubric 39 Evaluation Rubric B 41	Week 2 Inquiry Checklist, p. 216 Group Roles, p. 370 Evaluating Sources, p. 372
4.	Chain Organizer 36	
5.	Idea Tracker 34	Inquiry Planner, p. 217

Review Discussion Roles

Have students move into their Inquiry Groups and informally evaluate their discussions from the previous week. Write on the board the following question:

> Why is it important to make sure that you listen to what each group member is saying and wait your turn to speak?

- Review the group discussion roles and refer students to Group Discussion Roles (Practice Companion, p. 370).
- Ask group members to discuss any concerns they have about performing their chosen roles. **a**

ASSIGN **PRACTICE COMPANION 370**

Monitor Student Progress

Use the Collaboration Rubric (Resource Master 39) and the Inquiry Evaluation Rubric B (Resource Master 41) to monitor student progress throughout the project. Review the project expectations with students before beginning Inquiry Group work.

USE **RESOURCE MASTER 39, 41**

Minilesson: Collaboration

Write on the board and read aloud the following:

- Identify a common goal.
- Stay on topic during discussion.
- Summarize what has been said.

Tell students that group discussions can be a powerful way to gain new understandings when these three things happen. Say:

An example of a common goal for this week would be to confirm or revise your conjecture. Staying on topic means that everything said during discussion relates to whether the conjecture needs to be revised. When you stop to summarize what has been said so far, it helps to keep the discussion on topic.

With a volunteer, model staying on topic and going off topic during discussion. Then model summarizing what was discussed.

Have small groups practice staying on topic and summarizing a discussion. Give the groups a theme-related topic to discuss, such as what they would expect to see and do if they took a trip to Hawaii. After groups practice, discuss the process as a class.

Inquiry Groups

Continue to Collect Information *critical thinking* **analyze, evaluate**

- Remind students to complete an Investigation Sheet (Resource Master 35) for each relevant source they find.
- Have students refer to the Evaluating Sources Checklist (Practice Companion, p. 372). **b**
- Give time alerts for when to transition to the next step.

ASSIGN **RESOURCE MASTER 35**
PRACTICE COMPANION 372

4. Organize and Synthesize Information *critical thinking* **synthesize**

Organize Students take turns sharing information they collected independently.

- Remind students to use the Chain Organizer (Resource Master 36).

- Encourage students to identify at least three information chains as they organize their research.

- Group Recorders should be sure all important ideas are recorded.

ASSIGN RESOURCE MASTER **36**

Synthesize Encourage students to synthesize information until they can formulate a complete answer to their Inquiry Questions.

- Prompt group Checkers to monitor progress using the Week 2 Inquiry Checklist (Practice Companion, p. 216).

- Prompt Discussion Monitors to make sure that everyone listens respectfully to others.

- Prompt Questioners to encourage participation.

ASSIGN PRACTICE COMPANION **216**

5. Confirm or Revise Your Conjecture
 critical thinking **evaluate**

- Remind the Recorder to track important ideas and decisions using the Idea Tracker (Resource Master 34).

- Remind students to update the Question Board.

 etools 21 theme wall | Students can refer to the Theme Wall to view other posted questions.

- Students can list events to include in a time line or consider other possible formats to share their findings. **c**

- Groups should make plans to continue collecting information in the coming week. Encourage groups to share research tasks.

ASSIGN RESOURCE MASTER **34**

Record Action Plan

- Remind students to write their plans for independent work in the coming week using the Inquiry Planner (Practice Companion, p. 217).

- Students will share new information next week.

- Students place materials in their Inquiry folders.

ASSIGN PRACTICE COMPANION **217**

---

scaffolding options

a Literacy Builder
21st CENTURY SKILLS

LISTENING AND LEADERSHIP
Remind students to practice good listening and participation skills. Remind them that they should listen respectfully but that they should also encourage one another to contribute to the discussion. If they notice that a group member is not participating, they might encourage him or her to participate by asking: *How do you feel about being the group Recorder?* and then responding positively to the comments.

b Critical Thinking

EVALUATE
If students have difficulty evaluating sources, model applying the Evaluating Sources Checklist (Practice Companion, p. 372) to one of their sources. Continue to support students until they are able to use the checklist to evaluate their sources independently.

ASSIGN PRACTICE COMPANION **372**

c Challenge

REFLECT ON FORMATS
Challenge students to think of alternative ways to present their findings. Ask them to think about how using different formats would affect the way information is communicated. Ask:

- How would a written report communicate this information differently than a diagram or time line?

- How would a photo essay help you present this information?

Connect Ideas

Objectives
Students will:
- Share information across texts
- Use speaking and listening skills
- Make connections between the differentiated readers and Inquiry project

CONNECT DIFFERENTIATED READERS

Cross-Text Sharing

While students stay in their Inquiry Groups, announce Cross-Text Sharing time. Remind students that they have read about how geography and economy are connected in the Pacific States.

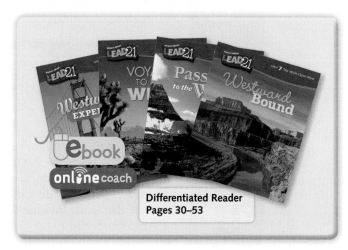

Differentiated Reader
Pages 30–53

- Prompt students to continue thinking of their Differentiated Readers as information sources for their Inquiry Projects.

- Have students from each differentiated group share the title of the selection they read, summarize the main ideas, and display the book as they tell what is happening in the photographs or pictures. Have students share any information that can be used to help answer their groups' Inquiry Questions. **a**

Monitor Student Progress

As you observe and work with each group, fill in your observations using the Collaboration Rubric (Resource Master 39).

USE RESOURCE MASTER **39**

Think Back

- Have students turn to **Think Back** page 54 in their Differentiated Readers.

- Tell students they will complete Practice Companion page 218 as they do Cross-Text Sharing.

ASSIGN PRACTICE COMPANION **218**

Check Understanding

Have students make a list of industries they read about and tell how geography and economy are connected in the places they read about. Intensive- and Strategic-level students can expand on the ideas they gathered on Day 4 during Prepare to Share.

Understand Text Features

Form mixed-level pairs within each Inquiry Group. Have each partner read the caption in his or her selection and tell how it describes the picture. Then have that student tell what information he or she would add to the caption. To facilitate the discussion, ask:

Is there anything you see in the photo that isn't described in the caption?

Share and Compare

Have students use their lists about the industries they read about to create a T-Chart (Resource Master 14) that shows which industries are dependent on water and which are dependent on land. Then have students compare their charts with their partners' charts.

ASSIGN RESOURCE MASTER **14**

Think Critically

Have each student give examples from his or her reading to answer the Theme Question: *What makes the West exceptional?* Tell students to compare their answers in their Inquiry Groups. For ideas, students can reference the ideas they gathered during the week's reading. Students can fill in their ideas on Practice Companion page 218. **b**

Connect to Inquiry

Before wrapping up Cross-Text Sharing, encourage groups to apply the information they gathered from their discussion to their Inquiry Questions. Ask:

- What new ideas did you learn from your discussion today?

- Can you use any of these ideas to help answer your Inquiry Question?

- Do you need to revise your conjecture to reflect any new understandings?

- Have students discuss their ideas, take notes using the Investigation Sheet (Resource Master 35), and put their notes into their Inquiry folders.

- Remind students to continue to work on their Inquiry Projects during Independent Practice and Self-Selected Reading time. **c**

ASSIGN | RESOURCE MASTER 35

scaffolding options

a ELL Support

SUMMARIZE
Have English language learners share their summaries with partners before sharing them with their groups. The partner can provide support with word choice and pronunciation.

b Intervention for Acceleration

USE PRIOR KNOWLEDGE
Remind students that they can also use their own knowledge and experience to help them answer the Theme Question. Ask:

- Have you ever visited a state in the West? What did you see or do there?

- Have you read stories that take place in the West? What were they about?

c Challenge

EXPLORE NEW IDEAS
Encourage students to note when other students' selections spark a personal interest during Cross-Text Sharing. Students may look for additional books or magazine articles about these topics during Self-Selected reading time or library time.

Share, Connect, Assess

Objectives
Students will:
- Perform fluent reading
- Spell words with final ə + l

Wrap Up the Week
whole group

Fluency Presentation

Have students turn to "Hiking in Redwood" on Practice Companion page 208. Each student will perform a reading of the procedural text for the class to demonstrate using good phrasing, expression, and pacing. Explain:

- Today we will be sharing the procedural text we have been working on all week by presenting it to the class. As you read aloud the text, focus on reading with appropriate expression, phrasing, and pacing.

- When you present the text to the class, make sure that you use an appropriate pace. Remember that it is sometimes helpful to read procedural texts more slowly so that listeners have time to understand each step.

- Students may choose another selection to perform for the class.

- You may wish to give students the option of performing this week's or another fluency selection to a caregiver at home.

- As students perform, use Assessing Oral Reading, Assessment Handbook pages 13–14, to evaluate and record each student's oral reading performance.

USE ASSESSMENT HANDBOOK **13–14**

Spelling Posttest

Remind students that their spelling words have the final *e* + *l* sound. Say a word, use it in a sentence, and say the word again. Students will write each word.

1. **towel** Don't forget your *towel* when you go to the beach.
2. **pedal** Malik put his foot on the bicycle *pedal*.
3. **riddle** My brother told me a funny *riddle*.
4. **metal** The *metal* pipe stuck out of the ground.
5. **simple** I had no problem doing the *simple* activity.
6. **ankle** She broke her *ankle* during the race.
7. **eagle** The *eagle* built a nest high in the tree.
8. **special** We had a *special* dinner for my brother's birthday.
9. **trouble** My little sister was in *trouble* for colring on the wall.
10. **marvel** The Grand Canyon is a *marvel* of nature.
11. **gravel** The new road was made out of *gravel* and sand.
12. **gentle** We enjoyed the *gentle* breeze as it blew through the trees.
13. **barrel** The wooden *barrel* was once used to hold water for horses.
14. **squirrel** The young *squirrel* searched for food for the winter.
15. **model** He was recognized as a *model* citizen in the community.
16. **tangle** The necklace chain has a small *tangle* in it.

Review Words
17. **violin** I have always wanted to learn how to play the *violin*.
18. **cereal** *Cereal* is my favorite breakfast food.

Frequently Misspelled Words
19. **around** The small dog ran *around* and around in circles.
20. **having** I enjoyed *having* my grandfather come to visit me on Saturday.

Objectives
Students will:
• Use key concepts
• Make text-to-self connections
• Write a description of a Pacific State
• Monitor their progress

Share Text Connections

Make Text-to-Self Connections Ask students to share the theme connections they made during Cross-Text Sharing time. Continue the Theme Concept Web for Unit 7 that you began in Week 1.

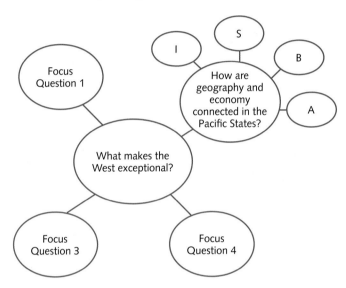

Write the Theme Question in the center circle and this week's Focus Question in one of the four connecting circles.

• For each Differentiated Reader, have students share a concept or main idea that connects to the Focus and Theme Questions.

• As students discuss their connections from their Differentiated Readers, fill in the outermost circles.

• Have students think about how this helps them address the Theme Question. Ask:

How are geography and economy connected in the Pacific States? How do the Pacific States help make the West exceptional?

• Save the Theme Concept Web and build on it over the next two weeks.

Think Ahead ▶

Have students open their Differentiated Readers to page 55 and begin thinking about the selection they will read next week.

Read aloud next week's Focus Question: *What is life like in the Mountain States?* Then read the **Selection Connection** and **Show What You Know** activities. Have students write their answers to these activities on Practice Companion page 219.

ASSIGN | PRACTICE COMPANION **219**

Daily Writing

Have students write a description of a Pacific State. Have them tell what they would see and do there.

Student Self Assessment

• You may want students to reflect on their learning by using My Daily Progress sheet, Resource Master 1.

• Remind students to note the concepts and skills for which they could use more support.

ASSIGN | RESOURCE MASTER **1**

Weekly Progress Monitoring

Use the following assessment tools to check students' weekly progress following independent and mixed-group work:
• **Practice Companion:** pp. 204–215
• **Fluency Presentation**
• **Spelling Posttest**
• **Think Back** and **Think Ahead, Differentiated Reader:** pp. 54–55
• **Assessing Oral Reading, Assessment Handbook:** pp. 13–14
• **Weekly Observation Record, Assessment Handbook:** p. 140
• **Assessment, Practice Companion:** pp. 227–228

Writing and Language Arts *whole group*

Science Fiction Story

Writing Traits

Organization — traits focus organization	**Ideas** — traits focus ideas	**Conventions** — traits focus conventions
Voice — traits focus voice	**Sentence Fluency** — traits focus sentence fluency	**Presentation** — traits focus presentation

Writing Highlights

- **Introduce** Science fiction story format
- **Reading/Writing Connection** Visualize, Monitor Comprehension
- **Talk About Text** Make connections between text and the characteristics of a science fiction story.
- **Grammar** Adverbs that Compare *(-er/-est),* Adverbs that Compare (more/most), Prepositions, Prepositional Phrases

Materials

Teacher Components
- Teacher's Lesson Guide, pp. 128–145
- Writing Models Chart, pp. 48–51

Student Components
- Practice Companion, pp. 220–226
- Writer's notebook

Digital 21

etools 21
- writing tool
- interactive glossary

Tips for Success

- Tell students that they will spend more time than usual on the drafting step for the science fiction story writing process lesson.
- Display the Writing Models Chart where students can see it clearly and refer to it as they work.
- You may wish to adapt the Pacing Guide to suit your scheduling needs from day to day and week to week.
- Guide students to make connections between reading and writing when they Talk About Text each day.
- Students will need their writer's notebooks for the writing process lesson.
- Remind students to refer to the Evaluation Rubric (Practice Companion, p. 221) as they draft, revise, and edit.

Pacing Guide: Science Fiction Story

Week 1	Student	Teacher's Lesson Guide
DAY 1 Lesson 1	**Prewrite** Study the writing model and set writing goals	pp. 130–131
DAY 2 Lesson 2	**Prewrite** Choose a topic and generate ideas	pp. 132–133
DAY 3 Lesson 3	**Prewrite** Organize ideas and develop plot; Grammar: Review Adverbs That Compare (*-er/-est*)	pp. 134–135
DAY 4 Lesson 4	**Draft** Write a first draft with character development; Grammar: Review Adverbs That Compare (more/most)	pp. 136–137

Week 2		
DAY 1 Lesson 5	**Draft** Write a draft with suspense and a climax	pp. 138–139
DAY 2 Lesson 6	**Revise** Revise the draft and conduct peer review; Grammar: Prepositions	pp. 140–141
DAY 3 Lesson 7	**Edit** Edit the model and the draft; Grammar: Prepositional Phrases	pp. 142–143
DAY 4 Lesson 8	**Publish and Present** Publish and present a final draft	pp. 144–145

Write a Science Fiction Story

Objectives
Students will:
• Identify the characteristics and organization of a science fiction story

Activate Prior Knowledge

• Begin by asking students what they already know about writing science fiction stories.

• Remind students that in Unit 1 they wrote a story. Invite them to discuss what they remember about the writing process for stories and what they learned the first time they wrote a story this year.

• Encourage students to talk about what they need to think about before they write a science fiction story.

• Record ideas on chart paper. Have students add to it as they learn more about writing a science fiction story.

• Post the chart near the Writer's Desk. For the next two weeks, students will develop their own science fiction stories.

Writing a Science Fiction Story	
Know About Science Fiction Stories	Need to Think About
• They have characters.	• Who are the characters in my story?
• They have settings that are often futuristic.	• Where will my story take place?
• Characters often face problems related to science or technology.	• What will happen to my characters?

Study the Writing Model

Read aloud *The Thief of the Northwest* on Writing Models Chart pages 48–49 as students follow along on  Practice Companion page 220. Invite students to respond to the science fiction story by asking them what they liked about it. Record students' responses on chart paper.

Writing Models Chart Pages 48–51

ASSIGN

PRACTICE COMPANION **220**

Talk About Text ★★★

Invite students to respond to the model. Ask:

• Why do you think the author wrote this science fiction story?

• For whom do you suppose the author wrote the science fiction story? How do you know?

• How can you tell this is a science fiction story?

Characteristics of Science Fiction

Record the characteristics of a science fiction story on chart paper. Have students point out examples of these characteristics and circle them on Practice Companion page 220.

Characteristics of a Science Fiction Story
A good science fiction story … 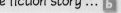
• Is made up by the author.
• Contains characters that may have special powers or may be aliens.
• Has a beginning, a middle, and an end.
• Tells events in the order in which they happened.
• Contains a setting that may be in the future or in outer space.

Writing and Language Arts *whole group*

Organization of Science Fiction

traits focus **organization**

Use Resource Master 23 to record information about the organization of a science fiction story.

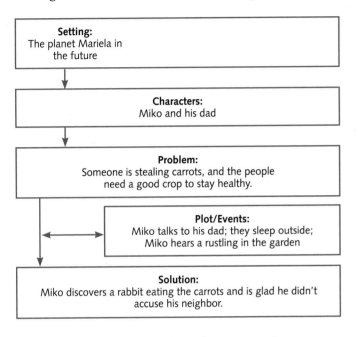

Setting:
The planet Mariela in the future

↓

Characters:
Miko and his dad

↓

Problem:
Someone is stealing carrots, and the people need a good crop to stay healthy.

↓

Plot/Events:
Miko talks to his dad; they sleep outside; Miko hears a rustling in the garden

↓

Solution:
Miko discovers a rabbit eating the carrots and is glad he didn't accuse his neighbor.

Invite students to discuss how the setting, characters, and plot reflect the characteristics of science fiction.

ASSIGN   RESOURCE MASTER **23**

Set Writing Goals

Have students begin to think about the purposes and audiences for the science fiction stories they will write.

Practice Companion Page 221

Have them jot down ideas in their writer's notebooks; remind them that their ideas should reflect science fiction characteristics.

Use Practice Companion page 221 to introduce the criteria listed on the Evaluation Rubric. Explain that students will use this rubric throughout the project to be sure their writing stays on track.

ASSIGN   PRACTICE COMPANION **221**

a Intervention for Acceleration

PARTNER FOR ACCELERATION
Some Intensive- and Strategic-level students may have less knowledge about writing a science fiction story. Pair Intensive- and Strategic-level students with Benchmark- and Advanced-level students. Have pairs think about science fiction stories that they've read in the past and then have them brainstorm the characteristics of this genre. Ask them to think about what makes a science fiction story different from a conventional short story or report. Then ask volunteers to share their ideas with the class.

b Critical Thinking

EVALUATE AND DISCUSS CHARACTERISTICS OF A GOOD SCIENCE FICTION STORY
Have students think of additional characteristics that make a good science fiction story. Add them to the list. Items could include unique characters (such as robots or androids), an interesting setting, a problem that relates to science or technology, and futuristic or unreal events. Then have students use the list to reevaluate the Writing Model.

Write a Science Fiction Story

Writing and Language Arts whole group

Objectives
Students will:
• Choose a topic
• Generate ideas

Study the Writing Model

Use the Writing Model *The Thief of the Northwest* (Writing Models Chart, pp. 48–49) to talk about what makes a good science fiction story idea or topic. Students should follow along using Practice Companion page 220. Ask:

Writing Models Chart
Pages 48–51

• What does the title tell you about the science fiction story? *(Possible response: It's about someone or something that steals or takes something.)*

• What topics are good for science fiction stories? *(Possible responses: topics that relate to science or technology; topics that involve the future, other worlds, or outer space)*

Point out that this is a good topic for a science fiction story because it is set in the future and in outer space.

Remind students that a story should have a problem and a solution. Say:

When you read a story, you soon find out that a character in the story has a problem. Something has happened that needs to be fixed. At the end of the story, the problem is resolved. This is the solution to the problem.

Explain that in science fiction, the problem and solution, like other story elements, are connected to science, technology, or the future. Ask students to share the problems and solutions from science fiction books or movies they have read or seen.

ASSIGN PRACTICE COMPANION **220**

Talk About Text ★★★

Have students respond to the model by asking:

Why do you think the writer chose this topic for his science fiction story? *(It is about farming, which people can relate to, but it has characters from another planet, which is new and interesting.)*

Choose a Topic traits focus ideas

Model your thoughts as you come up with an idea for a class science fiction story:

think aloud What subject will make a good science fiction story? I should find a subject that I will enjoy writing about and that lends itself to a future setting. I look at pictures of planets in outer space all the time. I think that one day, people will live in and visit outer space. I could write a story about that. What else can I write about?

Let students choose ideas that are interesting to them and others. Remind them that their science fiction stories should involve problems that get resolved at the end. Ask students to write down a few ideas in their writer's notebooks. Then ask volunteers to share ideas with the whole class. Write their ideas on the board. **a**

Reading/Writing Connection

Visualize Vivid descriptions help readers visualize what is taking place in a story. Good science fiction writers use descriptive language to help their readers visualize the new and exciting worlds they create in their stories. By using descriptive language, writers can make future outer space settings come to life. **b**

Generate Ideas

Explain that students can use a Story Map (Resource Master 23) to plan their science fiction stories. Review the meaning of the specific literary elements *setting*, *characters*, *plot*, *problem*, and *solution*. **c**

think aloud Now that you have some ideas to work with, let's develop a plan for our story. Look at the story map. I'm going to use the idea about living in outer space in the future. That will be the setting. Who are the characters? I will write about a group of students who take a field trip into outer space. Who else should be involved in the story?

Model talking through all the sections of the Story Map so students see how to complete it for their own stories.

ASSIGN RESOURCE MASTER **23**

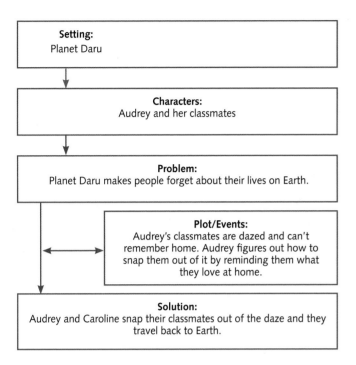

Setting:
Planet Daru

↓

Characters:
Audrey and her classmates

↓

Problem:
Planet Daru makes people forget about their lives on Earth.

↓

Plot/Events:
Audrey's classmates are dazed and can't remember home. Audrey figures out how to snap them out of it by reminding them what they love at home.

Solution:
Audrey and Caroline snap their classmates out of the daze and they travel back to Earth.

Write and Confer

Independent Writing

Allow students to work independently to generate story ideas and choose topics. Distribute Story Map Resource Master 23 for students to begin planning the setting, characters, and plots of their stories.

ASSIGN RESOURCE MASTER 23

Conference with Students

Meet with students individually to talk about their topics, ideas, and story maps. Assist them in generating ideas, outlining plot, and completing the organizer.

Reflect on Writing

Have students turn to the Evaluation Rubric (Practice Companion, p. 221). Ask them to read the goals for Ideas and Word Choice. In their writer's notebooks, have students reflect on the work they completed today and how they will apply these traits to their stories.

ASSIGN PRACTICE COMPANION 221

scaffolding options

a Intervention for Acceleration

BRAINSTORM

For students struggling to brainstorm ideas for their stories, have partners select fiction books from the classroom library. Ask the partners to look at the books and think about how they could retell the story as a science fiction story. Help them get started with the following questions:

What problem do the characters in the story face?

How do they solve the problem?

How could you connect these ideas to science, technology, the future, or outer space?

Have students jot down their ideas in their writer's notebooks.

b Intervention for Acceleration

READING/WRITING CONNECTION: VISUALIZE

To help students practice visualization, ask partners to take turns describing a scene in a book from the classroom library. One partner should shut his or her eyes while the other partner describes a scene from the book using descriptive language. After describing the scene, the partners can discuss how their visualizations matched the actual illustrations of the book. Then partners can switch roles so each partner has a chance to describe and visualize.

c ELL Support

ACADEMIC LANGUAGE

Assist students who have difficulty understanding the meaning of specific literary terms such as *setting*, *problem*, and *solution*. Explain these elements in terms that students will understand and use pictures to support your definitions. Place the pictures in the Writing Model next to where these literary elements appear, or use picture books with clear illustrations to point out setting, characters, and plot events. Students will begin to associate pictures with the definitions of the literary elements.

Write a Science Fiction Story

Objectives
Students will:
- Organize ideas
- Develop plot
- Review adverbs that compare

Writing and Language Arts
whole group

Study the Writing Model

Use the model science fiction story *The Thief of the Northwest* (Writing Models Chart, pp. 48–49) to review

Writing Models Chart Pages 48–51

the characteristics of a good science fiction story. Have students follow along on Practice Companion page 220. Use the chart paper list from Lesson 1 to remind students what elements a good science fiction story must include. Explain that during today's lesson, students will focus on plot and organization.

When should the reader introduce story elements such as setting, character, problem, and solution into the story?

Write down students' responses on chart paper.

- *The setting should come close to the beginning.*
- *The main character or characters should be introduced in the beginning.*
- *The problem should be introduced in the beginning.*
- *The solution must come at the end.*

Work with students to identify where certain story elements appear in the Writing Model. For example, mark the beginning of the model as follows:

> "Someone is stealing our carrots," I said to my father. It was
> *problem*   *character*
> our first summer in the Northwest Greenhouse, and the carrot
> *setting*   *setting*
> patch was my responsibility.

ASSIGN PRACTICE COMPANION **220**

Talk About Text ★ ★ ★

Invite students to respond to the model. Ask:

How does the organization of the Writing Model help you understand the story? *(Possible response: Knowing the characters and setting helps me understand the problem and plot.)*

Organize Ideas

Writer's Craft: Develop Plot   *traits focus* **organization**

Ask students to review what they know about story structure. Remind them that plot is the series of events that take place in the beginning, middle, and end of a story. Say:

- In the beginning of a story, the setting, characters, and problem are introduced.
- In the middle, key events show how the characters deal with the problem. The action builds up to a *climax*, or turning point. This is the most exciting part of the plot.
- In the end, the problem is solved; this is called the solution. The action winds down.

Tell students they can use Three-Column Chart Resource Master 15 to plan events for the beginning, middle, and end of their stories. Encourage them to use this chart in conjunction with the story maps they completed in Lesson 2 to flesh out their stories.

Think Aloud as you model how to fill in the chart.

 My main character is a fourth-grader named Audrey. She lives on Earth but is visiting Planet Daru, a planet outside of our solar system, with her classmates. The problem is that when people get there, they forget about their lives on Earth and want to stay forever. For some reason, this does not affect Audrey, and she has to figure out how to get her classmates back to Earth. Since we need to put setting, problem, and character at the beginning, I will include that information first.

Invite students to help you add events to the beginning, middle, and end of your chart.

- What events should build the action in the middle?
- What should the climax be?
- How should the problem be solved in the end?

ASSIGN RESOURCE MASTER **15, 23**

Write and Confer

Independent Writing

Have students work independently to complete their three-column charts. Remind them to chart what will happen at the beginning, in the middle, and at the end of their stories. Remind them to be sure their plans include a problem, key events, climax, and a solution.

Conference with Students

Meet with students individually and offer support to those who are having trouble developing plot.

Reflect on Writing

Direct students to the Evaluation Rubric (Practice Companion, p. 221). Highlight the goals for the writing trait Organization. Have students reflect in their writer's notebooks about how today's lesson will help them meet these goals.

ASSIGN PRACTICE COMPANION 221

Grammar ✓tested!

Review Adverbs That Compare
traits focus conventions

Review that adverbs modify verbs, adjectives, or other adverbs. Remind students that many shorter adverbs that compare end in *-er* and *-est*. Add *-er* to most adverbs to compare two things. Then explain that *-est* is added to most adverbs to compare one action with several others. Write both examples on the board.

> Andrea arrived earlier than I did.
> Sandra arrived earliest of all.

Practice

Have students practice using adverbs that compare by writing four sentences that compare science fiction stories with nonfiction stories. Have students underline the adverb in each sentence. c

ASSIGN PRACTICE COMPANION 223

---

scaffolding options

a Critical Thinking

ANALYZE PLOT SEQUENCE
Explain the importance of order in a science fiction story by asking students to think about stories that they've read in the past. Use a few versions of the model—one in which the beginning is removed, one in which the middle is removed, and one in which the end is removed. Ask students how this changed order affects the final story.

b Challenge

SEQUENCE PLOT
For some Benchmark- and Advanced-level students, story plotting and sequencing may be easy. Challenge those students to complete a reverse structure. Let them plot their story backwards while still including some of the critical literary elements. Make sure that their story begins with a strong sentence but that they they plan the beginning last instead of first. Encourage students to use literary elements such as flashbacks and foreshadowing. Allow pairs to work together to assist each other with the backwards structure.

c ELL Support

WORD STUDY
Support students who may still have difficulty using adverbs that compare. Use illustrations in the Differentiated Readers and compare things using adverbs. For example, on page 39 of the Intensive reader, you might say:

> The tree is taller than the man.

After you demonstrate making comparisons for the student, switch roles.

Write a Science Fiction Story

Objectives
Students will:
- Write a first draft
- Develop strong beginnings
- Develop character
- Review adverbs that compare

Study the Writing Model

Have students turn to the Writing Model on Practice Companion page 220 and review the characteristics of

a good science fiction story. Explain that today students will focus on strong beginnings and character development.

Ask students to look closely at the way character is developed in the Writing Model. Ask:

Writing Models Chart Pages 48–51

How does the writer develop the main characters?

Guide students to follow along on Practice Companion page 220. Have them circle words and phrases that give them insight into the main characters. Make similar annotations to Writing Models Chart pages 48–49.

ASSIGN **PRACTICE COMPANION 220**

Talk About Text ★★★

Encourage students to consider how the author brings the characters to life.

How does the writer get readers to visualize the characters in the story? (Possible response: He writes sentences that give readers information about what the characters think and do.)

Write a First Draft

Strong Beginnings traits focus voice

Explain that it is important for writers to develop strong openings for their story in order to grab their readers' attention. One way that writers do this is by establishing the setting right away with vivid descriptions. Since the settings of science fiction stories are particularly unique and interesting, this is a good tactic for drawing readers into the story.

Model your thinking as you begin the class draft.

 I know that my beginning is important, and I want to bring the reader into my story quickly. I need to grab the reader's attention with the first few sentences.

> Planet Daru was beautiful and inviting, just the place for a quick interplanetary picnic. But underneath its purple-tufted palm trees and sparkling orange waters lurked a dangerous secret.

Ask students to brainstorm other ways to develop a strong beginning. Remind them that their first sentences should pull the reader into the story.

Writer's Craft: Develop Character traits focus ideas

Explain that writers develop their characters' traits and voices to give readers insight into them. Even though characters in science fiction are not always human, they should have traits readers can relate to. To bring their characters to life, writers can:

- Use dialogue to show what a character says and how he or she says it.
- Use descriptive language to describe characters appearances, actions, thoughts, and feelings.
- Show what others think or say about a character.

Model how to develop character for the class draft.

 In my story about the class visit to Planet Daru, I want the reader to understand how Audrey thinks and feels. I want to show that she is initially worried about the trip because even though pictures of the planet are beautiful, there are no interviews from people who have actually been there. This makes her really nervous, but also curious. I need to express her traits, thoughts, and feelings in my story.

Have students help you write sentences for the class draft that describe Audrey's feelings. Encourage them to use description and dialogue.

Tell students they can use a Wheel (Resource Master 17) to plan their characters before they draft. They can write their character's name in the center of the Wheel and his or her traits, actions, behaviors, words, and feelings in the outer sections of the Wheel.

ASSIGN **RESOURCE MASTER 17**

Write and Confer

Independent Writing

Give students time to plan character traits and begin their drafts. Remind them they will have time to revise and edit their drafts later.

Conference with Students

Meet with students individually about their drafts. Encourage them to ask questions about developing strong beginnings and characters. **b**

Reflect on Writing

Ask students to consider what they have learned today and add details to the Writing a Science Fiction Story chart from Day 1.

Grammar *tested*

Review Adverbs That Compare

traits focus
conventions

Explain that adverbs with two or more syllables, such as adverbs that end in *-ly,* use the words *more* or *most* to compare. Write the following on the board:

> *The soup cooked more slowly than the chicken.*
> *The bread cooked most slowly of all.*

Tell students to use *more* when comparing one action with another and to use *most* when comparing one action with several others.

Practice

Have students practice using *more* and *most* by writing sentences for partners. Students should leave a blank where *more* and *most* appear in the sentences and then exchange with partners and fill in the blanks.

ASSIGN | PRACTICE COMPANION **224**

---

scaffolding options

a Literacy Builder

DEVELOP CHARACTER

As students plan their characters, reinforce that they don't have to write every single detail about a character (what he or she is wearing, what type of cereal he or she likes) unless it is important to the story. Also emphasize that students should give their characters unique voices that are different from their own when they use dialogue. Model writing effective dialogue for the class draft.

b Intervention for Acceleration

WRITING PROCESS: DRAFT

Support students struggling to write independently. Help them brainstorm words and phrases to describe their setting in their openings and to describe their characters. Then have them develop one interesting detail or sentence for each paragraph of their science fiction stories. Once they are comfortable with that, encourage them to add descriptive language to each paragraph. If they have problems remembering what to include, provide them with a checklist.

Students can also use the Writing Tool to get feedback on their drafts.

Write a Science Fiction Story

Objectives
Students will:
- Write a first draft
- Develop suspense and climax
- Develop a strong ending

Study the Writing Model

Use *The Thief of the Northwest* (Writing Models Chart, pp. 48–49) to review organization. Have students follow

Writing Models Chart Pages 48–51

along on Practice Companion page 220.

Talk about the importance of building action and suspense in a story and leading to the climax, or turning point, of the events. Review that after a climax is presented, the solution should occur.

Read the Writing Model aloud, asking students to underline the sentences that build suspense. Then have students draw a mountain next to the climax section of the story (when Miko hears a rustling in the garden and gets up to investigate it). Finally have students circle the solution that resolves the problem in the story (Miko discovers a rabbit was stealing the carrots, not his neighbor).

Prompt students with the following questions:

- How does suspense enhance the story? **a**

- How are the climax and solution of the story connected?

ASSIGN   **PRACTICE COMPANION 220**

Talk About Text ★★★

Invite students to respond to the model. Ask:

- Why is suspense required before the climax of the story is revealed? *(Possible response: To create a feeling in the reader that they can't wait to find out what happens next.)*

- Why is a solution important in a story? *(Possible response: The writer needs to give the reader a conclusion that wraps up the plot.)*

Write a First Draft

Writer's Craft: Develop Suspense and Climax [traits focus voice]

Explain that suspense is the sense that the reader does not know what will happen next. It builds readers' interest and makes them excited to find out what will happen next. In science fiction, suspense is especially useful, since the futuristic settings and events often create a sense of the unknown.

Writers develop suspense by:

- Introducing a problem that has an unclear solution.

- Changing the pacing of the story: fast-paced action excites readers; a slow pace draws out suspense.

- Providing readers with information that the characters don't know so that readers will wait eagerly to see how events unfold.

- Using exciting descriptive language.

Explain that writers build suspense up to the climax, or turning point, of their stories. The action should build up so that the climax is the most exciting point in the plot. The climax typically occurs just before the problem is solved.

Model your thinking aloud as you develop suspense and a climax for the class draft: **b**

 The problem of our story, "The Secret of Planet Daru," is that Audrey's classmates have forgotten about their lives on Earth. I will try to build suspense as Audrey deals with this problem, and then I will present the climax.

> Audrey studied her classmate Caroline. Caroline's eyes were cloudy and she gazed out listlessly. "Caroline! Listen to me!" Audrey pleaded. "You need to snap out of this so we can go home!" Caroline's silent stare remained unbroken. "Caroline, please! Think of your new baby sister at home. Don't you miss your family?"
>
> Just then Caroline's eyes flickered and the clouds melted away. Her eyes shown bright as she gasped, "My little sister? I need to get home right away!" Audrey had figured it out! She only needed to remind her classmates of what they loved most to snap them out of this curse.

Invite students to discuss how you built suspense.

- Which descriptions and dialogue build suspense? Why?

- What is the climax? Why is it exciting?

Guide students to see that the climax is when Caroline returns to normal and remembers her life on Earth. It comes just before the solution: Audrey's discovery of how she can restore her classmates' memories.

Strong Endings

Explain that after the solution is presented, the action of the story winds down. A strong ending leaves the reader with the sense that the problem is resolved. Often, but not always, this means loose ends in the story are tied up, or remaining questions are answered.

 In our story, Audrey figured out how to snap people out of the curse. I will wrap my story up by describing the result of her efforts.

> Audrey glanced around at the bright, smiling faces of her classmates. She overheard Paul talking excitedly about getting back to his grandparents. She was overcome with relief knowing that she had snapped everyone out of the curse. She couldn't wait to get home!

Ask students to discuss why this is a strong ending and how it provides resolution to the plot.

Write and Confer

Independent Writing

Ask students to complete their story drafts. Encourage them to build suspense in their plots.

Conference with Students

As students work, circulate and talk with them about what is going well with their writing and what they still need help with. Assist them with developing their climaxes and solutions.

Reflect on Writing

Revisit the Evaluation Rubric (Practice Companion, p. 221). Point out the goals for Organization and Voice. Have students use their writer's notebooks to reflect on how suspense is related to these traits.

ASSIGN   PRACTICE COMPANION **221**

---

scaffolding options

a Intervention for Acceleration

ORGANIZATION
On a large piece of paper, write a sample paragraph that includes examples of suspense, climax, and resolution. Then cut the sentences into strips, mix them up, and tape them to the board. Invite a volunteer to read aloud the mixed-up paragraph. Ask students if the paragraph makes sense. Have another volunteer come to the board and rearrange the paragraph into the correct order. Then ask another volunteer to reread the new paragraph and label each sentence with a S, C, or R. Discuss how the sentences are similar and different.

b ELL Support

CLASSROOM LIBRARY
Ask students to choose their favorite book from the classroom library. Have students point out examples of suspense, climax, and resolution in the stories. Ask students to discuss how they can include suspense, climax, and resolution in their science fiction stories.

 **etools 21**
writing tool
Students can use the Writing Tool to get feedback on their drafts.

Write a Science Fiction Story

Objectives
Students will:
- Revise a draft
- Use prepositions

Revise the Model

Remind students that experienced writers revise their science fiction stories until they feel that their writing expresses exactly what they want it to say. For a science fiction story, this means:

Writing Models Chart Pages 48–51

- Adding words and details to clarify the setting, events, or characters.
- Removing confusing words and details that distract from the plot.
- Rearranging sentences and paragraphs to make the plot flow smoothly.
- Replacing unclear words and phrases with descriptive ones.

Encourage students to ask themselves the following questions when they revise their stories:

- Does my story have a clear structure (beginning, middle, and end) with a problem, climax, and solution?
- Did I clearly develop my setting and characters?
- Is my language descriptive? **a**
- Did I use a variety of sentence types?
- Are there any words or phrases that are confusing or out of place?

Ask a volunteer to read the Revising and Editing Model (Writing Models Chart, p. 50). Then model your thinking as you rearrange, add, and change text. Remind students that they will edit for grammar, spelling, and punctuation after revising.

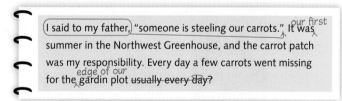

I said to my father, "someone is steeling our carrots." It was
our first
summer in the Northwest Greenhouse, and the carrot patch
was my responsibility. Every day a few carrots went missing
edge of our
for the gardin plot usually every day?

Introduce the Revising Checklist (Writing Models Chart, p. 51). Invite students to use it as a guide to suggest more changes to the model.

Revise the Draft

Present the class draft for student review. Ask students to look at the Peer Evaluation form on Practice Companion page 222. Direct students to use the prompts on this page to conduct a review of the class draft. Provide support as necessary, reminding students how to phrase comments constructively. Then revise the draft with students based on their comments.

ASSIGN PRACTICE COMPANION **222**

etools 21
interactive glossary
Students can use the Interactive Glossary as they revise word choice in their stories.

Peer Review

Assign students writing partners for peer review. Ask them to use the Peer Evaluation form (Practice Companion, p. 222) to review their partners' drafts. Restate the appropriate routine for peer review. **b**

- The writer shares his or her work.
- The reviewer tells what he or she liked about the work.
- The reviewer asks questions about the work.
- The reviewer makes suggestions for changes.
- The writer makes notes of the reviewer's comments.
- The partners switch roles.

ASSIGN PRACTICE COMPANION **222**

Author's Chair

Invite volunteers to read their science fiction stories aloud to the class. Remind students about the correct protocol for responding to others' writing.

- First, talk about what you found interesting or exciting.
- Then ask questions about what you heard.
- Finally, tell what you liked and why you liked it.

Encourage students to reflect on their peer reviews and their classmates' responses to improve their science fiction stories.

Write and Confer

Independent Writing

Encourage students to carefully consider the suggestions made by their writing partners on the Peer Evaluation form (Practice Companion, p. 222) and choose which comments to use during revision. Remind them to use the Revising Checklist (Writing Models Chart, p. 51) to guide their revisions.

ASSIGN | PRACTICE COMPANION **222**

Conference with Students

Talk with individual students to discuss their revisions.

Reflect on Writing

Ask students to reflect on the peer review process and how it improved their writing. Provide time for them to write in their writer's notebooks.

Grammar *tested*

Use Prepositions | traits focus conventions

Tell students that a preposition is a word that shows the relationship between a noun or pronoun and another word in the sentence. Write the following common prepositions and sentences on the board:

> among, between, at, with, beside, by, from behind, in, into, through, for, above, upon
> - A river runs between those mountains.
> - The actors are behind the curtain.
> - The apples from that orchard are great.
> - The road through the woods is curvy.
> - The squirrel crawls into its burrow.

With students, identify the prepositions in the above sentences. Ask them to determine between which words they show a relationship.

Practice

Ask partners to write sentences for five of the prepositions shown on the board. Then have them switch sentences and identify which nouns or pronouns and other words each preposition connects.

ASSIGN | PRACTICE COMPANION **225**

scaffolding options

a Challenge

USE DESCRIPTIVE LANGUAGE
Challenge students to replace common descriptive words in their stories such as *good*, *nice*, *big*, and *small* with more interesting descriptive words. Students can use a thesaurus or dictionary in their search for appropriate descriptive words. Explain that a thesaurus is a great source for finding synonyms and antonyms of words. Remind students that synonyms are words that mean the same thing and antonyms are words that mean the opposite.

b Literacy Builder

PEER REVIEW
Help students struggling to conduct an effective peer review. Provide examples of effective and ineffective feedback. Use the class draft or a student's draft as a model. Provide students with language to give effective feedback. Encourage them to use the following sentence starters:

I like this paragraph because . . .

I'm not sure I understand how this event is important. Let me see if I can summarize it. . . .

I can't picture this. Can you describe . . . ?

Week 3 Planner

Interactive Reading
WHOLE GROUP | 25–35 mins.

tested ✓

	Oral Language	Vocabulary	Read Together	Comprehension	Word Study and Phonics	Spelling	Fluency
Day 1	Discuss the Theme	Introduce ✓ Theme Vocabulary	• Model • Share • Read **Theme Reader,** pp. 409–423	Read about life in the Mountain States.	Introduce ✓ Three-Syllable Words	Spelling ✓ Pretest Introduce Three-Syllable Words	Introduce and Model "Roaring Downriver"
Day 2	Reinforce the Theme	Reinforce ✓ Theme Vocabulary	Read Theme Reader, pp. 424–438	Review ✓ Comprehension Strategy Make Predictions	Reinforce ✓ Three-Syllable Words	Practice ✓ Three-Syllable Words	Shared Choral Reading "Roaring Downriver"
Day 3	Reinforce the Theme	Introduce ✓ Vocabulary Strategy Descriptive Language	Reread Theme Reader, pp. 409–438	Review ✓ Comprehension Skill Sequence Events	Review ✓ Negative Prefixes 🖱epractice	Practice ✓ Three-Syllable Words	Paired Reading "Roaring Downriver"
Day 4	Extend the Theme	Extend ✓ Theme Vocabulary	Reread Theme Reader, pp. 409–438	Reinforce ✓ Comprehension Strategy Make Predictions	Reinforce ✓ Negative Prefixes 🖱epractice	Practice ✓ Three-Syllable Words	Personal Rehearsal "Roaring Downriver"

Day 5 — **Inquiry and 21st Century Skills** 🖱etools 21 | inquiry project

21st CENTURY SKILLS

Review Project Plan	Model the Inquiry Process	Continue Inquiry Group Work
Connect to the Theme	Share New Information	Review Discussion Roles
Discuss Previous Week	6. Develop Presentation	Monitor Student Progress
		Minilesson: Evaluate Sources

Theme Reader — Pages 409–438

Weekly Vocabulary
fulfill
treasure
exchange

🖱ebook
onl**i**ne coach

Selection 3: Differentiated Readers — Pages 56–79

Intensive

Weekly Vocabulary
wilderness
haul
knapsack
tough
buckle
canteen
stagger
canyon

🖱ebook
onl**i**ne coach

Strategic

Weekly Vocabulary
weary
astonish
stable
slumber
rejoice
obviously
tempt
wicked

🖱ebook
onl**i**ne coach

Differentiated Reading
SMALL GROUPS | 60–80 mins.

Read and Comprehend

Reinforce Theme Vocabulary ✓

Reread Theme Reader,
pp. 409–423

Introduce Differentiated Vocabulary ✓
Read about a clever plan in New Mexico, Paul Bunyan, skiing, or a folktale about turkeys in the first half of Selection 3.

Reinforce Comprehension Strategy ✓
Make Predictions

Introduce Differentiated Vocabulary ✓
epractice
Read about a clever plan in New Mexico, Paul Bunyan, skiing, or a folktale about turkeys in the second half of Selection 3.

Reinforce Comprehension Skill ✓
Sequence Events

Extend Vocabulary
epractice

Reread Differentiated Readers,
pp. 56–79

Reinforce Comprehension Strategy ✓
Make Predictions

Mixed Groups

Cross-Text Sharing

Think Back

Connect to Inquiry

Wrap Up
WHOLE GROUP | 5–10 mins.

Share, Connect, Assess

Share Text Connections

Daily Writing

Student Self Assessment

Daily Progress Monitoring

Home Connection

Share Text Connections

Daily Writing

Student Self Assessment

Daily Progress Monitoring

Home Connection

Share Text Connections

Daily Writing

Student Self Assessment

Daily Progress Monitoring

Home Connection

Share Text Connections

Daily Writing

Student Self Assessment

Daily Progress Monitoring

Home Connection

Weekly Assessment

Fluency Presentation ✓

Spelling Posttest ✓

Student Self Assessment

Weekly Progress Monitoring

Writing and Language Arts
WHOLE GROUP | 30 mins.

Writing Process and Grammar
Suggested Pacing Guide

etools 21
- theme wall
- writing tool
- story starter
- interactive glossary

Prewrite
Autobiography

Traits Focus ✓
Organization

Prewrite
Autobiography

Traits Focus ✓
Ideas

Prewrite
Autobiography

Traits Focus ✓
Organization
Conventions

Grammar ✓
Review Prepositions

Draft
Autobiography

Traits Focus ✓
Ideas
Voice
Conventions

Grammar ✓
Review Prepositional Phrases

Writing Models Chart

Writing Model
Autobiography,
pp. 52–55

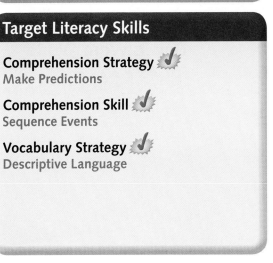
LEAD21
Writing Models Chart

Selection 3: Differentiated Readers
Pages 56–79

Benchmark	**Weekly Vocabulary**	**Advanced**	**Weekly Vocabulary**
Passage to the West	inn misplace slope creek responsible linger accuse mischievous	*Westward Bound*	peasant maiden sacred sympathy garment unlatched befriend recover

ebook online coach

ebook online coach

Target Literacy Skills

Comprehension Strategy ✓
Make Predictions

Comprehension Skill ✓
Sequence Events

Vocabulary Strategy ✓
Descriptive Language

Week 3 Planner

Daily Small-Group Rotation

	Small-Group, Teacher-Led Instruction	Independent Practice	Self-Selected Reading	Study Station Flip Charts
	When the teacher is with these groups...	these groups rotate through independent activities.		
Session 1	Intensive	Advanced	Benchmark	Strategic
Session 2	Strategic	Intensive	Advanced	Benchmark
Session 3	Benchmark	Strategic	Intensive	Advanced
Session 4	Advanced	Benchmark	Strategic	Intensive

Study Station Flip Charts, page 27

Day 1: Vocabulary Central

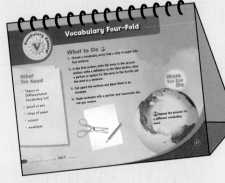

Students create and reassemble vocabulary word strips.

Day 2: Writer's Desk

Students write a poem about life in the Mountain States.

Day 3: Word World

Students add prefixes to words to change the meanings of sentences.

Day 4: Book Corner

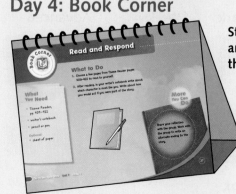

Students read and respond to the text.

Week 3 Day 1

Lesson Highlights

- Introduce the Literature Selection
- Introduce Theme Vocabulary: fulfill, treasure, exchange
- Spelling Pretest: Three-Syllable Words
- Prewrite an Autobiography, pp. 268–269

Materials

	Teacher's Lesson Guide	Student Components	Digital 21
Interactive Reading	pp. 150–153	• Theme Reader, pp. 409–423 • Practice Companion, pp. 229–230, 234–235, 240 • Resource Master 7	ebook onlinecoach
Differentiated Reading	pp. 154–159	• Theme Reader, pp. 409–423 • Practice Companion, p. 230 • Resource Masters 11, 25	ebook onlinecoach
Wrap Up	p. 160	• Resource Masters 1–3	etools 21 • theme wall • writing tool • story starter
Writing and Language Arts	pp. 268–269	• Writing Models Chart, pp. 52–53 • Practice Companion, pp. 268–269 • Resource Master 25	

Tips for Success

- You may wish to have students begin the Weekly Planner on Practice Companion page 229.
- Introduce the Study Stations (Flip Charts, p. 27) and arrange materials for the week.
- Use the Anticipation Guide on Practice Companion page 240.
- **21ST CENTURY SKILLS** Remind students to work on their Inquiry Projects during Independent Practice or Self-Selected Reading time.
- Set out theme-related reference materials for students to use during the week. Refer also to the Theme Bibliography, pages 304–305.

Oral Language and Vocabulary

Objectives
Students will:
• Discuss the theme
• Use theme vocabulary

Discuss the Theme

Recall the Theme Question: *What makes the West exceptional?* Ask students to recall a fact or idea that stood out to them in the previous week, and have them share why it stayed with them.

**Theme Reader
Pages 377–438**

Ask partners to choose a photograph from the Theme Reader that they found interesting and to share why.

Discuss the Inquiry Project

21ST CENTURY SKILLS

Have students recall their Inquiry Questions. Tell them that they will continue their investigations this week.

• Remind students to collect information during Independent Practice or Self-Selected Reading time.

• Encourage students to continue to post their ideas and questions on the Question Board.

etools 21
theme wall

Students can also use the Theme Wall to post ideas and images.

Activate Prior Knowledge

Talk with students about the role of ranching in the Western Region of the United States. Ask students to share what they know about ranches. List their ideas in a concept web on the board.

Prompt students with questions, such as:

• What do you know about ranches? What do people do on ranches?

• Where are most ranches found? What is the weather like there?

Introduce Theme Vocabulary

Theme Vocabulary
fulfill
treasure
exchange

Introduce the theme vocabulary words that students will read this week in their Theme Reader. Tell students that knowing these words will help them answer the Theme and Focus Questions.

Vocabulary Routine	
\multicolumn{2}{l}{Help students scan the selection to find the highlighted theme vocabulary words and have them read and pronounce the words after you. Then use the vocabulary routine below to discuss the meaning of each word.}	
Define	To **fulfill** (p. 422) is to carry out or finish.
Example	We can fulfill our neighbor's wish by cleaning up our yard.
Ask	What is a wish that you can fulfill?

Treasure (p. 422) means "to cherish or consider to have great value." *My parents treasure the homemade gifts that I give them each year.* What do you *treasure*? **a**

Exchange (p. 425) means "to give and receive things of the same kind." *I exchanged the sweater for a different color.* What kinds of things do you *exchange*?

ASSIGN | PRACTICE COMPANION **230**

Read and Comprehend

Objectives
Students will:
• Read a folktale about the West

Prepare to Read

Build Background

Today students will read pages 409–423 of *Juan Verdades: The Man Who Couldn't Tell a Lie*, a folktale about an honest ranch hand in the West.

Theme Reader
Pages 409–423

Preview/Predict/Set Purposes

Preview pages 409–423. Have students share predictions. Students will read to answer the Theme Question. Invite them to begin the Anticipation Guide (Practice Companion, p. 240).

ASSIGN PRACTICE COMPANION 240

MODELED AND SHARED READING

Read Together

Share your thinking as you begin reading *Juan Verdades: The Man Who Couldn't Tell a Lie*. Invite partners to continue reading. Pause periodically to check understanding of concepts and vocabulary.

PAGES 409–419 How does don Ignacio feel about Juan? How do you know? **b**

PAGES 420–423 What does Araceli want Juan to do? Why won't he fulfill her wish?

Respond

Review the predictions students made and the purposes they set. Discuss how the selection to this point answers the Theme Question.

Partner Talk

Ask partners to discuss Araceli and don Arturo's plan. How does the plan affect the students' view of these two characters? Have them discuss predictions for the rest of the story.

---

scaffolding options

a Intervention for Acceleration

WORD FORMS
Intensive- and Strategic-level students might have difficulty recognizing the word *treasure* as a verb. Create a chart for students that shows the word as a noun and a verb. Provide a sample sentence for the noun form of the word:

The word *treasure* can be used as a noun. A *treasure* is something that you find special or of great value.

b Literacy Builder

ACADEMIC LANGUAGE
Explain to students that characterization is the way an author presents a character. It includes the character's appearance, actions, thoughts, and feelings. Sometimes the author states this information explicitly, but other times readers need to infer what kind of person a character is based on context information. Invite students to select a character from the story. Create a four-column chart labeled *Appearance*, *Actions*, *Words*, and *Feelings*, and invite students to find information from the story about the character.

Literacy Builder

Students can use the eBook version of the Theme Reader for building literacy.

Word Work and Fluency

Interactive Reading
whole group

Objectives
Students will:
- Spell words with three syllables
- Analyze words with three syllables
- Practice fluent reading

Spelling and Word Study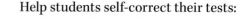

Pretest Three-Syllable Words

Say each word from the list, read the sentence, and say the word again. Then have students write the word.

1. **example** The students read the *example* sentence before they began writing their own sentences.
2. **deliver** I have to *deliver* this note to the principal.
3. **important** There is an *important* meeting that we must attend.
4. **history** The *history* of our town dates back to the 1880s.
5. **hospital** The doctors are very busy in the *hospital*.
6. **several** We have *several* books to choose from.
7. **vacation** My family is going on *vacation* during winter break.
8. **victory** The baseball team celebrated the *victory*.
9. **imagine** I often *imagine* what it would be like to travel to space.
10. **remember** I *remember* what it was like to be young.
11. **camera** She took lots of pictures with her new *camera*.
12. **library** There are many books in the *library*.
13. **tomato** There was a ripe, red *tomato* growing in the garden.
14. **memory** My favorite *memory* is the time I traveled to the mountains.
15. **president** The *president* of the company is having a special dinner for his employees.
16. **favorite** Strawberry ice cream is my *favorite* flavor.

Review Words

17. **squirrel** The *squirrel* gathered nuts for the winter.
18. **simple** I have a *simple* answer to your problem.

Frequently Misspelled Words

19. **probably** We will *probably* watch movies tonight, but we may play video games.
20. **suddenly** *Suddenly*, we heard a crash of thunder.

Explain that these words may seem easy to spell, but they are often misspelled by fourth-graders. 🅐

Help students self-correct their tests:

- Say the word, spell it aloud, and repeat the word.
- Students checkmark each correctly spelled word.
- Students circle each misspelled word and write the correct spelling next to it. Encourage students to note these words as the ones they should pay extra attention to this week.

Teach Three-Syllable Words

Remind students that words can be divided into syllables, and that each syllable has a vowel sound. Invite students to sound out words and look for spelling patterns they know to divide the words into syllables.

Write *hospital* on the board. Label each letter as a vowel or consonant. Then sound out the word as you model dividing it into syllables: hos | pi | tal.

Practice/Apply

Write the remaining spelling words on the board and invite volunteers to label the spelling patterns and sound out the words as they divide them into syllables.

i | mag | ine	vic | to | ry
pres | i | dent	va | ca | tion
his | to | ry	mem | o | ry
to | ma | to	cam | er | a
fa | vor | ite	de | liv | er

Fluency

Introduce and Model

Introduce the fluency selection for the week, "Roaring Downriver" (Practice Companion, pp. 234–235).

Practice Companion Pages 234–235

Remind students that becoming fluent readers will help them better understand what they read.

Tell students that throughout the week, they will practice reading the interview to be fluent readers.

Encourage students to look over the selection. Introduce white-water rafting, and ask students to share anything they know about it. Ask:

Have you gone white-water rafting? Would you ever want to try it? Why or why not?

Discuss challenging vocabulary in the selection.

- Find the word *towering*. What is the meaning of *towering*? *(very tall)*
- Now find the word *picturesque*. What is the root of the word? How does that help you figure out the meaning of *picturesque*? Why do you think the author describes the scene as *picturesque*?

Briefly discuss the meanings of *exhilarating* and *swerves*.

Read "Roaring Downriver" aloud twice with appropriate pace, phrasing, and expression. Ask students whether they enjoyed the reading, and why.

Practice

Read the fluency selection one sentence at a time and have students echo-read. Then divide the class into two groups. Assign one group the part of the reporter and the other group the part of the subject of the interview. **c**

---

scaffolding options

a Intervention for Acceleration

SPELLING AND WORD STUDY
Have students choose an unfamiliar word from the spelling list and complete a Word Skeleton (Resource Master 7) to explore the word's meaning. Allow students to use dictionaries as needed. Have partners share their word skeletons. Discuss the words as a class if desired.

ASSIGN   RESOURCE MASTER **7**

b Challenge

SPELLING AND WORD STUDY
Write each spelling word on a separate piece of paper. Cut the words on the paper to divide them into syllables. Shuffle the pieces and display them on a table, or tape them to a board. Invite students to select the parts that make up each word and write a sentence using that word. Encourage students to share their words and sentences with the group.

c ELL Support

FLUENCY
English language learners may benefit from additional fluency practice. Read the selection with them slowly, pronouncing challenging words and using gestures and sketches to explain the concepts.

Differentiated Reading small groups

Objectives
Students will:
• Reinforce the theme
• Reinforce theme vocabulary
• Reread a folktale that takes place in the West

Prepare to Read

Build Background

Recall the Theme Question: *What makes the West exceptional?* Guide students to consider how

Theme Reader Pages 409–423

geography, economy, history, and culture are demonstrated in the story. Create a four-column chart on the board labeled *Geography, Economy, History*, and *Culture*.

Support students as they discuss how what they've read so far tells them about the West. Record their ideas in the chart.

Have students read the completed chart chorally.

Reinforce Theme Vocabulary *tested*

To reinforce and assess students' understanding of the theme vocabulary, have them complete the following sentences by writing the correct vocabulary word.

• She wanted to … her mom's wish by doing something nice for her. *(fulfill)*

• I want to … this shirt for one that fits better. *(exchange)*

• Many people … their friends. *(treasure)*

Then write the word *fulfill* in the center of a Concept and Word Web (Resource Master 11). Ask students to describe the actions people take when they fulfill someone's wish.

Ask students to use the word *exchange* to talk about something they might exchange with their friends.

Finally, ask students to use the word *treasure* to describe important things they treasure.

ASSIGN

RESOURCE MASTER	11
PRACTICE COMPANION	230

Set Purposes

Students will revisit *Juan Verdades: The Man Who Couldn't Tell a Lie* to:

• Notice information or details they missed during the first reading.

• Help them understand parts of the text that didn't make sense the first time through.

• Find answers to the Theme Question.

Read

Explain that students will hear pages 409–423 of the selection again, but this time they will be closely guided to respond. To help students get started, model reading pages 412–413 as students follow along.

think aloud The illustration on page 412 makes me realize that this story doesn't happen in the present. I can see that the buildings look like something I have seen before in books or in movies. I also see words on page 413 that I do not recognize. For instance, the word *rancheros* is unfamiliar to me. It sounds like *ranchers*, though. I think that *rancheros* is a Spanish word for *ranchers*.

Guide Comprehension

Continue reading as students follow along. Pause after every few pages to check comprehension, using prompts such as the ones below. Encourage students to discuss their responses with partners before answering.

PAGES 409–414 What is don Ignacio most proud of? What is so special about it? *(his apple tree; his great-grandfather planted it, and it flourished and gave sweeter and more flavorful fruit than any other tree around.)*

Why does don Arturo believe that Juan would lie to don Ignacio? *(He believes that every worker would lie to his boss.)*

PAGES 415–418 Why does don Ignacio's wife become upset? Why is the ranch important to don Ignacio and his wife? *(She is afraid they will lose their ranch; the ranch is how they earn a living.)*

Don Ignacio's daughter, Araceli, isn't worried about losing the ranch. What does she suggest to her father that they do? *(stay with don Arturo to find out a way to win the bet)*

PAGES 419–423 On page 422, I see two important words that are highlighted: *fulfill* and *treasures*. How does the text on this page help you understand the meanings of these words? *(Possible response: The sentences "I could never give you that," and "He might agree to give you a basket of apples, but no more," show that don Ignacio treasures his apple tree and that Juan Verdades cannot fulfill, or give, Araceli what she wants.)*

Check Comprehension

1. Why does don Ignacio make a bet with don Arturo? *(Don Ignacio wants to prove that Juan would never lie to him.)* IDENTIFY CAUSE AND EFFECT **b**

2. Summarize what has happened so far in the story. *(Don Arturo makes a bet with don Ignacio that he can get don Ignacio's worker, Juan Verdades, to tell him a lie; don Arturo and his daughter, Araceli, plan to get Juan to fall in love with her; Araceli asks him for all the apples from el manzano real.)* SUMMARIZE **c**

Respond and Write

1. Have partners discuss the details they noticed this time but missed in the first reading, and then ask them to share with the group.

2. Return to the four-column chart. Encourage students to share additional ideas now that they have a more thorough understanding of the selection. Read the chart chorally.

scaffolding options

a ELL Support

PARTNER FOR SUPPORT
To help English language learners access the selection, encourage them to look over pages 409–423 of *Juan Verdades: The Man Who Couldn't Tell a Lie* to remind themselves of questions they had during the first reading. Have them share their questions with partners so that both can look for answers as they reread.

b Intervention for Acceleration

REREAD
If students are undecided about how to answer this question, have them reread the selection with a partner. Ask guiding questions to help students determine what makes people do what they do.

c Intervention for Acceleration

COMPREHENSION: SUMMARIZE
Remind students that summarizing involves using new words to restate important ideas in the selection. The first step in summarizing is to think about which events and details are most important.

ebook online coach
Intervention for Acceleration

Students can use the support features in the eBook version of the Theme Reader.

Read and Comprehend   Strategic

Objectives
Students will:
- Reinforce the theme
- Reinforce theme vocabulary
- Reread a folktale that takes place in the West

Prepare to Read

Build Background

Guide students to recall the Theme Question: *What makes the West exceptional?* Write *geography, economy, history,* and *culture* on the board and invite students to recall what each word means.

ebook
online coach

**Theme Reader
Pages 409–423**

Discuss *Juan Verdades: The Man Who Couldn't Tell a Lie* and encourage students to use these words as they share how the story tells them about the Western Region.

Have partners list questions they still have about what they read in the whole-group session and share their ideas with the group.

Reinforce Theme Vocabulary *tested*

To reinforce and assess students' understanding of the theme vocabulary, have them jot down responses on scrap paper to the following prompts.

- Do you **fulfill** a wish or a bowl? Why?
- Do people usually **exchange** gifts or chores? Why?
- Do you **treasure** an item you value or dislike? Why?

Next, have students create a short story or scenario using all three vocabulary words.

- Lead a group discussion to choose a scenario and decide what would be the best way to incorporate each word.

- Use Resource Master 25 as a sequence chart to help students plan where they will use each word. Label the cells *First, Next,* and *Last* as needed.

- Remind the group of examples and definitions as necessary.

ASSIGN

| RESOURCE MASTER | 25 |
| PRACTICE COMPANION | 230 |

Set Purposes

Explain that rereading helps readers understand how ideas fit together and gives readers a chance to think more deeply about a topic. Ask students to set their own purposes.

> What do you hope to find out by rereading *Juan Verdades: The Man Who Couldn't Tell a Lie*?

Encourage them to keep the Theme Question in mind as they read.

Read

Explain that students have heard the selection read, but now they will read it together with some guidance. To help students get started, model reading pages 413–414 as they follow along. As you read, model your thinking:

 I read that don Ignacio loves his apple tree. I can tell this tree will be important to the story because the author spends a lot of time describing it.

Guide Comprehension

Have partners continue reading. Circulate and listen as they read. Pause periodically to monitor understanding of the theme concepts and vocabulary. **a** **b**

PAGES 409–413 Why do the other ranchers hope to get a basket of apples from don Ignacio's tree? *(The apples are sweeter than any other apples.)*

PAGES 414–416 Who do you think is right regarding the argument about Juan Verdades: don Ignacio or don Arturo? Why? *(Responses will vary, but students should demonstrate an understanding of the argument.)*

On page 416, what does the author mean by "went on arguing good-naturedly?" *(Possible response: The argument was between friends, and neither man was very upset.)*

PAGES 417–423 What excuse does don Arturo tell don Ignacio when he asks if his family can stay with don Ignacio? *(The walls of his house are being mended and painted.)*

What is the plan that don Arturo and his daughter think of to try and get Juan Verdades to tell a lie? *(Araceli will make Juan fall in love with her and then ask him to give her all of the apples from the tree.)*

Why would Juan have to lie to don Ignacio if he gave Araceli the apples? *(Don Ignacio wouldn't allow him to give the apples to Araceli, so he would have to steal them and lie to don Ignacio about what happened.)*

Check Comprehension

1. What important things have happened so far in the story? *(Possible response: Araceli asks Juan Verdades to give her all of the apples from the tree so she can win the bet.)* DETERMINE IMPORTANT INFORMATION

2. What kind of person is Juan Verdades? How do you know? *(He is a hard worker and very honest person; his boss is willing to bet his ranch on Juan's character.)* ANALYZE

Respond and Write

1. Have partners return to the list of questions they had about *Juan Verdades: The Man Who Couldn't Tell a Lie*, and then ask them to share which questions they are able to answer after rereading.

2. Have students point out details in the story that support answers to the Theme Question: *What makes the West exceptional?*

scaffolding options

a Intervention for Acceleration

FEEDBACK
Circulate and listen as students partner-read the selection. If students struggle to answer the prompts, ask them to think about strategies they might use to help them understand what they read. You may wish to suggest strategies, such as visualizing, making connections, or asking and answering questions.

b Literacy Builder

WORDS FROM OTHER LANGUAGES
Explain to students that *Juan Verdades: The Man Who Couldn't Tell a Lie* includes many Spanish words. As students reread the selection, encourage them to use context clues to figure out the meanings of the words.

Intervention for Acceleration

Students can use the support features in the eBook version of the Theme Reader.

Share, Connect, Assess

Wrap Up
whole group

Objectives
Students will:
- Use key concepts and vocabulary
- Make text-to-self connections
- Write about telling the truth
- Monitor their progress

Share Text Connections

Make Text-to-Self Connections Bring students back together from their small groups to share what additional things they learned while reading about Juan Verdades.

- Encourage students to use theme and other academic vocabulary as they share their own insights about key concepts.

- Ensure that students from all groups have a chance to contribute to the discussion.

- Ask students to share their thoughts on how what they've read connects to their personal experiences.

Daily Writing

Have students reflect on why it is important to tell the truth. Encourage them to describe consequences to not telling the truth.

For additional writing practice, remind students to access the Story Starter from their student Home Page.

Student Self Assessment

- Remind students that they are responsible for their learning and that it is helpful to be aware of how well they understand what they are reading, writing, talking, and thinking about in the classroom.

- You may want students to reflect on their reading and learning by using their Personal Reading Logs and My Daily Progress sheets (Resource Masters 1, 3).

ASSIGN | RESOURCE MASTER **1, 3**

Daily Progress Monitoring

To ensure that students have mastered the day's skills and strategies, monitor their success in completing the following independent work:

- **Vocabulary:** Practice Companion, p. 230
- **Spelling:** Practice Companion, p. 232
- **Fluency:** Practice Companion, p. 234
- **Study Station Work Record:** Resource Master 2
- **Self Assessment:** Resource Masters 1–3

Distribute the Unit 7 Take-Home Activities from the Home Connection book. Tell students to complete the activities with their caregivers.

Day at a Glance

Lesson Highlights

- Review Comprehension Strategy: Make Predictions
- Spelling and Phonics: Three-Syllable Words
- Prewrite an Autobiography, pp. 270–271

Materials

	Teacher's Lesson Guide	Student Components	Digital 21
Interactive Reading	pp. 162–165	• Theme Reader, pp. 424–438 • Practice Companion, pp. 230, 232, 234, 236–237, 240, 242	ebook online coach
Differentiated Reading	pp. 166–171, 296–299 (ELL)	• Differentiated Readers • Resource Masters 4, 12	ebook online coach
Wrap Up	p. 172	• Resource Masters 1–3	etools 21 • theme wall • writing tool • story starter
Writing and Language Arts	pp. 270–271	• Writing Models Chart, pp. 52–53 • Practice Companion, pp. 268–269 • Resource Masters 13, 18	

Tips for Success

- Guide students to make connections between reading and writing (p. 163).
- You may wish to have students complete the Respond to Literature Practice Companion page 242.
- If students work on their writing during independent work time, have them use the Evaluation Rubric on Practice Companion page 269.
- Remind students to use their Study Station Work Records (Resource Master 2) throughout the week.
- **21st CENTURY SKILLS** Remind students to work on their Inquiry Projects during Independent Practice or Self-Selected Reading time.

Oral Language and Vocabulary

Interactive Reading *whole group*

Objectives
Students will:
- Reinforce the theme
- Reinforce theme vocabulary

Reinforce the Theme

Use Theme Reader pages 378–379 to reinforce the theme. Remind students of the unit title, *The Wide-Open West*, and discuss how the large photograph on page 379 illustrates what the geography of the West is like. Ask:

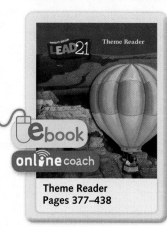

Theme Reader Pages 377–438

- What does this photograph tell you about the geography of the West?
- What do you notice in the other images on these pages? What do they make you think about?

Prompt students to use as many theme vocabulary words as they can in the discussion.

Activate Prior Knowledge

Explain that today students will continue reading *Juan Verdades: The Man Who Couldn't Tell a Lie.*

- Ask students to share what they've learned and what they already know about the importance of ranches in the West.

- Ask students to discuss what could cause people to lie to one another. Prompt students to tell the consequences for lying and why people should tell the truth.

Reinforce Theme Vocabulary

Theme Vocabulary	
fulfill	to carry out or finish
exchange	to give and receive things of the same kind
treasure	to cherish or consider to have great value

Display the list of vocabulary words and review their meanings. To reinforce understanding, ask students to think of sentences containing at least two of the words. Invite students to record their sentences on the board. Think aloud to help students get started. **a**

think aloud I know that *fulfill* means "to carry out or finish" and *exchange* means "to give and receive things of the same kind." I will write about a wish being fulfilled when something is being exchanged.

Write the following sentence on the board and encourage students to create other sentences that use both words. **b**

> Jenny's wish was fulfilled when she exchanged her old radio for a new one.

ASSIGN PRACTICE COMPANION **230**

model read share

Read and Comprehend

Objectives
Students will:
• Review making predictions

REVIEW **COMPREHENSION STRATEGY**

Make Predictions

Define

Remind students that readers make predictions by making an informed guess about what will happen, based on clues in the text and their prior knowledge. As they read, they confirm or revise their predictions.

Model

Write a T-chart, such as the one below, on chart paper. Ask students to turn to pages 422–423 of their Theme Readers as you model making predictions.

 Juan Verdades says that he cannot possibly give all of the apples on the tree to Araceli. Even though he wants to make her happy, he knows don Ignacio would be unhappy. I think Juan will find a way to make both people happy, because he is a very nice person.

Make Predictions	
Clues from the Story	Prediction
Juan wants to make Araceli happy.	Juan will find a solution to make both people happy.
Juan does not want to disappoint his boss.	

Collaborative Practice

Invite students to continue making predictions. Write students' predictions in the chart. Explain that they will check their predictions when they finish *Juan Verdades: The Man Who Couldn't Tell a Lie* today. **c**

Reading/Writing Connection

Explain that writers know readers need clues in order to predict. Authors give readers clues to help them make predictions and make the text interesting. Tell students that sometimes a reader's prediction might not be correct. Ask:

How do writers help readers predict? *(by giving them clues)*

ASSIGN   **PRACTICE COMPANION   236–237**

---

scaffolding options

a Intervention for Acceleration

VOCABULARY
For additional practice, encourage students to create Word Maps (Resource Master 6) for the theme vocabulary words they are learning this week.

ASSIGN   **RESOURCE MASTER   6**

b ELL Support

WORD ASSOCIATIONS
Encourage English language learners to make word associations based on their individual experiences in their home countries and corresponding translations in their native languages. Ask them to relate the new vocabulary words to other words they are more familiar with and can remember easily.

c Literacy Builder

COMPREHENSION: MAKE PREDICTIONS
Allow students additional opportunities to practice making predictions. Guide students to appropriate fiction selections in the classroom library. Have partners pause after each chapter or each page to make predictions. As they continue reading, ask partners to stop when they find information that they can use to confirm or revise their predictions.

Read and Comprehend (continued)

Interactive Reading whole group

Objectives
Students will:
• Read a folktale that takes place in the West
• Reinforce making predictions

Prepare to Read

Build Background

Remind students that yesterday they began reading a folktale about an honest man named Juan Verdades  who worked on a ranch in the West. Invite students to recap what has happened so far in the story. Ask them to discuss what Juan Verdades must be feeling as he struggles between satisfying Araceli's wish and maintaining his loyalty to don Ignacio.

Theme Reader Pages 424–438

Preview and Predict

Preview pages 424–438 of *Juan Verdades: The Man Who Couldn't Tell a Lie.* Point out the illustrations on each page and have students identify the characters and setting in each one. Ask:

> What do you think will happen in the last part of the story? Why do you think so?

Students will continue working on their Anticipation Guides (Practice Companion, p. 240).

ASSIGN PRACTICE COMPANION **240**

Set Purposes

Remind students that they will read to find answers to the Theme Question: *How is the West exceptional?*

Students should also set their own purposes for reading. Ask them to page through the rest of the selection and then suggest something they want to find out as they read today.

Read Together

Have students continue reading *Juan Verdades: The Man Who Couldn't Tell a Lie* independently. Pause periodically to discuss broad concepts and vocabulary.

PAGES 424–427 What does Juan Verdades decide to do about Araceli's request? Does this confirm your predictions, or do you need to revise them based on this new information? *(He goes and picks all the apples; responses will vary, but students should use the story to confirm or revise predictions.)*

PAGES 428–431 After students read page 428, ask:

Do you think Juan Verdades will tell the truth, or will he lie to don Ignacio? Why do you think so?

After page 430, ask students to predict what they think Araceli requested of don Ignacio.

PAGES 432–435 What does Juan tell don Ignacio? Why do you think he decided to tell the truth using a riddle?

PAGES 436–438 The author's note on page 438 tells us that this story first came from Europe and has been passed down through the generations, traveling from country to country. Does the information on that page change the way that you think or feel about the story?

Respond

Lead a brief class discussion about the folktale. Ask students if they enjoyed the story and to share their favorite parts. Revisit the predictions they made before reading and discuss whether students confirmed or revised their predictions.

Invite students to complete the Anticipation Guide on Practice Companion page 240 and share their responses with the class.

Partner Talk ★★

Provide these discussion points:

• What is the message of this folktale?

• What would you have done if you were Juan Verdades?

ASSIGN PRACTICE COMPANION **240**

Word Work and Fluency

Objectives
Students will:
- Practice spelling three-syllable words
- Practice fluent reading

Spelling and Word Study

Practice Three-Syllable Words

Remind students that this week they are practicing words with three syllables.

Have students use their spelling lists to write a sentence for each word, and then read their sentences to partners. Their partners spell the word and give its meaning. Then the partners switch roles.

ASSIGN PRACTICE COMPANION 232

Fluency

Shared Choral Reading

Have students turn to "Roaring Downriver" (Practice Companion, p. 234). Ask students to recall the structure of an interview. Then ask:

- What is the purpose of this interview?
- Is the interview informative?
- What is something you would like to ask the person being interviewed?

Explain that *phrasing* is when readers chunk the reading into smaller, meaningful parts to better understand what they read.

- Read the interviewer's first question without pausing. Then read it again, this time using proper phrasing.

- Have students note the differences in your readings. Lead a discussion about which reading was easier to understand.

- Read aloud the entire selection as students listen carefully to the phrasing you use. Then lead a choral reading of the selection, reminding students to be aware of their phrasing. **b**

ASSIGN PRACTICE COMPANION 234

scaffolding options

a Intervention for Acceleration

COMPREHENSION: MAKE PREDICTIONS
Intensive- and Strategic-level students may benefit from partnering with Benchmark- and Advanced-level students for practice making predictions. Encourage all students to support their predictions with clues from the selection.

b Intervention for Acceleration

FLUENCY
If Intensive- and Strategic-level students have difficulty with phrasing, encourage them to practice reading from their Differentiated Readers. Select a page that is familiar, and ask partners to take turns reading it aloud two or three times.

Read and Comprehend **Intensive**

Objectives
Students will:
- Use differentiated vocabulary
- Reinforce making predictions
- Read about Paul Bunyan

Prepare to Read

Build Background

Read with students the Focus Question: *What is life like in the Mountain States?* (Differentiated Reader, p. 5).

Differentiated Reader Pages 56–65

Prompt students to answer the question using information they already know from the whole-group reading or from their own lives.

Direct students to turn to page 56 and have the group read the title, *How Paul Bunyan Shaped the West*, aloud.

- Explain that the story is about Paul Bunyan and his ox, Babe.

- Encourage students to tell what they know about Paul Bunyan.

- Show illustrations or display books about Paul Bunyan and other tall tales.

- Start a KWL chart on chart paper. Elicit information to help students complete the "What I Know" and "What I Want to Know" columns. **a**

Introduce
Differentiated Vocabulary *tested* ✓

Have students complete the Vocabulary Rating Sheet (Resource Master 4).

- Find and pronounce with students the highlighted differentiated vocabulary words (pp. 56–65).

- Use the following routine to discuss each word's meaning.

- For each word, have students discuss answers to prompts with partners.

Vocabulary Routine

Define	**Wilderness** (p. 57) is a natural place where no people live.
Example	Many different types of wild animals can be found in the wilderness.
Ask	Can buildings be found in the wilderness? Why or why not?

Haul (p. 58) means "to pull or move with force." *Our neighbors helped us haul our furniture to our new house.* Does *haul* mean the same as *carry*? Why or why not?

A **knapsack** (p. 60) is a bag that is strapped on the back to carry supplies or personal belongings. *Marcus put water and snacks in his knapsack.* Are a backpack and a *knapsack* the same thing? Why or why not?

Continue the routine with *tough* (p. 64) and *buckle* (p. 65), using the Glossary definitions and sentences and asking questions.

ASSIGN **RESOURCE MASTER 4**

Preview and Predict

Have students preview pages 56–65 by turning each page and looking at the illustrations and chapter titles. Ask students to predict what they think will happen in the story.

Set Purposes

Remind students that readers set purposes to focus their attention as they read.

- Students will find answers to the questions they wrote in the KWL chart and discuss what they learned.

- Students will look for answers to the Focus Question.

REINFORCE COMPREHENSION STRATEGY

Make Predictions *tested* ✓

Remind students that readers predict as they read by using clues from the text and their own prior knowledge to guess what will happen next. Prompt students to tell why readers use this strategy.

To reinforce making predictions, use page 56 to model your thinking.

think aloud

The blue text on page 56 tells me who the story is about, Paul Bunyan. I wonder what we will read about him. I can predict that since this story is a folktale, he is a made-up character.

ASSIGN **PRACTICE COMPANION 236–237**

Read

Tell students that today they will read pages 56–65 of *How Paul Bunyan Shaped the West*. Model your thinking as you read page 57 to help students get started.

 After I read the first page, I reread the chapter title: "Meet Paul Bunyan." Paul Bunyan is a fictional character. I read that he was able to lift a table when he was three years old. A three-year-old couldn't really do that though. This is just one example of an event in the story that couldn't really happen. I will keep reading to find out about other events.

Guide Comprehension

Have partners continue reading pages 56–65 of the selection. Pause periodically to monitor understanding of theme concepts and vocabulary. Have students use sticky notes to respond to prompts prior to discussion.

PAGES 56–59 Read the **Strategy Tool Kit** on page 59. Have students jot down their thoughts before sharing their predictions with partners.

PAGES 60–61 Ask students to explain what happened when Paul and Babe traveled West to look for more forests to cut down. *(Their footsteps created lakes.)*

PAGES 62–65 Ask students to write synonyms for *tough*, the highlighted vocabulary word on page 64. Have them share their words with their partners. Discuss as a group which words students chose.

Check Comprehension

1. What are the main events of the story so far? SUMMARIZE

2. How do the events in the story compare to real events in other stories? COMPARE AND CONTRAST

3. What other stories have you read about made-up characters who did amazing things? MAKE CONNECTIONS

Respond and Write

1. Have partners discuss **Stop and Think** on page 65. Have them cite specific text evidence to support their answers. **b**

2. Have students add information to the "What I Learned" column of the KWL chart and write any new questions in the "Want to Know" column.

3. Discuss how the story so far has helped answer the Focus Question.

scaffolding options

ELL Support

See page 296 of this Teacher's Lesson Guide for vocabulary and instructional support of English language learners at the Intensive level.

a Critical Thinking

EVALUATE AND DISCUSS IDEAS
Have students work together in small groups to compare ideas and generate new ones. Encourage them to review selections in both the Theme and Differentiated Readers from the previous two weeks to refresh their memories as they fill in their charts.

b Intervention for Acceleration

SKIM
Before students answer **Stop and Think** on page 65, ask them to skim the selection from the beginning on page 56. Tell them that skimming text for a specific purpose, such as answering a question, is an effective strategy for finding information.

ebook online coach

Intervention for Acceleration

Students can use the support features in the eBook version of the Differentiated Reader.

Read and Comprehend **Strategic**

Objectives
Students will:
- Use differentiated vocabulary
- Reinforce making predictions
- Read about a man who finds sacks of gold

Differentiated Reading small groups

Prepare to Read

Build Background

Read with students the Focus Question: *What is life like in the Mountain States?* (Differentiated Reader, p. 5).

Differentiated Reader Pages 56–67

Encourage students to answer the question using their own prior knowledge.

Read aloud with students the title of the story on page 56, *Foolish Juan and the Sacks of Gold.*

- Explain that this is a folktale, a story that is passed down from generation to generation.

- Encourage students to tell what they know about folktales or to share any folktales they have read or heard in the past.

- Have students begin a KWL Chart (Resource Master 12) about what they know about folktales, and have them fill in the "What I Know" column before they begin reading.

ASSIGN   RESOURCE MASTER **12**

Introduce
Differentiated Vocabulary

Have students complete the Vocabulary Rating Sheet (Resource Master 4).

- Find and pronounce with students the highlighted differentiated vocabulary words (pp. 56–67).

- Use the following routine to discuss each word's meaning.

- For each word, have students discuss answers to prompts with a partner.

Vocabulary Routine	
Define	**Weary** (p. 57) means "very tired."
Example	The travelers were weary after their long journey.
Ask	What other activity might make you feel weary?

Astonish (p. 58) means "to surprise." *The huge mountains astonished us as we came around the bend.* What is a synonym for *astonish*?

Continue the routine with *stable* (p. 60), *slumber* (p. 64), and *rejoice* (p. 65), using the Glossary definitions and sentences and asking questions.

ASSIGN   RESOURCE MASTER **4**

Preview and Predict

Have students preview pages 56–67 by turning each page and looking at the illustrations and chapter titles. Ask students to predict what they think will happen in the story.

Set Purposes

Remind students that readers set purposes to focus their attention as they read.

- Students will read to add details to their KWL charts and fill in the "What I Want to Know" column.

- Students will look for answers to the Focus Question.

REINFORCE COMPREHENSION STRATEGY

Make Predictions

Remind students that readers make predictions as they read by using clues from the text and their own prior knowledge to make informed guesses about what will happen. Then model your thinking using pages 56–57.

 When I looked at the story's title and the illustrations on pages 56 and 57, I decided that the characters live in a place out west. When I read on page 57 that the man was not very clever but his wife was, I started making predictions in my mind about what his wife might be clever about. I know that when I am clever, I think about my choices before I act on them. Maybe that is what his wife does. Maybe that is how she is different from Juan. I think that Juan's wife will have to make some clever choices in the story. **b**

ASSIGN   PRACTICE COMPANION **236–237**

Read

Tell students that today they will read pages 56–67 of *Foolish Juan and the Sacks of Gold*. To help them get started, model your thinking as you read page 57.

 At the beginning of the story, I see that the *Monday* is in parentheses next to the word *Lunes*. I'm not sure what *Lunes* means, but the context clue of *Monday* makes me think that *Lunes* means "Monday" in Spanish. As I scan through the story, I see that each chapter is divided into days of the week, and the Spanish word for each day of the week is included.

Guide Comprehension

Have partners continue to read. Pause periodically to monitor understanding of theme concepts and vocabulary.

PAGES 56–59 Have students read the **Strategy Tool Kit** on page 59 and jot down their responses before sharing their predictions with the rest of the group.

PAGES 60–63 Ask students to share why they think Rosa spent all night making the buñuelos.

PAGES 64–67 Have students describe what happened when Juan woke up the next morning. *(There were buñuelos all over the lawn. Juan thought it had rained buñuelos.)*

Check Comprehension

1. Identify the most important information in the first half of the story. DETERMINE IMPORTANT INFORMATION

2. What happens after Juan brings home the sacks of gold? SEQUENCE EVENTS

3. What will probably happen next in the story? MAKE PREDICTIONS

Respond and Write

1. Have partners discuss **Stop and Think** on page 67. Ask them to cite specific examples in the text.

2. Have students complete the "What I Learned" column of their KWL charts. Encourage students to read aloud what they learned and share what they still want to find out.

3. Discuss how the selection to this point has helped answer the Focus Question.

scaffolding options

ELL Support

See page 297 of this Teacher's Lesson Guide for vocabulary and instructional support of English language learners at the Strategic level.

a Literacy Builder

MULTIPLE-MEANING WORDS
Remind students that some words have more than one meaning. You can determine meaning by the context in which the word is used. Say:

Juan went out to the stable to hitch up the mule. In this sentence, the word *stable* is a noun that names a building.

The house was stable. Here, the word is used as an adjective that describes the house.

Discuss the multiple meanings of *slumber*.

b Intervention for Acceleration

READ CHALLENGING TEXT
Have partners use a higher-level Differentiated Reader to practice making predictions.

ebook onlinecoach
Intervention for Acceleration

Students can use the support features in the eBook version of the Differentiated Reader.

Read and Comprehend Benchmark

Objectives
Students will:
• Use differentiated vocabulary
• Reinforce making predictions
• Read about missing ski poles

Prepare to Read

Build Background

Introduce the Focus Question: *What is life like in the Mountain States?* and the selection title, *The Mystery of*

Differentiated Reader Pages 56–65

the Missing Ski Poles (pp. 5, 56). Tell students that the story is about a family who goes skiing in the mountains. Have students share what they know about the Mountain States and the activities that people participate in there.

Have students begin a KWL Chart (Resource Master 12) and fill out the "What I Know" and "What I Want to Know" columns.

ASSIGN RESOURCE MASTER **12**

Introduce Differentiated Vocabulary *tested*

Have students complete the Vocabulary Rating Sheet (Resource Master 4).

Vocabulary Routine	
Define	An **inn** (p. 57) is a small hotel.
Example	The family decided to stay at the cozy mountain inn.
Ask	How is an inn different from an apartment?

Misplace (p. 58) means "to lose track of." *It is easy to misplace your keys.* What do you *misplace* easily?

Partners continue the routine with *slope* (p. 59) and *creek* (p. 64), using the Glossary definitions and sentences and asking questions.

ASSIGN RESOURCE MASTER **4**

Preview/Predict/Set Purposes

Students preview the selection to predict what they think will happen. They will read to answer the Focus Question and complete their KWL charts.

Read

Guide Comprehension

Partners will read pages 56–65 of *The Mystery of the Missing Ski Poles*. Monitor understanding of key concepts and vocabulary with the prompts below. Remind students to make predictions as they read.

PAGES 56–59 What will happen to Tyrone and Josh as the story progresses? **MAKE PREDICTIONS**

PAGES 60–65 Describe Josh and Tyrone's relationship. Make connections to other stories or experiences you've had with similar relationships. **MAKE CONNECTIONS**

Respond and Write

1. Have students discuss their predictions and how the first half of the story answers the Focus Question.

2. Ask students to make notes in the "What I Learned" column of their KWL charts.

ELL Support

See page 298 of this Teacher's Lesson Guide for vocabulary and instructional support of English language learners at the Benchmark level.

Literacy Builder *tested*

COMPREHENSION: MAKE PREDICTIONS
Challenge students to predict whether Tyrone's feelings will change about Josh, and if so, how. Encourage them to use details from the story to guide their predictions.

Objectives
Students will:
- Use differentiated vocabulary
- Reinforce making predictions
- Read about a young girl who tends to turkeys

Differentiated Reading
small groups

Prepare to Read

Build Background

Introduce the Focus Question: *What is life like in the Mountain States?* and the selection title, *The Turkey Maiden* (pp. 5, 56). Tell students that this is a story within a story. A grandfather tells his grandchildren a folktale about a girl who lived long ago in the mountains.

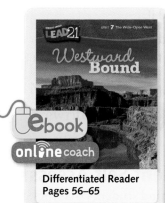

Differentiated Reader Pages 56–65

ebook
online coach

Have students do a quickwrite to jot down everything they know about folktales. Discuss students' ideas as a group, clarifying information as needed.

Introduce Differentiated Vocabulary

Have students complete the Vocabulary Rating Sheet (Resource Master 4).

Vocabulary Routine

Define	A **peasant** (p. 58) is a person who works on or owns a small farm.
Example	A peasant tended the flocks of the royal family.
Ask	What else might a peasant do?

A **maiden** (p. 59) is an unmarried girl or woman. *The folktale had a maiden as its main character.* What is a synonym for the word *maiden*?

Partners continue the routine with *sacred* (p. 62) and *sympathy* (p. 65), using the Glossary definitions and sentences and asking questions. **a**

ASSIGN | RESOURCE MASTER 4

Preview/Predict/Set Purposes

Students preview the selection to predict what they think will happen. Students will read to answer the Focus Question and add information to their quickwrites.

Read

Guide Comprehension

Students will read pages 56–65 of *The Turkey Maiden* independently. Remind them to make predictions as they read. After they read, discuss key concepts.

PAGES 56–61 Ask students how the turkeys might have known that the turkey maiden only wanted to protect them. MAKE INFERENCES

PAGES 62–65 Have students write down predictions of what will happen next in the story and share their ideas as a group. MAKE PREDICTIONS

Respond and Write

1. Invite students to discuss how the selection helps answer the Focus Question.

2. Ask students to add new information they learned today to their quickwrites.

scaffolding options

ELL Support

See page 299 of this Teacher's Lesson Guide for vocabulary and instructional support of English language learners at the Advanced level.

a Challenge

VOCABULARY
Have partners write sentences using all of the vocabulary words. Sentences should demonstrate word meaning. Ask pairs to share their sentences with the group.

Oral Language and Vocabulary

Interactive Reading whole group

Objectives
Students will:
- Reinforce the theme
- Analyze descriptive language

Reinforce the Theme

Use the Theme Reader (pp. 378–379) to revisit the Theme Question: *What makes the West exceptional?*

Theme Reader Pages 377–438

Lead a discussion about how *Juan Verdades: The Man Who Couldn't Tell a Lie* touches upon the theme concepts of geography, economy, history, and culture.

Ask prompts such as these:

Which concept do you think was most clearly demonstrated in the story?

Why? Use pictures or passages that stood out to you to explain your answer. *(Responses will vary, but students should be able to connect the concept to the illustrations and text from the reading.)*

Encourage students to recall and use new vocabulary and concepts they've learned throughout the unit.

INTRODUCE **VOCABULARY STRATEGY**

Use Descriptive Language

Define and Model

Explain that understanding descriptive language is a strategy that helps readers more deeply understand the text they read. Say:

Descriptive language helps the reader understand how things look, smell, feel, sound, or taste. Descriptive language creates a picture in the reader's mind, often causing the reader to think of things in a new way.

Have students turn to page 413 of the Theme Reader. Read aloud the first sentence on the page.

think aloud
The phrase *one late summer day* makes me picture what the light must have looked like as the ranchers were talking. I know that in the summer the sun doesn't begin to set until late in the day. When it does, the sky turns orange. The phrase *wealthy rancheros* makes me visualize that they are wearing very nice clothes and are well-groomed.

Practice

Challenge students to skim the first few pages of *Juan Verdades: The Man Who Couldn't Tell a Lie*, looking for descriptive language.

As they find examples, create a word bank on chart paper and add vivid verbs, adjectives, and nouns to it.

ASSIGN | PRACTICE COMPANION **238–239**

Objectives
Students will: • Review sequencing events

REVIEW COMPREHENSION SKILL
Sequence Events

Define and Model
Remind students that *sequence* is a way authors organize their writing to help readers understand the order in which events happen. Authors often use signal words, such as *first*, *after that*, *later*, *next*, and *finally* when writing about events.

Use Theme Reader page 413 to model the sequence of events. Use a T-chart on chart paper to record your ideas:

 The phrase *one late summer day* tells me when the story begins: late in the day during the summer.

Event(s)	Signal Word(s)
A group of wealthy rancheros gathered to talk.	One late summer day

Practice
Tell partners to continue paging through the story to look for signal words that show sequence. Pause periodically to elicit their ideas, adding events from the text to the T-chart in one column and signal words in the other column. Discuss students' ideas as a class. **b** **c**

Reading/Writing Connection

Explain that authors use signal words to help show readers the order of events.

What other ways do we know that time is passing during a story? *(Illustrations show events happening in sequence; authors use dates, times, and ages; verb tenses give clues about when events happen in relation to each other.)*

ASSIGN PRACTICE COMPANION 243

---

scaffolding options

a ELL Support

BUILD CONCEPTS
Help English language learners understand the theme by reinforcing the key concepts. Show pictures and illustrations that demonstrate various kinds of communities and types of geography in the western portion of the United States. Point out things that the communities have in common and things that make them different. As you show the pictures, explain how people use or interact with geographical features.

b Intervention for Acceleration

CHOICE FOR ACCELERATION
Invite Intensive- and Strategic-level students who are having difficulty sequencing events to choose a different selection from the classroom library. Have partners read the selection and note examples that show the sequence of events. Have them jot down any signal words they find that helped them identify the order of events.

c Literacy Builder

COMPREHENSION: SEQUENCE EVENTS
You may wish to distribute Time Lines (Resource Master 18) to help students identify the sequence of events in the story.

ASSIGN RESOURCE MASTER 18

Read and Comprehend (continued)

Objectives
Students will:
• Identify conflict and resolution
• Reinforce sequencing events
• Reread about Juan Verdades

Interactive Reading whole group

Prepare to Read

Use Literary Elements

Explain that authors use literary elements to express ideas in a meaningful way. Some elements, such as plot and setting, help create a story. Other elements, like similes and personification, sway the reader to think, feel, or visualize a certain way.

Theme Reader
Pages 409–438

Tell students that today they will reread *Juan Verdades: The Man Who Couldn't Tell a Lie* while focusing on how literary elements add meaning.

Literary Elements Minilesson: Plot—Conflict and Resolution

Turn to pages 413–414 of the Theme Reader and explain that an important part of a plot is the conflict resolution, or the way characters solve the main problem. Prompt students to name the conflict in the story and tell how the characters develop a plan to resolve it. Ask questions such as these:

• What was the conflict between don Ignacio and don Arturo? *(They disagreed about whether Juan Verdades would tell a lie, and they bet their ranches on it.)*

• What conflict did Juan Verdades have? *(Possible response: He had to decide whether to be loyal to his boss or to fulfill Araceli's wishes, whom he loved; he had to decide if he would lie or tell the truth.)*

• How were each of these conflicts resolved? *(Possible response: Don Ignacio won the bet, and Juan was rewarded for his honesty.)* **a**

ASSIGN   PRACTICE COMPANION 241

Set Purposes

Remind students that when they read, they will focus on how literary elements add meaning to the story.

Students should also set their own purposes for reading and look for answers to the Theme Question.

Read Together

Have students reread *Juan Verdades: The Man Who Couldn't Tell a Lie* independently. Pause periodically to discuss literary elements and the sequence of events. **b**

PAGES 413–416 What are the events that set up the conflict in this story? Which words help the reader put the events in order? *(The wealthy rancheros are talking and the subject of Juan Verdades not telling lies to his boss comes up; one summer day, when.)*

Encourage students to discuss how other literary elements, such as setting and mood, are important to the story.

PAGES 417–431 Which examples of descriptive language can you find on these pages? How are these words important to the plot of the story? *(Possible response: very bright and lively young woman; he greeted her politely; she thanked him very warmly, and his spirits rose for a moment; he had run gleefully. Possible response: These words give information about the characters' traits.)*

PAGES 432–437 What conflict does Juan face? How does he resolve it? *(He has given away the apples, and now he must decide if he will confess and pay the consequences or lie to try to get away with it; he tells the truth using a riddle because it is very difficult to confess what he did.)*

Respond

Ask students to discuss the descriptive language in the story. Have them tell how literary elements add meaning to the text. Then have partners discuss whether they achieved their purposes for reading and whether they found any new information to answer the Theme Question.

> ### Talk About Text ★★★
>
> **Provide these discussion points:**
>
> • What other resolution might the author have written to try to solve the conflict in the story? Do you think it would have been as effective? Why?
>
> • What does the resolution tell us about the message the author wants to share with readers?

model read share

Word Work and Fluency

Objectives
Students will:
- Practice spelling words with three syllables
- Review prefixes *un-, de-, dis-, counter-, mis-*
- Practice fluent reading

Spelling

Practice Three-Syllable Words
Have students turn to page 233 in their Practice Companions. Explain that they will proofread the paragraph to find and correct the misspelled words.

ASSIGN PRACTICE COMPANION **233**

Word Study

Review Prefixes *un-, de-, dis-, counter-, mis-*
Remind students that the prefixes *un-, de-, dis-, counter-,* and *mis-* mean "opposite" or "bad." These prefixes change the meanings of the words they are added to.

Teach/Model
Write *dismounted* from Theme Reader page 428 on the board. Circle the prefix *dis-*. Think aloud as you share the meaning of *mount* and use the meaning of the prefix to determine the meaning of *dismount*.

Practice/Apply
Write the following words on the board and have students identify their meanings: *untied, derailed, undid, descend.*

Ask partners to use a dictionary to find other words that have the *un-, de-, dis-, counter-,* or *mis-* prefixes. Invite students to share their lists with the class and use at least four of the words in sentences. **c**

ASSIGN PRACTICE COMPANION **244**
epractice
word study games

Fluency

Paired Reading
Read "Roaring Downriver" (Practice Companion, p. 234), modeling good expression. Then have partners practice. One partner takes on the role of the interviewer while the other reads the tour guide's lines. Then partners switch roles.

ASSIGN PRACTICE COMPANION **234**

scaffolding options

a Literacy Builder

USE LITERARY ELEMENTS
Review elements that are commonly found in fiction, such as figurative language and dialogue. Discuss each element and list it on the board. Ask students to look for certain elements when reading.

b Intervention for Acceleration

CHOICE FOR ACCELERATION
Some of your Intensive- and Strategic-level students might have difficulty accessing the selection independently. To help accelerate their reading, have them choose slightly less challenging texts from the classroom library to practice identifying a problem and its resolution.

c Challenge

WORD STUDY
As students use the dictionary to find additional words with the target prefixes, remind them that not every word beginning with *un-, de-, dis-, counter-,* or *mis-* actually uses the letters as a prefix. If students are unsure about a particular word, remind them that they can look up the root word in the dictionary.

Read and Comprehend Intensive

Objectives
Students will:
- Use differentiated vocabulary
- Reinforce sequencing events
- Reinforce analyzing descriptive language
- Reinforce literary elements
- Read about Paul Bunyan

Prepare to Read

Review

Review pages 56–65 of *How Paul Bunyan Shaped the West* as students page through the selection. Ask questions, such as:

ebook
online coach

Differentiated Reader
Pages 66–77

- Who are the characters in the story? How are they different from other characters you have read about?
- What is the setting? How is it important to the story?
- What unbelievable things does Paul Bunyan do?

Ask students to share what they learned about the Focus Question: *What is life like in the Mountain States?*

Introduce
Differentiated Vocabulary

Have students complete the Vocabulary Rating Sheet (Resource Master 4).

- Find and pronounce with students the highlighted differentiated vocabulary words (pp. 66–77).
- Use the following routine to discuss each word's meaning.
- For each word, have students jot down and explain their answers to the prompts.

Vocabulary Routine	
Define	A **canteen** (p. 67) is a small container for carrying water.
Example	The camper filled his canteen with water before he left for his trip.
Ask	What else could you put into a canteen?

Stagger (p. 70) means "to move unsteadily or unbalanced." *Emma staggered home from school after a long, tiring day.* Do you have lots of energy when you *stagger*? Why or why not?

A **canyon** (p. 71) is a deep, narrow valley with steep sides, often with a stream or river flowing through it. *The western part of the United States has many deep canyons.* Are valleys and *canyons* the same? Why or why not?

ASSIGN   RESOURCE MASTER **4**    **epractice**
vocabulary activities

Set Purposes

Display the KWL chart students contributed to on the previous day.

- Have students tell what they hope to learn from the rest of the selection today.
- Remind students to look for information that helps answer the Focus Question and complete the KWL chart.

REINFORCE COMPREHENSION SKILL

Sequence Events

Remind students that when readers look for a sequence of events, they determine the order in which events happen. Readers use clue words, such as *first*, *next*, and *finally*.

Help students recognize a sequence of events by modeling your thinking about page 67.

think aloud As page 67 begins, the author provides a clue to the sequence of the story. The phrase *just before Paul and Babe left their campfire* tells me the beginning of the sequence of this part of the story. I will keep looking for words and phrases like these as I read the story.

ASSIGN   PRACTICE COMPANION **243**

Read

Tell students that today they will read pages 66–77 of *How Paul Bunyan Shaped the West*. Model your thinking as you look back to yesterday's reading to help students get started.

think aloud Before I begin reading the second half of the story, I'm going to flip back one page to review the last thing I read. That will help me remember what happened in the first half. I see that when Paul and Babe moved rocks to build a fire, the Rocky Mountains were formed. This is one of the many unreal things that are included in the story.

Guide Comprehension

Have students continue reading pages 66–77 independently. Pause periodically to monitor understanding of theme concepts and vocabulary. Have students use Resource Master 25 as a sequence chart to keep track of the story's events. **b**

PAGES 66–69 Read the **Strategy Tool Kit** on page 69. Have students jot down their thoughts before sharing their predictions with partners.

PAGES 70–73 Discuss how the author incorporates places students have been reading and learning about during this unit.

PAGES 74–77 Ask students to look for examples of descriptive language on these pages. Once they are finished, guide them to study the illustrations and describe the pictures in their own words.

ASSIGN   RESOURCE MASTER **25**

Check Comprehension

1. What action of Paul's created the desert of Nevada? *(He sat down and all the plants died.)* VISUALIZE

2. Describe a conflict in this story. Tell how it was resolved. *(Paul was taking away work from the other loggers, so his boss sent him to find more trees to cut down. Paul eventually found plenty of forests in the Pacific Northwest.)* ANALYZE

3. In what order do the main events of the story occur? Use your sequence charts to share. SEQUENCE EVENTS

Respond and Write

1. Tell students to write personal responses to the story, stating main ideas and supporting their opinions with details from the text.

2. Have students add information to the KWL chart they began on Day 2. Read the chart chorally. Invite volunteers to share the most interesting facts or ideas they learned.

3. Ask students how what they learned helped them answer the Focus Question.

scaffolding options

ELL Support

See page 296 of this Teacher's Lesson Guide for vocabulary and instructional support of English language learners at the Intensive level.

a Literacy Builder

COMPREHENSION: SEQUENCE EVENTS
Guide students to list other words that authors can use to signal sequence, such as *then*, *later*, *soon*, *before*, and *again*.

b Intervention for Acceleration

FEEDBACK
Circulate and invite students to whisper-read. Listen for use of vocabulary strategies, fluency techniques, or comprehension strategies. Use an example as a starting point for discussion when you address the group after reading.

ebook online coach
Intervention for Acceleration

Students can use the support features in the eBook version of the Differentiated Reader.

Read and Comprehend

Strategic

Objectives
Students will:
- Use differentiated vocabulary
- Reinforce sequencing events
- Reinforce analyzing descriptive language
- Reinforce literary elements
- Read about Juan and Rosa

Differentiated Reading *small groups*

Prepare to Read

Review

Review the first half of *Foolish Juan and the Sacks of Gold* by asking questions such as these:

Differentiated Reader Pages 68–77

- What is the setting of the story? Why is it so important?
- What challenges have the characters faced?
- What surprised you about yesterday's selection?

Have students discuss what they found out about the Focus Question: *What is life like in the Mountain States?*

Introduce
Differentiated Vocabulary

Have students complete the Vocabulary Rating Sheet (Resource Master 4).

- Find and pronounce with students the highlighted differentiated vocabulary words (pp. 68–77).
- Use the following routine to discuss each word's meaning.
- For each word, have students jot down and explain their answers to the prompts.

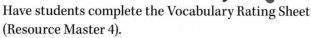

Vocabulary Routine	
Define	**Obviously** (p. 68) means "in an easily seen or understood way."
Example	She was obviously hurt by the rude remark.
Ask	What is a synonym for *obviously*?

Tempt (p. 71) means "to give someone ideas of doing something wrong." *I was tempted to eat the chocolate chip cookie.* What might *tempt* you?

Wicked (p. 75) means "very bad or evil." *The selfish man attempted wicked acts against others.* What is an antonym for the word *wicked*?

ASSIGN **RESOURCE MASTER 4**

vocabulary activities

Set Purposes

Invite students to review the KWL charts they began on Day 2.

- Ask students what they hope to learn from the second half of the selection. Invite them to add new questions to their charts.
- Remind students that the rest of the story will help them answer the Focus Question and add details to their KWL charts.

REINFORCE COMPREHENSION SKILL

Sequence Events

Remind students that stories are often written in the order, or sequence, in which events happen. Point out that sometimes the events are out of order. Students can look for dates, times, and clue words, such as *first, then, after that, finally,* and *next,* to help them determine sequence.

To help students understand a sequence of events, use page 64 to model your thinking.

think aloud This chapter begins with the sentence, "On Wednesday Juan woke early." This tells me when this part of the story takes place—early on Wednesday. I will look for more sequence words as I read the second half of the story.

ASSIGN **PRACTICE COMPANION 243**

Read

Tell students that today they will read pages 68–77 of *Foolish Juan and the Sacks of Gold.* To help students get started, model your thinking as you read pages 68–69.

think aloud Before I start reading, I'll look at the illustrations. I see Rosa holding the donkey, and the donkey has hay in its mouth. I know that donkeys like to eat hay. Why is this illustration important to the story? I will keep this question in mind as I read.

Guide Comprehension

Have students continue reading pages 68–77 on their own. Pause periodically to monitor understanding of theme concepts and vocabulary. Have students use sticky notes to respond to prompts before discussing them with the group. **a**

PAGES 68–71 Have students read the **Strategy Tool Kit** on page 71 and jot down their predictions before sharing them with the class.

PAGES 72–75 Ask students to recount the events, in the order they occurred, that Juan tells the thieves happened to him during his lucky week. Tell them in the order in which they occurred. *(Juan found gold on Monday, it rained buñuelos on Wednesday, and the mule started eating with its tail on Thursday.)*

PAGES 76–77 Ask students to study the illustrations on these pages. Encourage them to use descriptive language to discuss the pictures with partners.

Check Comprehension

1. How do the headings help you understand the story? *(They show the dates that events happen, making it easier to understand the sequence.)* USE TEXT FEATURES **b**

2. What descriptive language does the author use? How does it help you visualize the story? *(Responses will vary, but students should note that descriptive language creates a more detailed picture in the reader's mind.)* VISUALIZE

3. What was the conflict and resolution in this story? How would the resolution have been different if Rosa had not carried out her plan? *(Thieves came looking for the gold Juan had found. The thieves didn't believe Juan had the gold because of his strange stories. Juan and Rosa returned the gold to the bank; the thieves might have gotten the gold.)* ANALYZE

Respond and Write

1. Tell students to write a personal response telling about a time when they had to be smart and make wise decisions.

2. Have students add information to the KWL charts they began on Day 2. Discuss as a group the new ideas they discovered.

3. Ask students how what they learned helped them answer the Focus Question.

scaffolding options

ELL Support

See page 297 of this Teacher's Lesson Guide for vocabulary and instructional support of English language learners at the Strategic level.

a Critical Thinking

ANALYZE LITERARY ELEMENTS
Explain to students that characters are a literary element, and authors use dialogue and description to help readers understand what the characters are like. Have students analyze the text and give a character analysis that includes a physical description, age, how they act, what decisions they make, and how these decisions affect their lives.

b Intervention for Acceleration

MONITOR COMPREHENSION
Ask students to reread before answering the Check Comprehension Questions. Remind students that rereading is an effective strategy for helping them understand things that might have been confusing the first time they read the text.

ebook online coach

Intervention for Acceleration

Students can use the support features in the eBook version of the Differentiated Reader.

Read and Comprehend

Objectives
Students will:
- Use differentiated vocabulary
- Reinforce sequencing events
- Reinforce analyzing descriptive language
- Reinforce literary elements
- Read about missing ski poles

Prepare to Read

Review

Revisit pages 56–65 of *The Mystery of the Missing Ski Poles* with students.

ebook
online coach

Differentiated Reader Pages 66–77

Revisit the KWL charts students began on Day 2, and ask students to share what they've learned. Discuss how the selection answers the Focus Question: *What is life like in the Mountain States?*

Introduce Differentiated Vocabulary ✓ tested

Have students complete the Vocabulary Rating Sheet (Resource Master 4).

Vocabulary Routine	
Define	**Responsible** (p. 66) means "in charge of, able to be trusted with."
Example	Students must be responsible for their own homework.
Ask	What are you responsible for?

Linger (p. 70) means "to be slow to leave." *Grace and Jacqueline lingered after everyone else left.* What is another word or phrase that means the same as *linger*?

Accuse (p. 71) means "to blame or charge someone of a wrongdoing." *Don't accuse someone of something that you're not sure they did.* What reason might you have to *accuse* someone?

Partners continue the routine with *mischievous* (p. 74), using the Glossary definitions and sentences and asking questions.

ASSIGN   RESOURCE MASTER **4**   epractice vocabulary activities

Preview/Predict/Set Purposes

Display the KWL charts that students started yesterday and have them record what they want to learn as they read today. Preview the selection and have students predict what will happen. Remind students that they will also read to answer the Focus Question.

Read

Guide Comprehension

Students will read pages 66–77 of *The Mystery of the Missing Ski Poles* on their own. Remind students to use the skills and strategies they learned in whole group as they read. Circulate to reinforce concepts.

PAGES 66–72 How does the author's use of descriptive language help you visualize the story? **VISUALIZE**

PAGES 73–77 Prompt students to discuss how the sequence of the story helps them follow the plot more closely. **SEQUENCE EVENTS** **a**

Respond and Write

Have students complete their KWL charts and tell how the last half of the story answers the Focus Question.

scaffolding options

ELL Support

See page 298 of this Teacher's Lesson Guide for vocabulary and instructional support of English language learners at the Benchmark level.

a Challenge

CONFLICT AND RESOLUTION
Ask students to discuss the conflict and resolution in *The Mystery of the Missing Ski Poles*. Then challenge students to think of a different conflict and resolution that could have taken place in the same setting. Have them write brief summaries of their new conflict-resolution relationships.

Differentiated Reading
small groups

Objectives
Students will:
- Use differentiated vocabulary
- Reinforce sequencing events
- Reinforce analyzing descriptive language
- Reinforce literary elements
- Read about the turkey maiden

Prepare to Read

Review

Revisit pages 56–65 of *The Turkey Maiden* with students. Have them retell the main events and

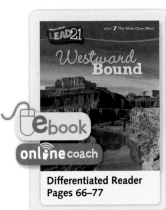

Differentiated Reader Pages 66–77

describe the setting and characters. Remind students of the quickwrite they began the day before and have them summarize what they wrote. As a group, discuss how the selection answers the Focus Question: *What is life like in the Mountain States?* Encourage students to use new vocabulary when discussing theme concepts.

Introduce
Differentiated Vocabulary

Have students complete the Vocabulary Rating Sheet (Resource Master 4).

Vocabulary Routine	
Define	A **garment** (p. 67) is a piece of clothing.
Example	The seamstress sewed a garment made of silk.
Ask	What is an example of a type of garment?

Unlatched (p. 70) means "opened or unlocked." *Terry unlatched the gate to let the dogs out.* Name two things in your house that can be *unlatched*.

Partners continue the routine with *befriend* (p. 72) and *recover* (p. 76), using the Glossary definitions and sentences and asking questions.

ASSIGN | RESOURCE MASTER 4 | 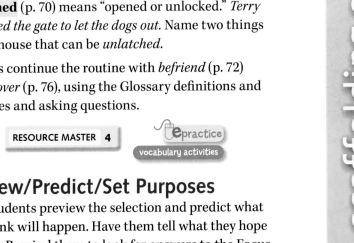 epractice vocabulary activities

Preview/Predict/Set Purposes

Have students preview the selection and predict what they think will happen. Have them tell what they hope to learn. Remind them to look for answers to the Focus Question and information to add to their quickwrites.

Read

Guide Comprehension

Students will finish reading *The Turkey Maiden* independently. Remind them to use the skills and strategies they learned in whole group as they read. After students read, use the following prompts:

PAGES 66–71 How does the author describe the way the maiden is transformed after she visits the turkey pen? How did the descriptive language improve this part of the story? **ANALYZE**

PAGES 72–77 How is the conflict resolved? Why was the resolution not necessarily a happy ending? **EVALUATE** [a]

Respond and Write

Ask students to add their final thoughts to their quickwrites and summarize how what they read today helps answer the Focus Question.

scaffolding options

ELL Support

See page 299 of this Teacher's Lesson Guide for vocabulary and instructional support of English language learners at the Advanced level.

[a] Literacy Builder

COMPREHENSION: SEQUENCE EVENTS
The Turkey Maiden is a story within a story. Have students list the sequence of events for each story in separate sequence charts. Then have them cut their sequence charts into individual strips and exchange with partners. Partners will assemble the correct sequence for the entire selection.

Share, Connect, Assess

Wrap Up
whole group

Objectives
Students will:
• Summarize selections
• Make text-to-world connections
• Write about changing their mind
• Monitor their progress

Share Text Connections

Building Classroom Community

Make Text-to-World Connections Bring students back together from their small groups to summarize their selections.

• Encourage students to use theme and other academic vocabulary in their summaries.

• As students discuss the texts, help them to make connections between texts and the world. For example, *How Paul Bunyan Shaped the West* is a folktale that talks about a character who helped shape the landforms in the West. Explain that many countries around the world have similar folktales.

• Ask students to share the activities they completed during Respond and Write.

• Have students share how what they've read answers the week's Focus Question.

etools 21
theme wall

Daily Writing

Have students write about a time they liked something after learning more about it. Encourage them to describe why they changed their mind.

For additional writing practice, remind students to access the Story Starter from their student Home Page.

etools 21
• writing tool
• story starter

Student Self Assessment

• Remind students that they are responsible for their learning and that it is helpful to be aware of how well they understand what they are reading, writing, talking, and thinking about in the classroom.

• You may want students to reflect on their reading and learning by using their Personal Reading Logs and My Daily Progress sheets (Resource Masters 1, 3).

ASSIGN **RESOURCE MASTER 1, 3**

Daily Progress Monitoring

To ensure that students have mastered the day's skills and strategies, monitor their success in completing the following independent work:

• **Vocabulary:** Practice Companion, pp. 238–239
• **Comprehension:** Practice Companion, p. 243
• **Word Study:** Practice Companion, p. 244
• **Spelling:** Practice Companion, p. 233
• **Fluency:** Practice Companion, p. 234
• **Study Station Work Record:** Resource Master 2
• **Self Assessment:** Resource Masters 1–3

epractice
reporting

Home Connection

Distribute the Unit 7 Take-Home Activities from the Home Connection book. Tell students to complete the activities with their caregivers.

Week 3 Day 4

Lesson Highlights

- Extend Vocabulary
- Reinforce Comprehension Strategy: Make Predictions
- Use Text Evidence
- Reinforce Word Study: Negative Prefixes
- Draft an Autobiography, pp. 274–275

Materials

	Teacher's Lesson Guide	Student Components	Digital 21
Interactive Reading	pp. 186–189	• Theme Reader, pp. 409–438 • Practice Companion, pp. 231–232, 234–237, 244 • Resource Masters 14, 21	**ebook** online coach · **epractice** word study games
Differentiated Reading	pp. 190–195, 296–299 (ELL)	• Differentiated Readers • Resource Masters 14, 18, 22	**ebook** online coach · **epractice** vocabulary activities
Wrap Up	p. 196	• Resource Masters 1–3	**etools 21** • theme wall • writing tool • story starter
Writing and Language Arts	pp. 274–275	• Writing Models Chart, pp. 52–53 • Practice Companion, pp. 268, 272	**etools 21** writing tool

Tips for Success

- Guide students to use multiple strategies as they read (Model Multiple Strategies, p. 187).
- If students work on their writing during Independent Practice, encourage them to make connections between reading and writing.

 Remind students to work on their Inquiry Projects during Independent Practice or Self-Selected Reading time.

Oral Language and Vocabulary

Interactive Reading whole group

Objectives
Students will:
• Extend the theme
• Extend theme vocabulary

Extend the Theme

Recall the Theme Question: *What makes the West exceptional?* Point out that this week students have been learning about the history and culture of the region. Say:

Theme Reader Pages 377–438

> How can stories help us understand things about real life? As you think about *Juan Verdades: The Man Who Couldn't Tell a Lie*, consider how the author used characteristics of the West in the story.
>
> Think about what you already know about the West, and ask yourself how the story adds to your understanding.

Have students share their thoughts in small groups. To help students get started, model your thinking:

> **think aloud**
> I could see from the illustrations that the story took place in another time because of the way people dressed, how the buildings looked, and the fact that there weren't any cars. People got around using carts pulled by animals. When I think about how the author portrays life in the West in the past, it helps me understand what defines the region.

Remind students to revisit the Theme Reader to guide their conversations.

Extend Theme Vocabulary

Distribute T-Charts (Resource Master 14) to partners. Draw a T-chart on chart paper, listing the vocabulary in the left column.

• Partners will first review the theme vocabulary definitions.

• Partners will use their own experiences or their Theme or Differentiated Readers to help them think of other words that relate to the theme vocabulary.

• Remind students that related words may be words that have related meanings, examples of the word, or words with similar word parts.

To help partners get started, model your thinking:

> **think aloud**
> When I look at the word *fulfill*, I think of the word *happy*. People who have dreams fulfilled must feel very happy. I can also add *dreams* to the chart, since I have often heard people say we should fulfill our dreams.

Theme Vocabulary	Related Words
fulfill	happy, dreams
exchange	
treasure	

After partners have completed their T-charts, have them form small groups to share what they wrote and explain their thinking to each other. **a**

ASSIGN

RESOURCE MASTER	14
PRACTICE COMPANION	231

model
read · share

Read and Comprehend

Objectives
Students will:
• Reinforce making predictions

REINFORCE **COMPREHENSION STRATEGY**

Make Predictions

Define

Ask students to recall how to make predictions. Revisit the T-chart used to record predictions on Day 2 and have students tell how it helped them understand what they read.

Remind students that readers use multiple strategies as they read. Invite students to share other strategies they know.

Model Multiple-Strategy Use

Use page 428 from the Theme Reader to model using multiple strategies:

 When I initially read this page, I asked questions to check my understanding. I wasn't sure who Juan Verdades was talking to. When I reread it, I answered this question when I realized that Juan Verdades was talking to himself to practice what he would say to don Ignacio about the apples.

I predicted that he wouldn't use these ideas when he did talk to don Ignacio because he just didn't seem happy with them. As I kept reading, I confirmed this prediction.

Guided Practice

Have partners record the strategies they use in Use Multiple Strategies (Resource Master 21) as they read pages 425–427.

• Circulate to provide support as needed, suggesting strategies and asking guiding questions.

• After partners have finished, lead a class discussion about the strategies they used.

Independent Practice

Have students independently continue to read the selection and apply multiple strategies.

Have them add information to Resource Master 21.

ASSIGN	RESOURCE MASTER	21
	PRACTICE COMPANION	236–237

scaffolding options

a Challenge

VOCABULARY
Challenge students to think of experiences or situations from their own lives, from their reading, or from the world that exemplify each word.

For example, students might share about a possession they treasured that they lost and then found, and how they felt about it.

b Challenge

MULTIPLE-STRATEGY USE
Challenge students to use multiple strategies as they read. Have students practice using the strategies with partners and model their thinking as they read together. Then encourage volunteers to share with the class their thought processes about using multiple comprehension strategies.

c ELL Support

MULTIPLE-STRATEGY USE
Pair English language learners with native English speakers. Have the native English speakers demonstrate their use of multiple strategies by thinking through their thought processes aloud. Ask the English language learners to explain their partners' uses of multiple strategies and to demonstrate their own uses by thinking aloud. Have the native English speakers provide support and feedback to their partners.

Read and Comprehend (continued)

Interactive Reading whole group

Prepare to Read

Use Text Evidence

Remind students that they have been reading *Juan Verdades: The Man Who Couldn't Tell a Lie* to answer the Theme Question: *What makes the West exceptional?* Explain to students that when readers read for specific information, they can use evidence from the text to support their answers.

**Theme Reader
Pages 409–438**

Explain that students will use a T-Chart (Resource Master 14) to record their text evidence.

Remind them to skim and scan the selection to find relevant information that relates to the Theme Question. **a**

ASSIGN   PRACTICE COMPANION   **14**

Set Purposes

Students will reread pages 409–438 to find text evidence that answers the Theme Question: *What makes the West exceptional?*

Read Together

Start a T-chart on chart paper. Model skimming pages 409–413 for text evidence and use the T-chart to record your findings. **b**

 think aloud The pictures at the beginning of the selection show wide-open spaces, which reminds me of the theme title, *The Wide-Open West*. I definitely think wide-open spaces are something that makes the West special, or exceptional. Even though it isn't put into actual words, this is text evidence that helps me answer the Theme Question.

Juan Verdades: The Man Who Couldn't Tell a Lie	
What makes the West exceptional?	
Page #	**Text Evidence**
409–411	The illustrations show wide-open spaces.
413	Ranchers lived far apart from one another.
414	There are many Spanish words here and throughout the story, which shows the culture and history of the region.
416	Don Arturo and his wife are worried about losing the ranch. This shows that ranching was an important way people made a living in the region.

- Have partners continue to read and complete their own charts.
- Pause students throughout the reading and encourage volunteers to add information they found to the chart paper.

Respond

Have partners share the text evidence they have gathered. Discuss how the ideas they recorded tell why the West is exceptional. Then ask:

How does using evidence help you better answer the Theme Question?

Writer's Response ★

Have students choose one activity:

- What do you think would have happened if Juan Verdades had decided to lie? Write about it.
- Write a letter to the author. Share what you enjoyed about the story, and ask any questions you might have.

model read share

Word Work and Fluency

Objectives
Students will:
- Practice spelling three-syllable words
- Reinforce prefixes *un-*, *de-*, *dis-*, *counter-*, *mis-*
- Practice fluent reading

Spelling

Practice Test

Have partners dictate the spelling words to one another. Then have them self-correct their papers. Remind them to focus their studying on words they misspelled.

ASSIGN | PRACTICE COMPANION **232**

Word Study

Reinforce Prefixes *un-*, *de-*, *dis-*, *counter-*, *mis-*

Review that the prefixes *un-*, *de-*, *dis-*, *counter-*, and *mis-* mean "opposite" or "not." Remind students that prefixes help readers understand a word's meaning. Provide examples and have partners discuss what each one means.

> deforestation   disappear
> dehydration   dishonest
> uncover   counterclockwise
> unfair   misunderstand

Practice/Apply

Have students write sentences using the example words and share them with their partners.

ASSIGN | PRACTICE COMPANION **244**
epractice
word study games

Fluency

Personal Rehearsal

Read "Roaring Downriver" (Practice Companion, p. 234) with appropriate pacing, speeding up slightly during the exciting descriptions of the rapids.

Ask partners to rehearse the selection and complete the Reading Response Form (Practice Companion, p. 235).

ASSIGN | PRACTICE COMPANION **234–235**

scaffolding options

a Intervention for Acceleration

USE TEXT EVIDENCE
Support students as they look for text evidence in a fiction selection by explaining:

> You can find evidence to answer the Theme Question in a fiction story by noticing how the setting, the characters' actions, and the problems characters face tell about the region.

b ELL Support

BUILD COMPREHENSION
If English language learners struggle to understand events and concepts in *Juan Verdades: The Man Who Couldn't Tell a Lie*, ask students to act out the story as others take turns reading parts of it aloud. Have students represent all characters: don Ignacio, don Arturo, Juan Verdades, Araceli, don Ignacio's wife, and the other rancheros.

Differentiated Reading
small groups

Read and Comprehend   Intensive

Objectives
Students will:
- Extend vocabulary
- Reread to find text evidence
- Reinforce making predictions
- Reinforce sequencing events

Prepare to Read

Extend Vocabulary   *tested*

Tell students that one way to extend their vocabulary knowledge is by linking words to other related words.

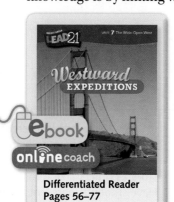

Differentiated Reader
Pages 56–77

Explain that words may be synonyms, antonyms, or have related word parts. One word might also be an example of another word.

Write the following word pairs on the board:

> wilderness/uselessness (related word parts)
> haul/carry (synonyms)
> knapsack/backpack (synonyms)
> tough/weak (antonyms)
> buckle/smooth (antonyms)
> canteen/water bottle (synonyms)
> stagger/stumble (synonyms)
> canyon/landform (example)

Have students describe the relationships between the words.

vocabulary activities

Set Purposes

Students will revisit *How Paul Bunyan Shaped the West* to find and record text evidence to support answers to the Focus Question: *What is life like in the Mountain States?*

Use Text Evidence

Distribute a T-Chart (Resource Master 14). When students find a fact or detail that might help them answer the Focus Question, they should record it in their charts.

Help students get started by reading aloud page 58. Model your thinking as you read.

think aloud As I skim the first pages of the story, I notice that all of the action takes place in Minnesota. I know from Unit 5 that Minnesota is part of the Midwest, so these pages will not help me answer the Focus Question. I will continue scanning for words that relate back to the Focus Question.

ASSIGN   RESOURCE MASTER **14**

Read

Guide Comprehension

Have partners continue to reread *How Paul Bunyan Shaped the West.* Ask pairs to skim and scan for text evidence to record in their charts. Students should pause to share their notes with the group and self-check their progress frequently. Use the prompts below to provide support as needed. **a**

PAGES 56–59 Have partners discuss why Paul Bunyan's boss sent him to look for other forests to cut down. *(He had cut down all of the trees in his section of the logging camp.)* IDENTIFY CAUSE AND EFFECT

PAGES 60–66 What are the important events that take place in Chapter 3? *(Babe ate all the grass in Nebraska, and Paul and Babe dragged rocks to make a fire, which formed the Rocky Mountains in Colorado.)* SEQUENCE EVENTS **b**

PAGES 66–73 Invite students to tell about the setting and characters, and how this information helps them understand what life was like in the Mountain States long ago. USE TEXT EVIDENCE

Have partners discuss how the illustrations add information to the text, and how they answer the Focus Question. USE GRAPHIC SOURCES

PAGES 74–77 Have partners discuss why they think the author wrote the selection. *(Possible response: to tell a fun story about Paul Bunyan)* DETERMINE AUTHOR'S PURPOSE

What do you think happened to Paul Bunyan and Babe once they got to the forests in the Pacific Northwest? *(Students' answers should reflect what they have already learned about Paul in the story.)* MAKE PREDICTIONS

Respond and Write

Have students look over the text evidence they've gathered and share one or two items with the group. Guide students to understand how the information from the text helps them answer the Focus Question.

Prepare to Share

Tell students they will discuss **Think Back** on page 78 of their Differentiated Readers tomorrow with their mixed groups.

1. **Check Understanding** After students have completed the activity independently, bring them together to share their ideas about what life was like in the Mountain States.

2. **Understand Literary Elements** Review with students that conflict is a problem in the story and that resolution is the solving of that problem. Have students share an example of a conflict and a resolution.

3. **Share and Compare** Have partners complete the activity. Discuss which characteristics the partners identified as the same, and which characteristics they identified as different.

4. **Think Critically** Complete this activity as a group. Emphasize that students should use their prior knowledge to help them answer the question.

scaffolding options

ELL Support

See page 296 of this Teacher's Lesson Guide for vocabulary and instructional support of English language learners at the Intensive level.

a Intervention for Acceleration

REREAD
If students have difficulty answering the prompts, have them reread the section of the text to scan for answers. You may wish to offer additional clues or answer choices to guide students.

b Literacy Builder

COMPREHENSION: SEQUENCE EVENTS
To help students understand the events in the story, have them complete a Time Line (Resource Master 18) for the selection. Have partners compare time lines and use them to retell the events of the story.

ASSIGN   RESOURCE MASTER **18**

ebook online coach

Intervention for Acceleration

Students can use the support features in the eBook version of the Differentiated Reader.

Read and Comprehend   Strategic

Objectives
Students will:
• Extend vocabulary
• Reread to find text evidence
• Reinforce making predictions
• Reinforce sequencing events

Prepare to Read

Extend Vocabulary

Explain that one way to expand vocabulary knowledge is to make word associations. List the differentiated

ebook
online coach

Differentiated Reader
Pages 56–77

vocabulary on the board: *weary, astonish, stable, slumber, rejoice, obviously, tempt, wicked.*

Say a vocabulary word aloud. Have students silently think and record the first word that comes to mind.

Model making an association by thinking aloud.

 The vocabulary word is *weary.* The first word that comes to my mind is *nap* because when I am weary, I want to take a nap.

Invite students to respond. Remind them that there are no right or wrong answers. Repeat the activity for the remaining words.

epractice
vocabulary activities

Set Purposes

Students will revisit *Foolish Juan and the Sacks of Gold* to find and record text evidence to support answers to the Focus Question: *What is life like in the Mountain States?*

Use Text Evidence

Distribute a T-Chart (Resource Master 14). When students find a fact or detail that might help them answer the Focus Question, they should record it in their charts.

Help students get started by reading aloud page 58. Model your thinking as you read.

think aloud The Focus Question is *What is life like in the Mountain States?* When I see something in the text that answers that question, I will write it in my chart. I read on page 58 that Juan and his wife live in an adobe house. I know that this is normal in some parts of the West because of the extreme temperatures there. I will write that in my chart because it is text evidence that answers the Focus Question. **a**

ASSIGN   RESOURCE MASTER **14**

Read

Guide Comprehension

Have partners continue to reread *Foolish Juan and the Sacks of Gold.* Have them work together to record text evidence in their charts. Use the prompts below to provide support as needed.

PAGES 56–59 What happened to Juan and his wife on Monday? *(Juan found some gold on the side of the road, and Rosa devised a plan to keep them safe from thieves.)* SUMMARIZE

PAGES 60–67 Guide students to identify and retell the sequence of events of Tuesday and Wednesday. SEQUENCE EVENTS

PAGES 68–75 Invite students to share the conflict that arose on these pages and what Rosa tries to do to help resolve the conflict. LITERARY ELEMENTS **b**

Assign students or partners paragraphs. Have students reread their paragraphs looking for answers to the Focus Question. Then ask students to share with the group any evidence they find that helps answer the Focus Question. USE TEXT EVIDENCE

PAGES 76–77 Think about how the resolution in the story helps you learn about life in the Mountain States. *(Possible response: Rosa and Juan go into town on a wagon, so they must be far away from town. Also, the bank uses a train to transport gold coins; gold was abundant in the West because of the gold rush.)* USE TEXT EVIDENCE

Based on what you know about Rosa, make a prediction about what she will do with the remaining 49 coins.
MAKE PREDICTIONS

Respond and Write

Have students look over the text evidence they've gathered and share one or two items with the group. Guide students to understand how the information from the text helps them answer the Focus Question.

Prepare to Share

Tell students they will discuss **Think Back** on page 78 of their Differentiated Readers tomorrow with their mixed groups.

1. **Check Understanding** After students have completed the activity independently, bring them together to share their ideas about what life was like in the Mountain States.

2. **Understand Literary Elements** Review with students that a conflict is a problem in a story, and a resolution is the solving of that problem. Have students share an example of a problem and a solution.

3. **Share and Compare** Have partners complete the activity. Discuss which characteristics the partners identified as the same, and which characteristics they identified as different.

4. **Think Critically** Complete this activity as a group. Emphasize that students should use their prior knowledge to help them answer the question.

scaffolding options

ELL Support

See page 297 of this Teacher's Lesson Guide for vocabulary and instructional support of English language learners at the Strategic level.

a Intervention for Acceleration

USE TEXT EVIDENCE
If students have difficulty understanding which information they should record, remind them that they are looking for text that will help them answer the Focus Question. Write the Focus Question on the board and have students refer to it while rereading the selection.

b Intervention for Acceleration

USE LITERARY ELEMENTS
To help students who may not clearly understand the idea of conflict resolution, have partners complete an Event Summary (Resource Master 22) about the story. Discuss the event's details as a group, and then ask students to name the conflict and how it was resolved.

ASSIGN   RESOURCE MASTER **22**

ebook onl?ne coach
Intervention for Acceleration

Students can use the support features in the eBook version of the Differentiated Reader.

Read and Comprehend Benchmark

Objectives
Students will:
- Extend vocabulary
- Reread to find text evidence
- Reinforce making predictions
- Reinforce sequencing events

Differentiated Reading *small groups*

Prepare to Read

Extend Vocabulary

Explain that one way to expand vocabulary is to pair words by their relationships, such as synonyms, antonyms, or examples. Read the following clues and have students name the related vocabulary.

LEAD21 *unit 7 The Wide-Open West*

Passage to the West

ebook
online coach

Differentiated Reader Pages 56–77

- A synonym for *hotel* (**inn**)
- An antonym for *found* (**misplaced**)
- A place where you would ski (**slope**)
- A synonym for *stream* (**creek**)
- Good students are this (**responsible**)

- A synonym for *stay behind* (**linger**)
- To charge with a crime (**accuse**)
- An antonym for *well-behaved* (**mischievous**)

epractice
vocabulary activities

Set Purposes

Students will revisit *The Mystery of the Missing Ski Poles* to find and record text evidence to support answers to the Focus Question: *What is life like in the Mountain States?*

Use Text Evidence

Distribute T-charts. Students will note facts that answer the Focus Question. Have students page through the selection and discuss any examples of text evidence that answer the Focus Question.

ASSIGN **RESOURCE MASTER 14**

Read

Guide Comprehension

Students work independently to complete their charts with further text evidence. Use the following prompts to monitor students' progress.

CHAPTER 1 How do the events in Chapter 1 help you answer the Focus Question? *(I know that people come to the West for vacation and to ski on the mountains.)*
USE TEXT EVIDENCE

CHAPTER 2 Have students identify the sequence of events in Chapter 2. What details does the author include to show how well Tyrone looked for the ski pole?
SEQUENCE EVENTS

CHAPTERS 3 AND 4 Ask partners to discuss the consequences of accusing someone of something he or she didn't do. Have them provide examples from other texts, movies, or personal experiences. **MAKE CONNECTIO**

Respond and Write

1. Have students use the text evidence they found today to write a response to the Focus Question.

2. Tell students they will discuss the **Think Back** activities on page 78 when they meet with their mixed groups tomorrow.

ELL Support

See page 298 of this Teacher's Lesson Guide for vocabulary and instructional support of English language learners at the Benchmark level.

Literacy Builder

COMPREHENSION: MAKE PREDICTIONS
Invite students to recall the predictions they made before reading the story. Discuss evidence from the text that led them to confirm or revise their predictions.

Objectives
Students will:
- Extend vocabulary
- Reread to find text evidence
- Reinforce making predictions
- Reinforce sequencing events

Prepare to Read

Extend Vocabulary *tested*

Explain that one way to expand vocabulary is to pair words by their relationships, such as synonyms, antonyms, or examples. Read the following phrases and ask students to identify the vocabulary words they relate to and to tell how the words and phrases are related.

ebook
online coach

Differentiated Reader Pages 56–77

- A farmhand from the past (*peasant*, example)
- An unmarried girl (*maiden*, example)
- The word *cherished* (*sacred*, synonym)
- Giving flowers at a funeral (*sympathy*, example)
- A costume (*garment*, example)
- The word *fastened* (*unlatched*, antonym)
- The word *ignore* (*befriend*, antonym)
- The word *uncover* (*recover*, word part)

epractice
vocabulary activities

Set Purposes

Students will reread *The Turkey Maiden* to record text evidence to answer the Focus Question: *What is life like in the Mountain States?*

Use Text Evidence

Have students draw T-charts. Tell them to skim and scan the selection to note facts that will help them answer the Focus Question.

ASSIGN   RESOURCE MASTER 14

Read

Guide Comprehension

Students will work on their own to complete their charts with text evidence. Use the following prompts to lead discussion after they read. **a**

PAGES 56-59 What do we learn about the characters and setting in this part of the story? **SUMMARIZE**

PAGES 60-69 Ask students to describe the story's conflict, the solution that the maiden discovers, and how this information helps answer the Focus Question. **USE LITERARY ELEMENTS**

PAGES 70-77 Have students retell the most important events that happened in the second part of the story. **DETERMINE IMPORTANT INFORMATION**

Ask students to make predictions about changes in the behavior of Elu and Lanon after learning the story of the turkey maiden. **MAKE PREDICTIONS**

Respond and Write

1. Have students use the text evidence they found today to write a response to the Focus Question.

2. Tell students they will discuss the **Think Back** activities on page 78 when they meet with their mixed groups tomorrow.

ELL Support

See page 299 of this Teacher's Lesson Guide for vocabulary and instructional support of English language learners at the Advanced level.

a Literacy Builder *tested*

COMPREHENSION: SEQUENCE EVENTS
Assign students different events in the story. Have them complete an Event Summary (Resource Master 22) about their event. Then have students share their event summaries in the order they occurred in the story.

ASSIGN   RESOURCE MASTER 22

Share, Connect, Assess

Wrap Up
whole group

Objectives
Students will:
- Use key concepts and vocabulary
- Use text evidence to answer essential questions
- Make text-to-text connections
- Write about finding text evidence
- Monitor their progress

Share Text Connections

Building Classroom Community

Make Text-to-Text Connections Bring students back together from their small groups to share how the text evidence they gathered from their Differentiated Reader selections helped them to answer the Focus Question: *What is life like in the Mountain States?*

- Encourage students to use theme and other academic vocabulary as they share their responses.

- Ensure that students from all groups have a chance to contribute to the discussion.

- As students share text evidence, help them make connections between texts. For example, illustrations help readers follow the story in all four Differentiated Readers.

etools 21
theme wall

Daily Writing

Ask students to write briefly about the strategy and method they used to find text evidence. Encourage them to describe how the text evidence helped them answer the Theme and Focus Questions.

For additional writing practice, remind students to access the Story Starter from their student Home Pag

etools 21
- writing tool
- story starter

Student Self Assessment

- Remind students that they are responsible for thei learning and that it is helpful to be aware of how well they understand what they are reading, writi talking, and thinking about in the classroom.

- You may want students to reflect on their reading a learning by using their Personal Reading Logs and Daily Progress sheets (Resource Masters 1, 3).

ASSIGN **RESOURCE MASTER 1, 3**

Daily Progress Monitoring

To ensure that students have mastered the day's skills and strategies, monitor their success in completing the following independent work:
- **Vocabulary:** Practice Companion, p. 231
- **Comprehension:** Practice Companion, pp. 236–237
- **Word Study:** Practice Companion, p. 244
- **Spelling:** Practice Companion, pp. 232–233
- **Fluency:** Practice Companion, pp. 234–235
- **Study Station Work Record:** Resource Master 2
- **Self Assessment:** Resource Masters 1, 3

epractice
reporting

Home Connection

Distribute the Unit 7 Take-Home Activities from the Home Connection book. Tell students to complete the activities with their caregivers.

Day at a Glance

Lesson Highlights

- Review Project Plan
- 21st Century Skills Minilesson: Evaluate Sources
- Cross-Text Sharing
- Fluency Presentation
- Spelling Posttest

Materials

	Teacher's Lesson Guide	Student Components	Digital 21
Inquiry	pp. 198–201	• Practice Companion, pp. 200, 245–246, 370, 373 • Resource Masters 25, 34–35, 37	etools 21 inquiry project
Cross-Text Sharing	pp. 202–203	• Differentiated Readers • Practice Companion, p. 247 • Resource Masters 11, 19, 26, 35	ebook online coach
Wrap Up	pp. 204–205	• Assessment Handbook, pp. 13–14, 140 • Differentiated Reader, p. 79 • Practice Companion, p. 248 • Resource Master 1	etools 21 • theme wall • writing tool • story starter

Inquiry Process Guide

Week 1, Day 5	Week 2, Day 5	Week 3, Day 5	Week 4, Day 5
1. Generate Ideas and Questions 2. Make a Conjecture 3. Make Plans to Collect Information	Days 1–4: Collect Information 4. Organize and Synthesize Information 5. Confirm or Revise Your Conjecture	Days 1–4: Collect Information 6. Develop Presentation	Days 1–4: Collect Information 7. Deliver Presentation

Tips for Success

- Provide Investigation Sheets (Resource Master 35) for students to use during the week.
- Provide Presentation Organizers (Resource Master 37) for students to use while they develop their presentations.

Develop Ideas

21ST CENTURY SKILLS

Objectives
Students will:
• Make connections between the theme question and the Inquiry project
• Review the format: time line
• Review the Inquiry process

Inquiry whole group

Review Project Plan

Connect to the Theme

Ask a volunteer to recall the Theme Question: *What makes the West exceptional?* and the Focus Question: *What is life like in the Mountain States?* Say:

> What aspects about living in a Mountain State appeal to you? How would it be the same as where you live now? How would it be different?

etools 21
inquiry project

Be sure students know to access Inquiry Project online from their student Home Page.

Discuss Previous Week

• Students take out their Inquiry folders.

• Review the Inquiry steps covered last week:

4. Organize and Synthesize Information

5. Confirm or Revise Your Conjecture

• Verify that each group has completed the items on the Week 2 Inquiry Checklist (Practice Companion, p. 216).

ASSIGN PRACTICE COMPANION **216**

Review the Format: Time Line

Tell students that a time line is one of the formats that they might consider using to share their Inquiry findings in this unit. Remind them that in a time line, events are arranged on a line in time order from left to right or from top to bottom. Review with students the time line example and characteristics on Practice Companion page 200.

Talk about time lines students may have seen or used in social studies or science textbooks. Have them tell how they were helpful.

ASSIGN PRACTICE COMPANION **200**

Model the Inquiry Process

Share New Information

Explain to students that, before planning their presentations, their groups should take turns sharing information collected independently over the past week. Remind them to revise their conjectures if necessary.

6. Develop Presentation

Choose a Format Tell students they will need to choose a format that best matches the understanding they have gained about their Inquiry Questions. Say:

> When you choose a format, think about the relationship among the ideas you are trying to show. A diagram might be a good way to show how something works, while a mural, photo essay or time line could be a good format for telling a story or showing how something changes over time.

• Use Presentation Formats (Practice Companion, page 373) to review formats students have studied previous units.

• Tell students that when they are showing a sequence of events, a time line, photo essay, mural, or play are all good ways to present their ideas.

• Talk with students about how they might use technology to help in developing their presentation formats. For example, they might make a multimedia time line or use a computer graphics program to create a diagram. [a]

• Tell students they will need to make plans for creating their presentation formats. For example, they have chosen a time line, they will need to decide what events to include, decide what section each group member will talk about, and plan and create visuals to support their time lines.

ASSIGN PRACTICE COMPANION **373**

Organize Presentation Remind students that each group will do a four to six-minute presentation to share its findings with the class. Review the Presentation Organizer (Resource Master 37) with students. Ask:

What are the main parts outlined in the Presentation Organizer? *(State Inquiry Question, Explain New Ideas and Understandings, List Sources)*

Use the sample Inquiry Question and Conjecture from Weeks 1 and 2 to model completing the Presentation Organizer. Reproduce or display on the board the format of the Presentation Organizer. For Explain New Ideas and Understandings, say:

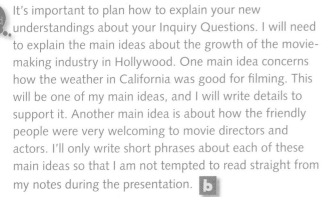 It's important to plan how to explain your new understandings about your Inquiry Questions. I will need to explain the main ideas about the growth of the movie-making industry in Hollywood. One main idea concerns how the weather in California was good for filming. This will be one of my main ideas, and I will write details to support it. Another main idea is about how the friendly people were very welcoming to movie directors and actors. I'll only write short phrases about each of these main ideas so that I am not tempted to read straight from my notes during the presentation. **b**

- Remind students that their Presentation Organizers should include whatever project formats they have chosen. If they have chosen a format such as a mural, the Explain New Understandings section of the Presentation Organizer will include a description of the mural and the main speaking points relating to it.

- Emphasize that all group members should have a speaking role in the presentations. Remind groups to decide who will deliver each section of the presentation and fill in the Presenters column in the Presentation Organizer. **c**

ASSIGN | RESOURCE MASTER 37

scaffolding options

a Literacy Builder

TECHNOLOGY FLUENCY
Students will have different levels of technology literacy. Make technology available to students in the classroom whenever possible. You may set aside time to demonstrate different technologies, such as computer graphics programs or video recorders. Or you may invite knowledgeable students to volunteer to plan their own demonstrations for the class. Encourage students to access the Inquiry Project online from their student Home Page where they will find additional instruction for using technology to develop their presentations.

b Critical Thinking

EVALUATE
Tell students that they have probably gathered a lot of information on their topics. Not all of the information needs to be included in their presentations, however. Have students determine which ideas help provide deeper understandings of their Inquiry Questions. They should include those ideas in their presentations. Then explain that they can add other ideas if they find their presentations are too short.

c ELL Support

SPEAKING SKILLS
Have each English language learner rehearse his or her portion of the presentation with a native English speaker. Have the native speaker provide support with word choice, pronunciation, and transitions.

Objectives
Students will:
- Review discussion roles
- Practice evaluating sources
- Share new information
- Choose a presentation format
- Plan their presentations
- Collaborate in Inquiry groups

Continue Inquiry Group Work

The following Resource Masters and Practice Companion pages will be used in this lesson.

Step	Resource Master	Practice Companion
All	Idea Tracker 34 Collaboration Rubric 39 Evaluation Rubric C 42	Week 3 Inquiry Checklist, p. 245 Group Roles, p. 370
6.	Investigation Sheet 35 Presentation Organizer 37	Time Line, p. 200 Inquiry Planner, p. 246 Presentation Formats, p. 373

Review Discussion Roles

Have students move into their Inquiry Groups and informally evaluate their discussions from the previous week. Write on the board the following questions:

> - Why is it important to stay on topic?
> - How can summarizing help your group stay on task?

- Review Group Discussion Roles (Practice Companion, p. 370).
- Give students the opportunity to ask clarifying questions about group roles.

ASSIGN | PRACTICE COMPANION **370**

Monitor Student Progress

Use the Collaboration Rubric (Resource Master 39) and the Inquiry Evaluation Rubric C (Resource Master 42) to monitor student progress throughout the project. Review the project expectations with students before beginning Inquiry Group work.

USE | RESOURCE MASTER **39, 42**

Minilesson: Evaluate Sources

Write on the board *relevance, currency, authority, objectivity,* and *accuracy.* Remind students that these are the five criteria for evaluating sources. Have volunteers give the definitions of each criteria. Say:

> Remember that if your source does not meet all five criteria, you may want to find a different, more reliable source for your Inquiry Question.

Have students get into their Inquiry Groups and use the Evaluating Sources Checklist (Practice Companion 372) to evaluate one source they are using for their Inquiry Projects. Have each group present the source it evaluated and explain whether it is a good source to use and why.

ASSIGN | PRACTICE COMPANION **372**

Inquiry Groups

Share New Information

- Have students take out their research notes to sha organize, and synthesize the new information.
- Students revise their conjectures as needed.
- Remind groups to follow the Week 3 Inquiry Checklist (Practice Companion, p. 245). Prompt th group Checkers to monitor their groups' progress.
- Group Discussion Monitors should prompt their groups to take turns speaking and keep the discussion on topic. **a**
- Prompt Recorders to track changes to their group conjectures using the Idea Tracker (Resource Master 34).

ASSIGN | RESOURCE MASTER **34**
| PRACTICE COMPANION **245**

6. Develop Presentation

critical thinking
make connections, evaluate

Choose a Format As students discuss what type of format to use, remind them to review Time Line and Presentation Formats (Practice Companion, pp. 200, 373) and any notes they took last week about format.

- Prompt students to consider the best format for the type of information they want to communicate.
- Guide students to identify and distribute tasks to create presentation formats. For a time line, students might first outline the events they want to include. Then they can decide who will talk about which events. **b** **c**
- Encourage students to use technology.
- Give periodic time alerts to keep groups on track.

ASSIGN PRACTICE COMPANION **200, 373**

Organize Presentation Remind the Questioners to ensure that all group members are involved in preparing the Presentation Organizers.

- As groups follow the Presentation Organizer (Resource Master 37) to plan their presentations, prompt the Group Recorder to make sure each student is assigned to a section.
- Students refer to their completed Idea Tracker (Resource Master 34) and Investigation Sheets (Resource Master 35) to plan their presentations.
- Some students may put information on note cards.
- Remind students that they will deliver their presentations next week.

ASSIGN RESOURCE MASTER **34, 35, 37**

Record Action Plan

- Remind students that they can continue to collect information and develop their presentations during independent time.
- Each student completes an Action Plan for the coming week on his or her Inquiry Planner (Practice Companion, p. 246) and places materials in his or her Inquiry folder.

ASSIGN PRACTICE COMPANION **246**

scaffolding options

a Literacy Builder

21st CENTURY SKILLS

COLLABORATION
Review with students that Inquiry Projects are a collaboration. Every group member needs to participate and be prepared. Ask:

- How does it affect the group if someone goes off topic?
- What happens when people don't do their part?

b Intervention for Acceleration

ORGANIZING IDEAS
If students are doing a time line or similar format, have them use Sequence Chart (Resource Master 25) to help them order their ideas and events before putting them on the time line.

ASSIGN RESOURCE MASTER **25**

c ELL Support

SPEAKING SKILLS
Suggest that English language learners have a visual to support their parts of the presentations. Having a visual cue can make it easier to discuss and describe the information.

Connect Ideas

Objectives
Students will:
• Share information across texts
• Use speaking and listening skills
• Make connections between the Differentiated Readers and the Inquiry project

CONNECT DIFFERENTIATED READERS

Cross-Text Sharing

While students stay in their Inquiry Groups, announce Cross-Text Sharing time. Remind students that they have read about what life is like in the Mountain States.

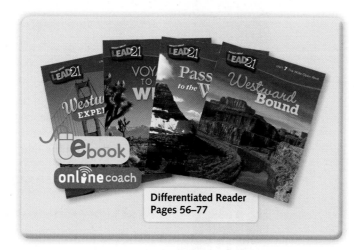

Differentiated Reader Pages 56–77

• Remind students that the four Differentiated Readers are possible sources of information to help investigate their Inquiry Questions.

• Have students from each differentiated group share the title of the selection they read, give a brief summary of the plot, and display photographs as they explain how they relate to their understanding of the story. Students may also summarize their ideas about how the selection relates to the groups' Inquiry Questions. **a**

Monitor Student Progress

As you observe and work with each group, fill in your observations using the Collaboration Rubric (Resource Master 39).

USE RESOURCE MASTER **39**

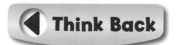

Think Back

• Have students turn to **Think Back** page 78 in the Differentiated Readers.

• Tell students they will complete Practice Companion page 247 as they do Cross-Text Shar[...]

ASSIGN PRACTICE COMPANION **247**

Check Understanding

On Practice Companion page 247, have students wr[...] about what life is like in the Mountain State they re[...] about and what they could do there. Intensive and Strategic-level students can expand on the ideas the[...] prepared on Day 4 during Prepare to Share.

Understand Literary Elements

Form mixed-level pairs within each Inquiry Group. Have each student describe the conflict, or problem[...] and solution in the story he or she read to a partner[...] Partners should discuss what challenge a character[...] faced and how he or she solved it. **b**

To facilitate discussion, ask:

• What is the conflict, or problem? What steps does [...] character take to solve it?

• How does the story end?

• Would you have solved the problem the same way? Why or why not?

Share and Compare

Have each student make a list of characteristics of t[...] Mountain States they read about. Then have partne[...] use a Venn Diagram (Resource Master 13) to compa[...] their lists.

ASSIGN RESOURCE MASTER **13**

Think Critically

Have each student give one example from his or her reading to answer the Theme Question: *What makes the West exceptional?* Have groups compare similarities and differences among their ideas and discuss which examples are given most often. For ideas, students can use the ideas that they gathered during the week's reading. Students can fill in their ideas on Practice Companion page 247. **c**

Connect to Inquiry

Before wrapping up Cross-Text Sharing, ask groups to connect what they learned in their sharing to their Inquiry Questions. Ask:

- How can you connect the ideas shared during your Cross-Text discussion to your Inquiry Question?
- What might you add to or change about your presentation, based on the discussion?

• Have groups talk about whether or not they will update their presentation plans based on what they have learned from their Differentiated Readers.

• Have students complete an Investigation Sheet (Resource Master 35) and, if needed, make any changes to their Action Plan for next week, and put their notes into their Inquiry folders.

ASSIGN   RESOURCE MASTER **35**

scaffolding options

a Intervention for Acceleration

SUMMARIZE
Have students use the Story Map (Resource Master 23) to help them summarize the selections. Students can use their completed Story Maps when they summarize for their groups.

ASSIGN   RESOURCE MASTER **23**

b ELL Support

ACADEMIC LANGUAGE
Tell Spanish speaking students that *conflict* and *conflicto* and *resolution* and *resolución* are cognates. Explain that they can use their knowledge of these words in their native language to help them understand and remember the English meaning.

c Challenge

SYNTHESIZE
Ask students to note similarities among the examples they give to answer the Theme Question. Challenge them to use the similarities to synthesize their ideas about the West and decide what things the different states in this region all have in common.

Share, Connect, Assess

Objectives
Students will:
• Perform fluent reading
• Spell three-syllable words

Wrap Up the Week
whole group

Fluency Presentation *tested*

Have students turn to "Roaring Downriver" on Practice Companion page 234. Each student will perform a reading of the interview for the class to demonstrate using good phrasing, expression, and pacing. Explain:

• Today we will be celebrating the interview we have been working on all week by presenting it to the class. As you read aloud the interview, remember to read with expression. Use your voice to show whether you are asking or answering a question.

• When you present the interview to the class, make sure that you speak at an appropriate pace. If you are presenting the interview with a partner, be sure to pause between questions and answers.

• Students may choose another selection to perform for the class.

• You may wish to give students the option of performing this week's or another fluency selection to a caregiver at home.

• As students perform, use Assessing Oral Reading, Assessment Handbook pages 13–14, to evaluate and record each student's oral reading performance.

USE ASSESSMENT HANDBOOK **13–14**

Spelling Posttest *tested*

Remind students that their spelling words have three syllables. Say a word, use it in a sentence, and say the word again. Students will write each word.

1. **example** The students read the *example* sentence before they began writing their own sentences.
2. **deliver** I have to *deliver* this note to the principal.
3. **important** There is an *important* meeting that we must attend.
4. **history** The *history* of our town dates back to the 1880s.
5. **hospital** The doctors are very busy in the *hospital*.
6. **several** We have *several* books to choose from.
7. **vacation** My family is going on *vacation* for winter break.
8. **victory** The baseball team celebrated their *victory*.
9. **imagine** I often *imagine* what it would be like to tr to space.
10. **remember** I *remember* what it was like to be youn
11. **camera** She took lots of pictures with her new *cam*
12. **library** There are many books in the *library*.
13. **tomato** There was a ripe, red *tomato* growing in the garden.
14. **memory** My favorite *memory* is the time I traveled the mountains.
15. **president** The *president* of the company is having special dinner for his employees.
16. **favorite** Strawberry ice cream is my *favorite* flavor.

Review Words
17. **squirrel** The *squirrel* gathered nuts for the winter.
18. **simple** I have a *simple* answer to your problem.

Frequently Misspelled Words
19. **probably** We will *probably* watch movies tonight, we may play video games.
20. **suddenly** *Suddenly*, we heard a crash of thunder.

Objectives
Students will:
- Use key concepts
- Make text-to-self connections
- Write a description of a job they might do in a Mountain State
- Monitor their progress

Share Text Connections

Make Text-to-Self Connections Ask students to share the theme connections they made during Cross-Text Sharing time. Continue the Theme Concept Web for Unit 7 that you began in Week 1.

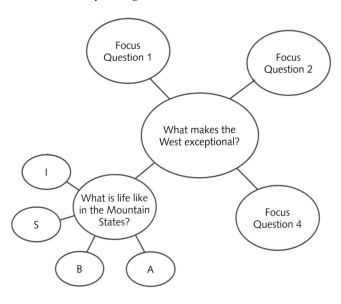

Write the Theme Question in the center circle and this week's Focus Question in one of the four connecting circles.

- For each Differentiated Reader, have students share a concept or main idea that connects to the Focus and Theme Questions.

- As students discuss their connections from their Differentiated Readers, fill in the outermost circles.

- Have students think about how this helps them address the Theme Question. Ask:

  How would you describe life in the Mountain States?
  What is exceptional about this part of the United States?

- Save the Theme Concept Web and build on it over the next week.

theme wall

Think Ahead

Have students open their Differentiated Readers to page 79 and begin thinking about the selection they will read next week.

Read aloud next week's Focus Question: *What is life like in the Pacific States?* Then read the **Selection Connection** and **Show What You Know** activities. Have students write their answers to these activities on Practice Companion page 248.

ASSIGN PRACTICE COMPANION 248

Daily Writing

Ask students to write a help-wanted ad for a job they might do in the Mountain States. Have them include specific details about the job.

- writing tool
- story starter

Student Self Assessment

- You may want students to reflect on their learning by using My Daily Progress sheet, Resource Master 1.

- Remind students to note the concepts and skills for which they could use more support.

ASSIGN RESOURCE MASTER 1

Weekly Progress Monitoring

Use the following assessment tools to check students' weekly progress following independent and mixed-group work:

- **Practice Companion:** pp. 230–244
- **Fluency Presentation**
- **Spelling Posttest**
- **Think Back** and **Think Ahead, Differentiated Reader:** pp. 78–79
- **Assessing Oral Reading, Assessment Handbook:** pp. 13–14
- **Weekly Observation Record, Assessment Handbook:** p. 140

reporting

Week 4 Planner

Interactive Reading
WHOLE GROUP | 25–35 mins.

tested ✓

	Oral Language	Vocabulary	Read Together	Comprehension	Word Study and Phonics	Spelling	Fluenc
Day 1	Build Theme Connections	Build ✓ Vocabulary Connections	Reread Theme Reader, pp. 380–438	Use Text Evidence	Introduce ✓ Silent Consonants	Spelling ✓ Pretest Introduce Silent Consonants	Introduce and Mode "At the Tra End"
Day 2	Build Theme Connections	Build ✓ Vocabulary Connections	Reread Theme Reader, pp. 380–438	Review ✓ Comprehension Strategy Determine Important Information	Reinforce ✓ Silent Consonants	Practice ✓ Silent Consonants	Shared Choral Reading "At the Tra End"
Day 3	Build Theme Connections	Use Multiple ✓ Vocabulary Strategies	Reread Theme Reader, pp. 380–438	Review ✓ Comprehension Skill Recall and Retell	Review ✓ Contractions epractice	Practice ✓ Silent Consonants	Paired Reading "At the Tra End"
Day 4	Build Theme Connections	Build ✓ Vocabulary Connections	Reread Theme Reader, pp. 380–438	Reinforce ✓ Comprehension Strategy Determine Important Information	Reinforce ✓ Contractions epractice	Practice ✓ Silent Consonants	Personal Rehearsal "At the Tra End"

Day 5 — Inquiry and 21st Century Skills

etools 21 — inquiry project

21st CENTURY SKILLS

Review Project Plan	Model the Inquiry Process	Continue Inquiry Group Work
Connect to the Theme	Share New Information	Review Discussion Roles
Discuss Previous Week	7. Deliver Presentation	Monitor Student Progress
	Minilesson: Consider Your Audience	Identify New Questions

Theme Reader — Pages 380–438

Weekly Vocabulary

extremes
irrigated
arid
missionary
film
rugged
fulfill
treasure
exchange

ebook
online coach

Selection 4: Differentiated Readers — Pages 80–10

Intensive

Weekly Vocabulary

hardship
rally
blistering
landmark
commotion
frail
ailing
wary

ebook
online coach

Strategic

Weekly Vocabulary

pristine
alert
muffle
stride
hideous
continenta
scrape
replenish

ebook
online coach

Differentiated Reading
SMALL GROUPS | 60–80 mins.

Wrap Up
WHOLE GROUP | 5–10 mins.

Writing and Language Arts
WHOLE GROUP | 30 mins.

etools 21
- theme wall
- writing tool
- story starter
- interactive glossary

Read and Comprehend

Share, Connect, Assess

Writing Process and Grammar Suggested Pacing Guide

Build Vocabulary Connections ✓

Read Across Texts

Share Text Connections

Daily Writing

Student Self Assessment

Daily Progress Monitoring

Home Connection

Draft
Autobiography

Traits Focus ✓
Word Choice
Sentence Fluency

Introduce Differentiated Vocabulary ✓
Read about Alaska, the Oregon Trail, railroad expansion, or a folktale about the sun in the first half of Selection 4.

Reinforce Comprehension Strategy ✓
Determine Important Information

Share Text Connections

Daily Writing

Student Self Assessment

Daily Progress Monitoring

Home Connection

Revise
Autobiography

Traits Focus ✓
Sentence Fluency
Conventions

Grammar ✓
Avoid Double Negatives

Introduce Differentiated Vocabulary ✓
🖱 practice
Read about Alaska, the Oregon Trail, railroad expansion, or a folktale about the sun in the second half of Selection 4.

Reinforce Comprehension Skill ✓
Recall and Retell

Share Text Connections

Daily Writing

Student Self Assessment

Daily Progress Monitoring

Home Connection

Edit
Autobiography

Traits Focus ✓
Conventions

Grammar ✓
Recognize Troublesome Word Groups

Extend Vocabulary
🖱 practice

Reread Differentiated Readers, pp. 80–103

Reinforce Comprehension Strategy ✓
Determine Important Information

Share Text Connections

Daily Writing

Student Self Assessment

Daily Progress Monitoring

Home Connection

Publish and Present
Autobiography

Traits Focus ✓
Presentation

Mixed Groups

Weekly Assessment

Cross-Text Sharing

Think Back

Connect to Inquiry

Fluency Presentation ✓

Spelling Posttest ✓

Inquiry Project Presentation ✓

Weekly Progress Monitoring

Writing Models Chart

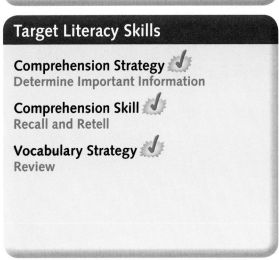

Writing Model
Autobiography,
pp. 52–55

Selection 4: Differentiated Readers   Pages 80–103

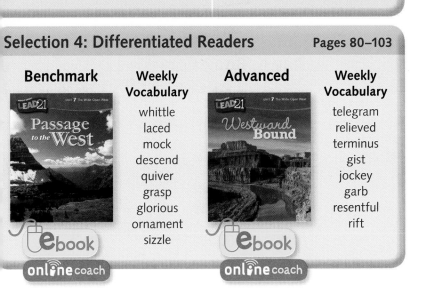

Benchmark

Weekly Vocabulary
whittle
laced
mock
descend
quiver
grasp
glorious
ornament
sizzle

Passage to the West

🖱 ebook
online coach

Advanced

Westward Bound

Weekly Vocabulary
telegram
relieved
terminus
gist
jockey
garb
resentful
rift

🖱 ebook
online coach

Target Literacy Skills

Comprehension Strategy ✓
Determine Important Information

Comprehension Skill ✓
Recall and Retell

Vocabulary Strategy ✓
Review

Daily Small-Group Rotation

	Small-Group, Teacher-Led Instruction	Independent Practice	Self-Selected Reading	Study Station Flip Charts
	When the teacher is with these groups…	these groups rotate through independent activities.		
Session 1	Intensive	Advanced	Benchmark	Strategic
Session 2	Strategic	Intensive	Advanced	Benchmark
Session 3	Benchmark	Strategic	Intensive	Advanced
Session 4	Advanced	Benchmark	Strategic	Intensive

Study Station Flip Charts, page 28

Day 1: Vocabulary Central

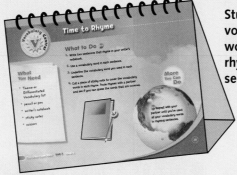

Students use vocabulary words in rhyming sentences.

Day 2: Writer's Desk

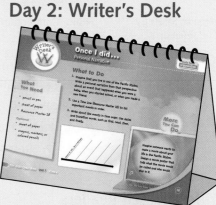

Students write a personal narrative.

Day 3: Word World

Students use contractions to tell what they have and have not done.

Day 4: Book Corner

Students listen to reading and ask and answer questions.

Week 4 Planner

Day at a Glance

Lesson Highlights

- Build Vocabulary Connections
- Read Across Texts
- Spelling Pretest: Silent Consonants
- Draft an Autobiography, pp. 276–277

Materials

	Teacher's Lesson Guide	Student Components	Digital 21
Interactive Reading	pp. 210–213	• Theme Reader, pp. 380–438 • Practice Companion, pp. 249–250, 254–255 • Resource Masters 6, 14	ebook online coach
Differentiated Reading	pp. 214–219	• Differentiated Readers • Resource Master 20	ebook online coach
Wrap Up	p. 220	• Resource Masters 1–3	etools 21 • theme wall • writing tool • story starter
Writing and Language Arts	pp. 276–277	• Writing Models Chart, pp. 52–53 • Practice Companion, pp. 268–269	etools 21 writing tool

Tips for Success

- You may wish to have students begin the Weekly Planner on Practice Companion page 249.
- Introduce the Study Stations (Flip Charts, p. 28) and arrange materials for the week.
- **21st CENTURY SKILLS** Remind students to work on their Inquiry Projects during Independent Practice or Self-Selected Reading time.
- Set out theme-related reference materials for students to use during the week. Refer also to the Theme Bibliography, pages 304–305.

Oral Language and Vocabulary

Interactive Reading whole group

Objectives
Students will:
• Make connections to the theme
• Make vocabulary connections

Build Theme Connections

Ask students to turn to page 378 of their Theme Readers and read the first Focus Question: *How are geography and economy connected in the Mountain States?*

Theme Reader Pages 377–438

Prompt students to make connections to the Focus Question by asking questions like these:

• Where else have you heard or read about this question? Have you read books or seen television programs that discuss the Mountain States? What did they say?

• Now that you've learned more about this question, what is your opinion of the Mountain States? **a**

To demonstrate how to begin a conversation, share your thinking:

 One thing I know about this question is that farming is still the main source of income for many families in the Mountain States. I know this because we have read several stories about life in the Mountain States.

Have partners discuss the questions before sharing their ideas with the class. Finally, lead a discussion about how answering the Focus Question helps students better understand what makes the West exceptional.

Discuss the Inquiry Project

 21ˢᵗ CENTURY SKILLS

Remind students that they will present their Inquiry findings this week.

• Remind students to continue to research and work on their presentations during Independent Practice or Self-Selected Reading time.

• Encourage students to continue to post their ideas and questions on the Question Board.

 etools 21 theme wall — Students can also use the Theme Wall to post ideas and images.

Build Vocabulary Connections

tested ✓

Write the theme vocabulary words on the board.

Theme Vocabulary		
extreme	fulfill	rugged
arid	exchange	film
irrigated	treasure	missionary

• Have students recall their definitions and examples. Record the information on the board.

• Ask students to make connections among the words by generating sentences that contain two of the words. Record their ideas on the board.

• Model a sentence to get them started. **b**

The *irrigated* crops did well even with the *extreme* temperatures this season.

ASSIGN PRACTICE COMPANION **250**

model read share

Read and Comprehend

Objectives
Students will:
- Connect themes across texts
- Reread to find text evidence

Prepare to Read

Use Text Evidence

Remind students that when they read to find answers to a question, they can skim and scan the text to find evidence. Remind students that they've been using T-charts to record text evidence throughout the unit.

Theme Reader
Pages 380–438

Set Purposes

Recall Focus Question 1: *How are geography and economy connected in the Mountain States?* Explain that students will use *A Tour of the Western Region* and *Juan Verdades: The Man Who Couldn't Tell a Lie* to find text evidence that answers this question.

ASSIGN RESOURCE MASTER **14**

Read Across Texts

Have students read independently or with partners to find text evidence. Ask questions such as these: **c**

PAGES 380–408 When I skim pages 386–387, I see that farming is essential to the Western Region. How else do people use the geography to earn a living?

PAGES 409–438 On page 413, the men standing around are identified as ranchers. What does this tell you about the geography and economy of the region?

Respond

Invite students to use the text evidence they've gathered to craft responses to the Focus Question.

Partner Talk

Provide these discussion points:
- Which selection was more interesting to you? Why?
- Which would you recommend to a friend? Why?

scaffolding options

a ELL Support

CONCEPT DEVELOPMENT
Build understanding of the Theme and Focus Questions by reviewing the key concepts of *geography* and *economy*. Ask students to name examples of geographical features and different ways that geography is connected to the economy in the West. List students' suggestions on the board and use their ideas to give examples that help answer the questions.

b Challenge

THEME VOCABULARY
Challenge students to represent connections among the theme vocabulary in a different format, such as a word pyramid or chart. Have partners create their own representations and present them to the class.

c Intervention for Acceleration

USE TEXT FEATURES
Explain to students that as they skim the text to look for text evidence, they should use text features as well. Tell students that captions, charts, and labels have information that can be used as text evidence to answer the Focus Question. Have students look at pages 398–399 and guide them to find text evidence to answer the Focus Question.

Word Work and Fluency

Interactive Reading *whole group*

Objectives
Students will:
- Spell words with silent consonants
- Analyze words with silent consonants
- Practice fluent reading

Spelling and Phonics

Pretest Silent Consonants

Say each word from the list, read the sentence, and say the word again. Then have students write the word.

1. **half** The brothers each ate *half* of the pizza.
2. **comb** The barber used a *comb* on the boy's hair.
3. **calm** It is important to remain *calm* in an emergency.
4. **often** We *often* eat rice with dinner.
5. **honor** The citizens of the country *honor* people who fought in wars.
6. **listen** She likes to *listen* to the orchestra.
7. **answer** My mother lets me *answer* the phone when she is busy.
8. **handsome** I think my grandpa is very *handsome*.
9. **knuckle** I slammed my *knuckle* in the door yesterday.
10. **wrinkle** That shirt has a *wrinkle* in it.
11. **yolk** Malik doesn't like to eat the *yolk* of an egg.
12. **folktale** We read a *folktale* last week.
13. **climb** I used to *climb* trees when I was younger.
14. **honest** My parents taught me to be *honest* and always tell the truth.
15. **limb** The kitten was stuck on a high *limb* in the tree.
16. **plumber** The *plumber* was able to fix the leaky faucet.

Review Words

17. **remember** Did you *remember* your homework today?
18. **hospital** My baby brother was born in the *hospital* yesterday.

Frequently Misspelled Words

19. **eighth** Our team came in *eighth* place last year.
20. **know** Do you *know* what time it is?

Explain that these words may seem easy to spell, but they are often misspelled by fourth-graders.

Help students self-correct their tests:

- Say each word, spell it aloud, and repeat the word
- Students checkmark each correctly spelled word
- Students circle each misspelled word and write the correct spelling next to it. Encourage students to note these words as the ones they should pay extra attention to this week.

Teach Silent Consonants

Explain that many words contain silent consonants letters that cannot be heard when a word is said. Tell students that they will need to memorize the spelling of these words.

- Write the words *calm* and *handsome* on the board. Invite students to say each word aloud.
- Ask students to identify the consonants in each word that are silent. Have them underline these letters.
- Continue with the remaining spelling words.

Practice/Apply

Word Sort Have students use word cards to sort the spelling words according to their silent consonant. **a** **b**

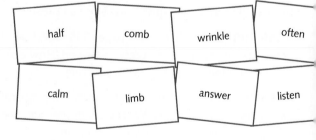

Fluency ✓tested

Introduce and Model

Introduce the fluency selection, "At the Trail's End," on Practice Companion page 254. Tell students that

Practice Companion Pages 254–255

throughout the week, they will practice reading the journal entry to become fluent readers.

To activate prior knowledge and build background, invite students to tell what they know about the mountain plains.

Encourage them to discuss what it might be like to live in the mountain plains or live in a time before modern conveniences were invented. Ask:

Do you think it was hard to live during this time? Why or why not?

Introduce, pronounce, and discuss words that may be unfamiliar, such as *stunning, insignificant, unleash,* and *frigid.*

Read aloud the selection two or three times. Model using good phrasing, pacing, and expression. Ask:

How would you describe the way I read the journal entry?

Practice

Lead an echo reading of the selection followed by a line-a-student choral reading in which each student reads one or two lines of text. **c**

---

scaffolding options

a Literacy Builder

VOCABULARY

Students may not be familiar with all of the spelling words or the words that the class brainstormed. Have students choose words that are unfamiliar to them and complete Word Maps (Resource Master 6) to learn more about the words' meanings and usages. Ask students to share what they learned with partners or in small groups.

ASSIGN RESOURCE MASTER **6**

b Challenge

SPELLING

Challenge students by encouraging them to look for other words with silent consonants in books from the classroom library, their Differentiated Readers, or a newspaper. Have them make lists of these words and share them with partners, who will check for silent consonants.

c Intervention for Acceleration

PARTNER FOR ACCELERATION

Pair students who struggle to read fluently with fluent readers and have them read the selection together several times. Invite them to make recordings to read along with for additional practice throughout the week.

Read and Comprehend

Objectives
Students will:
- Reinforce themes across texts
- Make vocabulary connections
- Read Strategic-level selection

Differentiated Reading
small groups

Prepare to Read

Build Background

Recall the Theme Question: *What makes the West exceptional?* Gather copies of Strategic-level

Differentiated Readers and list on the board the topics covered in each selection:

- Canyons and deserts of the Mountain States
- Farming in the Pacific Northwest
- A husband and wife living in New Mexico
- Working on a boat in Alaska

Ask students to note topics they know something about, and have them share examples with the group.

Ask students to recall the key concepts of farming, geography, and the economy. Discuss how these concepts might relate to each topic on the list.

Build Vocabulary Connections

Ask students to write the above topics and the theme vocabulary words on cards. Have them place the topic cards in a line across their tables. Then ask them to pair each word card with the topic they feel most closely relates to it.

Circulate and encourage discussion of how words were sorted and why they belong where students placed them.

- Why do you think these words belong with this topic?
- What do all the words in this group have in common?
- Could this word belong with another topic as well? Can you explain why (or why not)?
- What name would you assign to this group of cards?

ASSIGN PRACTICE COMPANION **250**

Ask students to discuss which words are easiest to remember and why they are easy, and which are difficult to remember and why. Guide them to identi strategies to help them remember difficult words, including antonyms, synonyms, examples, and sentences. You may wish to model choosing a strate

I think *hue* is an easy word to remember, because I have heard that word in art class before. The word *astounding* is not as familiar. I can remember it, thoug if I remember a synonym, such as *amazing*. When I re *astounding*, I will think *amazing*.

Review Vocabulary Strategies

Briefly review strategies students can use to figure the meanings of unfamiliar words:

- Use the Glossary for boldface, highlighted words.
- Use picture clues.
- Read the sentences directly before and after the word to see if they give more information.
- Use a dictionary.
- Look at word parts.

Set Purposes

Tell students that today they will choose a selection that interests them and read to find out how the selection answers the Theme Question: *What makes West exceptional?*

- Guide students to look at the selection title, chap titles, and illustrations or photographs.
- They might look to see if the selections are fiction nonfiction, and choose one based on their preferences.

Model choosing a selection:

I see that the Chapter 2 title of *Farming in the Pacific Northwest* is "Oregon." This topic is interesting to me because my grandparents are from Oregon. I think I w read this story to find out more about farming in Oreg

Read

Have partners read selections of their choosing. To help them get started, model beginning to read:

> The last sentence in the first paragraph of *Farming in the Pacific Northwest* contains the phrase *a one-stop farm stand*. If I'm not sure what this means, I can ask someone who has already read this selection. With a little help, I can understand this selection even if I don't know every single word or phrase.

Guide Comprehension

Before students read, invite them to use sticky notes to record questions they have, as well as answers to the Theme Question.

- Circulate to monitor comprehension and provide feedback as students read. Ask questions to monitor their understanding.
  - How do you like the story so far? Why?
  - Which parts have been challenging? Let's look at where you got stuck and talk about strategies you can use to better understand the selection.

If students have difficulty with their selection, remind them of fix-up strategies they can use to help them understand. **b**

- Reread the section.
- Keep reading to see if the author explains it further.
- Speed up or slow down.
- Use picture clues.
- Ask for help.

Respond and Write

1. Have partners share some of their sticky notes with the group, explaining what they marked and why they marked it.

2. Encourage partners to add to their lists of familiar topics, based on what they read today.

3. Ask students to journal about the selections they read, why they chose them, and what, if anything, surprised them.

scaffolding options

ELL Support

See pages 289, 293, 297, and 301 of this Teacher's Lesson Guide for vocabulary and instructional support of English language learners.

a Intervention for Acceleration

FEEDBACK
As students read, circulate to check their understanding and monitor their use of vocabulary and comprehension strategies. Ask students which strategies they are using and offer suggestions to help them with difficult passages. Use an example as a starting point for discussion when you come together to share ideas as a group.

b Literacy Builder

COMPREHENSION STRATEGY HANDBOOK
Refer students to the Comprehension Strategy Handbook on pages 502–513 of their Theme Readers for strategy definitions and uses.

ebook online coach
Intervention for Acceleration

Students can use the support features in the eBook version of the Differentiated Reader.

Objectives
Students will:
• Reinforce themes across texts
• Make vocabulary connections
• Read Benchmark-level selection

Differentiated Reading *small groups*

Prepare to Read

Build Background

Recall the Theme Question: *What makes the West exceptional?* Gather copies of Benchmark-level

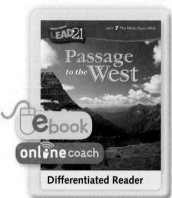

ebook
online coach
Differentiated Reader

Differentiated Readers, and list on the board the topics covered in each selection:

• Rocky Mountains

• Hawaii

• A mystery about missing ski poles

• A Native American folktale

Ask students to note topics they know something about, and have them share examples with the group.

Ask students to recall the key concepts of farming, geography, and the economy. Discuss how these concepts might relate to each topic on the list.

Build Vocabulary Connections *tested*

Ask students to write the topics mentioned above and the theme vocabulary words on word cards.

Have the group sort the words and topics into categories, based on their own criteria. Encourage discussion of how categories were chosen and why words or topics belong where students placed them.

• Why do you think these two cards belong in the same category?

• How are these cards different from those?

• Could this card belong in another category as well? Can you explain why (or why not)?

• What name would you assign to this category?

Invite the group to think of strategies for remembering the meanings of the more challenging words, such as making personal connections or using mnemonic devices.

ASSIGN   **PRACTICE COMPANION   250**

Review Vocabulary Strategies

Briefly review strategies students can use to figure the meanings of unfamiliar words:

• Use the Glossary for boldface, highlighted words

• Use picture clues.

• Read the sentences directly before and after the word to see if they give more information.

• Use a dictionary.

• Look at word parts.

Set Purposes

Tell students that today they will choose a selection that interests them and read to find out how the selection answers the Theme Question: *What makes West exceptional?*

• Guide students to look at the selection title, chap titles, and illustrations or photographs.

• They might look to see if the selections are fiction nonfiction and choose one based on their preferences.

Model choosing a selection:

 think aloud This selection with photographs of the Rocky Mounta looks interesting. It is titled *The Majestic Rockies*. I thi mountains are beautiful and would like to read more about them, so I will read this one. As I read, I will thin about how this topic might connect with the Theme Question.

Read

Students will partner-read selections of their choosi To help them get started, model this thinking as you begin to read *The Majestic Rockies:*

 think aloud The second paragraph has an unfamiliar word: *jagged* I'm not sure what *jagged* means, but if I look at the photographs, I can see that the tops of the mountains are spiky and uneven. I think this is what the settlers s therefore, *jagged* must mean "uneven" because it is u to describe mountains.

Intensive *Strategic* *Independent Practice* *class manager* *Self-Selected Reading* *Advanced* *Study Stations* *Benchmark*

Guide Comprehension

Before students read, invite them to use sticky notes to make predictions and record questions they have, as well as answers to the Theme Question.

Circulate to monitor comprehension and provide feedback as students read. Ask questions to monitor their understanding.

- How do you like the story so far? Why?
- Which parts have been challenging? Let's look at where you got stuck and talk about strategies you can use to better understand the selection.

If students have difficulty with their selections, remind them of fix-up strategies they can use to help them understand. **b**

- Reread the section.
- Keep reading to see if the author explains ideas further.
- Speed up or slow down.
- Use picture clues.
- Ask for help.

Respond and Write

1. Ask partners to discuss how the topics named earlier relate to the selections they read.

2. Encourage partners to share some of their sticky notes. Were their predictions correct? What questions did they have? Did they find answers?

3. Have students draw book jackets for the selections they read. Encourage them to include titles, names of authors and illustrators, and illustrations that show what the selection is about.

scaffolding options

ELL Support

See pages 290, 294, 298, and 302 of this Teacher's Lesson Guide for vocabulary and instructional support of English language learners.

a Intervention for Acceleration

FEEDBACK
As students read, circulate to check their understanding and monitor their use of vocabulary and comprehension strategies. Ask students which strategies they are using, and offer suggestions to help them with difficult passages. Use an example as a starting point for discussion when you come together to share ideas as a group.

b Intervention for Acceleration

COMPREHENSION STRATEGY HANDBOOK
Refer students to the Comprehension Strategy Handbook on pages 502–513 of their Theme Readers for strategy definitions and uses.

ebook online coach

Intervention for Acceleration

Students can use the support features in the eBook version of the Differentiated Reader.

Read and Comprehend   Benchmark

Objectives
Students will:
• Reinforce themes across texts
• Make vocabulary connections
• Read Advanced-level selection

Differentiated Reading
small groups

Prepare to Read

Build Background

Recall the Theme Question: *What makes the West exceptional?* Have students page through the

Differentiated Reader

Advanced-level Differentiated Readers and create a list of topics. Lead a discussion about what students already know about these topics.

Ask them to think about the key concepts they've read about during the unit, and how the concepts relate to each topic.

Build Vocabulary Connections *tested*

Ask students to think about how the theme vocabulary words relate to the selection topics. Write the topics across the board and have partners choose one or two to discuss, using all of the theme vocabulary words. Model the task:

• Both Mountain States and Pacific States have extreme weather conditions. How are their weather conditions similar? How are they different?

ASSIGN   PRACTICE COMPANION   **250**

Set Purposes

Students will choose a selection to read based on their personal interests. Students will read to:

• Find out how the selection they've chosen answers the Theme Question.

• Make connections across texts, to their own experiences, and to their prior knowledge.

Read

Guide Comprehension

As they read, students will make connections using Resource Master 20. Explain that as they read, they should stop periodically to take notes about how the text reminds them of something they read, experienced, or know about.

You may wish to model an example on the board.

Circulate to monitor students and provide feedback they read.

Remind students to use skills and strategies they know to figure out unfamiliar words and to better understand the text. **a**

ASSIGN   RESOURCE MASTER   **20**

Respond and Write

1. Invite students to share their thoughts about the selections they chose and discuss one or two of the notes.

2. Have students discuss how the selections connect the topics discussed earlier and how they help answer the Theme Question.

scaffolding options

ELL Support

See pages 291, 295, 299, and 303 of this Teacher's Lesson Guide for vocabulary and instructional support of English language learners.

a Literacy Builder

COMPREHENSION STRATEGY HANDBOOK
Students may wish to use the Comprehension Strategy Handbook on Theme Reader pages 502–513.

Literacy Builder

Students can use the support features in the eBook version of the Differentiated Reader.

Differentiated Reading · small groups

Objectives
Students will:
- Reinforce themes across texts
- Make vocabulary connections
- Read Benchmark-level selection

Prepare to Read

Build Background

Have students page through the Benchmark-level Differentiated Readers and identify the topics addressed in each selection. Lead a discussion about what students already know about these topics.

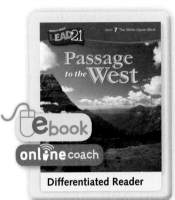
Differentiated Reader

Have students jot down the ways in which the topics might relate to the Theme Question: *What makes the West exceptional?*

Build Vocabulary Connections

Write the topics across the board and have each student choose one to discuss. Encourage them to use all of the theme vocabulary words in the discussion, and model the task:

> Many parts of the Mountain and Pacific States have extreme weather. Some parts of this region are extremely cold, while others are extremely hot. Coastal California is known for its balmy weather, while some desert areas are described as arid. Alaska is very cold, while Hawaii is very warm.

ASSIGN   PRACTICE COMPANION   250

Set Purposes

Students will choose selections to read based on their personal interests. Students will read to:

- Find answers to the Theme Question.
- Make connections across texts and to their own experiences and prior knowledge.

Students may choose more than one selection to read if they wish to do so.

Read

Guide Comprehension

Tell students that as they read, they will record connections they make using Resource Master 20. Explain that as they read, students should take notes about how the text reminds them of other things they have read, experienced, or know about.

ASSIGN   RESOURCE MASTER   20

Respond and Write

1. Invite students to share their thoughts about the selections they chose and discuss one or two of their notes. **a**

2. Have students synthesize what they learned from each selection into an answer to the Theme Question.

scaffolding options

ELL Support

See pages 290, 294, 298, and 302 of this Teacher's Lesson Guide for vocabulary and instructional support of English language learners.

a Challenge

COMPREHENSION: COMPARE AND CONTRAST
Encourage students to compare and contrast the selection they read today with a selection from their Advanced Differentiated Reader. They may wish to address the genre, the author's purpose, and the information and ideas presented.

Ask students to recommend one selection over the other and explain why they recommend it.

Share, Connect, Assess

Objectives
Students will:
- Use key concepts and vocabulary
- Make text-to-self connections
- Write about visiting someone in a different place
- Monitor their progress

Share Text Connections

Make Text-to-Self Connections Bring students back together from their small groups to share what additional things they learned while reading about life in the Pacific States.

- Encourage students to use theme and other academic vocabulary as they share their own insights about key concepts.

- Ensure that students from all groups have a chance to contribute to the discussion.

- Ask students to share their thoughts on how what they've read connects to their personal experiences.

etools 21
• theme wall

Daily Writing

Have students write a journal entry about a time th visited a relative or friend who lived in a different place. Encourage them to write about what they sav and what they did in the new place.

For additional writing practice, remind students to access the Story Starter from their student Home P

etools 21
• writing tool
• story starter

Student Self Assessment

- Remind students that they are responsible for the learning and that it is helpful to be aware of how well they understand what they are reading, writ talking, and thinking about in the classroom.

- You may want students to reflect on their reading learning by using their Personal Reading Logs and Daily Progress sheets (Resource Masters 1, 3).

ASSIGN **RESOURCE MASTER 1, 3**

Daily Progress Monitoring

To ensure that students have mastered the day's skills and strategies, monitor their success in completing the following independent work:
- **Vocabulary:** Practice Companion, p. 250
- **Spelling:** Practice Companion, p. 252
- **Fluency:** Practice Companion, p. 254
- **Study Station Work Record:** Resource Master 2
- **Self Assessment:** Resource Masters 1, 3

Home Connection

Distribute the Unit 7 Take-Home Activities from the Home Connection book. Tell students to complete the activities with their caregivers.

Day at a Glance

Lesson Highlights

- Review Comprehension Strategy: Determine Important Information
- Compare Genres
- Spelling and Phonics: Silent Consonants
- Revise an Autobiography, pp. 278–279

Materials

	Teacher's Lesson Guide	Student Components	Digital 21
Interactive Reading	pp. 222–225	• Theme Reader, pp. 380–438 • Practice Companion, pp. 250, 252, 254, 256–257 • Resource Masters 8, 13, 14	ebook online coach
Differentiated Reading	pp. 226–231, 300–303 (ELL)	• Differentiated Readers • Practice Companion, pp. 260–261 • Resource Masters 4, 11, 13, 14, 23	ebook online coach
Wrap Up	p. 232	• Resource Masters 1–3	etools 21 • theme wall • writing tool • story starter
Writing and Language Arts	pp. 278–279	• Writing Models Chart, pp. 54–55 • Practice Companion, pp. 270, 273	etools 21 writing tool

Tips for Success

- Guide students to make connections between reading and writing (p. 223).
- Remind students to use their Study Station Work Records (Resource Master 2) throughout the week.
- If students work on their writing during Independent Practice, have them use the Evaluation Rubric on Practice Companion page 269.

21st CENTURY SKILLS Remind students to work on their Inquiry Projects during Independent Practice or Self-Selected Reading time.

Oral Language and Vocabulary

Objectives
Students will:
• Make connections to the theme
• Make vocabulary connections

Interactive Reading *whole group*

Build Theme Connections

Ask students to turn to page 378 of their Theme Readers and read the second Focus Question:

online coach

Theme Reader
Pages 377–438

How are geography and economy connected in the Pacific States?

Prompt students to make connections to the Focus Question by asking questions like these:

• What have you read about in class that helps answer this question?

• Have you read about the Pacific States anywhere else?

• When you think of California, Washington, and Oregon, what geographical features do you think of? Why?

• When you think of Alaska and Hawaii, what comes to mind? Why?

• What are some things you know now that you didn't know before about the geography and economy of these states?

Share your thoughts to model starting a discussion:

think aloud When I think about this question, I remember reading about the crops that grow in the Pacific States, like apples. I know they are important to the area's economy, and because of the good amount of rainfall, the farmers can grow them successfully.

Have students discuss the questions with partners before sharing their ideas with the class. Finally, lead a discussion about how answering the Focus Question helps students determine what makes the West exceptional. **a**

Build Vocabulary Connections

tested

Remind students that they have been using vocabul related to the unit theme, *The Wide-Open West*. List theme vocabulary words on the board.

Theme Vocabulary

arid	irrigated
exchange	missionary
extreme	rugged
film	treasure
fulfill	

Explain that today students will make connections between the theme vocabulary and the vocabulary they have learned in their Differentiated Readers.

• Pair students from different small groups.

• Distribute Concept and Vocabulary Brainstormi charts (Resource Master 8).

• Have students write a theme vocabulary word at top and then brainstorm differentiated vocabula that relates to that word.

• Encourage partners to share the definitions of the differentiated vocabulary words they have learned and explain how they connect to the then vocabulary word.

Think aloud to model making connections:

think aloud I learned that *irrigated* means "watered with resources from another area." I read the word *ample* in *Hawaii: Beautiful Island State*. The farmers in this area probab do not have to worry much about irrigating their crops because Hawaii receives an ample amount of rain each year.

Invite volunteers to explain the connections they made. **b**

ASSIGN

RESOURCE MASTER	8
PRACTICE COMPANION	250

Read and Comprehend

REVIEW **COMPREHENSION STRATEGY**

Determine tested
Important Information

Define
Ask students to recall that readers determine the most important information the author wants them to remember or understand.

Model
Use Theme Reader page 385 to model determining important information. Begin a T-chart on chart paper and share your thoughts as you read.

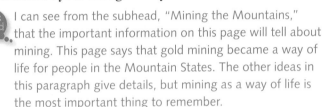

I can see from the subhead, "Mining the Mountains," that the important information on this page will tell about mining. This page says that gold mining became a way of life for people in the Mountain States. The other ideas in this paragraph give details, but mining as a way of life is the most important thing to remember.

Collaborative Practice
Have students continue reading page 386 to add information to the chart. Ask guiding questions such as these:

• What clues do the subhead, photographs, and captions give you about what is important on this page?

• What information do you think is most important to understand or remember about ranching?

Encourage students to share their thoughts as they add information to the chart. Remind students to look carefully for the most important information as they read today.

Reading/Writing Connection

Explain that authors include additional features to help readers understand which information in a text is the most important. Have partners page through *A Tour of the Western Region* and point out text features—such as chapter titles, subheads, and captions—that highlight important information. **c**

ASSIGN | PRACTICE COMPANION 256–257 |

scaffolding options

a ELL Support

THEME CONNECTIONS
Because the illustrations and photos in this selection feature culture-specific situations, this activity provides an opportunity for some English language learners to share their experiences, which may be quite different from those of other students. Ask them if geography and economy are different in their countries of origin, and if so, how.

b Critical Thinking

SYNTHESIZE VOCABULARY AND CONCEPTS
Have students use the vocabulary and concepts they've learned in this unit to create an informative poster, brochure, or diagram that illustrates one way geography and economy are connected in your area. Have them prepare a brief oral presentation about what they've made and share it with the class. Encourage students to ask questions and discuss connections to the unit and the selections they've read.

c Literacy Builder

COMPREHENSION: DETERMINE IMPORTANT INFORMATION
Explain to students that not all text features indicate the most important information on a page. Point out that some text features—such as the sidebar on page 399—give additional detailed information to help illustrate the main points.

Objectives
Students will:
- Compare informational text and folktale
- Reread to find text evidence
- Connect themes across texts

- Reinforce determining important information

Interactive Reading
whole group

Prepare to Read

Compare Genres:
Informational Text and Folktale

Explain that an informational text provides facts and details that explain a topic. Explain that a folktale is a story passed down within a culture for many generations. Many folktales have moral lessons.

Ask questions such as these to guide students in comparing the two genres:

**Theme Reader
Pages 380–438**

- Which selection tells facts about a topic?

- Which selection has characters and a plot?

- Why do you think *A Tour of the Western Region* uses photographs, while *Juan Verdades: The Man Who Couldn't Tell a Lie* uses illustrations? **a**

Set Purposes

Remind students that they will read to find answers to Focus Question 2: *How are geography and economy connected in the Pacific States?*

- They will gather text evidence from both *A Tour of the Western Region* and *Juan Verdades: The Man Who Couldn't Tell a Lie* to answer the Focus Question.

- They will consider how two different genres can address the same key concepts.

Tell students that they will use a T-Chart (Resource Master 14) to record text evidence as they read.

ASSIGN RESOURCE MASTER **14**

Read Across Texts

Students will revisit *A Tour of the Western Region* and *Juan Verdades: The Man Who Couldn't Tell a Lie* independently or with partners. Pause periodically a prompt them to determine important information. Remind students to record text evidence as they rea

PAGES 396–403 Which characteristics of this selection tell you it is informational text?

Why does California have the biggest state economy i the United States? *(It has 1,000 miles of coastline, a good climate, and a lot of land.)*

Why is tourism a big part of Hawaii's economy? *(The islands and warm climate make it a popular vacation spot.)*

What are some other connections you find between th geography and economy of the Pacific States? *(Possib responses: Growing crops, dairy farming, mining, wat transportation, timber, apple orchards, and tourism ar all industries that are connected to the geography.)*

PAGES 409–438 What is the lesson of this folktale? *(Possible response: It pays to be honest.)*

Which details in the selection show that the characters are using the geography around them to make a living *(Possible response: The wide open spaces provide plenty of room for ranching; don Arturo and his wife are worried about losing their ranch; the rancheros are wealthy.)*

Respond

Invite students to share the text evidence they have gathered and use it to formulate a response to the Focus Question. **b**

Word Work and Fluency

Objectives
Students will:
- Practice spelling words with silent consonants
- Practice fluent reading

Spelling and Phonics

Practice Silent Consonants

Remind students that this week they are learning to spell words with silent consonants.

Have students use their spelling lists to write a sentence for each word and then read their sentences to partners. The partner spells the word and gives its meaning. Then partners switch roles.

ASSIGN PRACTICE COMPANION **252**

Fluency

Shared Choral Reading

Have students turn to "At the Trail's End" on page 254 of their Practice Companions. Ask students to recall who is writing the journal entry and what they have to say. Then ask:

> Can you imagine what it would have been like to travel on the Oregon Trail? Describe what it might have been like.

Explain that *phrasing* is when readers chunk text into meaningful parts.

- Read the selection and invite students to mark the text in their Practice Companions to show the phrasing you model.
- Then lead a choral reading of the selection. Remind students to focus on their phrasing as they read. **c**

ASSIGN PRACTICE COMPANION **254**

scaffolding options

a Challenge

COMPREHENSION: MAKE CONNECTIONS
Challenge students to make connections to as many different concepts in the Theme Reader as possible. Have them record how many connections they make. Tally the number for each student after everyone is finished reading. Have the winner discuss his or her connections and label them as text-to-self, text-to-text, or text-to-world. Suggest making connections between both selections in the Theme Reader.

b Critical Thinking

ANALYZE GENRE
Ask students to compare one of the selections with another text of the same genre from the classroom library. Have students take notes on how the selections are similar or different in terms of characteristics. For example, students might point out that one informational text has many graphs while another does not. You may wish to have students use a Venn Diagram (Resource Master 13) to compare and contrast the texts.

ASSIGN RESOURCE MASTER **13**

c ELL Support

FLUENCY
To ensure that English language learners get the most from this activity, briefly go over academic language, such as *phrasing, punctuation, period, comma,* and *paragraph break.* As you discuss the latter four, have them point to examples in the selection.

Read and Comprehend **Intensive**

Differentiated Reading *small groups*

Objectives
Students will:
• Use differentiated vocabulary
• Reinforce determining important information
• Read about traveling west to Oregon

Prepare to Read

Build Background

Read with students the Focus Question: *What is life like in the Pacific States?* (Differentiated Reader, p. 5). Guide

Differentiated Reader Pages 80–89

students to answer using information they already know from classroom reading selections or from their own lives.

Have students turn to page 80 of *Onward to Oregon!* and read the title aloud with the group.

• Explain that the story is about settlers who travel west to settle in Oregon.

• Encourage students to tell what they know about western settlers. If necessary, remind them about the gold rush and westward expansion.

• Distribute Concept and Word Webs (Resource Master 11) and record student responses on chart paper. Guide students to use what they have been learning about the Pacific States to promote discussion.

ASSIGN RESOURCE MASTER 11

Introduce Differentiated Vocabulary *tested*

Have students complete the Vocabulary Rating Sheet (Resource Master 4).

• Find and pronounce with students the highlighted differentiated vocabulary words (pp. 80–89).

• Use the following routine to discuss each word's meaning.

• For each word, have students jot down and explain answers to prompts.

Vocabulary Routine	
Define	**Hardship** (p. 81) means "suffering."
Example	Settlers faced great hardships as they traveled west.
Ask	What is one hardship the settlers faced?

Rally (p. 83) means "to recover, to become stronger." *The team rallied in the 4th quarter and won the game.* What might cause a team or someone to *rally*?

Blistering (p. 84) means "very intense, strong, or severe." *The blistering summer heat made me misera* Could cold temperatures be *blistering*? Why?

Continue the routine with *landmark* (p. 85), *commo* (p. 85), and *frail* (p. 89), using the Glossary definition and sentences and asking questions.

ASSIGN RESOURCE MASTER 4

Preview and Predict

Have students preview the selection, looking at the illustrations and chapter titles. Ask students to mak predictions. Students will also begin the Anticipatio Guide on Practice Companion page 260.

ASSIGN PRACTICE COMPANION 260

Set Purposes

Remind students that readers set purposes to focus their attention and get more out of what they read.

• Students will add to their concept and word webs

• Students will look for answers to the Focus Question.

REINFORCE COMPREHENSION STRATEGY

Determine *tested* Important Informatio

Remind students that readers ask questions to determine which information is most important. Ha students tell why readers use this strategy.

To reinforce determining important information, us page 81 to model your thinking.

 The story starts with the narrator sharing that the Bryan family is moving to Oregon to begin a new life because they lost their farm in Missouri. This import information because it tells the reader right away why the family is heading west. I think that moving will be important idea in the story.

ASSIGN PRACTICE COMPANION 256–257

Read

Tell students that today they will be reading pages 80–89 of *Onward to Oregon!* Model your thinking as you read page 81 to help students get started.

think aloud

One of the first things I notice is that the story is told in the form of a play. Instead of chapters, the story has scenes. I can predict that I'm going to learn something that will help me answer the Focus Question because the title has *Oregon* in it, which is in the West. I'll pay special attention to information about moving westward as I read.

Guide Comprehension

Have partners continue reading pages 80–89. Pause periodically to monitor understanding of theme concepts and vocabulary. Have students jot down answers to prompts before discussing them. **a**

PAGES 80–85 Read the **Strategy Tool Kit** on page 85. Have partners find details in the text to help them make inferences.

PAGES 86–87 What problem does the family face? Make a prediction about what the family will do to overcome it. *(They come to a wide river; Possible response: They might float across it on the wagon.)*

PAGES 88–89 Who are the most important characters in the story? What are the important events that take place? *(The most important characters are Uriah and Jennie.)*

Have students explain why everyone working together is so important to the Bryan family's success. *(On the trail, there were too many hardships for people to be successful alone; a team effort was required.)* **b**

Check Comprehension

1. What words were new to you in this part of the story? How did you figure out their meanings? MONITOR COMPREHENSION

2. What things happen during the family's journey? Use the illustrations to discuss the events. SEQUENCE EVENTS

Respond and Write

1. Have students discuss **Stop and Think** on page 89. Ask students to add their answers to the concept and word web.

2. Discuss how the story so far has helped answer the Focus Question.

scaffolding options

ELL Support

See page 300 of this Teacher's Lesson Guide for vocabulary and instructional support of English language learners at the Intensive level.

a Intervention for Acceleration

MONITOR COMPREHENSION
To help students understand important elements in the story, you may wish to have them begin a Story Map (Resource Master 23). Ask pairs to complete the information about characters, setting, and so on. After students have finished reading, ask them to share their story maps with the group to compare what people wrote.

ASSIGN RESOURCE MASTER 23

b Literacy Builder

COMPREHENSION: SUMMARIZE
Encourage readers to pause for summarizing on content-rich pages, such as pages 84, 86, and 88. Have them use illustrations on these pages for support in their summarizing.

ebook onlinecoach
Intervention for Acceleration

Students can use the support features in the eBook version of the Differentiated Reader.

Read and Comprehend **Strategic**

Objectives
Students will:
• Use differentiated vocabulary
• Reinforce determining important information
• Read about working on a boat in Alaska

Prepare to Read

Build Background

Read with students the Focus Question: *What is life like in the Pacific States?* (Differentiated Reader, p. 5). Have

Differentiated Reader Pages 80–90

students answer using information from classroom reading selections or from their personal experiences and prior knowledge.

Have students turn to page 80 of *Deckhands*. Read the title aloud with the group.

• Explain that this story is about two cousins who work on a boat in Alaska for the summer.

• Distribute Concept and Word Webs (Resource Master 11) and ask students to write what they know about Alaska. Record their answers on chart paper. Provide images of different scenes from Alaska or a descriptive poem about Alaska to help students.

ASSIGN RESOURCE MASTER **11**

Introduce
Differentiated Vocabulary

Have students complete the Vocabulary Rating Sheet (Resource Master 4).

• Find and pronounce with students the highlighted differentiated vocabulary words (pp. 80–90).

• Use the following routine to discuss each word's meaning.

• For each word, have students jot down and explain answers to prompts.

Vocabulary Routine	
Define	**Pristine** (p. 83) means "pure, clean."
Example	The park was so beautiful and pristine.
Ask	Is a garbage dump pristine? Why or why not?

Alert (p. 88) means "attentive or watching carefully." *The captain stayed alert to watch for the approaching storm.* What are other situations in which you need be alert? Why?

Muffle (p. 89) means "to lower or hold back a sound." *Jacob tried to muffle a groan when he realized he had forgotten to do his homework.* What is another word muffle?

ASSIGN RESOURCE MASTER **4**

Preview and Predict

Have students page through the selection to preview the illustrations and chapter titles. Ask students to make predictions. Invite students to begin the Anticipation Guide on Practice Companion page 26(

ASSIGN PRACTICE COMPANION **260**

Set Purposes

Remind students that readers set purposes to focus their attention and get more out of what they read.

• Students will read to find details to include in the concept and word webs.

• Students will look for answers to the Focus Question.

REINFORCE COMPREHENSION STRATEGY

Determine
Important Informatio

Remind students that readers try to determine which information is most important in order to better understand the text. Have students tell why readers use this strategy.

To reinforce determining important information, us page 80 to model your thinking.

think aloud The story starts by telling why Roberto travels to Alask This is important information because it tells the reader what events might happen in the rest of the story.

ASSIGN PRACTICE COMPANION **256–257**

Read

Tell students that today they will read pages 80–90 of *Deckhands*. To help them get started, model your thinking as you begin reading.

think aloud From looking at the title, I don't know much about being a deckhand. The illustrations show people on a boat, and I know that the deck of a boat is where people stand or sit. A deckhand must work on that part of the boat.

Guide Comprehension

Invite partners to continue reading. Encourage them to make predictions. Pause periodically to check understanding of theme concepts and vocabulary. **b**

PAGES 80–83 What do you see pictured on pages 82 and 83? *(the characters getting onto a water taxi)*

Why do they use this mode of transportation? *(Possible response: Alaska has a lot of waterways, and many people use boats to get around.)*

PAGES 84–85 Have students determine important information based on the **Strategy Tool Kit** on page 85. Encourage them to jot down their responses before sharing them with the group.

PAGES 86–90 What did Roberto think of his first morning in Alaska? *(He was surprised at how light it was so early in the morning.)*

Check Comprehension

1. What is Chapter 1 mostly about? SUMMARIZE

2. What are the most important events in Chapter 2? DETERMINE IMPORTANT INFORMATION

Respond and Write

1. Invite students to add information from their reading to the concept and word web. Together, discuss which parts of the story they've enjoyed most, and why.

2. Ask students to discuss **Stop and Think** on page 90. Have students briefly make Venn diagrams to illustrate the similarities and differences between Alaska and Arizona.

ASSIGN RESOURCE MASTER 13

---

scaffolding options

ELL Support

See page 301 of this Teacher's Lesson Guide for vocabulary and instructional support of English language learners at the Strategic level.

a Critical Thinking

CONCEPT DEVELOPMENT
Encourage students to combine information from different sources. Ask:

What books have you read about Alaska? What movies about Alaska have you seen?

Have students visualize the land and animals and make educated guesses about what kinds of problems would exist there.

b Intervention for Acceleration

COMPREHENSION: MAKE PREDICTIONS
Encourage students to use T-Charts (Resource Master 14) labeled *Clues from the Story* and *Predictions* to help them make predictions as they read *Deckhands*.

ASSIGN RESOURCE MASTER 14

ebook online coach
Intervention for Acceleration

Students can use the support features in the eBook version of the Differentiated Reader.

Read and Comprehend **Benchmark**

Differentiated Reading *small groups*

Objectives
Students will:
• Use differentiated vocabulary
• Reinforce determining important information
• Read a Native American folktale

Prepare to Read

Build Background

Introduce the Focus Question: *What is life like in the Pacific States?* and share the selection title, *Mink and the Sun* (pp. 5, 80). Tell students that the story is a Native American folktale about the sun. Have students share what they know about Native American folktales.

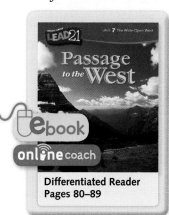

Differentiated Reader
Pages 80–89

Distribute Concept and Word Webs (Resource Master 11) and ask students to jot down what they know about the sun. Record their answers on chart paper.

Introduce Differentiated Vocabulary *tested*

Have students complete the Vocabulary Rating Sheet (Resource Master 4).

Vocabulary Routine	
Define	**Whittle** (p. 81) means "to shape something, especially wood, with a knife."
Example	Being able to whittle something out of wood is a special talent.
Ask	What objects can be made by whittling?

Laced (p. 83) means "marked with streaks of color or mixed." *The weaver made a blue silk scarf laced with soft purples.* What is a synonym for the word *laced*?

Partners continue the routine with *mock* (p. 85) and *descend* (p. 89), using the Glossary definitions and sentences and asking questions.

ASSIGN RESOURCE MASTER **4, 11**

Preview/Predict/Set Purposes

Invite students to preview the selection. Have them predict what they think will happen. Students will also begin their Anticipation Guides.

ASSIGN PRACTICE COMPANION **261**

Read

Guide Comprehension

Partners will read pages 80–89 of *Mink and the Sun*. Monitor understanding of key concepts and vocabulary with the prompts below. Remind studen[ts] to determine important information as they read.

PAGES 80–83 How does the descriptive language help you visualize the information on these pages? How is t[his] important to the story? VISUALIZE

PAGES 84–89 Have partners identify the most importa[nt] events in the story to this point. Invite them to share which characters are most important to the story.
DETERMINE IMPORTANT INFORMATION **a**

Respond and Write

Invite students to add new ideas from the story to th[e] concept webs. Then have students discuss how the fi[rst] half of the story answers the Focus Question.

scaffolding options

ELL Support

See page 302 of this Teacher's Lesson Guide for vocabulary and instructional support of English language learners at the Benchmark level.

a Literacy Builder

COMPREHENSION: MAKE PREDICTIONS
Have students use information in the selection to predict what will happen next in the story.

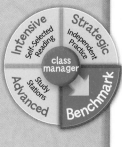

Read and Comprehend [Advanced]

Objectives
Students will:
- Use differentiated vocabulary
- Reinforce determining important information
- Read about building railroads in the 1800s

Prepare to Read

Build Background

Introduce the Focus Question and read aloud the selection title, *The Mystery of the Railroad Letters* (pp. 5, 80). Explain that the story takes place in the 1800s and describes life then.

Differentiated Reader
Pages 80–89

Provide images from the 1800s and ask students what they know about the building of railroads in the 1800s. Distribute Concept and Word Webs (Resource Master 11) and record students' ideas on chart paper.

Introduce Differentiated Vocabulary

Have students complete the Vocabulary Rating Sheet (Resource Master 4).

Vocabulary Routine	
Define	A **telegram** (p. 82) is a message sent by telegraph, which uses a series of electric sounds.
Example	Long ago, people sent messages in telegrams.
Ask	What would you say in a telegram to a relative who lived far away?

Relieved (p. 84) means "feeling better, especially after being anxious." *I was relieved to hear that today's test had been postponed.* What is a synonym for *relieved*?

Partners continue the routine with *terminus* (p. 86) and *gist* (p. 88), using the Glossary definitions and sentences and asking questions.

ASSIGN [RESOURCE MASTER **4**]

Preview/Predict/Set Purposes

Invite students to preview the selection. Have them predict what they think will happen. Students will also begin their Anticipation Guides.

ASSIGN [PRACTICE COMPANION **261**]

Read

Guide Comprehension

Students will read pages 80–89 of *The Mystery of the Railroad Letters* independently. Have them determine important information and discuss key concepts.

PAGES 80–85 Ask students to discuss the similarities and differences between life in the 1800s and life today. COMPARE AND CONTRAST

PAGES 86–89 Have students note the important details about the proposed railway terminus.
DETERMINE IMPORTANT INFORMATION

Why are the men of Tacoma interested in the terminus? Why wouldn't it be a joint project? MAKE PREDICTIONS

Respond and Write

Invite students to add new ideas from the story to their concept webs. Students will discuss how the selection helps answer the Focus Question. **ⓐ**

ELL Support

See page 303 of this Teacher's Lesson Guide for vocabulary and instructional support of English language learners at the Advanced level.

ⓐ Challenge

COMPREHENSION: MAKE CONNECTIONS
Challenge students to consider what it would be like to live in the time before modern conveniences, such as e-mail, were invented. Have them write short stories describing what that would be like, and then ask them to share with the group.

Share, Connect, Assess

Wrap Up
whole group

Objectives
Students will:
- Use key concepts and vocabulary
- Make text-to-text connections
- Write about their impressions of the Pacific States
- Monitor their progress

Share Text Connections

Building Classroom Community

Make Text-to-Text Connections Bring students back together from their small groups to talk about their Differentiated Reader selections.

- Invite students to share the topic of their selections and something interesting they've read so far. Encourage them to share some of the differentiated vocabulary words they read.

- Ask students what they know about the topics that other groups are reading about. As they discuss the texts, point out connections. For example, both *Onward to Oregon!* and *The Mystery of the Railroad Letters* talk about historical events (traveling the Oregon Trail and the expansion of the railroad).

- Have students share how what they've read and discussed answers the week's Focus Question.

etools 21
theme wall

Daily Writing

Have students write about their impressions of the Pacific States. How do they feel when they hear abou the Pacific States? What images come to mind?

For additional writing practice, remind students to access the Story Starter from their student Home Pa

etools 21
- writing tool
- story starter

Student Self Assessment

- Remind students that they are responsible for the learning and that it is helpful to be aware of how well they understand what they are reading, writi talking, and thinking about in the classroom.

- You may want students to reflect on their reading a learning by using their Personal Reading Logs and Daily Progress sheets (Resource Masters 1, 3).

ASSIGN RESOURCE MASTER **1, 3**

Daily Progress Monitoring

To ensure that students have mastered the day's skills and strategies, monitor their success in completing the following independent work:

- **Vocabulary:** Practice Companion, p. 250
- **Comprehension:** Practice Companion, pp. 256–257
- **Spelling:** Practice Companion, p. 252
- **Fluency:** Practice Companion, p. 254
- **Study Station Work Record:** Resource Master 2
- **Self Assessment:** Resource Masters 1, 3

Home Connection

Distribute the Unit 7 Take-Home Activities from the Home Connection book. Tell students to complete the activities with their caregivers.

Day at a Glance

Lesson Highlights

- Use Multiple Vocabulary Strategies
- Review Comprehension Skill: Recall and Retell
- Analyze Author's Purpose
- Review Word Study: Contractions
- Edit an Autobiography: pp. 280–281

Materials

	Teacher's Lesson Guide	Student Components	Digital 21
Interactive Reading	pp. 234–237	• Theme Reader, pp. 380–438 • Practice Companion, pp. 250, 253–254, 258–259, 262–263 • Resource Masters 11, 14, 25	ebook online coach epractice word study games
Differentiated Reading	pp. 238–243, 300–303 (ELL)	• Differentiated Readers • Practice Companion, pp. 260–261 • Resource Masters 4, 8	ebook online coach epractice vocabulary activities
Wrap Up	p. 244	• Resource Masters 1–3	etools 21 • theme wall • writing tool • story starter
Writing and Language Arts	pp. 280–281	• Writing Models Chart, pp. 54–55 • Practice Companion, pp. 269, 274	

Tips for Success

- Guide students to make connections between reading and writing (p. 235).
- Remind students to use their Study Station Work Records (Resource Master 2) throughout the week.
- You may wish to set out the Writing Models Chart where students can see it and refer to it during their Independent Practice.

21st CENTURY SKILLS Remind students to work on their Inquiry Projects during Independent Practice or Self-Selected Reading time.

Objectives
Students will:
• Make connections to the theme
• Make vocabulary connections

Interactive Reading *whole group*

Build Theme Connections

Ask students to turn to pages 378–379 of their Theme Readers and read the third Focus Question: *What is life like in the Mountain States?*

Encourage small groups of students to make connections to the Focus Question by asking questions like these:

ebook
online coach

Theme Reader Pages 377–438

• We've read a lot about this question in class. Where else have you read or heard about the Mountain States?

• Have you seen movies or read stories that take place there? What did you learn from these other sources?

• What people, places, special days, or events do you know that relate to life in the Mountain States?

Model this thinking to help students begin their discussions:

think aloud When I think about what life is like in the Mountain States, I remember reading about the Native Americans who first lived in the area long ago. I know from visits to the Southwest that Native American culture is a big part of the area.

Many people visit the area to learn about Native American culture, and many stores sell Native American items, such as jewelry and blankets.

Have students discuss the questions in small groups before sharing their ideas with the class. Then lead a discussion about how answering the Focus Question helped students better understand what makes the West exceptional.

Use Multiple ✓tested Vocabulary Strategie

Have students recall the definition of the vocabular strategies they have learned in this unit, and tell ho to use the strategies when reading.

Synonyms: words that mean the same or almost the same

Context Clues: words, sentences, pictures, and other clues on the page that help readers figure out a word

Descriptive Language: words that help the reader visualize or feel a certain way

Remind students that they can use multiple strateg when they read to help them better understand the meanings of words.

• Have partners look back through the Theme Rea to find places where they can apply each strategy

• Have students share their examples with the clas Write on the board examples of how students use each strategy and discuss each one. **b**

ASSIGN **PRACTICE COMPANION 258–259**

model
read share

Objectives
Students will:
• Review recalling and retelling

REVIEW **COMPREHENSION SKILL**

Recall and Retell tested ✓

Define and Model
Remind students that retelling ideas in one's own words makes it easier to understand and remember what has been read. Model retelling the information about Hawaii on Theme Reader page 406.

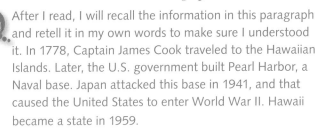 After I read, I will recall the information in this paragraph and retell it in my own words to make sure I understood it. In 1778, Captain James Cook traveled to the Hawaiian Islands. Later, the U.S. government built Pearl Harbor, a Naval base. Japan attacked this base in 1941, and that caused the United States to enter World War II. Hawaii became a state in 1959.

Practice
Guide students through using Resource Master 25 as a sequence chart to help them retell information on pages 406–407.

• Encourage them to think aloud as they practice recalling and retelling.

• Remind students to pause now and then for retelling as they read. **c**

Reading/Writing Connection

Share with students that writers explain ideas in a clear and orderly way so that readers can understand and remember what they read.

What kind of order does the author use to describe the addition of Hawaii and Alaska to the United States? *(The events are described in the order they occurred.)*

ASSIGN

| RESOURCE MASTER | 25 |
| PRACTICE COMPANION | 262 |

---

scaffolding options

a ELL Support

COMPREHENSION: MAKE CONNECTIONS
For students without prior knowledge of the Mountain States, provide a series of pictures that shows scenes of life there to help them make connections beyond what they've read in the classroom. Have students use the pictures to make connections to their reading.

b Intervention for Acceleration

USE VOCABULARY STRATEGIES
If students have difficulty remembering how to use one or more of the vocabulary strategies, return to the whole-group lesson earlier in the unit and quickly review/reteach it. Then ask students to give an example of where this strategy could be used in the Theme Reader or their Differentiated Reader.

c Intervention for Acceleration

COMPREHENSION: RECALL AND RETELL
Encourage students to use familiar passages from their Differentiated Readers to practice retelling. Have them skim the passages for ideas, write a few words in the retelling chart about each idea, and then use the chart in their retelling.

Read and Comprehend (continued)

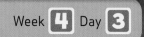

Interactive Reading whole group

model
read
share

Objectives
Students will:
• Analyze author's purpose
• Reread to find text evidence
• Connect themes across texts

• Reinforce recalling and retelling

Prepare to Read

Analyze Author's Purpose: Bias

Explain that when readers think about why an author writes a selection, they become better readers and writers.

**Theme Reader
Pages 377–438**

Explain that *bias* is a writer's personal feelings on the topic he or she is writing about. Readers can identify bias by:

• Examining word choice and connotations.

• Noticing what type of information is included or left out. **a**

• Looking for claims that aren't supported with facts or examples.

Point out that writers of informational text try to avoid bias. Explain:

The purpose of informational text is to share facts, not opinions. If writers show bias about their topic, then readers should question whether or not the writer is presenting an accurate picture of the topic.

Then ask students:

• Do you think the author of *A Tour of the Western Region* wants you to feel a certain way about the region? How do you know? *(No; the author presents facts but doesn't say how she feels about them.)*

• How does the author of *Juan Verdades: The Man Who Couldn't Tell a Lie* feel about honesty? How do you know? *(He thinks it's good; Juan is a good character, and he is rewarded for being honest.)*

Set Purposes

Students will revisit *A Tour of the Western Region* and *Juan Verdades: The Man Who Couldn't Tell a Lie*, using T-Charts (Resource Master 14) to gather text evidence to answer Focus Question 3: *What is life like in the Mountain States?* Encourage students to think about the authors' purposes as they read.

ASSIGN   RESOURCE MASTER **14**

Read Across Texts

Have students reread *A Tour of the Western Region* and *Juan Verdades: The Man Who Couldn't Tell a Lie* independently or with partners. Pause periodically guide students to find text evidence and analyze the authors' purposes.

PAGE 382 How does the introduction help you determ the author's purpose for writing this selection? *(It giv readers an idea of what they will learn, which is most facts about the region.)*

PAGES 392–393 How have Native Americans defined the history and culture of the Mountain States? *(The have lived there for thousands of years; many Pueblo and Navajo still live throughout the region today and contribute their art to the culture of the region.)*

PAGES 394–395 How can the history of the Mountain States be seen in its culture today? *(Possible response Museums preserve Montana's way of life; cultural eve teach about Native Americans; tourists visit historical mining towns.)*

PAGES 409–438 What does this folktale tell you about the history and culture of the region? *(Possible responses: Ranch foremen were usually not allowed to marry the daughters of wealthy rancheros; illustration show the way people dressed and their houses.)*

What do you think was the author's purpose in writing about Juan? How do you know? *(Possible response: T author wanted to share a story about the importance honesty; the author wrote that Juan was rewarded fo being honest.)*

Respond

Have partners discuss the authors' purposes for writing each story, as well as how text evidence help them answer the Focus Question. Ask if students think the authors were thinking about the history a culture of the Mountain States as they wrote. **b**

Talk About Text ★★★

Provide these discussion points:

• What was your favorite part of *A Tour of the Western Region*? Why?

• What would you like to learn more about?

Word Work and Fluency

Spelling

Practice Silent Consonants

Have students turn to page 253 in their Practice Companions. Explain that they will proofread the paragraph to find and correct the misspelled words.

ASSIGN PRACTICE COMPANION 253

Word Study

Review Contractions

Remind students that contractions are words that are formed by two words joined together by an apostrophe.

Practice/Apply

List on the board the following contractions.

• Have students identify the two words that form each contraction and name its meaning.

• Then invite them to use each contraction in a sentence.

haven't	wouldn't
hadn't	would've

ASSIGN PRACTICE COMPANION 263   word study games

Fluency

Paired Reading

Read "At the Trail's End" (Practice Companion, p. 254), once with appropriate expression and once in a monotone voice. Ask students which reading they enjoyed more and why.

Have partners practice reading the selection with expression. Circulate to offer feedback and positive comments about students' readings. **c**

ASSIGN PRACTICE COMPANION 254

---

scaffolding options

a Intervention for Acceleration

AUTHOR'S PURPOSE
Support Intensive- and Strategic-level students' understanding of author's purpose by encouraging them to discuss how the authors of the two selections achieved their purposes:

• Which author provided more explanations and facts?

• Which author told a story that appealed to your five senses?

b Critical Thinking

EVALUATE TEXT
Have students make judgments about which selection best answers Focus Question 3 and why. Ask them to fill in a concept web that shows how the selection answers the question. Have them write the question in the middle circle and include the supporting details around it.

ASSIGN RESOURCE MASTER 11

c Intervention for Acceleration

MISCUE ANALYSIS
As students read, circulate and listen for their miscues. Use one of the miscues for feedback on what type of error to avoid when you reconvene with the whole group.

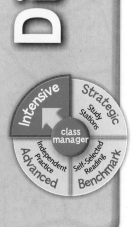

Differentiated Reading
small groups

Objectives
Students will:
- Use differentiated vocabulary
- Reinforce recalling and retelling
- Reinforce using multiple vocabulary strategies
- Read about traveling west to Oregon

Prepare to Read

Review

Review pages 80–89 of *Onward to Oregon!* by asking questions such as these:

ebook
onli**ne** coach

**Differentiated Reader
Pages 90–102**

- What is the setting of the story? What is the land like there?
- What do the characters do on their way to Oregon? How is working together important to the group?
- What did you think was interesting about the story?

Have students discuss any answers they found to the Focus Question: *What is life like in the Pacific States?*

Introduce
Differentiated Vocabulary

Have students complete the Vocabulary Rating Sheet (Resource Master 4).

- Find and pronounce with students the highlighted differentiated vocabulary words (pp. 90–102).
- Use the following routine to discuss each word's meaning.
- For each word, have students jot down and explain answers to prompts.

Vocabulary Routine	
Define	**Ailing** (p. 96) means "being ill."
Example	It is important to take care of an ailing person.
Ask	What could you do to help take care of an ailing person?

Wary (p. 99) means "alert, watchful." *The wary travelers wondered what could possibly happen to them next.* What is a synonym for the word *wary*?

ASSIGN   RESOURCE MASTER **4**

epractice
vocabulary activities

Set Purposes

Display the concept webs students began on Day 2.

- Have partners tell each other what they included their webs so far. Explain that today they will ad new information from the reading.
- Remind students to look for answers to the Focu Question.
- Students will continue working on their Anticipation Guides (Practice Companion, p. 26(

ASSIGN   PRACTICE COMPANION **260**

REINFORCE COMPREHENSION SKILL

Recall and Retell

Remind students that retelling ideas helps readers understand and remember what they've read. Whe retelling, they should focus on important ideas and retell them in the order they occurred.

Have students turn to pages 88–89 as you model retelling the events on the page. **a**

 think aloud
The family realizes that they can't get across the river. They decide that the only way to get across is to take wheels off the wagons and float the wagons across. T have to do this before sundown so they don't lose a d

ASSIGN   PRACTICE COMPANION **262**

Read

Tell students that today they will read pages 90–102 of *Onward to Oregon!* Model your thinking as you re page 90 to help students get started. **b**

 think aloud
The first thing I notice is the title of the second scene: "Safe and Sound." This tells me that the people must have made it across the river safely. I wonder what otf obstacles they will have to overcome as they travel to Oregon. This makes me think about how brave early settlers must have been to travel to new places under unknown, and sometimes unsafe, conditions.

Guide Comprehension

Have students continue reading pages 90–102 independently. Pause periodically to monitor understanding of theme concepts and vocabulary. Have partners discuss their ideas before sharing with the group.

PAGES 90–91 Have students retell what happened on these pages. *(They made it across the river, Hiram felt better, and Jennie gave Annabel her doll.)*

PAGES 92–97 Read aloud the **Strategy Tool Kit** on page 97 to students. Have students jot down their responses before sharing them with the group.

PAGES 98–102 Have students retell the most important events that led up to the story's conclusion. Then have them discuss whether they liked the way the story ended, and why.

What are some examples of descriptive language the author uses? How does understanding descriptive language help you better understand the story?

Check Comprehension

1. Why do you think the author decided to write about early settlers who traveled to Oregon? *(Possible response: to show how difficult life was back then and how they had to depend on each other)*
DETERMINE AUTHOR'S PURPOSE

2. What crushed the family's dream? *(The Byran's house burned down.)* IDENTIFY CAUSE AND EFFECT

3. Why do you think the other families traveling with the Bryans came to help them? MAKE INFERENCES

Respond and Write

1. Ask students how what they learned helped them answer the Focus Question, and have them complete their Anticipation Guides.

2. Have students revisit the concept webs they began on Day 2. Discuss what they learned today about traveling west, and have students add details to their webs.

3. Ask students to tell which character from the story they would most like to meet, and why. What would they ask the person, and what kinds of activities would they like to do together?

scaffolding options

ELL Support

See page 300 of this Teacher's Lesson Guide for vocabulary and instructional support of English language learners at the Intensive level.

a Intervention for Acceleration

READ CHALLENGING TEXT
When students appear comfortable retelling and recalling, have them work with partners to apply the skill to a higher-level Differentiated Reader.

b Literacy Builder

ACADEMIC LANGUAGE
Explain to students that the way an author portrays a character is called *characterization*, which can be either direct or indirect. Point out that direct characterization includes descriptions of how a character looks or acts, as in a boy who is *tall* or speaks *fearfully*. Have partners skim through the selection to find additional examples of characterization.

ebook online coach

Intervention for Acceleration

Students can use the support features in the eBook version of the Differentiated Reader.

Objectives
Students will:
• Use differentiated vocabulary
• Reinforce recalling and retelling
• Reinforce using multiple vocabulary strategies
• Read about working on a fishing boat in Alaska

Differentiated Reading
small groups

Prepare to Read

Review

As students look back over pages 80–90 of *Deckhands*, review the concepts of the selection by asking questions such as these:

**Differentiated Reader
Pages 91–102**

• Where was Roberto traveling to at the beginning of the story? What was it like there?

• What were the cousins going to do for the summer? Why did they decide to do that?

Have students discuss what they found out about the Focus Question: *What is life like in the Pacific States?*

Introduce Differentiated Vocabulary *tested*

Have students complete the Vocabulary Rating Sheet (Resource Master 4).

• Find and pronounce with students the highlighted differentiated vocabulary words (pp. 91–102).

• Use the following routine to discuss each word's meaning.

• For each word, have students jot down and explain answers to prompts.

Vocabulary Routine	
Define	A **stride** (p. 91) is a long step.
Example	My father always strides when he walks.
Ask	What is the difference between a stride and a shuffle?

Hideous (p. 92) means "very ugly." *The strange creature looked hideous.* What is an antonym for the word *hideous*?

Continue the routine with *continental* (p. 95), *scrape* (p. 97), and *replenish* (p. 99), using the Glossary definitions and sentences and asking questions.

ASSIGN   RESOURCE MASTER 4    *epractice* vocabulary activities

Set Purposes

Remind students of the concept webs they began on Day 2.

• Tell students they will add new information they learn while reading to their concept webs.

• Have students continue working on their Anticipation Guides (Practice Companion, p. 260).

• Remind students to look for answers to the Focus Question.

ASSIGN   PRACTICE COMPANION   260

REINFORCE COMPREHENSION SKILL

Recall and Retell *tested*

Guide students to recall the definition of the comprehension skill recall and retell. Help them explain that readers recall and retell in order to better understand and remember what they've read.

Ask students to turn to page 86 while you model retelling the text.

think aloud Anna and Roberto woke up early to meet Captain Ron at the docks. Roberto was surprised at how bright it was outside. Anna explained that it is that way in the summer. It gets light early and doesn't get dark until later at night.

ASSIGN   PRACTICE COMPANION   262

Read

Tell students that today they will read pages 91–102 of *Deckhands*. Model your thinking as you read page 91 to help students get started.

think aloud The first thing I notice on this page is the chapter title: "Captain Ron." I know from the first half of the story that Captain Ron is the captain of the boat that Anna and Roberto will be working on. As I read the first paragraph, I see how the author describes Captain Ron. I wonder if Captain Ron will be nice to Anna and Roberto, or if he will be tough.

Guide Comprehension

Have students continue reading independently. Pause periodically to monitor understanding of theme concepts and vocabulary.

PAGES 91–93 Read the **Strategy Tool Kit** on page 93 and have students share their responses with partners before sharing them with the group.

PAGES 94–95 Ask partners to identify context clues that helped them determine the meaning of *continental*. *(Possible response: The text uses the phrase "the Lower Forty-eight" and talks about the United States, so it must mean the states not including Alaska and Hawaii.)*

PAGES 96–102 Why doesn't Captain Ron use nets to catch salmon? *(Nets scrape the fish, so they don't command as high a price.)*

Check Comprehension

1. What events happen on pages 91–93? *(Roberto and Anna meet Captain Ron, and Captain Ron asks Roberto a lot of questions.)* SEQUENCE EVENTS

2. Why did Captain Ron have a sad look on his face when he talked about oil spills? Why was Roberto surprised to see this look? *(Possible response: When there is a spill, it harms the ocean and the fish; Roberto thought Captain Ron was too tough to show this emotion.)* RECALL AND RETELL

3. What connections did you make with the story? Do you think you would like to work on a fishing boat in Alaska? Why or why not? MAKE CONNECTIONS [b]

Respond and Write

1. Tell students to write personal responses about unfamiliar activities they would like to do over the summer.

2. Have students add information to the concept webs they began on Day 2. Discuss the new information they learned.

3. Ask students to tell how what they learned from the reading today helped them answer the Focus Question, and have them complete their Anticipation Guides.

---

scaffolding options

ELL Support

See page 301 of this Teacher's Lesson Guide for vocabulary and instructional support of English language learners at the Strategic level.

[a] Intervention for Acceleration

VOCABULARY
To help students understand the concept of *replenish*, have them complete a Vocabulary Brainstorming chart (Resource Master 8). Have the group brainstorm words related to *replenish* and list them on the board. Then have partners choose the six words they think are most relevant. Have volunteers explain the words they chose, discussing their reasoning and giving examples as needed.

ASSIGN RESOURCE MASTER 8

[b] Critical Thinking

EVALUATE TEXT AND GRAPHIC SOURCES
Ask partners to look at the illustrations in the selection. Have them evaluate whether the illustrations are reflective of the main ideas on each page, and if not, what the illustration should show instead. Discuss as a group how the illustrations help readers determine the most important information.

ebook online coach
Intervention for Acceleration

Students can use the support features in the eBook version of the Differentiated Reader.

Read and Comprehend [Benchmark]

Differentiated Reading *small groups*

Objectives
Students will:
- Use differentiated vocabulary
- Reinforce recalling and retelling
- Reinforce using multiple vocabulary strategies
- Read a Native American folktale

Prepare to Read

Review

Review pages 80–89 of *Mink and the Sun* with students. Have students look back over the pages and tell about

Differentiated Reader Pages 90–102

the characters, setting, and important events in the story so far. Prompt students to discuss how the selection thus far has helped answer the Focus Question: *What is life like in the Pacific States?*

Introduce
Differentiated Vocabulary *tested*

Have students complete the Vocabulary Rating Sheet (Resource Master 4).

Vocabulary Routine	
Define	**Quiver** (p. 90) means "to shake or tremble slightly."
Example	The scared puppy sat quivering in the corner.
Ask	What would make you quiver?

Partners continue with *grasp* (p. 91), *glorious* (p. 94), *ornament* (p. 95), and *sizzle* (p. 100), using the Glossary definitions and sentences and asking questions.

ASSIGN   RESOURCE MASTER **4**   *epractice vocabulary activities*

Set Purposes

Students will read to add to the concept webs they started on Day 2. Remind students to look for answers to the Focus Question as they read. Students will also complete the Anticipation Guide.

ASSIGN   PRACTICE COMPANION **261**

Read

Guide Comprehension

Students read pages 90–102 of *Mink and the Sun* on their own, using skills and strategies they learned i whole group. Use the prompts to check understand

PAGES 90–95 Have students retell the events on these pages. *(Mink shot arrows in the sky and a rope forme He climbed the rope. He met his aunts, cousins, and father, who asked him to do his duties.)* RECALL AND R

Why wasn't Mink afraid to climb the golden rope?
MAKE INFERENCES

PAGES 96–102 Ask students to write down questions about the story and discuss them with partners.
MONITOR COMPREHENSION **a**

Respond and Write

Have students share their Anticipation Guides and discuss how the story answers the Focus Question.

scaffolding options

ELL Support

See page 302 of this Teacher's Lesson Guide for vocabulary and instructiona support of English language learners a the Benchmark level.

a Challenge

USE MULTIPLE VOCABULARY STRATEGIES
Invite partners to turn back through the selection and point out places where they applied vocabulary strategies to figure out unknown words or to better understand what they read.

Objectives
Students will:
- Use differentiated vocabulary
- Reinforce recalling and retelling
- Reinforce using multiple vocabulary strategies
- Read about building a railroad in the 1800s

Differentiated Reading · small groups

Prepare to Read

Review

Revisit pages 80–89 of *The Mystery of the Railroad Letters* with students. Ask students to describe the characters and setting, and retell the events of the story so far. Have students tell how the selection answers the Focus Question: *What is life like in the Pacific States?*

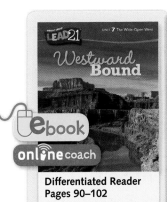

ebook
online coach

Differentiated Reader Pages 90–102

Introduce Differentiated Vocabulary

tested

Have students complete the Vocabulary Rating Sheet (Resource Master 4).

Vocabulary Routine

Define	**Jockey** (p. 92) means "to maneuver to get a better advantage in something."
Example	The fastest runners tried to jockey for a position near the front of the pack.
Ask	Where else might people jockey for position?

Partners continue the routine with *garb* (p. 94), *resentful* (p. 95), and *rift* (p. 100), using the Glossary definitions and sentences and asking questions.  **a**

ASSIGN **RESOURCE MASTER 4**

epractice
vocabulary activities

Set Purposes

Remind students of the concept webs they started on Day 2. Tell students that they will read pages 90–102 to:

- Add information to their concept webs.
- Look for answers to the Focus Question.
- Complete their Anticipation Guides (Practice Companion, p. 261).

ASSIGN **PRACTICE COMPANION 261**

Read

Guide Comprehension

Students finish reading *The Mystery of the Railroad Letters* on their own, using skills and strategies they learned in whole group. After students read, use the following prompts:

PAGES 90–97 Have partners retell the events that Henry shared with his cousin in his letters. **RECALL AND RETELL**

PAGES 98–102 Which information on these pages was more important: Tacoma being awarded the new terminus or Clara stealing the letters? Support your answers. **DETERMINE IMPORTANT INFORMATION**

Respond and Write

Have students add details to their concept webs and summarize how what they read today helps answer the Focus Question. Students will also finish their Anticipation Guides.

scaffolding options

ELL Support

See page 303 of this Teacher's Lesson Guide for vocabulary and instructional support of English language learners at the Advanced level.

a Challenge

VOCABULARY: USE SYNONYMS
Challenge partners to identify synonyms for each vocabulary word. As they read, invite them to consider how the meaning of the story would change if the author chose to use one of the synonyms instead.

Share, Connect, Assess

Objectives
Students will:
- Summarize selections
- Make text-to-world connections
- Write about their place in history
- Monitor their progress

Wrap Up
whole group

Share Text Connections

Building Classroom Community

Make Text-to-World Connections Bring students back together from their small groups to summarize their selections.

- Encourage students to use theme and other academic vocabulary in their summaries.

- As students discuss the texts, help them to make connections between texts and the world. For example, students have learned about people traveling the Oregon Trail. Point out that pioneers helped settle many of the areas in what is now the United States, and Americans benefit from their adventures.

- Ask students to share the activities they completed during Respond and Write.

- Have students share how what they've read answers the week's Focus Question.

etools 21
theme wall

Daily Writing

Invite students to think about a way they would like contribute to American history. Encourage them to creative in thinking of new modes of transportation solution to pollution problems, and so on.

For additional writing practice, remind students to access the Story Starter from their student Home P

etools 21
- writing tool
- story starter

Student Self Assessment

- Remind students that they are responsible for th learning and that it is helpful to be aware of how well they understand what they are reading, wri talking, and thinking about in the classroom.

- You may want students to reflect on their reading learning by using their Personal Reading Logs and Daily Progress sheets (Resource Masters 1, 3).

ASSIGN RESOURCE MASTER **1, 3**

Daily Progress Monitoring

To ensure that students have mastered the day's skills and strategies, monitor their success in completing the following independent work:
- **Vocabulary:** Practice Companion, pp. 258–259
- **Comprehension:** Practice Companion, p. 262
- **Word Study:** Practice Companion, p. 263
- **Spelling:** Practice Companion, p. 253
- **Fluency:** Practice Companion, p. 254
- **Study Station Work Record:** Resource Master 2
- **Self Assessment:** Resource Masters 1, 3

epractice
reporting

Home Connection

Distribute the Unit 7 Take-Home Activities from the Home Connection book. Tell students to complete the activities with their caregivers.

Day at a Glance

Lesson Highlights

- Build Vocabulary Connections
- Reinforce Comprehension Strategy: Determine Important Information
- Use Text Features
- Reinforce Word Study: Contractions
- Publish and Present an Autobiography, pp. 282–283

Materials

	Teacher's Lesson Guide	Student Components	Digital 21
Interactive Reading	pp. 246–249	• Theme Reader, pp. 380–438 • Practice Companion, pp. 251–252, 254–257, 263 • Resource Masters 11, 14, 18, 21	ebook online coach / epractice word study games
Differentiated Reading	pp. 250–255, 300–303 (ELL)	• Differentiated Readers • Resource Master 14	ebook online coach / epractice vocabulary activities
Wrap Up	p. 256	• Resource Masters 1–3	etools 21 • theme wall • writing tool • story starter
Writing and Language Arts	pp. 282–283	• Writing Models Chart, pp. 52–53 • Practice Companion, p. 269	

Tips for Success

- Guide students to make use multiple strategies as they read (Model Multiple Strategies, p. 247).
- You may wish to use the Assessment on Practice Companion pages 275–276 to monitor student progress on skill and strategy use over the past two weeks.

21st CENTURY SKILLS Remind students to work on their Inquiry Projects during Independent Practice or Self-Selected Reading time.

Oral Language and Vocabulary

Objectives
Students will:
• Make connections to the theme
• Make vocabulary connections

Build Theme Connections

Use Theme Reader pages 396–397 to read Focus Question 4: *What is life like in the Pacific States?* Draw

a Concept and Word Web (Resource Master 11) on the board and label it *Life in the Pacific States*. Point out that students have read a lot of information throughout the unit that answers this question. Ask students to help you add to the web by thinking about other texts, experiences, or knowledge that relate to the question.

**Theme Reader
Pages 377–438**

To prompt discussion, ask questions such as:

• What experiences do you have with the people and places of the Pacific States?

• What else have you read about this topic? Have you seen any articles or television shows about it?

Begin a discussion by modeling this thinking:

 One of the first things I think about when I think of the Pacific States is how amazing the scenery is there. From its majestic mountains to its beautiful coastline, it is really like nowhere else in the country. **a**

Bring students back together as a class to discuss their responses. Then invite students to discuss how answering the Focus Question helps them understand what makes the West exceptional.

ASSIGN | RESOURCE MASTER | **11**

Build Vocabulary Connections

Remind students that they have been using vocabu related to the unit theme, *The Wide-Open West*.

• To deepen understanding of the theme and differentiated vocabulary that students have bee learning, explain to students that they will classi words.

• Have students use T-Charts (Resource Master 14 and label the columns "Easy" and "Challenging."

• Invite students to list words they find easy to remember in the "Easy" column and words they challenging to remember in the "Challenging" column.

Discuss with students the words they know pretty

• Which strategies did you use to remember the meanings of these words?

• Do you use any of these words regularly?

Discuss with students strategies they can use to remember difficult words.

• Do any of these words remind you of other words?

• Are there any other words you see that can help yo remember the meanings of the challenging words?

Have partners continue to discuss strategies they c use. **b**

ASSIGN | RESOURCE MASTER | **14**
| PRACTICE COMPANION | **251**

Read and Comprehend

Objectives
Students will:
- Reinforce determining important information

REINFORCE **COMPREHENSION STRATEGY**

Determine ✔tested
Important Information

Define

Ask students to recall that readers determine important information to better understand what they read.

Remind students that readers use more than one strategy as they read. Invite students to share other strategies they know.

Model Multiple-Strategy Use

Use page 413 from the Theme Reader to model using multiple strategies.

> I can see that the apple tree is important to the story because the story begins with a lengthy discussion of the tree. Also, the tree is called *el manzano real*, which the text tells me means "the royal apple tree." I know the royal family in England is important, so the apple tree in the story must be important too.

Guided Practice

Have partners complete Use Multiple Strategies (Resource Master 21) to support them as they apply multiple comprehension strategies while reading pages 414–415.

- Circulate to provide support as needed, suggesting strategies that may work and asking guiding questions.

- After partners have finished, lead a class discussion about the strategies students used as they read. **c**

Independent Practice

Have students continue to read the selection and apply multiple strategies. Encourage them to record strategy use on Resource Master 21.

ASSIGN	RESOURCE MASTER	21
	PRACTICE COMPANION	256–257

scaffolding options

a Literacy Builder

CONCEPT DEVELOPMENT
Ask students to draw pictures of something related to the Focus Question. Then have them share their pictures with partners. Have them explain what the pictures show and how they relate to the Focus Question. Ask partners to compare and contrast their pictures to see what is similar about them and what is different.

b Critical Thinking

ANALYZE VOCABULARY CONNECTIONS
After students have sorted through words on their own to make decisions about how to classify them, allow them to work in pairs to share their reasoning. Point out that understanding the logic in a partner's reasoning can help students compare the similarities and differences among words. Have students share their thoughts about the words with the class.

c Challenge

USE MULTIPLE STRATEGIES
Challenge students to demonstrate their use of multiple strategies by having them think through their thought processes aloud with partners. Once they've done this, invite volunteers to share their thinking with the class.

Read and Comprehend (continued)

Objectives
Students will:
- Analyze text structure
- Reread to find text evidence
- Connect themes across texts
- Reinforce determining important information

Prepare to Read

Use Text Structure

Remind students that writers organize information in different ways. One way to organize text is *sequence*, or telling events in the order they happened.

**Theme Reader
Pages 377–438**

Point out that *Juan Verdades: The Man Who Couldn't Tell a Lie* uses sequence to tell the events of the story.

Ask a volunteer to read page 418. Then ask:

- What signal words do you see on page 418? *(the next day, that afternoon, then)*

Point out that the selection *A Tour of the Western Region* includes more than one type of text structure, but the chapters that explain historical events use sequence. **a**

Ask students to turn to page 392. Guide them to locate the signal words *many years later* and *today*.

Set Purposes

Encourage students to think about how text structure helps communicate ideas and information as they revisit *A Tour of the Western Region* and *Juan Verdades: The Man Who Couldn't Tell a Lie.*

Students will use T-Charts (Resource Master 14) to find and record text evidence that answers Focus Question 4: *What is life like in the Pacific States?*

ASSIGN   **RESOURCE MASTER 14**

Read Across Texts

Have students read independently or with partners find and record text evidence in their T-charts. Pau periodically to prompt them to find text evidence a note the text structure of the selections.

PAGES 404–405 What signals does the author use to show sequence on these pages? *(dates and signal wo such as "By the 1830s" and "In the 1880s and 1890.*

What was life like for the Inuit? *(It was too cold and snowy to farm, so they mostly hunted; they wore clothing made from furs; homes were made from sto sod, or snow.)*

What did you find out about the history of California? *(The Gold Rush brought about 300,000 people there in the 1800s.)*

PAGES 406–407 Which context clues help you deterr the meaning of the word *folly*? *(Possible response: T fact that some people disagreed with the purchase or Alaska, so* folly *must mean something foolish.)*

What is the culture of the Pacific States like?

PAGES 409–438 Look through *Juan Verdades: The M Who Couldn't Tell a Lie* and identify words or phrase that indicate sequence.

ASSIGN   **RESOURCE MASTER 14**

Respond

Have partners discuss why the authors chose to use sequence in these selections, and how noting the te structure helped students better understand what they read. Guide students to use the text evidence t gathered to respond to the Focus Question.

Writer's Response

Have students choose one activity:

- What are the most important ideas or concepts you have learned from both selections? Write about them and explain why they are important.

- Use what you've learned about the Focus Question to write a paragraph about life in the Pacific States.

model
read
share

Word Work and Fluency

Objectives
Students will:
- Practice spelling words with silent consonants
- Reinforce contractions
- Practice fluent reading

Spelling

Practice Test

Have partners dictate spelling words to one another. Then have them self-correct their tests. Remind them to focus on any words they misspelled.

ASSIGN | PRACTICE COMPANION **252**

Word Study

Reinforce Contractions

Lead students to recall that contractions are made up of two words and are joined by an apostrophe. Offer an example, such as *haven't*, and have students name the two words that make up the contraction.

Practice/Apply

Ask volunteers to identify contractions in both *A Tour of the Western Region* and *Juan Verdades: The Man Who Couldn't Tell a Lie*, and have them write the words on the board.

Pronounce each word, ask students to identify the original words, and discuss each contraction's meaning.

ASSIGN | PRACTICE COMPANION **263** | ePractice word study games

Fluency

Personal Rehearsal

Remind students that reading too fast or too slow makes the text hard to understand. Model reading "At the Trail's End" (Practice Companion, p. 254) with proper pacing.

- Read it again very fast, and a third time very slow.
- Ask students to discuss how reading at a good pace aids understanding.
- Have students rehearse the selection and complete the Reading Response Form (Practice Companion, p. 255).

ASSIGN | PRACTICE COMPANION **254–255**

---

scaffolding options

a Intervention for Acceleration

USE TEXT STRUCTURE
Allow students who are visual learners or need help organizing ideas to use a Time Line (Resource Master 18) to note the events that happen in each selection. Have them write the event, the date or time, and any signal words or time-order cues they find in the text.

ASSIGN | RESOURCE MASTER **18**

b Intervention for Acceleration

CONTRACTIONS
Provide students with the following contractions and work together to write them as two words:
- Shouldn't
- Hadn't
- Would've
- Could've

Read and Comprehend [Intensive]

Differentiated Reading *small groups*

Objectives
Students will:
• Extend vocabulary
• Reread to find text evidence
• Reinforce determining important information
• Reinforce recalling and retelling

Prepare to Read

Extend Vocabulary ✓*tested*

Explain to students that one way to expand vocabulary knowledge is to understand the relationships between words.

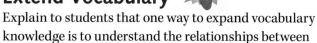

Differentiated Reader Pages 80–102

What is a synonym for the word *pretty*? *(beautiful)*

Pretty and *beautiful* are related words.

Provide word pairs for students. Have them discuss how the words are related.

The words *hardship* and *obstacle* are related words because they are synonyms. Look at the other words and think about how they are related.

hardship	obstacle (Synonym)
rally	weaken (Antonym)
blistering	severe (Synonym)
landmark	mountain (Example)
commotion	calm (Antonym)
frail	weak (Synonym)
ailing	healthy (Antonym)
wary	nervous (Synonym)

epractice
vocabulary activities

Set Purposes

Students will revisit *Onward to Oregon!* to find and record text evidence to support answers to the Focus Question: *What is life like in the Pacific States?*

Use Text Evidence

Distribute T-Charts (Resource Master 14). When students find a fact or detail that might help them answer the Focus Question, they should record it in their charts.

Help students get started by reading aloud page 81. Model your thinking as you read.

think aloud
The Focus Question is *What is life like in the Pacific States?* I read that the Bryan family lost their farm in Missouri and that is why they were traveling to Oregon to begin a new life. I know that's the reason many people long ago took a chance and traveled west. The Pacific States must have offered something to these families that other areas didn't.

ASSIGN [RESOURCE MASTER **14**]

Read

Guide Comprehension

Have partners reread *Onward to Oregon!* Pairs should work together to record text evidence in their charts. Students should share their notes with the group after each chapter. Use the prompts below to provide support as needed. **a**

PAGES 80–85 Invite students to determine which information is important on these pages.
DETERMINE IMPORTANT INFORMATION
Ask students to identify how this information helps them answer the Focus Question. USE TEXT EVIDENCE

PAGES 86–89 What do the illustrations help you understand about life on the trail? USE GRAPHIC SOURCES

PAGES 90–97 What did the Bryans want to do at Independence Rock? RECALL AND RETELL
Have students identify text that answers the Focus Question and record it in their charts. USE TEXT EVIDENCE

PAGES 98–102 What happened when the Bryans got to Oregon City? DETERMINE IMPORTANT INFORMATION
Guide students to use this information to help them answer the Focus Question. USE TEXT EVIDENCE

Respond and Write

Have students look over the text evidence they've gathered and share one or two items with the group. Guide students to understand how the information from the text helps them answer the Focus Question.

Prepare to Share

Tell students they will discuss **Think Back** on page 103 of their Differentiated Readers tomorrow with their mixed groups.

1. **Check Understanding** After students have completed the activity independently, bring students back together to share their ideas with the class.

2. **Understand Literary Elements** Explain that students will look at the dialogue in the story and then share their ideas of how the dialogue provides information about each character.

3. **Share and Compare** Explain that when students meet tomorrow with their groups, they will be comparing summaries of their stories with partners and identifying how the summaries are the same and different. **b**

4. **Think Critically** Complete the activity as a group. Explain that students should think about examples of how the West is exceptional.

scaffolding options

ELL Support

See page 300 of this Teacher's Lesson Guide for vocabulary and instructional support of English language learners at the Intensive level.

a Literacy Builder

FIND TEXT EVIDENCE
Encourage partners to listen for evidence they did not record and add it to their own charts. Encourage them to analyze the evidence they missed and connect it to the Focus Question.

b Intervention for Acceleration

COMPARE AND CONTRAST
You may wish to have partners complete a Venn diagram to organize their thoughts about the characters. As needed, ask guiding questions to help students identify information.

ebook **online coach**

Intervention for Acceleration

Students can use the support features in the eBook version of the Differentiated Reader.

Read and Comprehend   Strategic

Objectives
Students will:
- Extend vocabulary
- Reread to find text evidence
- Reinforce determining important information
- Reinforce recalling and retelling

Prepare to Read

Extend Vocabulary
Write the differentiated vocabulary words on the board and ask students to sit in a circle.

ebook

online coach

Differentiated Reader Pages 80–102

- Explain that today they will use differentiated vocabulary words to make connections with other words.

- Say the vocabulary word *pristine* and model sharing the first word that comes to mind.

think aloud The word *pristine* makes me think of the word *clear* because I have seen water that was so clear and pristine, it almost didn't look real. Silently think of the first word that comes to your mind when you hear the word *pristine*.

Ask students to take turns sharing their word associations, and have them explain why they associate their answers with *pristine*. Explain that there are no right or wrong answers. Have students continue with the remaining vocabulary words.

alert	continental
muffle	scrape
stride	replenish
hideous	

epractice
vocabulary activities

Set Purposes
Tell students that today they will reread the selection *Deckhands* to find text evidence that will help them answer the Focus Question: *What is life like in the Pacific States?*

Use Text Evidence
Distribute T-Charts (Resource Master 14). When students find facts or details that might help them answer the Focus Question, they should record the their charts.

Help students get started by reading aloud page 81. Model your thinking as you read.

think aloud The Focus Question is *What is life like in the Pacific States?* The text tells me that the people in the story to take a water taxi into town. This is not something I've ever done, but it is obviously a part of life in certa parts of Alaska. I will write this in my chart.

ASSIGN   RESOURCE MASTER 14

Read

Guide Comprehension
Partners should reread *Deckhands* to find and add evidence to their charts. Pause periodically to chec comprehension with prompts, such as the following

CHAPTER 1 Which word on page 84 signals that information on this page is organized in sequence? *(Af* **IDENTIFY TEXT STRUCTURE**

What did Anna tell Roberto he would be doing for th first week of his visit? How was Anna's explanation different from Aunt Sarah's? *(working on a fishing bc Aunt Sarah made it sound like a lot of work with a m captain)* **RECALL AND RETELL**

What does this chapter tell you about what life is like the Pacific States? *(Many people fish as a livelihood.)* **USE TEXT EVIDENCE**

CHAPTER 2 Explain what Roberto noticed that was different about Alaska. *(Possible response: The sun came up earlier in the day than where he was from.)* **USE TEXT EVIDENCE**

CHAPTERS 3 AND 4 What are the important events Chapters 3 and 4? *(Students should discuss what Ann and Roberto experienced during their time fishing.)* **DETERMINE IMPORTANT INFORMATION**

Respond and Write

Have students look over the text evidence they've gathered and share one or two items with the group. Guide students to understand how the information from the text helps them answer the Focus Question.

Prepare to Share

Tell students they will discuss **Think Back** on page 103 of their Differentiated Readers tomorrow with their mixed groups.

1. **Check Understanding** After students have completed the activity independently, bring them back together to share their ideas with the class.

2. **Understand Literary Elements** Explain that students will look at the dialogue in the story and then share their ideas of how the dialogue provides information about each character.

3. **Share and Compare** Explain that when students meet tomorrow with their groups, they will be comparing summaries of their stories with partners and identifying how the summaries are the same and different.

4. **Think Critically** Complete the activity as a group. Explain that students are thinking about examples of ways that the West is exceptional.

scaffolding options

ELL Support

See page 301 of this Teacher's Lesson Guide for vocabulary and instructional support of English language learners at the Strategic level.

a Intervention for Acceleration

FEEDBACK
As students reread with their partners, circulate and listen for their use of text structure and text evidence. Use an example as a starting point for discussion when you address the group together.

b Intervention for Acceleration

AUTHOR'S PURPOSE
Remind students that authors write for many reasons. Have them reread the text and think about the author's message. Have them ask themselves:

Is the author trying to make me laugh?

Is the author trying to teach me something?

What does the author want me to learn from reading the text?

ebook **online coach**

Intervention for Acceleration

Students can use the support features in the eBook version of the Differentiated Reader.

Read and Comprehend   Benchmark

Objectives
Students will:
- Extend vocabulary
- Reread to find text evidence
- Reinforce determining important information
- Reinforce recalling and retelling

Differentiated Reading
small groups

Prepare to Read

Extend Vocabulary

Explain that students can broaden their vocabulary by making connections among words.

**Differentiated Reader
Pages 80–102**

Write differentiated vocabulary words on the board. Invite students to name related words by asking questions or giving prompts. Relationships may include synonyms, antonyms, examples, and word parts. For example, you might ask:

What is a synonym for *whittled*? *(Possible answer: cut)*

whittle	ornament
laced	sizzle
mock	descend
quiver	grasp
glorious	

Set Purposes

Tell students that today they will reread the selection *Mink and the Sun* to find text evidence that will help them answer the Focus Question: *What is life like in the Pacific States?*

Use Text Evidence

Students will use T-Charts (Resource Master 14) to record text evidence that answers the Focus Question. Invite volunteers to page through the selection and point out examples of text evidence.

ASSIGN **RESOURCE MASTER 14**

Read

Guide Comprehension

Students will reread *Mink and the Sun* to record text evidence. You may wish to use the following prompt

CHAPTERS 1–2 Ask students how Mink's mother prov to him who his father was. *(She showed him the golden arrows the sun had sent down when Mink wa. born.)* DETERMINE IMPORTANT INFORMATION ⓐ

CHAPTERS 3–4 What caused Earth to catch fire? *(Mink ran across the sky and moved the clouds to see mother, showing himself completely.)* RECALL AND RETEL

Respond and Write

1. Lead students to discuss any text evidence they found that helps them answer the Focus Question

2. Explain that they will discuss **Think Back** when they meet with their mixed groups tomorrow.

scaffolding options

ELL Support

See page 302 of this Teacher's Lesson Guide for vocabulary and instructional support of English language learners at the Benchmark level.

ⓐ Critical Thinking

ANALYZE AUTHOR'S PURPOSE
Suggest that the author could have started the story when Mink was already born. Ask students to think about the author's purpose for starting the selection with Mink's mother's story. How would their views of Mink and his mother be different if they did not know the background provided by the author?

Differentiated Reading small groups

Objectives
Students will:
- Extend vocabulary
- Reread to find text evidence
- Reinforce determining important information
- Reinforce recalling and retelling

Prepare to Read

Extend Vocabulary ✓tested

To broaden understanding of vocabulary words, lead students in relating vocabulary to other words or phrases.

[Differentiated Reader cover: LEAD 21 unit 7 The Wide-Open West — Westward Bound]

ebook
online coach

Differentiated Reader Pages 80–102

Write differentiated vocabulary words on the board.

Challenge students to select a vocabulary word and then give a related word or phrase and state how it is related to the vocabulary word.

For example, students might say *e-mail* for the word *telegram*. Students should state that these are both examples of communication.

telegram	rift
relieved	terminus
gist	jockey
garb	resentful

epractice
vocabulary activities

Set Purposes

Explain that today students will reread the selection *The Mystery of the Railroad Letters* to find text evidence that helps them answer the Focus Question: *What is life like in the Pacific States?*

Use Text Evidence

Ask why using text evidence to answer questions is important. Invite students to use T-charts to record text evidence that answers the Focus Question: *What is life like in the Pacific States?*

ASSIGN   RESOURCE MASTER   14

Read

Guide Comprehension

Have students reread *The Mystery of the Railroad Letters* independently. After the reading, you may wish to check comprehension with the following prompts:

PAGES 80–85   Have students identify what John and Henry shared with one another through their letters. DETERMINE IMPORTANT INFORMATION

PAGES 86–102   How do the letters between the cousins help answer the Focus Question? USE TEXT EVIDENCE

Respond and Write

1. Invite partners to compare the text evidence they found today that answers the Focus Question. **a**

2. Explain that they will discuss **Think Back** when they meet with their mixed groups tomorrow.

scaffolding options

ELL Support

See page 303 of this Teacher's Lesson Guide for vocabulary and instructional support of English language learners at the Advanced level.

a Challenge ✓tested

COMPREHENSION: RECALL AND RETELL
Ask students to retell a part of the story that they feel expresses what the author's purpose was. How would the story have been different if told by a third-person narrator? If told by one of the cousins?

Share, Connect, Assess

Objectives
Students will:

- Use key concepts and vocabulary
- Use text evidence to answer essential questions
- Make text-to-text connections
- Write about finding text evidence
- Monitor their progress

Wrap Up
whole group

Share Text Connections

 Building Classroom Community

Make Text-to-Text Connections Bring students back together from their small groups to share how the text evidence they gathered from their Differentiated Reader selections helped them to answer the Focus Question: *What is life like in the Pacific States?*

- Encourage students to use theme and other academic vocabulary as they share their responses.

- Ensure that students from all groups have a chance to contribute to the discussion.

- As students share text evidence, help them make connections between texts. For example, both Mink in *Mink and the Sun* and Roberto in *Deckhands* go to visit relatives.

 **etools 21**
• theme wall

Daily Writing

Ask students to write briefly about the strategy and method they used to find text evidence. Encourage them to describe how the text evidence helped them answer the Theme and Focus Questions.

For additional writing practice, remind students to access the Story Starter from their student Home Pa

 **etools 21**
• writing tool
• story starter

Student Self Assessment

- Remind students that they are responsible for the learning and that it is helpful to be aware of how well they understand what they are reading, writ talking, and thinking about in the classroom.

- You may want students to reflect on their reading learning by using their Personal Reading Logs and Daily Progress sheets (Resource Masters 1, 3).

ASSIGN **RESOURCE MASTER 1, 3**

Daily Progress Monitoring

To ensure that students have mastered the day's skills and strategies, monitor their success in completing the following independent work:

- **Vocabulary:** Practice Companion, p. 251
- **Comprehension:** Practice Companion, pp. 256–257
- **Word Study:** Practice Companion, p. 263
- **Spelling:** Practice Companion, pp. 252–253
- **Fluency:** Practice Companion, pp. 254–255
- **Study Station Work Record:** Resource Master 2
- **Self Assessment:** Resource Masters 1, 3

 **epractice**
reporting

 Home Connection

Distribute the Unit 7 Take-Home Activities from the Home Connection book. Tell students to complete the activities with their caregivers.

Day at a Glance

Lesson Highlights

- Review Project Plan
- Minilesson: Consider Your Audience
- Cross-Text Sharing
- Fluency Presentation
- Spelling Posttest

Materials

	Teacher's Lesson Guide	Student Components	Digital 21
Inquiry	pp. 258–261	• Practice Companion, pp. 264–265, 370, 373 • Resource Masters 37, 38	etools 21 inquiry project
Cross-Text Sharing	pp. 262–263	• Differentiated Readers • Practice Companion, p. 267 • Resource Masters 14, 35	ebook online coach
Wrap Up	pp. 264–265	• Assessment Handbook, pp. 13–14, 140 • Differentiated Reader, p. 103 • Practice Companion, p. 266 • Resource Master 1	etools 21 • theme wall • writing tool • story starter

Inquiry Process Guide

Week 1, Day 5	Week 2, Day 5	Week 3, Day 5	Week 4, Day 5
1. Generate Ideas and Questions 2. Make a Conjecture 3. Make Plans to Collect Information	Days 1–4: Collect Information 4. Organize and Synthesize Information 5. Confirm or Revise Your Conjecture	Days 1–4: Collect Information 6. Develop Presentation	Days 1–4: Collect Information 7. Deliver Presentation

Tips for Success

- Prepare any technology that students might need for their Inquiry presentations.
- Provide Presentation Rubrics (Resource Master 38) for students to use while they critique the Inquiry Presentations.
- Monitor student weekly progress on skills and strategy use, by using the Assessment on Practice Companion pages 275–276.

Develop Ideas

Objectives
Students will:
- Make connections between the theme question and Inquiry project
- Review the Inquiry process
- Practice considering your audience

Inquiry whole group

Review Project Plan

Connect to the Theme

Ask a volunteer to recall the Theme Question: *What makes the West exceptional?* and the Focus Question: *What is life like in the Pacific States?* Say:

What was the most interesting thing you learned about life in the Pacific States? What is one word you would use to describe life in these states?

ebook
online coach

**Theme Reader
Pages 380–438**

Be sure students know to access Inquiry Project online from their student Home Page.

Discuss Previous Week

- Students take out their Inquiry folders.
- Review the Inquiry steps covered last week:

6. Develop Presentation

- Choose a Format
- Organize Presentation

- Verify that each group has completed the items on the Week 3 Inquiry Checklist (Practice Companion, p. 245).

ASSIGN PRACTICE COMPANION **245**

Model the Inquiry Process

Share New Information

Explain to students that, before rehearsing their presentations, their groups should take turns sharing information collected over the past week. Give students time to revise their presentation plans as needed.

7. Deliver Presentation

Rehearse Presentations Tell groups they will have several minutes to rehearse their presentations. **a**

- Remind students to use their Presentation Organizers and/or note cards as they rehearse their presentations.
- Remind students to practice speaking clearly and loud enough for everyone to hear while using appropriate gestures.

Deliver and Critique Presentations Assign each group a partner group to work with.

- Review the Presentation Rubric (Resource Master 38) with students. Make sure that students understand how to use the rubric for each evaluation category. **b**
- Explain that after each presentation, members of both groups will use their Presentation Rubrics to critique both their own presentations and their partner groups' presentations.

Model giving a critique that demonstrates positive feedback and constructive comments:

I thought the group was well-prepared. Everyone had their notes and had an equal speaking part. One thing I noticed was that some members looked at their notes all the time and did not make eye contact with the audience. Remember to look at your notes only from time to time, rather than reading from them directly.

ASSIGN RESOURCE MASTER **38**

Revise Presentations Remind students that they will have a second chance to present their findings—this time to the whole class. They should use the feedback from their self critiques and their partner groups' critiques to revise and refine their presentations. Model this process:

Look for ways to improve in the categories in which you scored a 1 or a 2. For example, if you need improvement in the use of notes, practice giving your speech to your group. Focus on making eye contact with your audience. You may want to make notes on your cards to remind yourself to look up at the audience. **c**

Minilesson: Consider Your Audience

Tell students that when they give their presentations, they need to think about how to make their information interesting and easy for their audience to understand. Say:

Start your presentation by explaining the most basic ideas about your topic. You need to make sure to include background information about your topic as well. Think about what ideas might be difficult for your audience to understand and decide on a way to make them clearer. For example, a diagram, photograph, or numbered list might help your audience better understand the information you are presenting.

Model reading a recipe to students. Then present the same recipe with numbered steps and a picture of the finished product. Ask them which presentation was easier to understand and why.

Have students work in their groups to choose one challenging concept from their presentations. Tell them to decide how to support that information. Then invite volunteers from each group to present the information to the class. Discuss as a group how the information was easier to understand with the support provided.

scaffolding options

a Literacy Builder

SHARE STRENGTHS
Have students who are more confident speakers pair with less confident students to rehearse their presentations. The more confident speaker can provide advice, feedback, and support to the speaker who does not feel as comfortable speaking in front of a group.

b ELL Support

BUILD ORAL LANGUAGE
Help students provide constructive critiques by giving them sentence frames such as "I liked the way your group ..." and "Next time, try to ... so that ... . Provide assistance completing the frames if necessary.

c Intervention for Acceleration

SUPPORT REVISION
Tell students who feel upset or uncertain about the revision process that all writers and performers revise their work to make it better. Help students prioritize their revisions and break down what they need to do into steps. Suggest that they start with their lowest scoring area and save minor changes for last.

Collaborate and Communicate

21st CENTURY SKILLS

Objectives
Students will:
- Review discussion roles
- Rehearse and deliver presentations
- Critique and refine presentations
- Collaborate in Inquiry groups

Inquiry
mixed groups

Continue Inquiry Group Work

The following Resource Masters and Practice Companion pages will be used in this lesson.

Step	Resource Master	Practice Companion
All	Collaboration Rubric 39 Evaluation Rubric C 42	Week 4 Inquiry Checklist, p. 264 Group Roles, p. 370
7.	Presentation Organizer 37 Presentation Rubric 38	Inquiry Planner, p. 265

Review Discussion Roles

Have students move into their Inquiry Groups. Have groups informally evaluate their discussions from the previous week. Write on the board the following questions:

> - Why is it important for everyone to contribute to the discussion?
> - What have you learned about sharing your ideas in a respectful way?

- Review the group discussion roles and refer students to Group Discussion Roles (Practice Companion, p. 370).
- Give students the opportunity to ask clarifying questions about group roles.

ASSIGN PRACTICE COMPANION **370**

Monitor Student Progress

Use the Collaboration Rubric (Resource Master 39) and the Inquiry Evaluation Rubric C (Resource Master 42) to monitor student progress throughout the project. Review the project expectations with students before beginning Inquiry Group work.

USE RESOURCE MASTER **39, 42**

Inquiry Groups

Share New Information

- Have students take out their research notes to sha organize, and synthesize any new information.
- Have students share any independent work done the presentation formats.
- Students revise their presentation plans as neede
- Prompt group Checkers to monitor progress on th Week 4 Inquiry Checklist (Practice Companion, p. 264).

ASSIGN PRACTICE COMPANION **264**

7. Deliver Presentation
critical thinking make connections

Rehearse Presentations Remind students that when they deliver their presentations, they need to make sure that their visual aids are large enough to be read by their audience, even from the back of the classroom.

- Have group members who aren't speaking watch group members who are talking and give feedbac about expression and gestures.
- Point out that students must be careful not to sta in front of the information they are presenting or their viewers will not be able to see it.
- Give time alerts for when to transition to the next step.

Deliver and Critique Presentations Students should refer to the Presentation Rubric (Resource Master 38). Each student will follow this rubric to write on separate sheets of paper scores for both his or her own group's and the partner group's presentations.

- Make sure each group takes several minutes after each presentation to compare individual evaluations to come up with an overall evaluation for its partner group. **b** **c**

- Group Questioners prompt each member for his or her feedback.

- The group Recorder creates an overall evaluation to present to the partner group.

- Have groups wait until after both have presented to exchange their written evaluations and give verbal feedback.

- Remind students to be respectful of the other groups and to offer their peers encouragement.

ASSIGN RESOURCE MASTER **38**

Revise Presentations Prompt groups to use the information from their self critiques and their peer critiques to refine their presentations, addressing the areas that scored lowest.

- Give students time to discuss the feedback they received, fill out new Presentation Organizers (Resource Master 37) or revise their note cards, and revise any visual aids as needed.

- Prompt Discussion Monitors to help keep their groups focused and on track.

- Remind students that their revisions are another form of collaboration, and they need to keep their discussions on topic.

ASSIGN RESOURCE MASTER **37**

Identify New Questions

Explain to students that they may continue to investigate their Inquiry topics after Unit 7 is complete. Have students list any new questions they may have on the Week 4 Inquiry Planner (Practice Companion, p. 265) for future investigation on their own.

ASSIGN PRACTICE COMPANION **265**

scaffolding options

a Critical Thinking

SYNTHESIZE
Remind students that to synthesize new information, they should think about how it relates to the ideas they already have gathered. Have students look for repeated words, concepts, and connections among ideas and guide them to recognize how the ideas are related.

b Critical Thinking

EVALUATE
Remind students that when they evaluate presentations, they are making judgments about what they see and hear. Point out that judgments are neither right nor wrong but should be supported with specific examples. Tell students to note examples to support their evaluations as they listen to other students' presentations.

c Literacy Builder

ACTIVE LISTENING
Tell students that active listening will help them evaluate the presentations. Suggest that they clear their desk from any distraction, focus on each speaker, and try to put what the speakers say into their own words to confirm their understandings.

Connect Ideas

Objectives
Students will:
- Share information across texts
- Use speaking and listening skills
- Make connections between the Differentiated Readers and the Inquiry project

Cross-Text Sharing
mixed groups

CONNECT **DIFFERENTIATED READERS**

Cross-Text Sharing

While students stay in their Inquiry Groups, announce Cross-Text Sharing time. Remind students that they have read about what life is like in the Pacific States.

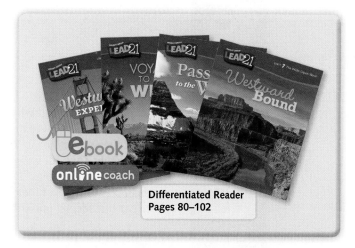

ebook
online coach

Differentiated Reader
Pages 80–102

- Remind students that all Differentiated Readers can be considered a source of information to answer their Inquiry Questions. **a**

- Have students from each differentiated group share the title of the selection they read, summarize the plot, and use the illustrations to help them retell the story. Have students share any information that can be used to help answer their groups' Inquiry Questions. **b**

Monitor Student Progress

As you observe and work with each group, fill in your observations using the Collaboration Rubric (Resource Master 39).

USE RESOURCE MASTER **39**

 **Think Back**

- Have students turn to **Think Back** page 103 in th Differentiated Readers.

- Tell students they will complete Practice Companion page 267 as they do Cross-Text Shari

ASSIGN PRACTICE COMPANION **267**

Check Understanding

Have students fill in Practice Companion page 267 list what they learned about life in the Pacific States based on what they read. Intensive- and Strategic-le students can expand on the information they gathe on Day 4 during Prepare to Share.

Understand Literary Elements

Form mixed-level pairs within each Inquiry Group. Explain that dialogue is the conversation between characters in a story. Say:

Sometimes authors don't directly tell us what characte are like. They use their words and actions to show rea what the characters are like.

Then have each student share an example of dialogu from his or her reading and explain what it tells us about the characters.

Share and Compare

Have each student write a summary about his or he selection, using the list he or she compiled about life in the Pacific States. Then have the mixed-level pair share their summaries and compare the details in them. Students may want to use a T-Chart (Resourc Master 14) to compare and contrast their summarie

ASSIGN RESOURCE MASTER **14**

Think Critically

Have each student give at least one example from his or her reading to answer the Theme Question: *What makes the West exceptional?* Have students discuss how many different examples can all answer the same question. For ideas, students can use the ideas they gathered during the week's reading. Students can fill in their ideas on Practice Companion page 267. **c**

Connect to Inquiry

Before wrapping up Cross-Text Sharing, have student groups think about their Inquiry Projects. Ask:

> How does what you learned from your discussion relate to your Inquiry Project?

- Have students discuss their ideas. Point out that even though students have already prepared their presentations, they can still continue to investigate their Inquiry Questions to gain deeper understandings.

- If students find the Differentiated Readers to be a source to help them answer their Inquiry Questions, have them fill out an Investigation Sheet (Resource Master 35). Have students place any notes in their Inquiry folders.

ASSIGN | RESOURCE MASTER **35**

Ask:

- Based on what you discussed, what questions do you still have?
- Which of these questions would you most like to investigate further?

If necessary, give students time to update their presentations according to their new understandings.

a Intervention for Acceleration

READ CHALLENGING TEXT
Encourage students to note when other students' selections spark personal interests during Cross-Text Sharing. Students may read these selections during Self-Selected Reading time next week. Remind students that they may use the eBook version to support them as they read more difficult texts.

b ELL Support

SUMMARIZE
Some English language learners may have difficulty summarizing their selections. Encourage them to look at the illustrations in their selections. Ask them to write sentences that describe the pictures. Then have them use these sentences to create summaries of the stories. Have students share their summaries with their groups.

c Literacy Builder
21st CENTURY SKILLS

LISTENING
As students participate in Cross-Text Sharing, remind them that successful groups practice good listening skills and collaborate together. Ask students to make sure each member gets to share his or her ideas, and remind them to stay focused and on topic. Suggest they summarize one another's ideas to stay on task.

Share, Connect, Assess

Objectives
Students will:
- Perform fluent reading
- Spell words with silent consonants

Wrap Up the Week
whole group

Inquiry Project Presentation

Invite groups to present the findings in their Inquiry Project. Remind students of good listening skills. Say:

> As the group presents, I will focus my ears and eyes on the speaker. I will not look at the people sitting around me because I could distract the presenters.

Ask students to respond to the presenters using these starters:

- "I really like how you . . ."
- "Could you please tell me more about . . ."
- "Could you repeat the part about . . ."

Have students share new questions related to the theme or the Inquiry Project. Post them on the Question Board.

Fluency Presentation

Have students turn to "At the Trail's End" on Practice Companion page 254. Each student will read the journal entry for the class to demonstrate using good phrasing, expression, and pacing. Explain:

> Today we will present the journal entry we have been working on all week to the class. As you read aloud, use your voice to capture the drama of traveling on the trail.

Students may perform a different selection for the c or to a caregiver at home.

As students perform, use Assessing Oral Reading in the Assessment Handbook to evaluate and record ea student's oral reading performance.

USE | ASSESSMENT HANDBOOK **13–14**

Spelling Posttest

Remind students that their spelling words have sile consonants. Say a word, use it in a sentence, and say the word again. Students will write each word.

1. **half** The brothers each ate *half* of the pizza.
2. **comb** The barber used a *comb* to fix the boy's hair.
3. **calm** It is important to remain *calm* in an emergenc
4. **often** We *often* eat rice with dinner.
5. **honor** The citizens of the United States *honor* peop who fought in wars.
6. **listen** She likes to *listen* to the orchestra.
7. **answer** My mother lets me *answer* the phone whe she is busy.
8. **handsome** I think my grandpa is very *handsome*.
9. **knuckle** I slammed my *knuckle* in the door yesterd
10. **wrinkle** That shirt has a *wrinkle* in it.
11. **yolk** Malik doesn't like to eat the *yolk* of an egg.
12. **folktale** We read a *folktale* last week.
13. **climb** I used to *climb* trees when I was younger.
14. **honest** My parents taught me to be *honest* and alv tell the truth.
15. **limb** The kitten was stuck on a high *limb* in the tre
16. **plumber** The *plumber* was able to fix the leaky fau

Review Words

17. **remember** Did you *remember* your homework tod
18. **hospital** My baby brother was born in the *hospital* yesterday.

Frequently Misspelled Words

19. **eighth** Our team came in *eighth* place last year.
20. **know** Do you *know* what time it is?

Objectives
Students will:
- Use key concepts
- Make text-to-self connections

- Write about what life is like in the Pacific States
- Monitor their progress

Share Text Connections

Make Text-to-Self Connections Ask students to share the theme connections they made during Cross-Text Sharing time. Continue the Theme Concept Web for Unit 7 that you began in Week 1.

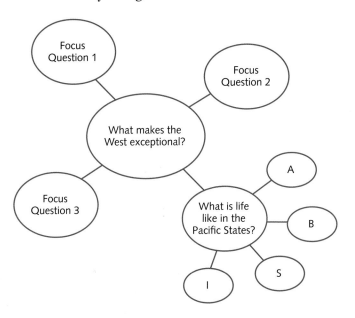

Write the Theme Question in the center circle and this week's Focus Question in one of the four connecting circles.

- For each Differentiated Reader, have students share a concept or main idea that connects to the Focus and Theme Questions.

- As students discuss their connections from their Differentiated Readers, fill in the outermost circles.

- Have students think about how this helps them address the Theme Question. Ask:

In what ways are the Focus Questions related to each other?

How has each of the Focus Questions helped you answer the Theme Question?

Daily Writing

Have students imagine that they are living in the future in a state they read about. Have them write about what job they have, what city they live in, and what they like about living there.

Student Self Assessment

- You may want students to reflect on their learning by using My Daily Progress sheet, Resource Master 1.

- For **Inquiry Self Assessment,** have students complete the Self-Assessment Rubric on Practice Companion, page 266.

ASSIGN

| RESOURCE MASTER | 1 |
| PRACTICE COMPANION | 266 |

Weekly Progress Monitoring

Use the following assessment tools to check students' weekly progress following independent and mixed-group work:
- **Practice Companion:** pp. 250–263
- **Fluency Presentation**
- **Spelling Posttest**
- **Think Back, Differentiated Reader:** p. 103
- **Assessing Oral Reading, Assessment Handbook:** pp. 13–14
- **Weekly Observation Record, Assessment Handbook:** p. 140
- **Assessment, Practice Companion,** pp. 275–276
- **Self-Assessment Rubric, Practice Companion:** p. 266

Unit Assessments
- Administer the **Differentiated Unit Assessment** for Unit 7
- Administer the **Reading Progress Assessment** for Unit 8, **Assessment Handbook,** pp. 113–122

Autobiography

Writing Traits

Organization `traits focus organization`	**Ideas** `traits focus ideas`	**Conventions** `traits focus conventions`
Voice `traits focus voice`	**Word Choice** `traits focus word choice`	**Sentence Fluency** `traits focus sentence fluency`
Presentation `traits focus presentation`		

Writing Highlights

- **Introduce** Autobiography format
- **Reading/Writing Connection** Determine Important Information, Sequence Events
- **Talk About Text** Make connections between text and the characteristics of an autobiography
- **Grammar** Review Prepositions, Review Prepositional Phrases, Avoid Double Negatives, Recognize Troublesome Word Groups

Materials

Teacher Components	Student Components	 Digital 21
• Teacher's Lesson Guide, pp. 266–283 • Writing Models Chart, pp. 52–55	• Practice Companion, pp. 268–274 • Writer's notebook	etools 21 • writing tool • interactive glossary

Tips for Success

- Tell students that they will focus on arranging their autobiographies in a logical order.
- Display the Writing Models Chart where students can see it clearly and refer to it as they work.
- You may wish to adapt the Pacing Guide to suit your scheduling needs from day to day and week to week.
- Guide students to make connections between reading and writing when they Talk About Text each day.
- Students will need their writer's notebooks for the writing process lesson.
- Remind students to refer to the Evaluation Rubric (Practice Companion, p. 269) as they draft, revise, and edit.

Writing and Language Arts *whole group*

Pacing Guide: Autobiography

Week 3	Student	Teacher's Lesson Guide
DAY 1 Lesson 1	**Prewrite** Study the writing model and set writing goals	pp. 268–269
DAY 2 Lesson 2	**Prewrite** Choose a topic and select purpose	pp. 270–271
DAY 3 Lesson 3	**Prewrite** Organize information by sequencing events; Grammar: Review Prepositions	pp. 272–273
DAY 4 Lesson 4	**Draft** Write a first draft with a strong introduction; Grammar: Review Prepositional Phrases	pp. 274–275
Week 4		
DAY 1 Lesson 5	**Draft** Write a first draft with descriptive language and time order words	pp. 276–277
DAY 2 Lesson 6	**Revise** Revise the draft and conduct peer review; Grammar: Avoid Double Negatives	pp. 278–279
DAY 3 Lesson 7	**Edit** Edit the model and the draft; Grammar: Recognize Troublesome Word Groups	pp. 280–281
DAY 4 Lesson 8	**Publish and Present** Publish and present a final draft	pp. 282–283

Write an Autobiography

Objectives
Students will:
• Identify the characteristics and organization of an autobiography

Activate Prior Knowledge

Ask students to share what they know about autobiographies.

• What are some elements of autobiographies?

• Why do people write autobiographies?

Record students' ideas on chart paper. Students may continue adding ideas as they learn more about writing autobiographies.

Post the chart near the Writer's Desk. Over the next two weeks, students will develop ideas and compose their own autobiographies.

Writing an Autobiography

What	Why
• Tells about important events in the writer's life	• To share an important experience with the reader
• Tells information in order	• To tell a true story
• Is told in first person using the pronoun *I* or *me*	• To provide the reader with a firsthand account of a person's life

Study the Writing Model

Display *Life in a Small Town* (Writing Models Chart, pp. 52–53). Ask students to think about the audience and purpose of the autobiography as you read it aloud. Students should follow along on Practice Companion page 268. Ask:

Writing Models Chart Pages 52–55

• What was interesting about this autobiography?

• What didn't you like about this autobiography?

• For whom do you suppose the author wrote this?

ASSIGN PRACTICE COMPANION **268**

Talk About Text ★★★

Invite students to respond to the model. Ask:

• What features of the writing tell you that it is an autobiography?

• What was the author's purpose in writing this autobiography?

Characteristics of Autobiographies

Tell students that they will spend time looking at the model to decide what makes a good autobiography. Remind them that they will include these characteristics in their own writing. Ask guiding questions to help students identify features of the form. Write the characteristics of an autobiography on chart paper and post it near the Writer's Desk.

• What events did the author include?

• Is the text written in first person or third person? **b**

Characteristics of an Autobiography

A good autobiography …

• *Tells about the important events and experiences in the writer's life.*

• *Tells why these experiences are important to the writer.*

• *Usually tells events in the order in which they happened.*

• *Is written in the first person; uses the pronouns I and me.*

Organization of Autobiographies traits focus **organization**

Remind students that autobiographies include a series of important events or experiences that are told in order. Use Resource Master 25 as a Sequence Chart to demonstrate the organization of autobiographies. Explain that writers can organize their autobiographies by placing each important event they will write about in one box of the chart.

• Reread the writing model and have students identify important experiences and events.

• Have volunteers suggest where each event belongs the sequence chart.

• Model filling in the sequence chart.

Writing and Language Arts *whole group*

think
oud

First, the reader is told that the author lives in Seattle with her family. She loves living there. These examples are important to include on the chart because they affected the author's life. **c**

- Continue modeling how to fill in the chart and invite students to identify other important events from the autobiography.

The author lived in Seattle with her parents.

↓

She loved living there, but her mother did not.

↓

The family moved to a small town in Alaska.

↓

The author realizes that she likes her new life in the small town.

ASSIGN RESOURCE MASTER 25

Set Writing Goals

Have students think about the purposes and audiences of their autobiographies. They may brainstorm events

Practice Companion Page 269

from their lives that they want to write about and record them in their writer's notebooks. Remind students to select events they are comfortable sharing.

Have students turn to Practice Companion page 269 to read the criteria listed on the evaluation rubric for writing an autobiography.

Remind students that they will refer to this rubric throughout the project to make sure their writing stays focused.

ASSIGN PRACTICE COMPANION 269

scaffolding options

a Intervention for Acceleration

GENRE: UNDERSTANDING TEXT STRUCTURE
Have students pay close attention to the features of an autobiography. Show them that certain words, such as *I* and *me*, are important in autobiographies. Show students that the events in an autobiography are usually revealed in the order that they happen. Finally, students should know that an autobiography is a story about true events. Students should talk about this as they think about features of an autobiography.

b ELL Support

ACADEMIC LANGUAGE
Help students understand the difference between first-person and third-person point of view. Use the first paragraph of *Life in a Small Town* to illustrate. Read it aloud and then say:

When Mimi was very small, she lived with her parents in Seattle, Washington.

Ask:

Is the paragraph written in first person or third person? When I summarized it, did I talk about it in first person or third person?

Continue by changing the rest of the paragraph to third person and working with students to compare it with the first-person narration of the model. Help students identify the pronouns that provide clues about the point of view.

c Critical Thinking

EVALUATE IMPORTANT EVENTS
Guide students to see that the important events in an autobiography made a significant impact on the writer. Some details may be interesting, but the truly important events are those that stand out for having changed or affected the writer's life. Looking back through the sequence chart, ask:

Are all of the events and experiences that we included in the sequence chart important to the story that the writer tells?

Ask students to look back at the model and see if it would make sense without these events. Ask them to explain how it would affect readers if these events were not included in the autobiography.

Write an Autobiography

Objectives
Students will:
- Choose a topic for an autobiography
- Understand audience and purpose

Study the Writing Model

Use the writing model *Life in a Small Town* (Writing Models Chart, pp. 52–53) to talk about choosing a topic

Writing Models Chart Pages 52–55

for an autobiography. Students should follow along using Practice Companion page 268. Ask:

- What does the title tell us about this autobiography? *(Possible response: It will tell about the author's life in a small town.)*

- What topics are good for autobiographies? *(Possible responses: an interesting story that someone has to tell about his or her life; a retelling of just the most important events from the writer's life that readers would want to learn more about)*

Point out that when writers choose topics for autobiographies, they must decide how much of their lives they want to retell. An autobiography often covers a string of major events from the writer's birth to the present. But an autobiography may also focus on just one important period of time in the writer's life.

ASSIGN **PRACTICE COMPANION 268**

Talk About Text ★★★

Invite students to respond to the model. Ask:

- Does the model cover the writer's whole life or an important period of time? *(an important period of time)*

- Why do you think the author chose this topic? *(Possible response: It is something she experienced that she wants to share with others.)*

- Why is life in a small town a good topic for an autobiography? *(Possible response: It was a period of time that changed the writer's life, and readers may relate to her feelings about moving away to an unknown place.)*

Choose a Topic

traits focus **ideas**

Audience and Purpose

An autobiography is a narrative of interesting and important events from a writer's life or from one period of a writer's life. If an autobiography is about one period, it usually covers a longer period of time, such as a year or more, rather than a single event or experience.

To select purposes and topics for autobiographies, writers should think about how much of their lives they want to narrate. Then they should consider wh events from that period of time will be interesting t their readers. Invite students to ask themselves thes questions:

- Do I want to tell about the major events from my b until now, or do I want to focus more closely on on period of my life? How many years of my life will m autobiography cover?

- Will the major events from this period interest my audience?

Demonstrate how to brainstorm possible topics for autobiography. Model your thinking aloud as you w ideas on the board.

 I need to represent true events from my life, but how much time should I cover? I could write generally abo events from my whole life; or I could focus on one per of time, like my childhood. I could write about my par and siblings. Other periods I could write about are my years of schooling, or my years as a teacher. My first f time job had a big influence on my life. That would be interesting topic if I want to write about a shorter peri of time.

1. The main events of my life
2. My family
3. My education from kindergarten through college
4. My first full-time job
5. My life as a teacher

Are these good topics for an autobiography? Which o do you think would be most interesting?

After students have evaluated your topics, have ther contribute topic ideas for their own autobiographie Add their ideas to the board.

Reading/Writing Connection

Determine Important Information Readers must determine which information in the text is the most important as they read. Writers must decide which events and experiences from their lives are important enough to include in their autobiographies. This means sorting through all the events and selecting those that most impacted their lives.

Write and Confer

Independent Writing

Allow students to work in groups to continue brainstorming topics. Students can ask partners to evaluate whether their topics are appropriate for autobiographies. Circulate as students work to make sure they brainstorm topics that fit the criteria you discussed as a group. Suggest that students develop at least three possible topics by the end of independent writing. **b**

Conference with Students

Meet with students individually to talk about the topics for their autobiographies. Encourage students to ask any questions they have and discuss what is going well in the prewriting process. **c**

Reflect on Writing

Have students turn to the Evaluation Rubric (Practice Companion, p. 269). Have students look at the Ideas section of the rubric. Refer back to the list of characteristics of an autobiography that you created in Lesson 1. Ask students to share any new information they have learned about writing autobiographies.

ASSIGN PRACTICE COMPANION 269

scaffolding options

a Literacy Builder

WRITING FORM: AUTOBIOGRAPHY
Some students might have trouble understanding how an autobiography is a narrative form of writing. Explain that students will narrate events from their lives in sequence, but that autobiographies do not have to have all the features of narrative fiction, such as a conflict and resolution. Invite partners to compare and contrast the process of planning an autobiography with that of planning a fictional story. They might use a Venn Diagram (Resource Master 13) to record their ideas and share them with the class.

ASSIGN RESOURCE MASTER 13

b Critical Thinking

EVALUATE AND DISCUSS TOPICS
Have students work in pairs to evaluate each topic they develop. In their evaluations, they should determine whether the topic covers a significant period of time in the writer's life and whether readers would be interested in reading about it. Have students discuss their evaluations, determine which topics are the best choices, and eliminate topics that do not make sense for the writing form.

c Intervention for Acceleration

WRITING PROCESS: PREWRITING
To help students who are struggling to think of topics, have them consider the following:

• The top five events in their lives

• Their time in school or a certain school year

• A series of events that taught them something

You might suggest that students use a Time Line (Resource Master 18) to list the most important events from their lives. This may help them decide what to write about.

ASSIGN RESOURCE MASTER 18

Write an Autobiography

Objectives
Students will:
- Organize information
- Select important events to include in an autobiography
- Sequence events for an autobiography
- Review prepositions

Study the Writing Model

Use the writing model *Life in a Small Town* (Writing Models Chart, pp. 52–53) to review the organization of

Writing Models Chart Pages 52–55

an autobiography. Review the characteristics of an autobiography and the sequence chart from Lesson 1 to remind students that good autobiographies include important events that are told in sequence. Have students look at Practice Companion page 268 to evaluate the order of events in the model.

What type of events does the author include in the autobiography? How are the events ordered?

Students should underline the important events in the model. Remind them that an event is important when it affects the writer's life and helps advance the story.

ASSIGN   PRACTICE COMPANION **268**

Talk About Text ★★★

Invite students to respond to the model. Ask:

How does the sequence of events help the reader understand the writer's story? *(Possible response: Sequence helps the reader connect to the story. It makes the events of the autobiography clearer.)*

Organize Information

Select Important Events

Remind students that all events in an autobiography should be important. Therefore, students should look back at the topics they have chosen and select important events associated with those topics to include in their autobiographies.

Model brainstorming events for an autobiography. Write them on the board or chart paper.

I have decided to write my autobiography about my y[ear] as a teacher. There are so many events and experience[s] associated with this time. I could write about applying [for] my first job, or about my first day as a teacher and ho[w] anxious I felt. I could also describe my first parent-tea[cher] conference. Ordering supplies for the classroom and setting up bulletin boards are common experiences I'v[e] had too. It might be interesting to describe the play th[at] my class put on one year and how much fun that was[.]

Invite students to help you rank these events and experiences and determine which are most importa[nt.] Circle the most important events so you can includ[e] them in the class draft.

Sequence Events

Explain that after writers decide which important events to include in their autobiographies, they organize them. Emphasize that most autobiographi[es] are organized by time order, or chronologically. **a**

Explain that students may use a Sequence Chart (Resource Master 25) to order the events for their autobiographies. If they are writing about their enti[re] lives or long periods of time, students may want to include dates on their sequence charts. They could a[lso] use a Time Line (Resource Master 18) as an alternat[e] prewriting organizer.

Model how to organize the events you selected for t[he] class draft and invite students to offer feedback.

ASSIGN   RESOURCE MASTER **25, 18**

Reading/Writing Connection

Sequence Readers follow and recall the sequence of narratives and other texts to help them comprehend ideas and events. Writers make concrete plans for the sequence of their autobiographies to help their reader[s] clearly understand what happened and when it happened.

Write and Confer

Independent Writing

Ask students to brainstorm important events and organize them using sequence charts or time lines, depending on the scope of their narratives. Remind students to order their events chronologically.

Conference with Students

Confer with individual students. Encourage them to ask questions about organizing their autobiographies. Invite them to share their sequence plans with you.

Reflect on Writing

Ask students to review the Evaluation Rubric (Practice Companion, p. 269). Have them reflect in their writer's notebooks on how their prewriting plans will help them meet the goals for Organization and Ideas.

ASSIGN | PRACTICE COMPANION **269**

Grammar *tested*

Review Prepositions
traits focus conventions

Remind students that a preposition is a word that shows the relationship between a noun or pronoun and another word in the sentence. Prepositions can show position and direction.

Write the following paragraph from *Life in a Small Town* on the board. Ask students to fill in prepositions.

> I said good-bye _____ my friends and packed up everything _____ my room. I watched _____ the moving van as the Space Needle disappeared behind me. I cried.

Practice

Ask students to write their own fill-in-the-blank paragraphs. Each preposition should be replaced with a blank. Have students swap their paragraphs with partners to fill in the correct prepositions.

ASSIGN | PRACTICE COMPANION **271**

---

scaffolding options

a Challenge

WRITING TRAIT: ORGANIZATION
Explain to students that while all writers of autobiographies use sequence, some writers might decide to organize their writing using a pattern other than time order. For example, a writer might start with a more recent event in his or her life and then write a flashback to earlier events. Ask students to consider whether there are other logical ways that autobiographies could be organized. Encourage them to try using a more challenging sequence for their drafts.

b Intervention for Acceleration

**INDEPENDENT WRITING:
SELECT IMPORTANT EVENTS**
Support students who may have difficulty brainstorming important events to include in their autobiographies. Provide them with a Concept and Word Web (Resource Master 11). Ask them to write the topic of their autobiography in the center oval. All of the important events and experiences associated with the topic may go in the connecting ovals. When students have completed their concept webs, suggest that they cross out any events or experiences that do not connect to their main topics. Help them understand that they should be determining the most important information to include.

ASSIGN | RESOURCE MASTER **11**

Write an Autobiography

Objectives
Students will:
- Write a first draft
- Develop strong introductions
- Use first-person point of view
- Review prepositional phrases

Study the Writing Model

Use the writing model *Life in a Small Town* (Writing Models Chart, pp. 52–53), asking students to follow

Writing Models Chart Pages 52–55

along on Practice Companion page 268. Inform students that today's lesson will focus on strong introductions and point of view.

Ask a volunteer to reread the introduction to *Life in a Small Town*. Encourage students to pay close attention to the opening sentence and descriptions. Have them circle appealing phrases or sentences on Practice Companion page 268.

ASSIGN   PRACTICE COMPANION **268**

Talk About Text ★★★

Invite students to respond to the model. Ask:
- Why do you think the author started this way?
- How does the introduction fit into the model's sequence?
- Does the introduction grab your attention? Why or why not?

Write a First Draft

Strong Introductions

Explain that, like any other story, an autobiography should capture readers' interest right away. Invite students to share ways they can create attention-grabbing introductions to their autobiographies.

Depending on students' topics, they might begin their drafts in different ways. Some may describe their birth or infancy, while others may start with a memorable event that began an important time period. **a**

Ask students to evaluate the strength of the followi opening sentences and explain their judgments:

> I was born in Philadelphia on October 27, 1979.
>
> My mom always says I was born with a head full of red hair and a sassy attitude to match it.
>
> Have you ever known a baby who never cries and always giggles? Well, I was that kind of baby.

Draft an introduction to an autobiography about teaching on chart paper. Model this thinking aloud

 How can I make readers interested in my writing? Ma I should make the first sentence something they can relate to. Not everyone has been a teacher, but most people have been students. I'll write, "The first day of school had always been an exciting time for me." The explain how I felt entering the classroom on my first of teaching. I want to use words to show how nervou felt.

> The first day of school had always been an exciting time for me. But on August 12, 2002, I entered the classroom for the first time as a teacher instead of as a student. Wow, was I nervous. There were butterflies fluttering in my anxious stomach, and I felt as if they would fly right out whe I opened my mouth. After setting my materials on the huge empty desk, I wrote my name on the chalkboard. I was so flustered I dropped the chalk three times and almost forgot my name! The rest of my first day was just as terrifying.

Explain that your introduction presents the first ma event of your autobiography by painting a vivid sce Ask students to discuss whether this is effective.

Point of View traits focus voice

Since autobiographies are narratives of the writer's life experiences, using first-person point of view is important. Ask students to look back at the model c your class draft to identify the pronouns *I*, *me*, and *

Ask students to discuss how using these pronouns a first-person point of view affects readers' sense of th writer's voice and the tone of the writing. **b**

How does point of view affect your connection to the writer and story? How would the autobiography be different if it were written in third-person point of vie

Writing and Language Arts — whole group

Write and Confer

Independent Writing

Remind students to follow their sequence charts or time lines from prewriting to begin drafting. Suggest that they start their introductions with vivid scenes, questions, surprising facts about themselves, or other interesting approaches.

Conference with Students

Talk with students about what is going well with their writing. Help them evaluate their introductions.

Reflect on Writing

Have students reflect in their writer's notebooks on why point of view is important in autobiographies.

Grammar ~tested~

Review Prepositional Phrases traits focus **conventions**

Remind students that a preposition always has at least one noun or pronoun as an object. The preposition, its object, and any modifers of the object make up a prepositional phrase. Write the following sentences from the writing model on the board. Have students identify each prepositional phrase.

> Now I have lived <u>in Yakutat</u> <u>for two years</u>. Life here is very different. My mom still works <u>with airplanes</u>, but now she works <u>in a tiny airport</u> and has plenty <u>of time</u> off.

Practice

Have partners write sentences with prepositional phrases, exchange them, and underline the prepositional phrases.

ASSIGN **PRACTICE COMPANION 272**

---

scaffolding options

a Challenge

STRONG INTRODUCTIONS

Ask partners to examine the first paragraphs of professional autobiographies in the classroom or school library. Have them discuss how each author captures readers' attention in the opening sentence or sentences. Invite students to select one or two introductions to read aloud and discuss with the class. Encourage students to use the professional writing as models for their own introductions.

b Critical Thinking

WRITING TRAIT: VOICE

Ask students to consider why voice is particularly important in autobiographies. Point out that in addition to using first-person point of view, students can focus on expressing their individual voices and unique points of view on their experiences. Writers express their personal thoughts, feelings, and reflections in their autobiographies so readers can connect to and understand their experiences. Invite students to list ways they can develop voice and help their readers relate to them. Students might suggest that they use vivid word choices to describe emotions and events.

c Intervention for Acceleration

WRITING PROCESS: DRAFT

Support students struggling to write independently. Help students use the sequence charts from their prewriting to focus on how to begin drafting. Have them use the detail in the first box to begin their draft. Explain that they should use the same process for writing the remainder of the autobiography.

 Students can use the Writing Tool to get feedback on their drafts.

Write an Autobiography

Objectives
Students will:
• Write a first draft
• Use descriptive language
• Use time-order words and transitions

Study the Writing Model

Display the writing model *Life in a Small Town* (Writing Models Chart, pp. 52–53). Ask students to follow along on Practice Companion page 268.

Writing Models Chart Pages 52–55

Inform students that you will be talking about word choice in today's lesson. Ask them to underline the descriptive language that the author of the model uses to paint a picture for the reader.

• Which words and phrases from *Life in a Small Town* help you visualize the writer's experiences? *(Possible responses: an apartment in the middle of downtown, where life rushed around us; standing by the window to watch people, dogs, and cars pass; fresh vegetables)*

• What time-order words and transitions did the author use to help the reader understand the sequence of her story? *(Possible responses: the word* when *in the first sentence;* every weekend *in the first paragraph;* one day *to start the third paragraph;* now *to start the last paragraph)*

ASSIGN PRACTICE COMPANION **268**

Talk About Text ⭐⭐⭐

Invite students to respond to the model. Ask:

• Are there any words you would add to improve the model? If so, what are they?

• Why is it important to use descriptive language and time-order words in an autobiography?

etools 21 *writing tool* Students can use the Writing Tool to get feedback on their drafts.

Write a First Draft

Descriptive Language [traits focus word choice]

Explain that writers use descriptive language in their autobiographies to help readers visualize their experiences. Strong descriptive words include precise nouns, action verbs, and vivid adjectives and adverb

Encourage students to also use sensory details and figurative language, such as similes and metaphors in their autobiographies. These types of details are particularly useful in helping readers visualize and understand a writer's unique perspective. **a**

Have students compare the strength of the word choices in the following sentences:

> During my first year teaching, I had a lot of planning and grading. But each day my students' faces made me happy.

> During my first year teaching, I was buried under a mountain of lesson planning and paper grading. But each day, my students' bright smiles and curious eyes sent my spirits soaring.

Time-Order Words [traits focus sentence fluency]

Tell students that using time-order words and transitions in their writing will help it flow. In an autobiography, time-order words make the sequence events and amount of time that passes clear to read

Ask students to share words that signal time and or Write their responses on the board or chart paper fo the class to reference during drafting. **b**

What are some time-order words you can use in your autobiography? *(Possible responses: first, then, earlie later, after, when, finally, while, during, before, now)*

Explain that writers use transitional phrases and sentences to signal new events or the passage of tim Often these are found at the beginnings or ends of paragraphs. Point out transitions in *Life in a Small Town*, such as the opening of the final paragraph *(N I have lived in Yakutat for two years)*. Ask students ho transitions help the story flow.

What would it be like to read the model if these transitions were not included? *(Possible response: It would be harder to know when things happened.)*

Model writing a middle paragraph of your class draft about teaching. Think aloud about how you use time-order words and transitions to help the writing flow.

think aloud

My beginning told about my first year of teaching, so I need to open this new paragraph with a transition. If I don't, my readers might still think I am talking about the first year. I want to show that time has passed.

> *After my first year of teaching, I didn't feel anxious very often. I had learned a lot about planning my time in the classroom and making learning fun. I worked with so many great teachers in my early years, and they helped me by sharing things that had happened to them and giving me advice. As time passed, I found that new teachers were coming to me for advice. That was a great feeling!*

Have students identify and discuss each transition you used.

Write and Confer

Independent Writing

Provide time for students to write a conclusion to their drafts. Remind them to use descriptive and time-order words to help readers visualize and understand the sequence of events. Reinforce that students will have time to revise and edit their drafts at a later stage. **c**

Conference with Students

Confer with students individually to discuss what is going well with their drafts and what still needs additional work.

Reflect on Writing

Revisit the Evaluation Rubric (Practice Companion, p. 269). Have students reflect on how today's lesson will help them meet goals on the rubric.

- How will your descriptive language help your reader?
- How do time-order words relate to organization?

ASSIGN PRACTICE COMPANION **269**

scaffolding options

a Challenge

WRITING TRAIT: WORD CHOICE
Emphasize that students should avoid repeating bland adjectives in their writing. They should look for fresh words. For example, instead of repeating *exciting*, they could use *exhilarating* or *thrilling*. As students develop their drafts, work with them to identify bland words they use too often. Suggest that they record these words in order to avoid reusing them in later writing. Show students how to use a thesaurus to find alternative word choices. Encourage them to record the new words in the Words section of their writer's notebooks and select the best words to use in their drafts.

b Challenge

WRITING TRAIT: TIME-ORDER WORDS
Ask students to write a paragraph using the following time-order words. Tell them they can use them in any order, as long as they fit each one into the content of the paragraph.

Finally

First

Now

Then

Before

c Intervention for Acceleration

WRITING TRAIT: ORGANIZATION
Students should see conclusions as important parts of a writing selection. In an autobiography, where a person is telling a story of his or her life, the conclusion generally brings a sense of closure for the reader. As writers, students should ask themselves:

- Did I tie up all of the loose ends that I introduced?
- Did I provide closure by the end of my autobiography?

Students should make sure that they leave the reader with a sense of completion after finishing the autobiography.

Write an Autobiography

Objectives
Students will:
- Revise a draft
- Avoid double negatives

Revise the Model `traits focus` `sentence fluency`

Remind students that experienced writers revise until their writing expresses exactly what they want it to say.

Writing Models Chart Pages 52–55

For an autobiography, this means:

- Adding vivid words and details to clarify experiences and events.

- Substituting bland words and phrases for clearer ones.

- Adding time-order words and transitions where needed.

- Rearranging sentences and paragraphs to make the sequence clearer.

- Deleting unimportant ideas and events that disrupt the flow of the narrative and distract the reader.

Model making changes to the Revising and Editing Model (Writing Models Chart, p. 54). Remind students that they will edit for grammar, spelling, and punctuation after revising. Ask:

- Are the events of your autobiography told in order?

- Do you capture the reader's attention in your introduction?

- Do you use descriptive language?

- Do you use the first-person pronouns *I* and *me*?

> When I was very small,
> I lived with my parents in seattle, Washington. My
> mother worked for a company that made airplanes and
> (was an engineer) and was good at it. We have an apartment
> in the middle of downtown, I used to love standing by the
> where life rushed around us.
> window too watch people dogs and cars pass. We went to
> Pike place market to buy fresh vegtables (every weekend,) and
> street
> I listened to, musicians and watched boats on the water,
> in the sea.

Introduce the Revising Checklist (Writing Models Chart, p. 55). Invite students to use it to suggest additional changes to the model.

Revise the Draft

Display the autobiography about teaching that you drafted on chart paper. Ask students to look at the [Peer] Evaluation Form on Practice Companion page 270. Direct them to use the peer review prompts, as well [as] the Revising Checklist (Writing Models Chart, p. 55[)] evaluate the class draft. Provide support as necessa[ry] reminding students how to phrase comments constructively. Revise the draft with students based on their comments.

ASSIGN | PRACTICE COMPANION **270**

Peer Review

Assign students writing partners for peer review. Have students use the Peer Evaluation Form (Practi[ce] Companion, p. 270) to review their partners' drafts. Remind students to follow the routine for peer revie[w].

- The writer shares his or her work.
- The reviewer tells what he or she liked about the wo[rk]
- The reviewer asks questions about the work.
- The reviewer makes suggestions for changes.
- The writer makes notes of the reviewer's comments
- Partners switch roles. **c**

ASSIGN | PRACTICE COMPANION **270**

Author's Chair

Have volunteers read their autobiographies aloud to the class. Remind students about the correct guidelines for responding to others' writing.

- First, talk about what you found interesting or excit[ing]
- Then, ask questions about what you heard.
- Finally, tell what you liked and why you liked it.

Encourage students to reflect on their peer review and use the class response to improve their autobiographies.

Writing and Language Arts *whole group*

Write and Confer

Independent Writing

Encourage students to consider the comments made by their writing partners on the Peer Evaluation Form (Practice Companion, p. 270). Make sure students consider all of the comments and decide which ones to use during revision. Remind them to use the Revising Checklist (Writing Models Chart, p. 55) to guide their revisions.

ASSIGN PRACTICE COMPANION 270

Conference with Students

Talk with students about what is going well in their revisions and answer any questions they have.

Reflect on Writing

Ask students to reflect on the revision process in their writer's notebooks.

Grammar *tested* ✓

Avoid Double Negatives *traits focus* conventions

Explain to students that negative words are a common part of everyday language. These words include the modifiers *no*, *not*, *never*, and *hardly*. Explain that a double negative is the use of two or more negative words to express one negative idea (e.g., *can't hardly*, *not never*, etc.). Write the following sentence on the board and have students fill in the correct negative.

> I loved Seattle, but my parents _____ happy there.

Practice

Have students write sentences using negatives and then swap sentences with partners. Partners should check to make sure no double negatives were used.

ASSIGN PRACTICE COMPANION 273

---

scaffolding options

a ELL Support

WORD STUDY

Review with students that first-person pronouns *I* and *me* are appropriate for an autobiography. Have students volunteer one sentence from their autobiographies that includes these pronouns. Have them discuss with the group why using these pronouns was correct.

b Challenge

CRITERIA FOR AUTOBIOGRAPHIES

Some students may see errors in the class draft more easily than others. In pairs, challenge those students to create a new rubric for evaluating an autobiography. Which items would they keep on the rubric? What would they add? What would they change? Invite students to share their rubrics with the class and consider making photocopies for others to use. When students share their new rubrics, make sure they can justify their decisions.

c Intervention for Acceleration

PARTNER FOR ACCELERATION

Encourage students who have a hard time evaluating their writing by pairing them with a Benchmark- or Advanced-level student. Make sure that both students are clear on the requirements for peer review. Also, remind students that this is the same way that they will talk about a text during Author's Chair.

 **etools 21** interactive glossary — Students can use the Interactive Glossary as they revise their writing.

Write an Autobiography

Objectives
Students will:
- Edit a draft
- Recognize troublesome word groups

Edit the Model [traits focus **conventions**]

Remind students that editing involves carefully checking for correct spelling, punctuation, and

Writing Models Chart Pages 52–55

grammar. Explain that editing a draft is the part of the process in which students can catch mistakes that they made while drafting. Tell students that editing is important because readers might think an autobiography is poorly written if it is full of errors.

Use the Revising and Editing Model and the Editing Checklist (Writing Models Chart, pp. 54–55) to demonstrate proofreading for errors. Explain or review each proofreading mark as you use it to show changes. **a**

Think aloud as you demonstrate how to edit the model with students. Make each type of edit in a different color.

 I'm going to read this draft out loud several times, but each time I will look for a different kind of error. This way, I can focus on finding one kind of mistake at a time.

Discuss the first steps in the process, and invite students to participate in finding errors.

First, I am going to read each sentence to find any spelling mistakes. Do you see spelling errors? *(vegetables)*

Next, I will make sure I used correct punctuation and capitalization. What punctuation or capitalization errors can you find? *(Seattle should be capitalized, and so should Place Market; there should be commas after people and dogs.)*

Discuss the final step in the editing process. Encourage students to examine the model for possible errors connected to their recent grammar lessons.

Finally, I am going to look for mistakes in grammar and usage. For example, I will make sure that I used the appropriate verb tense to tell about events. I see that *have* in the third sentence should be *had* because this is an event from the past. Do you see any errors with prepositions or double negatives? *(too should be to)*

When I was very small, I lived with my parents in seattle, Washington. My mother was an engineer for a company that made airplanes. We had have an apartment in the middle of downtown, where life rushed around us. I used to love standing by the window too to watch people, dogs, and cars pas Every weekend, we went to Pike place market to buy fresh vegetables, and I listened to street musicians and watched boats on the water.

After students have helped you make edits, refer th to the Editing Checklist (Writing Models Chart, p. 5 Have them verify that the class has addressed all requirements on the checklist.

Edit the Draft

Display your class draft about teaching. Invite stude to use the Editing Checklist (Writing Models Chart, p. 55) as they make edits on the chart paper. Remind students to make sure that words are spelled correc and that prepositions and prepositional phrases are used properly. You might also remind students to ch for double negatives and troublesome word groups.

Write and Confer

Independent Writing

Have students use the Editing Checklist (Writing Models Chart, p. 55) as a guide while they edit their autobiographies. Encourage them to read their autobiographies several times, focusing on one type of error each time. **b**

Conference with Students

Meet individually with students to discuss question they have about writing an autobiography. Assist students who might be struggling to edit their writi

Reflect on Writing

Refer students to the Evaluation Rubric (Practice Companion, p. 269). Have students use their writer's notebooks to reflect on how they have met the goals on the rubric so far.

ASSIGN   PRACTICE COMPANION   **269**

Grammar

Recognize Troublesome Word Groups

traits focus
conventions

Explain to students that there are some English words that are commonly confused with each other and used in the wrong way in writing; these words are sometimes called *troublesome pairs* or *word groups*.

Write the following troublesome words on the board:

> among/between
> accept/except
> to/too/two
> there/their/they're
> sit/set
> lie/lay

Practice

Work with students to look through *Life in a Small Town* and identify troublesome word groups that could be written in an incorrect way.

ASSIGN   PRACTICE COMPANION   **274**

scaffolding options

a Critical Thinking

ANALYZE PROOFREADING MARKS
Write a list of commonly used proofreading marks on the board (caret, strikethrough, three underlines, and so on). Invite students to describe how each mark helps with the editing process. Ask them to share why they think these marks have the features that they do. Encourage students to think of other effective ways to proofread papers and invite them to share personalized editing tips.

b Intervention for Acceleration

PARTNER FOR ACCELERATION
Some students may still struggle to see errors in their own work. Let these students work in pairs with a Benchmark- or Advanced-level student who is a successful editor. Ask students to read their drafts aloud while they are editing and look for the various types of mistakes they should correct. Tell students to model the editing process while reading aloud. Eventually, students who are struggling will internalize this process.

Write an Autobiography

Objectives
Students will:
• Publish and present a final draft

Study the Writing Model

Revisit the writing model *Life in a Small Town* (Writing Models Chart, pp. 52–53) to discuss what authors do

Writing Models Chart Pages 52–55

when they are ready to publish and present their writing.

Direct students' attention to specific features of the model. Point out that a published piece of writing:

• Is neat and easy to read.

• Has proper margins.

• Has an interesting title.

Remind students that writers go through several drafts before a piece is ready to be published. Show students some examples of published autobiographies from the classroom or media center.

Remind students that all of the published pieces they have read and studied have a professional level of presentation that students will want to achieve in their autobiographies.

Talk About Text ★★★

Show students the Writing Model *Life in a Small Town* (Writing Models Chart, pp. 52–53).

Why did the author choose to publish her autobiography in this format? *(Possible response: It is neat and easy to read, which lets the reader focus on the story.)*

Publish Final Draft [traits focus presentation]

Choose a Format

Remind students that the way a work is published should align with the writer's audience and purpose. Ask students to review the audiences and purposes their autobiographies.

Explain that students should consider how their published work will represent their lives to their readers. Encourage them to consider using photo albums or scrapbooks to supplement their written work with photographs, illustrations, past school w and other items from their pasts. Students could sh these books with family members. Students who w about their whole lives may also wish to create tim lines to support their writing.

Ask students to share other ideas for publishing the drafts that are appropriate for their audiences and purposes. Write the ideas on the board.

> Create a photo album or scrapbook
> Create a time line
> Make a digital photo collage
> Make an autobiographical comic book
> Record a video

Review Evaluation Rubric

Before students make final drafts of their autobiographies, review the criteria on the Evaluati Rubric (Practice Companion, p. 269).

Encourage students to read each statement careful and honestly evaluate their work based on the statements. Remind them that experienced writers back many times to revise and edit their writing.

Allow time for students to make final drafts of their autobiographies. Remind them to include any visua or other items they have collected to help readers understand important people, events, or experience from their lives. **b**

ASSIGN [PRACTICE COMPANION **269**]

Writing and Language Arts *whole group*

Present Final Draft

Author's Chair

Invite volunteers to share their autobiographies by reading them aloud to the class. Encourage students to respond to each autobiography by using the protocol for responding to others' writing:

- First, talk about what you found interesting about the autobiography.
- Then, ask any questions you have about what you heard.
- Finally, tell what you liked about the autobiography and why you liked it.

Classroom Visit traits focus presentation

Many students will be particularly invested in their autobiographies because they are about themselves, and some may want to share information about their lives with their peers. Arrange for a classroom visit to another class in your school so that students may present their writing.

Encourage students to practice presenting their autobiographies before the class visit. Remind them to read with expression so their individual voices and personalities come through in the reading. Remind students that they should speak directly to their audience and make eye contact. Suggest that students stop at appropriate intervals to show photographs or visuals if they have included them.

Reflect on Writing

Revisit the chart that students started in Lesson 1 showing the *what* and *why* of an autobiography. Have students add any new information to the chart. Save it to reuse the next time students write an autobiography.

Have students reflect on the writing process for an autobiography in their writer's notebooks.

- What did you learn about writing an autobiography?
- What would you do differently the next time you write an autobiography?

Invite students to share their reflections.

a Critical Thinking

EVALUATE PROFESSIONAL PRESENTATION
Help students connect what professional authors do with published works to what they should do with their own writing. Encourage students to look at professional autobiographies in the school library or media center. Have students look over each model and ask, "What can I learn from this that will help me publish?" Ask them to make checklists of the elements that are most important or appealing in the presentation of an autobiography. Encourage them to use as many of these elements as possible as they publish and to evaluate their presentations using their checklists.

b Literacy Builder

WORD STUDY
Students can work in pairs to volunteer descriptive words they have used in their autobiographies. One student should say a word and the partner should tell what the word means. Then have students switch roles.

Preteaching Vocabulary

Preteaching vocabulary to English language learners is critical to comprehension. Before students read or a teacher reads aloud, it is vital to preteach words that are key to comprehending the topic. LEAD21 incorporates a routine that ensures ELLs have sufficient vocabulary support before reading. The 7-Step Vocabulary Routine is a preteaching process that integrates second-language strategies, academic language sentence structures, and redundancy in hearing and using the word. Step 6 of the following 7-step routine appears within each English language learner lesson.

7-Step Vocabulary Routine	
1.	The teacher says the word.
2.	The teacher states the word as it is found in the context of the text.
3.	The teacher provides a definition or key definitions from the glossary or dictionary.
4.	The teacher provides another example of the word in a way that clarifies the word's meaning in student-friendly terms.
5.	The teacher asks students to repeat the word at least three times to build a phonological representation of the word and model pronunciation.
6.	The teacher ensures that all students become engaged with the word through oral language activities. • The production activity is most effectively carried out with a partner. • The teacher says "Turn to your partner" and "Tell me what your partner said" to have all students use the word at the same time and hear it several times from others. • When students report to the teacher what their partners said, they apply the word again from a different reference point and context, using it with related words and phrases. • This discourse sequence helps English language learners anchor their knowledge of the word, and it helps native English speakers achieve higher levels of specificity. It also develops listening and paraphrasing skills, third-person subject-verb agreement ("My partner says…"), and other grammatical structures.
7.	The teacher points out a special characteristic of the word, such as a cognate, multiple meaning, tense, spelling, or affix.

Read, Discuss, and Write

English language learners need to read, discuss, and write immediately after vocabulary instruction to support student recall and anchor newly learned words. The LEAD21 ELL lessons achieve this methodology in the following ways:

- **Think Alouds** Teachers think aloud using reading strategies, and then ELLs apply these reading strategies with a partner for reinforcement. This practice allows teachers to monitor the appropriate application of reading strategies.

- **Read Alouds** Teachers read aloud texts, allowing ELLs to shadow read and practice fluency, prosody, and word recognition.

- **Partner Reading and Cooperative Learning** These activities give students opportunities to practice their newly acquired language skills in safe contexts with peers.

- **Writing** Writing activities that are related to the reading reinforce new vocabulary words within each ELL lesson.

Read and Comprehend

English Language Learners
small groups

Objectives
Students will:
- Reinforce theme concepts
- Use differentiated vocabulary
- Read about farms and ranches in the Mountain States
- Review using text features

Prepare to Read

Build Background

On a U.S. map, locate the Mountain States. Show pictures of the Rocky Mountains and the short-grass prairies. Ask students how people in the Mountain States might earn a living. Provide the words *prairie*, *ranches*, and *dry climate*.

ebook
online coach

Differentiated Reader
Pages 6–27

Preteach Differentiated Vocabulary

tested ✓

Use the 7-Step Vocabulary Routine (p. 287) and the Step 6 activities below.

Point out the Spanish cognates.

Step 6 Activity	
range noun, p. 15	Show pictures of cattle grazing on the range. Students describe things they might see, hear, and feel on the range.
barbed adjective, p. 16	Students sketch a barbed wire fence used to keep animals in or people out. They describe the picture to partners.
endure verb, p. 18	Students tell partners about something that has endured a long time. Then they share their partners' responses.
integral adjective, p. 19 integral	Partners act out an activity that is an integral part of their day. Other students guess what the activity is and tell why it is an integral part of their day.
supplement verb, p. 21	Ask: "What are some ways you can supplement what you learn in school?" (read books from the library, go to museums, talk to experts on a subject)
widespread adjective, p. 23	Students sketch a plant or animal that is widespread in your state. Then they explain their choices.
preserve verb, p. 23 preservar	Students describe ways that people preserve old photographs. (put them in frames or photo albums, laminate them)
initiative noun, p. 25 la iniciativa	Ask: "What kind of initiative could we start to help improve our town?"

Preview and Set Purposes

Preview the selection, pointing out titles, captions, photos, and labels. Guide discussion about them. T students they will read to find answers to the Focu Question: *How are geography and economy connect* *the Mountain States?*

Read

Model

Read aloud the title. Model fluent reading of the selection. Pause to discuss on-page supports and te features. Model strategies and your thinking as you read.

- Use gestures and sketches to explain *tornadoes*, *herd*, *wandering*, and *roundup*.
- Explain *take advantage of* (p. 16), *wide-open spac* (p. 16), and *keep track of* (p. 17). Explain how multiple-meaning words *base* (p. 7), *driven* (p. 18 and *mount* (p. 22) are used.

Guide Comprehension

Now that students have heard the selection read to them, partners read it together. To help them get started, model your thinking:

think aloud In the selection title, the words *mountain plains* are confusing at first. Mountains are high and pointed, bu plains are flat. When I look at the photo on page 6, though, I understand. I see that mountain plains are f grassy areas right below the mountains.

PAGES 6–17 Use the map on page 8 to help students locate the short-grass prairies of the Mountain States. Help students interpret the line graph on page 12.

PAGES 18–27 Use the photos on page 19 to discuss *branding*. On page 26, explain *stewardship* and *allian*

PAGES 12, 17, 19, 20 Review on-page supports.

Respond and Write

1. Students tell partners why they would or would like to visit a dude ranch. Then they share their partners' responses with the class.

2. Students sketch and label people raising crops or animals on the mountain plains. Discuss how the sketches answer the Focus Question.

Objectives
Students will:
- Reinforce theme concepts
- Use differentiated vocabulary
- Read about canyons and deserts in the Mountain States
- Review using text features

(sidebar) **English Language Learners** small groups

Prepare to Read

Build Background
Show pictures of the Grand Canyon and the Painted Desert. Say that both places are in the Mountain States. Ask which place students would like to visit, and why. Provide useful words to aid discussion: *steep, view, landscape,* and *wildlife.*

Differentiated Reader Pages 6–27

Preteach Differentiated Vocabulary *(tested)*
Use the 7-Step Vocabulary Routine (p. 287) and the Step 6 activities below. Point out the Spanish cognates.

Step 6 Activity	
sustain *verb, p. 9* *sostener*	Ask: "What are some things that sustain the life of plants?" *(sunlight, water, soil, air)*
mesa *noun, p. 11* *la mesa*	Sketch a mesa. Ask how it is different from a mountain peak *(it's flat on top)* and how it is different from a plain *(it's higher in elevation).*
pillar *noun, p. 11* *el pilar*	Students sketch a building with pillars. Then they describe the pillars to partners.
surge *verb, p. 12*	Move your hand up and down to show surging. Ask: "What might happen if a river surges?"
ominous *adjective, p. 15* *ominoso(a)*	Students describe something ominous that they might see or hear in a scary movie.
astounding *adjective, p. 20*	Partners act out seeing something astounding. Other students guess what the actors see. They explain how they could tell the actors were astounded.
devise *verb, p. 21*	Partners imagine a solution they would like to devise to solve an everyday problem. Then they share their idea.
hue *noun, p. 22*	Students use crayons or markers to sketch an outdoor scene. They describe the different hues they used in their sketches.

Preview and Set Purposes
Preview the selection, pointing out titles, captions, photos, and labels. Guide discussion about them. Tell students they will read to find answers to the Focus Question: *How are geography and economy connected in the Mountain States?*

Read

Model
Read aloud the title. Model fluent reading of the selection. Pause to discuss on-page supports and text features. Model strategies and your thinking.

- Use sketches to explain *arches, canyon, rim, steep, cliffs, canals,* and *horseshoe.*
- On page 26, explain the idioms *leading the way* and *over the long run.* Also explain the homograph *conduct* (p. 25). Clarify how *wore* (p. 12) is used in context.

Guide Comprehension
Now that students have heard the selection read to them, partners read it together. To help them get started, model your thinking:

 The title tells me I'll learn about two kinds of landscapes in the Mountain States. The photos show me the Grand Canyon and a close-up of a cactus. The map on page 7 shows me where the Grand Canyon and the Painted Desert are located.

PAGES 6–15 Use the map on page 11 to help students locate the four major deserts. Use the photo on page 15 to help them distinguish between a *mesa* and a *butte.*

PAGES 16–27 Use the line graph on page 21 to discuss tourism in the Grand Canyon.

PAGES 9, 11, 15, 21, 23 Review on-page supports.

Respond and Write

1. Students tell partners about a place they would like to visit in the Mountain States. Then they share their partners' responses with the class.

2. Students sketch a scene for a postcard they might buy in the Mountain States. On the back, they write a message. Discuss how the postcards relate to the Focus Question.

Read and Comprehend

Objectives
Students will:
- Reinforce theme concepts
- Use differentiated vocabulary
- Read about the Rocky Mountains
- Review using text features

English Language Learners small groups

Prepare to Read

Build Background

On a map of the United States, locate the Rocky Mountains, and tell how high they are. Show pictures of the Rockies, and have students list words to describe them. Provide the words *steep*, *snow-capped*, *huge*, *dramatic*, and *impressive*.

Differentiated Reader Pages 6–27

ebook
online coach

Preteach Differentiated Vocabulary

tested

Use the 7-Step Vocabulary Routine (p. 287) and the Step 6 activities below. Point out the Spanish cognates.

Step 6 Activity	
jagged adjective, p. 7	Sketch a jagged shape. Students give examples of things that might have a jagged edge.
excursion noun, p. 9 la excursión	Partners act out going on an excursion to a particular place. Other students guess where the actors are going on their excursion.
barrier noun, p. 12 la barrera	Have students line up to form a barrier between you and part of the room. Think aloud about how you will find a way around the barrier. Students describe barriers that they have seen.
introduce verb, p. 16	Introduce yourself to the group. Then have partners introduce each other to the group.
journal noun, p.18	Students write a journal entry about something that happened this week. Then they share their journal entries.
overwhelm verb, p. 20	Partners act out being overwhelmed by a new place. Other students explain how they could tell the actors were overwhelmed.
dedicate verb, p. 24 dedicar	Show a picture of a public official dedicating a building or memorial. Make a word web: *open*, *public*, *speech*, *honor*, *audience*, *news*. Put the word *dedicate* in the middle. Have volunteers tell how the words are related.
maintain verb, p. 27 mantener	Describe how a teacher maintains respect and order in the classroom. Have students describe how they maintain good grades.

Preview and Set Purposes

Preview the selection, pointing out titles, captions, photos, and labels. Guide discussion about them. T students they will read to find answers to the Focu Question: *How are geography and economy connecte the Mountain States?*

Read

Model

Read aloud the title. Model fluent reading of the selection. Pause to discuss photos and text features Model strategies and your thinking.

- Use gestures to explain *rapids*, *white-water raftir* and how the Rockies were formed by shifting pla
- Explain idioms: *on the other hand* (p. 11), *breakin the surface* (p. 15), *paved the way* (p. 17), *from far wide* (p. 22), *going strong* (p. 23), and *pitch in* (p. 2 Also explain the homograph *felt* (p. 16).

Guide Comprehension

Now that students have heard the selection read to them, have partners read it together. To help them g started, model your thinking:

think aloud

The title says the Rockies are majestic. *That means th are great, grand, and impressive. The photo shows me how majestic they are. The chapter titles tell me I'll lea about the Rockies' geography, history, and economy.*

PAGES 6–14 Use the map on page 8 to discuss the Rockies' four sections and the Continental Divide. Poi out the related words *vary* (p. 10), *varied* (p. 11), and *various* (p. 14).

PAGES 15–27 Use the map and journal entries on pag 18–19 to discuss Lewis and Clark. Use the line graph page 25 to discuss tourism in Yellowstone National Pa

Respond and Write

1. Students tell partners why the Rocky Mountain Youth Corps is important. Then they share their partners' responses.

2. Students sketch an ad to attract tourists to the Rockies. Then they write a headline and a persua paragraph. Discuss how the ads answer the Focu Question.

Objectives
Students will:
- Reinforce theme concepts
- Use differentiated vocabulary
- Read about the Colorado River
- Review using text features

Prepare to Read

Build Background

On a U.S. map, trace the path of the Colorado River. Point out that there are several deserts along the river's route. Ask why the river might be important to people who live in the cities and countryside along its path. Provide the words *arid*, *irrigation*, *crops*, and *drinking water*.

ebook
online coach

Differentiated Reader
Pages 6–27

Preteach Differentiated Vocabulary

tested

Use the 7-Step Vocabulary Routine (p. 287) and the Step 6 activities below. Point out the Spanish cognates.

Step 6 Activity	
sediment noun, p. 7 el sedimento	Pour sand or coffee grounds into a clear bowl to show sediment. Ask when and where sediment might settle in a river.
tributary noun, p. 8	Sketch a river and its tributaries. Ask why it is important to protect a river's tributaries.
momentum noun, p. 13 el momento	Make ramps of various heights and lengths. Place a toy car at the top of each, and let it go. Have students compare the momentum the car gains on each ramp.
fierce adjective, p. 14 fiero(a)	Have partners act out being in a fierce wind or a fierce river current. Other students explain how they could tell that the wind or water was fierce.
trophy noun, p. 16 el trofeo	Students sketch a trophy that they would like to receive. Then they describe the trophy to a partner.
monument noun, p. 18 el monumento	Show a picture of the Washington Monument, and make a word web for *monument*: place, person, historic, scenic, honor, remember. Students each say a sentence to describe a monument.
vicinity noun, p. 20 la vecindad	Students draw a map to show places in the vicinity of your school. They share and compare their maps with the rest of the group.

Continue with *achievement* (p. 23) and *retain* (p. 26).

Preview and Set Purposes

Preview the selection, pointing out titles, captions, photos, and labels. Guide discussion about them. Tell students they will read to find answers to the Focus Question: *How are geography and economy connected in the Mountain States?*

Read

Model

Read aloud the title. Model fluent reading of the selection. Pause to discuss on-page supports and text features. Model strategies and your thinking.

- Use sketches to explain *funnels*, *pedestal*, and *catwalks*.
- Explain the metaphor *ribbon of sandpaper* (p. 15). Clarify how *volume* (p. 8) and *worn* (p. 15) are used. Explain the homographs: *winding* (p. 16) and *concrete* (p. 23).

Guide Comprehension

Now that students have heard the selection read to them, partners read it together. To help them get started, model your thinking:

think aloud The selection title tells me I'll learn about the Colorado River. The Chapter 1 title tells me the river is grand. The other chapter titles tell me two main ideas: The river is important for recreation and is a power source.

PAGES 6–17 Use the map on page 9 to discuss the Colorado's tributaries. Have students use the key to find dams and national parks.

PAGES 18–27 Ask students why the line graph on page 25 is alarming. Have them use context clues to figure out *unpredictable* (p. 22), *divert* (p. 23), and *revitalize* (p. 26).

Respond and Write

1. Students tell partners about two things that they would like to do in the Mountain States. Then they share their partners' responses.

2. Partners sketch and write ads to attract tourists or businesses to the Mountain States. Then they discuss how their ads answer the Focus Question.

English Language Learners small groups

Read and Comprehend   ELL | Intensive

Objectives
Students will:
• Reinforce theme concepts
• Use differentiated vocabulary
• Read about the California coast
• Review using text features

English Language Learners *small groups*

Prepare to Read

Build Background
Show pictures of tourist attractions such as Big Sur, Hollywood, and the Golden Gate Bridge. Ask what the places have in common. Guide a talk about why so many people live in or like to visit the California coast. Provide the words *beaches*, *coastline*, *climate*, and *harbors*.

ebook
online coach

Differentiated Reader Pages 30–53

Preteach Differentiated Vocabulary

tested ✓

Use the 7-Step Vocabulary Routine (p. 287) and the Step 6 activities below. Point out the Spanish cognates.

Step 6 Activity	
differ verb, p. 31 *diferir*	Hold up two pens or two cups, and ask how they differ. Then ask, "How does basketball differ from soccer?"
carve verb, p. 32	Show a picture of carved wood and tell how it was shaped. Then show a jagged coastline and ask, "What carved this coastline?" *(wind and water)*
variety noun, p. 34 *la variedad*	Have students list their favorite desserts, sports, and TV shows. Then discuss the variety of their choices.
contribute verb, p. 34 *contribuir*	Have the group plan a brief skit or talent show. As group members plan, have them discuss how each member can contribute to the performance.
tremendous adjective, p. 36 *tremendo(a)*	Students sketch a person standing next to something tremendous. Then they explain the picture to partners.
leisurely adjective, p. 38	Partners act out taking a leisurely walk. Other students explain how they could tell the walk was leisurely.
balmy adjective, p. 49	Students tell partners what they like to do when the weather is balmy. Then they share their partners' responses.
accustomed adjective, p. 51 *acostum-brado(a)*	Students talk about things they are accustomed to doing in school.

Preview and Set Purposes
Preview the selection, pointing out titles, photos, captions, and labels. Guide discussion about them. students they will read to find answers to the Focus Question: *How are geography and economy connected the Pacific States?*

Read

Model
Read aloud the title. Model fluent reading of the selection. Pause to discuss on-page supports and te features. Model strategies and your thinking.

• Use gestures to explain the shifting and colliding plates of rock. Act out *sightseeing* and *breathtaking*
• Explain the phrases *fish for sport* (p. 47) and *Ligh camera, action!* (p. 50). Also explain the homogra *bill* (p. 38) and *bass* (p. 47).

Guide Comprehension
Now that students have heard the selection read to them, partners read it together. To help them get started, model your thinking:

 The title tells me I'll learn about the California seacoa The photo on page 30 shows me an amazing view of coastline. Look how well it matches the map on page

PAGES 30–39 Use the photo on page 33 to discuss *erosion*. Have students use context clues to figure out *identified* (p. 36) and *prospered* (p. 38).

PAGES 40–53 Have students return to the map on page 31 to locate places described in Chapters 3–4. Use the photo on page 43 to discuss *aquarium* and *marine biologist*. Point out the cable car shown on page 45.

PAGES 33, 39, 45, 50 Review on-page supports

Respond and Write

1. Students tell partners which part of the Californi coast they would like to visit, and why. Then they share their partners' responses with the class.

2. Students sketch a postcard they might buy on the California coast. On the back, they write a messa to a friend. Discuss how their postcards relate to Focus Question.

Objectives
Students will:
- Reinforce theme concepts
- Use differentiated vocabulary
- Read about farms in the Pacific Northwest
- Review using text features

Prepare to Read

Build Background

Show some apples. Ask students to guess which state grows the most apples. Locate Washington state on a

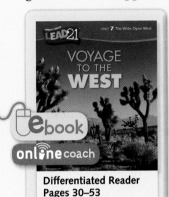

Differentiated Reader Pages 30–53

U.S. map. Guide a talk about why so many fruits and vegetables grow in the Pacific Northwest. Provide the words *rainfall*, *river valleys*, *irrigation*, and *dams*.

Preteach Differentiated Vocabulary

Use the 7-Step Vocabulary Routine (p. 287) and the Step 6 activities below. Point out the Spanish cognates.

Step 6 Activity	
inland *adverb, p. 32*	Show a map of the Western United States. Ask which cities students would come to if they went inland from Seattle or Portland.
origin *noun, p. 35* *el origen*	Talk about the origins of your ancestors. Then have each student describe his or her country of origin.
critical *adjective, p. 37* *crítico(a)*	Have partners list things that are critical to being a good student or a good athlete. Then have them share and compare their lists as a group.
pasture *noun, p. 41* *la pastura*	Students sketch animals grazing in a pasture. Then they describe their pictures to partners.
occur *verb, p. 48*	Hand out the schedule for your school year. Ask questions: "When did the first day of school occur?" "When will the last day of school occur?"
bushel *noun, p. 49*	Show a picture of or bring in a quart-sized fruit basket. Explain that a bushel is eight of those. Ask how many would make a half a bushel.
reservoir *noun, p. 51*	Show a picture of a reservoir. Ask how people use the water. *(for drinking, irrigation, recreation)*

Preview and Set Purposes

Preview the selection, pointing out titles, photos, captions, and labels. Guide discussion about them. Tell students they will read to find answers to the Focus Question: *How are geography and economy connected in the Pacific States?*

Read

Model

Read aloud the title. Model fluent reading of the selection. Pause to discuss on-page supports and text features. Model strategies and your thinking.

- Sketch a farm stand. Act out planting, pruning, picking, cleaning, and packing fruit in an orchard.

- Explain the phrases *in particular* (p. 49), *ahead of time* (p. 51), and *make do* (p. 51). Also explain the homographs *concrete* (p. 37), *sound* (p. 39), and *produce* (pp. 43, 44). Clarify how *key* (pp. 32, 41) is used.

Guide Comprehension

Now that students have heard the selection read to them, partners read it together. To help them get started, model your thinking:

The title tells me I'll learn about farming in the Pacific Northwest. The chapter titles tell me that Washington and Oregon are the states in this region. The map on page 34 shows me where these states are located.

PAGES 30–39 Have students trace the Columbia River's route on the map on page 34. Have them use context clues to figure out *ideal* (p. 31), *carved* (p. 32), *remained* (p. 32), *hydroelectric* (p. 38), and *international* (p. 38).

PAGES 40–53 Have students refer to the map on page 34 to locate the *Yakima Valley* (p. 47). Have them use context clues to figure out *seasonal* (p. 44).

PAGES 35, 41, 44, 52 Review on-page supports

Respond and Write

1. Students tell partners about their favorite food from the Pacific Northwest. Then they share in a group.

2. Students sketch and label workers doing jobs in a Pacific Northwest orchard. Discuss how the sketches answer the Focus Question.

Read and Comprehend

Objectives
Students will:
- Reinforce theme concepts
- Use differentiated vocabulary
- Read about Hawaii's geography and economy
- Review using text features

English Language Learners small groups

Prepare to Read

Build Background

Show a pineapple, a banana, and a mango. Have students guess which state produces all these foods (Hawaii). Ask what students know about Hawaii. Guide a talk about how it is different from other states. Provide the words *islands*, *tropical*, and *tourism*.

ebook
online coach

Differentiated Reader Pages 30–53

Preteach Differentiated Vocabulary

tested

Use the 7-Step Vocabulary Routine (p. 287) and the Step 6 activities below. Point out the Spanish cognates.

Step 6 Activity	
mainland noun, p. 30	On a U.S. map, point out islands off the coast of the mainland. Ask: "How can people get to these islands from the mainland?"
ample adjective, p. 32 amplio	Ask: "How do plants look when there is ample rainfall?"
upward adverb, p. 40	Use hand motions to show moving upward and downward. Students call out when your hand moves upward.
garland noun, p. 45	Students sketch someone wearing a garland. Then they describe the picture to partners.
premise noun, p. 46 la premisa	Ask: "What is the premise of United States democracy?" (All citizens have equal rights and an equal voice in choosing their leaders.)
concern noun, p. 46	Students act out showing concern for someone. Others say how the actor showed concern.
summit noun, p. 52	Sketch a mountain, and label the summit. Students describe the view they might see from the summit.
generate verb, p. 52 generar	Ask: "How do TV shows generate interest in next week's episode?"

Preview and Set Purposes

Preview the selection, pointing out titles, photos, captions, and labels. Guide discussion about them. students they will read to find answers to the Focus Question: *How are geography and economy connecte the Pacific States?*

Read

Model

Read aloud the title. Model fluent reading of the selection. Pause to discuss pictures and text feature Model strategies and your thinking.

- Act out reacting to breathtaking views.
- Explain the phrases *dance the night away* (p. 38) a *as well as* (p. 38). Clarify how *string* (p. 30), *waves* (p. 34), *forks* (p. 37), *mouth* (p. 37), and *base* (p. 40) are used in context.

Guide Comprehension

Now that students have heard the selection read to them, partners read it together. To help them get started, model your thinking:

The selection title tells me I will learn about Hawaii. Th chapter titles tell me the three main parts of Hawaii's economy: tourism, agriculture, and research. I wonder what kinds of research they do in Hawaii.

PAGES 30–41 Use the map on page 36 to help studen locate Hawaii's six main islands. Have them use contex clues to figure out *unique* (p. 31), *moisture* (p. 31), *thr* (p. 32), *souvenirs* (p. 34), *major* (p. 36), *inactive* (p. 40 *gigantic* (p. 40), and *erupted* (p. 40).

PAGES 42–53 Use the photo on page 42 to discuss Polynesia and Polynesians. Use the photo on page 47 discuss ecotourism. On page 50, have students compa and contrast agriculture and aquaculture.

Respond and Write

1. Students tell partners why they think ecotourism Hawaii is or is not a good idea. Then they share th partners' responses.

2. Students imagine they are tourists in Hawaii and write entries for a travel diary. They discuss how t diary entries relate to the Focus Question.

English Language Learners small groups

- Reinforce theme concepts
- Use differentiated vocabulary
- Read about technology in the Pacific States
- Review using text features

Prepare to Read

Building Background

Encourage students to provide names of companies with businesses that relate to technology. Ask what students know about the companies. Guide a talk about high-tech industries in the Pacific States. List the words *technology*, *advanced*, *communication*, and *engineers* to use during discussion.

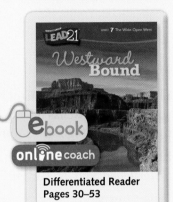

ebook
online coach

Differentiated Reader
Pages 30–53

Preteach Differentiated Vocabulary

Use the 7-Step Vocabulary Routine (p. 287) and the Step 6 activities below. Point out the Spanish cognates.

Step 6 Activity	
entertainment *noun, p. 30* el entretenimiento	Students tell partners about their favorite kind of entertainment. Then they share their partners' responses.
enable *verb, p. 32*	Students describe machines that enable us to know about events happening in faraway places.
alumni *noun, p. 33*	Ask students to pretend they have graduated from high school and are now alumni. Have partners discuss why alumni are important to a school.
enhance *verb, p. 43*	Ask: "How do computers enhance our everyday lives?"
expand *verb, p. 47* expandirse	Spread your hands wide as you say *expand*. Students copy the motion and complete this sentence: "When air and metal are heated, they _____."
contract *verb, p. 47* contraerse	Bring your hands closer together as you say *contract*. Students copy the motion and complete this sentence: "When air and metal are cool, they _____."
turbine *noun, p. 47* la turbina	Students sketch a turbine powered by water or wind. Then they explain the sketch to a partner.
dormant *adjective, p. 52* dormido(a)	Ask: "Could people safely explore a dormant volcano? Why or why not?"

Preview and Set Purposes

Preview the selection, pointing out titles, photos, captions, and labels. Guide discussion about them. Tell students they will read to find answers to the Focus Question: *How are geography and economy connected in the Pacific States?*

Read

Model

Read aloud the title. Model fluent reading of the selection. Pause to discuss pictures and text features. Model strategies and your thinking.

- Sketch film reels and frames, and a zigzag pattern. Explain *3-D* by showing the dimensions of a classroom object.
- Explain the phrases *came up with* (p. 35), *paved the way* (p. 36), *bear little resemblance* (41), *paid off* (p. 42), *worlds apart from* (p. 43), and *has done wonders* (p. 48).

Guide Comprehension

Now that students have heard the selection read to them, partners read it together. To help them get started, model your thinking:

 The title tells me I'll learn about technology in the Pacific States. In the Chapter 1 title, I see the term *high-tech*, which means "advanced technology." The other chapter titles name places and industries in the Pacific States.

PAGES 30–43 Use the photos on pages 42–43 to help students contrast early animation with how animators work today.

PAGES 44–53 On page 46, have students use the map to explain why the Trans Alaska Pipeline was needed. On page 48, have them use context clues to figure out *permanently* and *permafrost*.

Respond and Write

1. Students tell partners about a high-tech industry in the Pacific States they would like to work in.

2. Students write a business letter requesting information about high-tech careers in the Pacific States. Discuss how the letters answer the Focus Question

Read and Comprehend   ELL | Intensive

Objectives
Students will:
- Reinforce theme concepts
- Use differentiated vocabulary
- Read a folktale about Paul Bunyan
- Review using text features

Prepare to Read

Build Background
Say that students will read a folktale. Ask them to describe any folktale heroes they know about. Then guide a talk about Paul Bunyan, a hero of stories about the Mountain States. Provide the words *lumberjack, axe, ox,* and *giant.*

Differentiated Reader
Pages 56–77

Preteach Differentiated Vocabulary
Use the 7-Step Vocabulary Routine (p. 287) and the Step 6 activities below. Point out the Spanish cognates.

Step 6 Activity	
wilderness *noun, p. 57*	Students sketch what you might find in the wilderness. Then they describe their pictures.
haul *verb, p. 58*	Partners act out hauling something heavy. Other students guess what the actors are hauling.
knapsack *noun, p. 60*	Partners imagine that they are planning a hike in the wilderness. They make a list of things that they would pack in their knapsacks. Then they share and compare their lists in a group.
tough *adjective, p. 64*	Students describe real or fictional heroes who are tough.
buckle *verb, p. 65*	Make a bridge using a strip of cardboard between stacks of books. Students predict how many small objects they can place on the bridge before it buckles. Test their predictions.
canteen *noun, p. 67* *la cantimplora*	Students use the words *canteen* and *knapsack* in the same sentence.
stagger *verb, p. 70*	Act out *staggering.* Students tell reasons that a person might stagger.
canyon *noun, p. 71* *el cañón*	Students sketch people exploring a canyon. Then they share and compare their pictures as a group.

Preview and Set Purposes
Preview the selection, pointing out the titles and pictures. Guide discussion about them. Tell student they will read to find answers to the Focus Questio *What is life like in the Mountain States?*

Read

Model
Read aloud the title. Model fluent reading of the selection. Pause to discuss on-page supports and te features. Model strategies and your thinking.

- Use gestures to explain *snapped, forefinger, back forth, flattened,* and *backed up.*

- On page 57, explain *almost immediately, outgrown t house, from then on,* and *grown man.* On page 68, explain *a bit off track* and *from time to time.* On pag explain *lost track of* and *had something to do with.*

Guide Comprehension
Now that students have heard the selection read to them, partners read it together. To help them get started, model your thinking:

When I read the title, I recognize the name Paul Buny a hero of tall tales, or exaggerated folktales. I know th story won't be realistic, or true to life. It will probably funny. Looking at the chapter titles, I can predict whe Paul Bunyan will travel in the Mountain States.

PAGES 56–65 Use the picture map on page 61 to disc Minnesota's nickname and how Paul supposedly form the state's lakes.

PAGES 66–77 Use the pictures on pages 70–73 to disc how Paul made the Grand Canyon. Have students use context clues to figure out *gushed* (p. 67) and *exhaust* (p. 69).

PAGES 59, 65, 69, 75 Review the on-page supports.

Respond and Write

1. Students tell partners their favorite part of the st Then they share their partners' responses.

2. Students sketch and label the landforms and bod of water that Paul Bunyan formed. Discuss how t sketches relate to the Focus Question.

English Language Learners · small groups

Objectives
Students will:
- Reinforce theme concepts
- Use differentiated vocabulary
- Read a Hispanic folktale from New Mexico
- Review using text features

Prepare to Read

Build Background

Ask students what stories from their culture have been passed down to them. Guide a talk about folktales with characters who are wise or foolish. Provide the words *confused, comical, trick,* and *outsmart.*

Differentiated Reader Pages 56–77

Preteach Differentiated Vocabulary   *tested*

Use the 7-Step Vocabulary Routine (p. 287) and the Step 6 activities below. Point out the Spanish cognates.

Step 6 Activity

weary *adjective, p. 57*	Act out being weary. Students tell what might make them feel weary.
astonished *adjective, p. 58* atónito(a)	Partners act out being astonished. Other students say how they could tell the actors were astonished.
adobe *adjective, p. 58*	Show pictures of adobe homes. Students say sentences to describe the adobe homes.
stable *noun, p. 60* el establo	Students sketch animals in a stable. Then they describe their pictures to partners.
slumber *verb, p. 64*	Ask: "How long do you slumber each night? How do people act when they do not slumber long enough?"
rejoice *verb, p. 65* regocijarse	Students describe events that might cause them to rejoice.
tempt *verb, p. 71* tentar	Ask: "What can you do when a friend tempts you to do something you shouldn't?" Discuss making good choices when tempted.
wicked *adjective, p. 75*	Students use the words *wicked* and *tempt* in the same sentence.

Preview and Set Purposes

Preview the selection, pointing out the titles and pictures. Guide discussion about them. Tell students they will read to find answers to the Focus Question: *What is life like in the Mountain States?*

Read

Model

Read aloud the title. Model fluent reading of the selection. Pause to discuss on-page supports and text features. Model strategies and your thinking.

- Act out the steps of making buñuelos, as well as the words *stretched, yawned,* and *shrugged.*

- Explain the idioms *keep a secret* (p. 57), *from day to day* (p. 57), *good with his hands* (p. 58), *rightful owners* (p. 58), *all worn out* (p. 62), *all mixed up* (p. 63), *from time to time* (p. 64), and *it would never do* (p. 77).

Guide Comprehension

Now that students have heard the selection read to them, partners read it together. To help them get started, model your thinking:

think aloud The story's title tells me that the main character is foolish. I see that the chapter titles name the days of the week in order. That tells me that the story events happen over a period of seven days. The days of the week are in Spanish and English. That tells me the characters speak Spanish.

PAGES 56–67 Have students use the picture on pages 62–63 to predict what Rosa's plan is, and the picture on pages 64–65 to confirm or modify their predictions.

PAGES 68–77 Have students explain what is happening in the pictures on pages 72 and 75. Discuss how and why Rosa's clever plan is successful.

PAGES 59, 67, 71, 75 Review the on-page supports.

Respond and Write

1. Students tell partners about the funniest part of the story. Then they share their partners' responses.

2. Students write sentences to describe Juan and Rosa's house and farm. Discuss how their sentences answer the Focus Question.

Objectives
Students will:
- Reinforce theme concepts
- Use differentiated vocabulary
- Read a mystery set in Sun Valley, Idaho
- Review using text features

English Language Learners small groups

Prepare to Read

Build Background

Ask students what winter sports they know about. Tell them the story is about skiing. Write the word. Then

Differentiated Reader Pages 56–77

sketch and label some ski gear: *skis, poles, helmet, boots,* and *parka*. Ask why some Mountain States are good places for skiing *(high mountains, cold winters).*

Preteach Differentiated Vocabulary

Use the 7-Step Vocabulary Routine (p. 287) and the Step 6 activities below. Point out the Spanish cognates.

Step 6 Activity	
inn noun, p. 57	Make a word web for *inn: small, hotel, rooms, vacation, reservation.* Students each use the word *inn* in a sentence.
misplace verb, p. 58	Act out misplacing something that you use every day. Ask students how people can avoid misplacing things they need.
slope noun, p. 59	Students sketch skiers on a slope. Then they describe their picture to a partner.
creek noun, p. 64	Students describe things they might see, hear, and do in and around a creek.
responsible adjective, p. 66 responsable	Students list things that fourth graders might be responsible for. (doing homework, getting to school on time, doing chores, taking care of possessions)
linger verb, p. 70	Ask: "Why might people linger at the table after a meal? Linger in a theater after the movie ends?"
accuse verb, p. 71 acusar	Describe how you feel when someone has accused you of something you didn't do. Have students suggest other words similar to the word accuse.
mischievous adjective, p. 74	Ask which of these people might be described as mischievous, and why: a criminal, an active four-year-old child, a dangerous driver, a practical joker.

Preview and Set Purposes

Preview the selection, pointing out the titles and pictures. Guide discussion about them. Tell student they will read to find answers to the Focus Question *What is life like in the Mountain States?*

Read

Model

Read aloud the title. Model fluent reading of the selection. Pause to discuss pictures and text featur Model strategies and your thinking.

- Use sketches to explain *chairlift, steep, ski rack, tow.*
- Explain the idioms *looked forward to* (p. 59), *slee like a baby* (p. 64), *on a gut feeling* (p. 64), and *hit slopes* (p. 66). Clarify how *deal* (p. 57), *pretty* (p. and *tore* (p. 61) are used.

Guide Comprehension

Now that students have heard the selection read to them, partners read it together. To help them get started, model your thinking:

The title tells me this story is a mystery. I love myster As I read, I'll look for clues about the missing ski pole and make predictions. I hope I can solve the mystery before the story characters figure it out.

PAGES 56–65 Have students use context clues to figu out *exclaimed* (p. 56) and *tidy* (p. 57). Explain the Chapter 2 title, "Where'd It Go?" (p. 60).

PAGES 66–77 Use the picture on page 68 to explain *superpipe.* On page 77, discuss Tyrone's comment "T what we get for jumping to conclusions." Have stude use context clues to figure out *exited* and *thief* (p. 7

Respond and Write

1. Students tell partners when they were able to so the mystery and how they figured it out. Then th share their partners' responses.

2. Students write a persuasive headline and parag for a brochure promoting Sun Valley as a vacatic destination. Discuss how the brochure answers Focus Question.

Read and Comprehend

Objectives
Students will:
- Reinforce theme concepts
- Use differentiated vocabulary
- Read a Zuni folktale from New Mexico
- Review using text features

Prepare to Read

Build Background

On a map of the United States, locate New Mexico. Ask what students know about Native American cultures in the Mountain States. Guide a talk about how Native Americans lived in its arid deserts and mountains. List the words to use in discussion, such as *irrigation*, *adobe*, and *pueblo*.

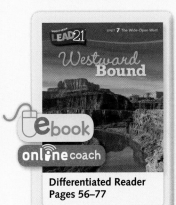

Differentiated Reader
Pages 56–77

Preteach Differentiated Vocabulary

Use the 7-Step Vocabulary Routine (p. 287) and the Step 6 activities below. Point out the Spanish cognates.

Step 6 Activity	
peasant noun, p. 58	Students sketch peasants working on a farm. Then they describe their pictures to partners.
maiden noun, p. 59	Explain that *maiden* is an old-fashioned word. Students describe maidens whom they have read or heard about in folktales and fairy tales.
sacred adjective, p. 62 *sagrado(a)*	Show pictures of sacred objects from different religions. Then make a word web for *sacred*: *holy, respect, cherish, worship, church, temple, mosque*. Students each use the word *sacred* in a sentence.
sympathy noun, p. 65	Partners act out one person showing sympathy for another. Other students say how they could tell the actor felt sympathy.
garment noun, p. 67	Hand out a clothing catalog, and have students choose their favorite garment. Have them describe the garment to a partner.
unlatched adjective, p. 70	Ask: "Why might you leave a door unlatched? What might happen if you left your seatbelt unlatched?"
befriend verb, p. 72	In a group, students discuss good ways to befriend a new classmate.
recover verb, p. 76	Ask: "If you lose something at school, how might you recover it?"

Preview and Set Purposes

Preview the selection, pointing out the pictures. Guide discussion about them. Tell students they will read to find answers to the Focus Question: *What is life like in the Mountain States?*

Read

Model

Read aloud the title. Model fluent reading of the selection. Pause to discuss pictures and text features. Model strategies and your thinking.

- Use gestures and sketches to explain *headdress, roosted, gobbling, gobbler, beak, pen, brood,* and *shooed.*
- Explain the idioms *taking stock of* (p. 57), *I can count on you* (p. 60), *turn my back on you* (p. 66), and *let us down* (p. 74). Point out irregular past-tense verb forms: *shone* (p. 68), *mistook* (p. 72), *misled* (p. 72), *withdrew* (p. 73).

Guide Comprehension

Now that students have heard the selection read to them, partners read it together. To help them get started, model your thinking:

 The word *maiden* in the title hints that this is an old story. The picture on pages 57–58 shows modern-day people, but the other pictures show Native Americans from long ago. The man on page 57 must be telling the folktale.

PAGES 56–63 Have students use context clues to figure out *satisfied* (p. 57). On page 60, help them decode comparative forms, such as *steadier* and *speediest*.

PAGES 64–77 Use the last sentence on page 75 to discuss the story's theme. Have students use context clues to figure out *deserve* (p. 64), *mistreated* (p. 66), *flattered* (p. 72), *companionship* (p. 73), and *dissatisfied* (p. 77).

Respond and Write

1. Students tell partners how this story reminds them of other folktales or fairy tales they know. Then they share their partners' responses.

2. Partners write a different ending for the folktale. Discuss how the tale relates to the Focus Question.

English Language Learners · small groups

Read and Comprehend  ELL Intensive

Objectives
Students will:
• Reinforce theme concepts
• Use differentiated vocabulary
• Read about pioneers on the Oregon Trail
• Review using text features

English Language Learners
small groups

Prepare to Read

Build Background

Ask what students know about the Oregon Trail. Show a map of the trail, and guide conversation about the

ebook
online coach

**Differentiated Reader
Pages 80–102**

settlers who went west on it in the 1850s. Provide the words *pioneers*, *homestead*, *covered wagon*, and *wagon train*.

Preteach Differentiated Vocabulary

Use the 7-Step Vocabulary Routine (p. 287) and the Step 6 activities below.

Point out the Spanish cognates.

Step 6 Activity	
hardship *noun, p. 81*	Make a word web to show some causes of hardship: danger, lack of food or money, illness, accident, loneliness. Then have students read and complete this sentence: "When a friend experiences hardship, you should _____."
rally *verb, p. 83*	Ask: "If your team rallied during a game, why would you be happy?"
blistering *adjective, p. 84*	Students tell what people should do to stay safe on a day of blistering heat.
landmark *noun, p. 85*	Students sketch a map from your school to another place in town, labeling important landmarks along the way. Then they give oral directions to a partner, describing the landmarks.
commotion *noun, p. 85* *la conmoción*	Students describe events that might cause a commotion at school.
frail *adjective, p. 89*	Ask: "Why is being frail a hardship? How can you help someone who is frail?" Have students describe characteristics of someone who is frail.
ailing *adjective, p. 96*	Ask: "Who might take care of you if you are ailing?" Then have students use *ailing* and *frail* in the same sentence.
wary *adjective, p. 99*	Partners act out being wary. Other students say how they could tell the actors were wary.

Preview and Set Purposes

Preview the selection, pointing out titles and pictu
Guide discussion about them. Tell students they w
read to find answers to the Focus Question: *What*
like in the Pacific States?

Read

Model

Read aloud the title. Model fluent reading of the selection. Pause to discuss on-page supports and t features. Model strategies and your thinking.

• Use gestures to explain *audience*, *shrugs*, *whoa*, *yonder*, and *panting*.

• On page 83, explain the idioms *it's up to us*, *exte hand*, *pitch in*, and *one for all and all for one*. Cla how *mark* (p. 85), *pass* (p. 86), *strains* (p. 95), *cle* (p. 98), *bound* (p. 99), and *sorely* (p. 102) are used

Guide Comprehension

Now that students have heard the selection read to them, partners read it together. To help them get started, model your thinking:

 I can tell the selection is a play. On page 80, I see the Cast of Characters. On page 81, I see the headings A and Scene 1. I also see stage directions in parenthese and a character's name, followed by dialogue.

PAGES 80–91 On page 81, explain *narrator* and *exit*. the picture on pages 88–89 to explain *ferry* and *wad*

PAGES 92–102 Have students use the pictures on pages 95–97 to summarize the episode with the Shos boy. Have them use context clues to figure out *expen* (p. 92), *disaster* (p. 99), and *engulfed* (p. 100).

PAGES 85, 87, 89, 97, 102 Review on-page support

Respond and Write

1. Students tell partners about the worst hardship Bryan family faced. Then they share their partne responses.

2. Students read the narrator's words about hardsl on page 81. They write a paragraph about how th statement applies to the Bryan family. Discuss h their paragraphs relate to the Focus Question.

Objectives
Students will:
- Reinforce theme concepts
- Use differentiated vocabulary
- Read a story about salmon fishing in Alaska
- Review using text features

English Language Learners · small groups

Prepare to Read

Build Background

Locate Alaska on a map of North America. Point out its coastline, and ask students how they think many Alaskans earn their living. Guide a talk about the fishing industry. Provide the words *commercial*, *nets*, *lines*, *bait*, and *trolling*.

Differentiated Reader
Pages 80–102

Preteach Differentiated Vocabulary

 tested

Use the 7-Step Vocabulary Routine (p. 287) and the Step 6 activities below.

Point out the Spanish cognates.

Step 6 Activity	
pristine *adjective, p. 83* *pristino(a)*	Students explain why pristine water is a valuable resource. *(for drinking water, animal habitats)*
alert *adjective, p. 88* *alerta*	Ask: "Why do you need to be alert at school? What are some other times when people need to be alert?" *(driving a car, crossing a street)*
muffle *verb, p. 89*	Students describe and demonstrate ways that they can muffle their voices.
stride *noun, p. 91*	Partners walk across the room together. Then they compare their strides.
hideous *adjective, p. 92*	Students sketch something hideous. Then they describe their sketches to partners.
continental *adjective, p. 95* *continental*	Hand out maps of the continental United States. Students trace its borders with their fingers. Then they each say a sentence to describe the continental United States.
scrape *verb, p. 97*	Ask: "What should you do after you scrape your knee on something sharp?"
replenish *verb, p. 99*	Ask: "How do we replenish the gasoline in our cars?"

Preview and Set Purposes

Preview the selection, pointing out titles and pictures. Guide discussion about them. Tell students they will read to find answers to the Focus Question: *What is life like in the Pacific States?*

Read

Model

Read aloud the title. Model fluent reading of the selection. Pause to discuss on-page supports and text features. Model strategies and your thinking.

- Use gestures to explain *winking*, *shivering*, and *shock*. Sketch a trolling boat.
- Explain *lined up* (p. 80), *up for it* (p. 85), *take advantage of* (p. 87), *made his way* (p. 88), and *up to it* (p. 91). Clarify how *light* (p. 86), *brightly* (p. 87), *run* (p. 89), *schools* (p. 90), *fire* (p. 92), and *tracks* (p. 99) are used.

Guide Comprehension

Now that students have heard the selection read to them, partners read it together. To help them get started, model your thinking:

> **think aloud** The title tells me that parts of this story take place on a boat. I know that a deck is where people walk on a boat. *Hands* sometimes means "workers." I predict that the characters will be workers on a boat.

PAGES 80–90 Have students use context clues to figure out *exit* (p. 81), *population* (p. 82), and *prompted* (p. 84).

PAGES 91–102 On pages 94–95, discuss the meaning of the *Lower Forty-eight*. On pages 96–97, have students explain the connection between oil and fishing.

PAGES 83, 85, 90, 93, 97 Review the on-page supports.

Respond and Write

1. Students tell partners the most surprising thing that they learned about Alaska. Then they share their partners' responses.

2. Students imagine they are Roberto. They write an e-mail to a friend telling what they have learned about Alaska. Discuss how their e-mails answer the Focus Question.

Objectives
Students will:
- Reinforce theme concepts
- Use differentiated vocabulary
- Read a Native American folktale
- Review using text features

English Language Learners *small groups*

Prepare to Read

Build Background
On a U.S. map, show the Pacific Northwest. Point out its mountains and rivers. Ask what students know about the region's climate. Guide a talk about how its cool, rainy climate affects life there. Provide the words *forests, lumber, fruits,* and *agriculture.*

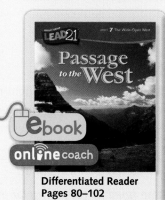

ebook
online coach

**Differentiated Reader
Pages 80–102**

Preteach Differentiated Vocabulary
Use the 7-Step Vocabulary Routine (p. 287) and the Step 6 activities below. Point out the Spanish cognates.

Step 6 Activity	
whittle *verb, p. 81*	Model the motion of whittling. Show a picture of an object whittled out of wood. Have students name things that might be whittled today.
laced *adjective, p. 83*	Students sketch something laced with colors. Then they describe their pictures to the group.
mock *verb, p. 85*	Students discuss safe ways to respond when someone mocks them.
descend *verb, p. 89* *descender*	Use hand motions to contrast the words *ascend* and *descend.* Students compare and contrast ascending and descending a mountain.
quiver *verb, p. 90*	Model quivering. Students explain when people might quiver.
grasp *verb, p. 91*	Students use the words *grasp* and *descend* in the same sentence.
glorious *adjective, p. 94* *glorioso(a)*	Students sketch something glorious. Then they describe their picture to a partner.
ornament *noun, p. 95* *el ornamento*	Students describe something they have seen that had ornaments.
sizzle *verb, p. 100*	Model a sizzling sound. Students tell about something that sizzles as it cooks.

Preview and Set Purposes
Preview the selection, pointing out titles and pictur... Guide discussion about them. Tell students they wi... read to find answers to the Focus Question: *What i... like in the Pacific States?*

Read

Model
Read aloud the title. Model fluent reading of the selection. Pause to discuss pictures and text featur... Model strategies and your thinking.

- Use gestures, sketches, and sound effects to expl... *rattle, snickered, gasped, booming,* and *rainbow.*
- Explain the idioms *made preparations* (p. 81), *be... his mother knew it* (p. 83), *hit its mark* (p. 90), *catching his breath* (p. 93), and *paid them no hee...* (p. 99). Discuss the homophone *fir* (p. 82) and the... homograph *bow* (p. 89). Clarify how *needles* (p. 8... and *patch* (p. 89) are used.

Guide Comprehension
Now that students have heard the selection read to... them, partners read it together. To help them get started, model your thinking:

 The selection title is mysterious. I know there is a furr... animal called a mink, but I don't see any pictures of f... animals. Mink must be a person. The Chapter 1 title i... puzzling, too. How can someone be the child of the s...

PAGES 80–89 Use the picture on page 80 to explain... *figurine.* Have students use context clues to figure ou... *strands* (p. 81), *opposites* (p. 83), *inseparable* (p. 84), *embarrassed* (p. 87).

PAGES 90–102 Have students use the pictures on pages 90–94 to summarize how Mink visits his father...

Respond and Write

1. Students tell partners what happened when Min... tried to look down at his mother. Then they share... their partners' responses with the class.

2. Students write an epilogue about Mink's return... the sky kingdom. Discuss how the folktale answe... the Focus Question.

Objectives
Students will:
- Reinforce theme concepts
- Use differentiated vocabulary
- Read a story about life in Washington state in the 1870s
- Review using text features

Prepare to Read

Build Background

Ask students how life in the United States was different in the 1870s than it is today. Guide a talk about

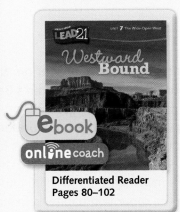

eBook
online coach

Differentiated Reader
Pages 80–102

improvements in transportation, communication, and other technology. Say that the story is told in letters between two cousins who lived in Washington State in the 1870s.

Preteach Differentiated Vocabulary *(tested)*

Use the 7-Step Vocabulary Routine (p. 287) and the Step 6 activities below. Point out the Spanish cognates.

Step 6 Activity	
telegram noun, p. 82 el telegrama	Ask: "Why don't people send many telegrams these days?"
relieved adjective, p. 84	Students describe how they feel when they are relieved.
terminus noun, p. 86 el término	Show a map of the Interstate Highway System. Have students identify the termini of different routes.
gist noun, p. 88	In several sentences, describe your feelings about e-mail, cell phones, or video games. Then have students restate the gist of your opinion.
jockey verb, p. 92	Students tell partners about how contestants in a reality TV show jockey for position. Then they share their partners' responses.
garb noun, p. 94	Students sketch someone wearing fashionable garb. Then they describe the garb to the group.
resentful adjective, p. 95 resentido(a)	Partners act out one person expressing resentful feelings and the other responding to the resentment. Other students explain why one person felt resentful.
rift noun, p. 100	Students tell about actions that might cause a rift in a friendship.

Preview and Set Purposes

Preview the selection, pointing out the letters and pictures. Guide discussion about them. Tell students they will read to find answers to the Focus Question: *What is life like in the Pacific States?*

Read

Model

Read aloud the title. Model fluent reading of the selection. Pause to discuss photos and text features. Model strategies and your thinking.

- Act out *sniffles*, *clams up*, *scowling*, and *having second thoughts*.
- Explain the idioms *nose to the grindstone* (p. 80), *slow as molasses* (p. 84), *gets swept up* (p. 86), *burning a hole in his pocket* (p. 92), *keep … under your hat* (p. 93), and *be of several minds* (p. 94). Discuss the homographs *object* (p. 87) and *contract* (p. 100).

Guide Comprehension

Now that students have heard the selection read to them, partners read it together. To help them get started, model your thinking:

 The title tells me a lot: There will be a mystery to solve, the story is told through friendly letters, and the subject of the letters is a railroad. On pages 80–81, I see a letter from Henry to John. The heading shows that he lives in Tacoma in 1872. On pages 82–83, I see John's reply.

PAGES 80–89 Have students note the dates in the letters to keep track of passing time. Have them use context clues to figure out *correspondence* (p. 82), *dependable* (p. 82), *conversing* (p. 84), *relaying* (p. 86), *transformed* (p. 86), *coincidence* (p. 88), and *conspiring* (p. 88).

PAGES 94–102 Ask how pages 98–101 look different from the rest of the story. Discuss what the mystery is.

Respond and Write

1. Students tell partners what surprised them most about life in the Pacific States in the 1870s. Then they share their partners' responses with the class.

2. Have partners write e-mails between two cousins in the Pacific Northwest today. Relate the story and the e-mails to the Focus Question.

The Wide-Open West

The LEAD21 Theme Bibliography presents leveled books that relate to the Unit 7 Theme *The Wide-Open West*, and that address the essential Theme Question: *What makes the West exceptional?* You may wish students to have access to these books for their Self-Selected Reading time. Students may also find useful information in these books as they work on their Inquiry Projects.

Intensive

Fleming, Denise. *Buster Goes to Cowboy Camp.* Henry Holt and Company, 2008. Buster the dog must stay at Sagebrush Kennels while his owner is traveling, but the humorous happenings at the Kennel's Cowboy Camp dude ranch keep Buster too busy with gathering wood for the campfire, creating paw-print posters, and steeping himself in cowboy culture to feel any pangs of homesickness. (Lexile AD 680) *fiction*

Lassieur, Allison. *The Wild West: An Interactive History Adventure.* Capstone Press, 2009. This text, filled with historical details, allows readers to create the structure and characters of a story set in the West in the 1880s; readers choose from characters such as a lawman, an outlaw, and a fortune seeker, and choose plots that might involve cowboy conflict resolution, stagecoach robbery, or travel to the Dakota Territory to mine for a fortune, and then choose from a variety of endings. (Lexile 630) *nonfiction*

Lowell, Susan. *Cindy Ellen: A Wild Western Cinderella.* HarperCollins, 2001. In this retelling of the Cinderella tale set in the Wild West, Cindy Ellen's fairy godmother, a quintessential granny cowgirl, dresses Cindy Ellen in classy cowgirl attire, complete with diamond-studded stirrups, in preparation for the cattle king's square dance and rodeo, where Cindy Ellen meets the cattle king's son Joe Prince; they fall in love. (Lexile 650) *fiction*

Strategic

Grupper, Jonathan. *Destination: Rocky Mountain.* National Geographic Children's Books, 2001. Featuring the natural resources and zones of the Rocky Mountains, this book presents readers with a hike up through the mountains to the majestic heights of the tallest peaks, and during the journey readers investigate the wildlife and vegetation that live in the mountain habitat and learn how different animals and plants have adapted to reside in the higher altitude. (Lexile 790) *nonfiction*

Lowell, Susan. *I Am Lavina Cumming.* Milkweed Editions, 2005. Lavina lives in the Arizona Territory where she enjoys riding horses, playing with her brothers, and helping on the ranch, but her father thinks life there is too wild for her and sends Lavina to her aunt's home in California, where she experiences firsthand the San Francisco earthquake of 1906, bravely enduring the ordeal and helping save the life of another victim. (Lexile 750) *fiction*

Miller, Debbie S. *Disappearing Lake: Nature's Magic in Denali National Park.* Walker Books for Young Readers, 1998. Presenting the concept of vernal lakes and featuring Alaska's Denali National Park, this book explains the effect of seasonal changes and how melting snow brings high water levels and attracts water-loving animals and birds and how dry summer weather brings lower lake levels that leave muddy lake bottoms exposed and causes grasses and flowering plants to flourish. (Lexile AD 650) *nonfiction*

Benchmark

McGowen, Tom. *African-Americans in the Old West.* **Children's Press, 1999.** Part of the Cornerstones of Freedom series, this book presents historical tales and photographs from historical center archives throughout the West and explains how brave African American men and women, many of whom were former enslaved people, performed key roles as cowboys, soldiers, and other professionals as they helped build the West. (Lexile 790) *nonfiction*

Miller, Debbie S. *The Great Serum Race: Blazing the Iditarod Trail.* **Walker Books for Young Readers, 2006.** Presenting the Arctic and its blue-white, snow-covered terrain, this book features the 1925 diphtheria outbreak; shows the Iditarod Trail Sled Dog teams bringing antitoxin serum to Nome, Alaska, when it faces a severe serum shortage; and also provides background on the different dogs and teams and the heroic rescue effort. (Lexile AD 910) *nonfiction*

Nolen, Jerdine. *Thunder Rose.* **Harcourt, 2003.** Born during a thunderstorm, Thunder Rose, a feisty cowgirl in the Wild West, lives up to her name and accomplishes amazing feats, such as lifting cows, capturing lightning and forming it into a ball, stopping a stampede, and transforming a tornado into a light rainfall; in addition to these exploits, she shows her creativity and ingenuity by inventing barbed wire. (Lexile AD 910) *fiction*

Advanced

Lourie, Peter. *Rio Grande: From the Rocky Mountains to the Gulf of Mexico.* **Boyds Mills Press, 2000.** In this photo essay, Lourie presents the Rio Grande; shows how it originates in the mountains of Colorado and travels 1,885 miles to the Gulf of Mexico; describes real-life characters from the Wild West, such as Pancho Villa and Billy the Kid; and explores the natural terrain of the region along the river as well as its historic towns and the pueblos of New Mexico. (Lexile 930) *nonfiction*

Markel, Rita J. *Your Travel Guide to America's Old West.* **Lerner Publishing Group, 2004.** In cartoon style, Markel presents an amusing yet informative view of the men and women of the American West in the 1800s, describing pioneer and Native American women, miners and their gear, scenes from the lives of ordinary people of the time, descriptions and close-up views of artifacts, and amusing bits of trivia. (Lexile 940) *nonfiction*

Paulsen, Gary. *The Legend of Bass Reeves: Being the True and Fictional Account of the Most Valiant Marshal in the West.* **Laurel Leaf, 2008.** Incorporating historical facts, Paulsen tells the story of Bass Reeves, an African American hero of the West, who was born an enslaved person in North Texas, and describes how as a child Reeves learned to hunt; how after the Emancipation Proclamation, he moved to Arkansas, where he became a rancher; and how at age 51 he was appointed a federal marshal, helping to bring order to the Indian Territory. (Lexile 950) *fiction*

Lexile® Measurements

A Lexile® is a measure of reading materials using the widely adopted Lexile Framework® for reading. The Lexile uses two predictors of text difficulty—word frequency and sentence length—to determine the Lexile measure of a book. The higher the Lexile measure, the more difficult the book is to comprehend.

	Selections	Lexile®
Theme Reader		
Concept Selection	A Tour of the Western Region	940
Literature Selection	Juan Verdades: The Man Who Couldn't Tell a Lie	650
Differentiated Readers		
INTENSIVE	*Westward Expeditions*	
Week 1	Living and Working on the Mountain Plains	710
Week 2	The California Coast	730
Week 3	How Paul Bunyan Shaped the West	680
Week 4	Onward to Oregon!	NP
STRATEGIC	*Voyage to the West*	
Week 1	Canyons and Deserts of the Mountain States	820
Week 2	Farming in the Pacific Northwest	840
Week 3	Foolish Juan and the Sacks of Gold	670
Week 4	Deckhands	710
BENCHMARK	*Passage to the West*	
Week 1	The Majestic Rockies	940
Week 2	Hawaii: The Beautiful Island State	960
Week 3	The Mystery of the Missing Ski Poles	770
Week 4	Mink and the Sun	770
ADVANCED	*Westward Bound*	
Week 1	The Colorado River in the Mountain West	1030
Week 2	Technology in the Pacific States	1060
Week 3	The Turkey Maiden	910
Week 4	The Mystery of the Railroad Letters	990

NP: Non-Prose

D

E

Index

Illustration Credits

Cover ©The McGraw-Hill Companies, Inc./Janet Atkinson; **vi** ©The McGraw-Hill Companies, Inc./Loly & Bernardilla; **285** ©The McGraw-Hill Companies, Inc./Janet Atkinson.

Photo Credits

Cover ©Brand X Pictures/Getty Images; **vi** ©Nicholas Pitt/Getty Images; **viii** (tr) ©Stephen Simpson/Getty Images, (tl) ©Digital Stock/Corbis, (bl) ©Bruce C. Murray/Shutterstock, (br) ©Tom Till/Getty Images; **1** © U.S. Fish and Wildlife Service, Alaska; **9** ©Whit Richardson/Getty Images; **22** ©Fotosearch; **23** ©Whit Richardson/Getty Images; **34** ©RubberBall Productions/Getty Images; **35** ©Whit Richardson/Getty Images; **46** ©Fotosearch; **47** ©Whit Richardson/Getty Images; **58** ©RubberBall/SuperStock; **59** ©Whit Richardson/Getty Images; **66** ©Rich Legg; **71** ©Corbis; **82** ©Relaximages/Punchstock; **83** ©Corbis; **94** ©RubberBall Photography/Veer; **95** ©Corbis; **106** ©RubberBall/SuperStock; **107** ©Corbis; **118** ©Comstock Images/Getty Images; **119** ©Corbis; **126** ©Photodisc/Punchstock; **129** ©Corbis; **149** ©Corbis RF/Alamy; **160** ©Photodisc/Punchstock; **161** ©Corbis RF/Alamy; **172** ©Rich Legg; **173** ©Corbis RF/Alamy; **184** ©Fotosearch; **185** ©Corbis RF/Alamy; **196** ©RubberBall/SuperStock; **197** ©Corbis RF/Alamy; **204** ©Comstock Images/Getty Images; **209** ©BananaStock/Punchstock; **220** ©Fotosearch; **221** ©BananaStock/Punchstock; **232** ©RubberBall Productions/Getty Images; **233** ©BananaStock/Punchstock; **244** ©RubberBall Photography/Veer; **245** ©BananaStock/Punchstock; **256** ©Relaximages/Punchstock; **257** ©BananaStock/Punchstock; **264** ©RubberBall/SuperStock; **267** ©BananaStock/Punchstock; **285** ©Brand X Pictures/Getty Images; **305** ©Fotosearch.

Acknowledgments

Notes

Notes

Notes

Notes

Notes

Notes

Notes

Notes